AF707129

SEARCH AND SEIZURE

Other Books in the *Essentials of Canadian Law* Series

International Trade Law

Family Law

Copyright Law

The Law of Sentencing

Administrative Law

Computer Law 2/e

International Human Rights Law

Franchise Law

Legal Ethics and Professional Responsibility 2/e

Public International Law 2/e

Individual Employment Law 2/e

Civil Litigation

Canadian Telecommunications Law

Intellectual Property Law 2/e

Animals and the Law

Income Tax Law 2/e

Youth Criminal Justice Law 3/e

Bank and Customer Law in Canada 2/e

The Law of Equitable Remedies 2/e

Remedies: The Law of Damages 3/e

Freedom of Conscience and Religion

The Law of Trusts 3/e

Ethics and Criminal Law 2/e

Insurance Law 2/e

Immigration Law 2/e

Bankruptcy and Insolvency Law 2/e

Legal Research and Writing 4/e

Canadian Maritime Law 2/e

Public Lands and Resources in Canada

Conflict of Laws 2/e

Statutory Interpretation 3/e

Constitutional Law 5/e

Land-Use Planning

Detention and Arrest 2/e

Refugee Law 2/e

Religious Institutions and the Law 4/e

The Law of Partnerships and Corporations 4/e

Environmental Law 5/e

Fundamental Justice 2/e

International and Transnational Criminal Law 3/e

The Law of Torts 6/e

Mergers, Acquisitions, and Other Changes of Corporate Control 3/e

Criminal Procedure 4/e

Information and Privacy Law in Canada

The Law of Evidence 8/e

The Law of Contracts 3/e

National Security Law 2/e

Canadian Competition Law and Policy

The Law of Property

Pension Law 3/e

The Charter of Rights and Freedoms 7/e

Personal Property Security Law 3/e

Criminal Law 8/e

Securities Law 3/e

ESSENTIALS OF
CANADIAN LAW

SEARCH AND SEIZURE

ROBERT DIAB
Faculty of Law, Thompson Rivers University

CHRIS D.L. HUNT
Faculty of Law, Thompson Rivers University

IRWIN LAW

Search and Seizure
© Irwin Law Inc., 2023

All rights reserved. No part of this publication may be reproduced, stored in a retrieval system, or transmitted, in any form or by any means, without the prior written permission of the publisher or, in the case of photocopying or other reprographic copying, a licence from Access Copyright (Canadian Copyright Licensing Agency), 56 Wellesley Street, Suite 320, Toronto, ON, M5S 2S3.

Published in 2023 by

Irwin Law Inc.
14 Duncan Street
Suite 206
Toronto, ON
M5H 3G8

www.irwinlaw.com

ISBN 978-1-55221-706-1 (print) | 978-1-55221-707-8 (PDF) | 978-1-55221-708-5 (epub)

Library and Archives Canada Cataloguing in Publication

Title: Search and seizure / Robert Diab, Faculty of Law, Thompson Rivers University, Chris D.L. Hunt, Faculty of Law, Thompson Rivers University.
Names: Diab, Robert, author. | Hunt, Chris, 1979– author.
Series: Essentials of Canadian law.
Description: Series statement: Essentials of Canadian law | Includes bibliographical references and index.
Identifiers: Canadiana (print) 20230548539 | Canadiana (ebook) 20230548571 | ISBN 9781552217061 (softcover) | ISBN 9781552217078 (PDF) | ISBN 9781552217085 (EPUB)
Subjects: LCSH: Searches and seizures—Canada.
Classification: LCC KE9270 .D53 2023 | DDC 345.71/0522—dc23

Canada

ONTARIO CREATES | ONTARIO CRÉATIF

Printed and bound by CPI Group (UK) Ltd, Croydon, CR0 4YY

1 2 3 4 5 27 26 25 24 23

SUMMARY TABLE OF CONTENTS

DETAILED TABLE OF CONTENTS

FOREWORD

I was delighted to be asked to write the foreword to this excellent book, which provides a precise and digestible presentation of the right to privacy and the jurisprudence interpreting section 8 of the *Canadian Charter of Rights and Freedoms*.

The book is both well written and eminently helpful. Its systematic presentation will be appreciated both by students new to the study of section 8 of the *Charter* and experienced practitioners looking to efficiently navigate the extensive body of jurisprudence in this important area. It contains lucid, organized, and comprehensive discussions of the legal principles surrounding search and seizure accompanied by astute commentary on how this area of law has developed. While maintaining a sleek presentation, the authors manage to capture the spirited debates that have come to characterize the section 8 jurisprudence. The result is a concise and academically rigorous text.

At the heart of *Charter* jurisprudence lies an ever-present tension between collective security and individuals' right to be free from state intrusions upon their liberty and privacy interests. The authors do not shy away from this tension. They instead ground their analysis of the jurisprudence with a philosophical discussion on the nature of privacy and its normative value. This illuminating discussion is sophisticated yet accessible. A range of perspectives are canvassed and the authors invite the reader to consider not only how privacy is protected within the criminal justice system, but *why* its protection is important to society and to the administration of justice.

I have no doubt that this book will prove to be a well-used resource by students, instructors, practitioners, and jurists alike, and I am grateful to Professors Diab and Hunt for producing what will be an enduring contribution to the literature on section 8 of the *Charter*.

The Honourable Sheilah L. Martin
Justice of the Supreme Court of Canada

PREFACE

This book offers a comprehensive account of section 8 of the *Canadian Charter of Rights and Freedoms*. It begins with the origins and antecedents of the right "to be secure against unreasonable search or seizure" and debates about the meaning and importance of privacy. It looks at the seminal early caselaw on the right and provides a brief overview of how courts apply section 8 in practice. The main chapters of the book examine the various elements of section 8 and caselaw on point. A concluding chapter surveys remedies for an unreasonable search under section 24 of the *Charter*.

The book is aimed at two kinds of readers: those new to section 8 of the *Charter*, and those who are familiar with it but looking for an easily navigated source to refresh their memory of a case, a rule, or a test. Since most of the fundamentals of section 8 are well settled—how to determine whether one has a reasonable expectation of privacy in a place or thing, whether a search or seizure is reasonable—we hope this book will be of enduring value and utility to both kinds of reader. The focus in this book is primarily on decisions of the Supreme Court of Canada and federal legislation, yet we do refer to many lower court cases and various provincial statutes throughout.

Although this was a collaborative effort, Professor Hunt drew on his work in privacy theory and his interest in a reasonable expectation of privacy in making a primary contribution to chapters 1 and 4. Professor Diab drew on his experience and expertise in criminal law (and time on sabbatical) to write the remaining chapters. We wish to thank our families for their support and encouragement, and Jeffrey Miller, Lesley Steeve, and Dale Clarry at Irwin Law.

Robert Diab & Chris D.L. Hunt
Kamloops, British Columbia

CHAPTER 1

INTRODUCTION: WHAT IS PRIVACY AND WHY DOES IT MATTER?

A. INTRODUCTION

When the framers of the *Canadian Charter of Rights and Freedoms* chose to include a guarantee that "[e]veryone has the right to be secure against unreasonable search or seizure," they sought to protect a right with deep historical roots.[1] As far back as 1604, the King's Bench in *Semayne's Case* declared that "the house of everyone is to him as his castle and fortress."[2] A sheriff must "signify the cause of his coming" and "make request to open doors."[3] In 1765, in *Entick v Carrington*, Lord Camden held that "our law holds the property of every man so sacred, that no man can set his foot upon his neighbour's close without his leave: if he does he is a trespasser, though he does no damage at all; if he will tread upon his neighbour's ground, he must justify it by law."[4] The framers of the American Bill of Rights, in response to decades of intrusive conduct by British authorities using "general" or open warrants, entrenched "the right of the people to be secure in their persons, houses, papers, and effects, against unreasonable searches and seizures" and the requirement that

1 *Canadian Charter of Rights and Freedoms*, Part I of the *Constitution Act, 1982*, being Schedule B to the *Canada Act 1982* (UK), 1982, c 11 [*Charter*].

2 *Semayne's Case* (1604), 77 ER 194.

3 *Ibid*, cited in James A. Fontana & David Keeshan, *The Law of Search and Seizure in Canada*, 12th ed (Toronto: LexisNexis Canada, 2021) at 3.

4 *Entick v Carrington*, [1765] EWHC KB J98.

warrants be issued on probable cause.[5] In the United Nations' *Universal Declaration of Human Rights*, the *European Convention on Human Rights* and other sources of international human rights law in the twentieth century, similar protections would be extended to "privacy" more broadly.[6]

When it came to be entrenched in Canada's *Charter of Rights and Freedoms*, the scope of the guarantee in section 8 against "unreasonable search or seizure" was not clear.[7] The section says nothing about protecting people's privacy in a broader sense. We might infer this broader intention for section 8 from the fact that an early draft of the *Charter* had included a freestanding "right to privacy," which the framers removed in later versions of the document that included section 8.[8] Soon after the *Charter* came into force in 1982, however, the Supreme Court of Canada in *Hunter v Southam Inc* made the broader scope of section 8 explicit by following American jurisprudence on point.[9] For a good part of its history, the protection in the Fourth Amendment against "unreasonable searches and seizures" had applied only to intrusions on a person's property.[10] In 1967, in *Katz v United States*, the US Supreme Court vastly expanded the scope of the Amendment by taking the view that it should protect "people, not places" and, more specifically, things over which one has a "reasonable expectation of privacy."[11] Adopting this approach in *Hunter*, Dickson J, as he then was, held that "[l]ike the Supreme Court of the United States, I would be wary of foreclosing the possibility that the right to be secure against unreasonable search and seizure might

5 US Const amend IV. William John Cuddihy, *The Fourth Amendment: Origins and Original Meaning, 1602-1791* (Oxford: Oxford University Press, 2009) at 441, cited in Simon Stern, "Textual Privacy and Mobile Information" (2018) 55:2 *Osgoode Hall Law Journal* 398 at 431 [Stern, "Textual Privacy"].

6 Article 12 of the *Universal Declaration of Human Rights*, GA Res 217A (III) UNGAOR, 3rd Sess, Supp No 13, UN Doc A/810 (1948) states that "No one shall be subjected to arbitrary interference with his privacy, family, home or correspondence, nor to attacks upon his honour and reputation. Everyone has the right to the protection of the law against such interference or attacks." See also Article 17 of the *International Covenant on Civil and Political Rights*, 19 December 1966, 999 UNTS 171 at 176 (entered into force 23 March 1976, accession by Canada 19 May 1976); and Council of Europe, *European Convention for the Protection of Human Rights and Fundamental Freedoms, as amended by Protocols Nos 11 and 14*, 4 November 1950, ETS 5, Article 8.

7 *Charter*, above note 1.

8 Robin Elliot, "Interpreting the *Charter*—Use of the Earlier Versions as an Aid" (1982) *University of British Columbia Law Review* 11 at 14.

9 *Hunter et al v Southam Inc*, [1984] 2 SCR 145 [*Hunter*].

10 See, e.g., *Olmstead v United States*, 277 US 438 at 465–66 (1928).

11 *Katz v United States*, (1967) 389 US 347 [*Katz*]. We discuss this transition in more detail at the beginning of Chapter 4.

protect interests beyond the right to privacy, but . . . I am satisfied that its protections go at least that far."[12]

Before we endeavour to explore section 8 in detail, we focus in this chapter on two fundamental questions that shape all of the law relating to section 8. What is privacy? And why does it matter? While there are no definitive answers to these questions, conceptual clarity on them is important to making sense of how section 8 works and what it aims to do. The debate among scholars and courts on the nature and scope of the normative values underpinning the right to privacy is a lively one, and it helps us understand how much is at stake in the meaning of section 8.

B. WHAT IS PRIVACY?

Scholars frequently lament the difficulties of defining of privacy. Nearly fifty years ago, the prominent philosopher Judith Jarvis Thomson observed that the "most striking thing about the right to privacy is that nobody seems to have any clear idea what it is."[13] Since then, there has been a vast outpouring of literature attempting to refine the concept,[14] but difficulties of definition continue to trouble the theoretical literature.[15] The Supreme Court of Canada, for its part, has acknowledged the "theoretical disarray" of the subject,[16] and referred to privacy as an "evanescent"[17] and "protean"[18] concept.

What follows is a review of some leading theoretical conceptions of privacy. It is important to emphasize that these accounts are not posited as legal tests. A purely theoretical definition "does not of itself 'solve' any

12 *Hunter*, above note 9 at 159. See the discussion in Chapter 4, Section C(1) and Section C(4)(f) of the expansion of s 8 protections to include an interest in anonymity.

13 Judith Jarvis Thomson, "The Right to Privacy" (1975) 4:4 *Philosophy & Public Affairs* 295 at 295.

14 For a detailed discussion of leading conceptual accounts, of which the following is drawn, see Chris D.L. Hunt, "Conceptualizing Privacy and Elucidating Its Importance: Foundational Considerations for the Development of Canada's Fledgling Privacy Tort" (2011) 37:1 *Queen's Law Journal* 167 [Hunt, "Conceptualizing Privacy"].

15 See Neil Richards, *Why Privacy Matters* (New York: Oxford University Press, 2022) at 17 [Richards, *Why Privacy Matters*]; Robert C. Post, "Three Conceptions of Privacy" (2001) 89:6 *Georgetown Law Journal* 2087 [Post, "Three Conceptions"] who writes at 2087 that he "sometimes despair[s] whether [privacy] can be usefully addressed at all."

16 *R v Spencer*, 2014 SCC 43 at para 35 [*Spencer*].

17 *Dagg v Canada (Minister of Finance)*, [1997] 2 SCR 403 at para 67.

18 *R v Tessling*, 2004 SCC 67 at para 25 [*Tessling*].

privacy problems."[19] At most it tells us that something is private, conceptually speaking; but it does not dictate any particular legal result. Nevertheless, reflecting on some theoretical definitions is important, since we need an idea of what privacy is before we can attempt to value it or craft legal doctrine to protect it.[20]

1) Right to Be Let Alone

One of the earliest and most influential definitions of privacy comes from Warren and Brandeis in a seminal article written in 1890.[21] The authors spoke of privacy as the "right to be let alone," which is anchored fundamentally in what they termed the individual's "inviolate personality."[22] This conception of privacy has been influential in American jurisprudence[23] and was referenced by Dickson J in *Hunter*.[24] Despite its longevity, their formulation has attracted critics, who note its inherent vagueness[25] and consequent potential for overbreadth.[26]

2) Control Based Conceptions

Later theorists have crafted narrower definitions of privacy, focusing especially on the control of information. Charles Fried, for example, posited that "privacy is not simply an absence of information about us in the minds of others; rather, it is the *control we have over information about ourselves*."[27] A difficulty here concerns the meaning of control. If

---

19 Edward J. Bloustein, "Privacy as an Aspect of Human Dignity: An Answer to Dean Prosser" (1964) 39:6 *New York University Law Review* 962 at 1004 [Bloustein, "Privacy"]. See also Stanley I. Benn, "Privacy, Freedom, and Respect for Persons" in J. Roland Pennock & John W. Chapman, eds, *Nomos XIII: Privacy* (New York: Atherton Press, 1971) at 13 [Benn, "Privacy, Freedom, and Respect"].

20 See generally, Julie Dickson, *Evaluation and Legal Theory* (Oxford: Hart, 2001) at 63–64; Ronald Dworkin, *Taking Rights Seriously* (Cambridge: Harvard University Press, 1977) at 14–15.

21 Samuel Warren & Louis Brandeis, "The Right to Privacy" (1890) 4:5 *Harvard Law Review* 193.

22 *Ibid* at 205.

23 *Katz*, above note 11; *Time, Inc v Hill*, 385 US 374 (1967), Fortas J, dissenting, at 413: "[the right to privacy] is, simply stated the right to be let alone."

24 *Hunter*, above note 9 at 159.

25 Daniel J. Solove, "Conceptualizing Privacy" (2002) 90:4 *California Law Review* 1087 at 1101 [Solove, "Conceptualizing Privacy"].

26 Ruth Gavison, "Privacy and the Limits of Law" (1980) 89:3 *Yale Law Journal* 421 at 438 [Gavison, "Privacy"].

27 Charles Fried, "Privacy" (1968) 77:3 *Yale Law Journal* 475 at 482 [emphasis in original] [Fried, "Privacy"]; similarly, see: Arthur R. Miller, *The Assault on Privacy:*

it is understood to mean actual control, and privacy is thus a state of controlling information, it follows that one who cannot exercise such control is not entitled to privacy, no matter how sensitive the information is or how it was acquired.[28] This is unduly narrow. One problem is that it fails to distinguish between a loss of privacy and the mere threat of a loss. This is illustrated if we imagine a computer hacker who has the ability to access X's emails. Mere possession of this device means X no longer has exclusive control over this information, but it is odd to characterize X as suffering an invasion of privacy if the hacker never in fact uses the device.[29] Moreover, on Fried's definition privacy rights are lost once information is obtained by a third party and hence no longer in the subject's exclusive control—a position reflected in American law.[30] A preferable control-based definition was offered by Alan Westin, another influential early theorist, as the "*claim* of individuals . . . to determine for themselves when, how and to what extent information about them is known to others."[31] By emphasizing "claim," this formulation shifts the definition from a descriptive to a normative account, and thereby avoids the criticisms identified above as one's factual ability to control access to their information is not a precondition to their entitlement to do so. Westin's account continues to influence the Supreme Court of Canada's approach to informational privacy,[32] and helps to explain the Court's rejection of American law, which treats factual control of information as dispositive of one's right to privacy.[33]

Normative control-based definitions have been subjected to other criticisms, however. As with the right to be let alone, scholars note

---

Computers, Data Banks and Dossiers (Ann Arbour: University of Michigan Press, 1971) at 25; and Hyman Gross, "Privacy and Autonomy" in J. Roland Pennock & John W. Chapman, eds, *Nomos XIII: Privacy* (New York: Atherton Press, 1971) at 169 [Gross, "Privacy and Autonomy"].

28 W.A. Parent, "A New Definition of Privacy for the Law" (1983) 2:3 *Law & Philosophy* 305 at 326–7 [Parent, "New Definition"].

29 See Nicole Moreham, "Privacy in the Common Law: A Doctrinal and Theoretical Analysis" (2005) 121:4 *Law Quarterly Review* 628 at 638 [Moreham, "Privacy in the Common Law"].

30 *United States v Miller*, 425 US 435 (1976).

31 Alan F. Westin, *Privacy and Freedom* (New York: IG Publishing, 1967) at 7 [emphasis added] [Westin, *Privacy and Freedom*].

32 *Tessling*, above note 18 at para 23.

33 See *R v Marakah*, 2017 SCC 59 [*Marakah*] (one may retain a privacy interest in text messages sent to and seized from a third party's phone); *R v Reeves*, 2018 SCC 56 [*Reeves*] (one does not lose their privacy interest in a computer simply because it is shared with another person). For a critical discussion of *Marakah*, see Stern, "Textual Privacy," above note 5.

inherent ambiguity and consequent overbreadth.[34] This stems from the fact that many authors fail to identify with precision when information falls within this conception. Simply put, defining privacy as a claim to control personal information does not illuminate what types of information are in fact private. On a plain reading, it could mean that any information about a person is private, including the colour of their eyes or even their name—information that few would regard as warranting that characterization. Moreover, insofar as control-based definitions are focused on information, they are plainly too narrow. Privacy can be invaded in manners having little to do with access to information, such as where a person is strip searched, monitored, or peered at by a peeping Tom. The underlying complaint in such cases is no doubt an intrusion upon privacy;[35] but notice that this is true regardless of the information, if any, that may have been gleaned as a result.[36] Notably, most leading privacy theorists now recognize that privacy can be invaded *either* by gaining *information* about a person or through non-informational *physical* intrusions, such as spying or touching.[37] The Supreme Court of Canada has recognized this as well.[38]

3) Access to the Individual

Ruth Gavison has attempted to overcome the criticisms set out above, first by refining the concept of privacy into three components, and hence narrowing the conceptual focus; and second by foregrounding that non-informational intrusions can compromise individual privacy.[39] She begins by conjuring an admittedly artificial notion of "perfect privacy" and then considers how this state may be compromised, thus suggesting a loss of privacy.[40] Perfect privacy exists when a person is "completely inaccessible to others," which, according to Gavison, consists of three "independent components":

---

34 Solove, "Conceptualizing Privacy," above note 25 at 1114; Tom Gerety, "Redefining Privacy" (1977) 12:2 *Harvard Civil Rights-Civil Liberties Law Review* 233 at 263 [Gerety, "Redefining Privacy"].

35 For a discussion, see Moreham, "Privacy in the Common Law," above note 29 at 651.

36 Richard Parker, "A Definition of Privacy" (1974) 27:2 *Rutgers Law Review* 275 at 280 [Parker, "Definition of Privacy"].

37 For elaboration, with leading sources, see Nicole Moreham, "Beyond Information: Physical Privacy in English Law" (2014) 73:2 *Cambridge Law Journal* 350 at 3, n 10; and see Megan Richardson, *Advanced Introduction to Privacy Law* (Cheltenham: Edward Elgar, 2020) at 30–32 [Richardson, *Advanced Introduction*].

38 See *Tessling*, above note 18 at para 24.

39 Gavison, "Privacy," above note 26.

40 *Ibid* at 428.

> [I]n perfect privacy [1] no one has any information about X, [2] no one pays attention to X, and [3] no one has physical access to X. . . . [Accordingly, a] loss of privacy occurs as others obtain information about an individual, pay attention to him, or gain access to him.[41]

Gavison refers to these components of privacy as secrecy, anonymity, and solitude. They are independent, because each can be compromised without a breach of another; yet they are related, since at bottom, the compromise of each state is a violation of privacy. *Secrecy,* Gavison says, captures the sense of intrusion one suffers when their private information is disclosed to others without consent. It is the disclosure itself, regardless of how the information was obtained, that violates privacy.[42] *Anonymity*, according to Gavison, is the loss of privacy one experiences when attention is focused on them, such as where a celebrity, blending initially into a crowd of people, is recognized and their name is called out. No other information is given, but none is required: privacy is compromised by virtue of the attention paid.[43] *Solitude*, Gavison concludes, is violated when people gain sensorial access to another, whether by touching, looking, eavesdropping, or the like. The essence of the privacy invasion here turns not on the nature of the information gleaned (as with secrecy) or because attention has been paid (as with anonymity); but rather because "spatial aloneness has been diminished."[44]

Gavison's approach has been influential, but critics have warned of its apparent overbreadth. One concern here is that Gavison's state of "perfect privacy," with solitude at the core, begins to collapse the concept of privacy into that of isolation, though the two ideas are not necessarily the same. Regarding the lonely person on a desert island as enjoying a state of privacy is rather conceptually inapt.[45] As Delany and Carolan explain:

> Privacy is . . . a relational rather than a solipsistic concept. To be private, a matter must be private against another party. Solitude, on the other hand, is a self-regarding and self-supporting concept. Whereas privacy presumes the existence of others, no other is needed to be alone.[46]

---

41 *Ibid.*

42 *Ibid* at 429.

43 *Ibid* at 432. As Westin explains, blending into the "situational landscape," by being anonymous in public places, is necessary for freedom and relaxation in modern democracies: Westin, *Privacy and Freedom*, above note 31 at 34.

44 Gavison, "Privacy," above note 26 at 433.

45 Fried, "Privacy," above note 27 at 482.

46 Hilary Delany & Eoin Carolan, *The Right to Privacy: A Doctrinal and Comparative Analysis* (Dublin: Thompson Round Hall, 2008) at 9.

Moreover, from a practical perspective, Gavison's account, like those discussed above, offers little guidance as to when a matter will be private. She does offer some assistance by developing the three states of privacy, but within each component we are left without any guiding principles.

4) Foregrounding Subjectivity

Nicole Moreham's work maintains the broad categorization of invasions offered by Gavison but provides further guidance by centring the individual's subjective desire to be free from the intrusion in question.[47] She defines privacy as "desired 'inaccess'" or "freedom from unwanted access," which she explains as follows:

> [A] person will be in a state of privacy if he or she is only seen, heard, touched or found out about if, and to the extent that, he or she wants to be seen, heard, touched or found out about. Something is therefore "private" if a person has a desire for privacy in relation to it: a place, event or activity will be "private" if a person wishes to be free from outside access when attending or undertaking it and information will be "private" if the person to whom it relates does not want people to know about it.[48]

This emphasis on subjective preferences has certain advantages.[49] By foregrounding privacy as a normative claim, Moreham displaces arguments that one's entitlement to privacy depends on their factual ability to control access to themselves or their information. Simply stated, the desire to limit access is a "means of bringing privacy about rather than . . . privacy itself."[50] In this way, it also distinguishes between an actual loss of privacy and a mere threatened loss.[51] Moreover, by framing privacy as a claim, rather than as an existential state, it overcomes the difficulty in Gavison's theory of collapsing the concept of privacy into that of isolation. In short, "aloneness . . . becomes privacy when it is chosen

---

47 Moreham, "Privacy in the Common Law," above note 29 at 651.

48 *Ibid* at 636.

49 Subjectivity has been noted by other scholars as well: see Parent, "New Definition," above note 28 at 306–7, emphasizing something can be private if the person is acutely sensitive about it despite not being something most others would regard as private; Michael A. Weinstein, "The Uses of Privacy in the Good Life" in J. Roland Pennock & John W. Chapman, eds, *Nomos XIII: Privacy* (New York: Atherton Press, 1971) at 94–95, emphasizing desires and choice for privacy as aspects of its theoretical conception.

50 Moreham, "Privacy in the Common Law," above note 29 at 639.

51 *Ibid.*

or desired."[52] Centring subjective preferences also provides a simple mechanism for testing whether privacy has been compromised through access without having to engage in the fraught exercise of categorizing something as "private" in the abstract. Such abstract classification is notoriously problematic. Any such list of private matters would have to be incredibly nuanced to avoid arbitrary results. Most people would regard medical information as quintessentially private, but there is a big difference between having a serious disease and suffering from a cold.[53] Moreover, different individuals sometimes have widely divergent understandings of privacy. Westin uses the following examples:

> Y, the impecunious academic, might regard her annual income as an intensely private matter while X, the braying City banker, will boast about his to anyone who will listen. Conversely, X might regard the intimate details of his medical misadventures as intensely private while Y will recount hers to the barest of acquaintances.[54]

Moreham's answer to this problem is simple and elegant: a matter is private if the subject desires that others do not access it. But is it convincing? On Moreham's account, completely innocuous or trivial access is treated as raising a *privacy* claim based solely on the individual's desire to be free from such access. Arguably, this simply does not accord with our intuitive understanding of privacy. Few people would regard it as a violation of privacy if a fleeting glance is cast their way on a public street, or if fellow passengers stand close to them on a crowded bus, even if, in each example, they would in fact prefer not to be looked at or stood next to. The same is true if someone disseminates innocuous information, such as revealing the colour of one's eyes. There is a danger here that if *anything* can be private, the concept becomes stripped of independent meaning. It is also something of a tautology to say "I don't want you to look because it is private; and it is private because I don't want you to look." A preference not to be looked at is not *necessarily* an assertion of privacy. Despite these criticisms, the Supreme Court of Canada continues to draw on the individual's subjective expectations of privacy as part of its overall privacy analysis under section 8 of the *Charter*.[55]

---

52 *Ibid* at 637.

53 See Mark Warby et al, eds, *The Law of Privacy and the Media*, 2d ed (Oxford: Oxford University Press, 2011) at 64.

54 Westin, *Privacy and Freedom*, above note 31.

55 *R v Edwards*, [1996] 1 SCR 128, para 45; *Tessling*, above note 18 at para 32.

5) Social Norms and Practices as Guiding Precepts

Other scholars have appealed to social norms, which are themselves reflective of shared intuitions about privacy, to discipline the overbreadth of a purely subjective approach.[56] One prominent account comes from Helen Nissenbaum, who explained invasions of informational privacy as acts which violate "contextual integrity."[57] Most people, she asserts, "have a robust sense of the information about them that is relevant, appropriate, or proper to particular circumstances, situations, or relationships." When these social norms are respected, contextual integrity is maintained; but where these norms are trenched on, by accessing information about an individual not appropriate to that context, "contextual integrity has been violated."[58]

Nissenbaum's work continues to influence contemporary theorists. Robert Post has argued that "[w]e can conceive privacy as identifying socially sanctioned expectations" reflected in "social norms that define the forms of respect that we owe each other,"[59] which he later termed the "decencies of civilization."[60] More recently, Kirsty Hughes has advanced what she calls a "behavioural understanding of privacy."[61] Hughes identifies privacy violations as those which cross "privacy barriers."[62] Three such barriers exist: (1) *physical barriers* (meaning "such things as walls, doors, hedges, lockers and safes"); (2) *behavioural barriers* (meaning the various ways a person communicates a desire for privacy, through express words, body language, or actions, such as retreating from public view); and (3) *normative barriers* (meaning the various social norms and conventions about privacy that people rely upon on a daily basis).[63]

---

56 See Thomas Scanlon, "Thomas on Privacy" (1975) 4:4 *Philosophy & Public Affairs* 315 at 316; Parker, "Definition of Privacy," above note 36 at 276–77; Benn, "Privacy, Freedom and Respect," above note 19 at 2; Gerety, "Redefining Privacy," above note 34 at 236; Robert C. Post, "The Social Foundations of Privacy: Community and Self in the Common Law Tort" (1989) 77 *California Law Review* 957 at 961–62; and see Hamish Stewart, "Reasonable Expectations of Privacy as Rights" in C.D.L. Hunt & R. Diab, eds, *The Last Frontier: Digital Privacy and the Charter* (Toronto: Thomson Reuters, 2021) at 55, discussing social norms as important guides for whether privacy claims should arise in public places.

57 Helen Nissenbaum, "Protecting Privacy in an Information Age: The Problem of Privacy in Public" (1998) 17 *Law & Philosophy* 559.

58 *Ibid* at 582.

59 Post, "Three Conceptions," above note 15 at 2092.

60 *Ibid* at 2093.

61 Kirsty Hughes, "A Behavioural Understanding of Privacy and Its Implications for Privacy Law" (2012) 75:5 *Modern Law Review* 806 [Hughes, "Behavioural Understanding"].

62 *Ibid* at 812.

63 *Ibid* at 812–13.

These barriers may overlap in any given situation, and the first two may be subsumed under the third.[64] Nevertheless, each is important in its own right: the first two reflect the ways in which people in fact manifest their desire for privacy, which builds upon the subjective core of the right;[65] and the third is essential in those daily situations where people desire some measure of privacy, but, perceiving no particular threat, do not employ physical or behavioural barriers. Instead, they rely on social norms pertaining to a particular place and situation, trusting they will not be intruded on in certain ways.[66]

Drawing on shared intuitions as reflected in social norms has two appreciable advantages for conceptualizing privacy. First, as Richard Parker has argued, it is important, as an epistemological matter, that any conceptual definition "fit[s] the data," which is to say it resonates with "intuitions of when privacy is gained or lost."[67] As Tom Gerety has noted, while conceptual certainty based on intuition may appear unduly subjective, "*shared* certainties" are "inter-subjective"; "if enough people share them—and act on them—we say we *know* them to be so."[68] Second, from a practical perspective, appealing to social norms has the further advantage of some (albeit imperfect) empirical verification. One can point to what privacy *is*, as actually practised in a given context, rather than appeal to what privacy *should be* based on one's preferred (and essentially contested) *a priori* theoretical frame.[69] Interestingly, in *R v Jarvis*[70] a majority of the Supreme Court of Canada recently endorsed

---

64 Hughes gives the example of X using a public toilet. The stall represents a physical barrier; X's choice to seek out this place represents a behavioural barrier; and social norms are such that X would not expect Y to have installed a secret camera in the stall. Y's failure to respect each of these barriers constitutes an invasion of privacy: *ibid* at 813.

65 *Ibid* at 810–12. This builds upon the insights of Nicole Moreham, who conceptualized privacy as an inherently subjective claim to "desired inaccess": Moreham, "Privacy in the Common Law," above note 29 at 636. Hughes's approach explains how a subjective desire for privacy, in Moreham's sense, is manifested by the subject.

66 Hughes, "Behavioural Understanding," above note 61 at 812: "we assume we are not being secretly filmed . . . ; we assume that our postal workers are not reading our mail; and we assume that our rubbish collectors are not rooting through our rubbish bags and taking note of items that we discard."

67 Parker, "Definition of Privacy," above note 36 at 276–77.

68 Gerety, "Redefining Privacy," above note 34 at 236.

69 For a discussion of this point, see Avner Levin, "Ought from Is: Towards Truly Reasonable Expectations of Privacy" in C.D.L. Hunt & R. Diab, eds, *The Last Frontier: Digital Privacy and the Charter* (Toronto: Thomson Reuters, 2021).

70 *R v Jarvis*, 2019 SCC 10 [*Jarvis*]. The case involved criminal voyeurism, not s 8 of the *Charter*. Nevertheless, the majority was explicit that it was anchoring its approach to privacy in the *Charter* jurisprudence at para 59. For a detailed discussion, see C. Hunt, "Voyeurism and the *Charter*: A Comment on the Supreme

drawing on "fundamental shared ideals about privacy," "our everyday experiences,"[71] and a "common sense understanding"[72] guided by the "norms of conduct in our society"[73] to assess the reasonableness of a person's expectation of privacy.

6) Supreme Court of Canada's Key Privacy Principles

The discussion above is offered as a short primer on some leading theoretical conceptions of privacy. Of course, whichever theoretical approach one finds attractive, it cannot simply be transposed to the legal context without refinement. It would be intolerably broad to say, for instance, that individuals have a right to control any and all access to themselves or to their information, or that their subjective preferences for privacy must prevail in all contexts.

Chapter 4 of this book is devoted to a detailed discussion of the Supreme Court of Canada's approach to testing whether a *Charter* protected privacy interest arises under section 8. As we shall see, in novel situations or where a privacy interest in a place or thing is debatable, the Court applies a four-stage analysis:

1) What was the subject matter of the evidence obtained by the police?
2) Does the claimant have a direct interest in the subject matter?
3) Did the claimant have a subjective expectation of privacy in the subject matter?
4) Was the subjective expectation of privacy objectively reasonable?[74]

The contours of this analysis are shaped by a variety of considerations, especially regarding the fourth point, above, which has been the subject of extensive judicial elaboration. If the claimant has a reasonable expectation of privacy, on the above analysis, to any degree, and the search or seizure was carried out by a state agent, section 8 of the *Charter* is engaged. Importantly, privacy rights exist in a spectrum. How high or low an expectation of privacy is becomes important at later stages of a constitutional challenge to a search. It plays a role in assessing whether a law authorizing a search is reasonable or was conducted reasonably, and

Court of Canada's Privacy Principles in *R v Jarvis*" in C.D.L. Hunt & R. Diab, eds, *The Last Frontier: Digital Privacy and the Charter* (Toronto: Thomson Reuters, 2021) [Hunt, "Voyeurism"].

71 *Jarvis*, above note 70 at para 59.

72 *Ibid* at para 60.

73 *Ibid* at para 68.

74 See *Tessling*, above note 18 at para 19; *Marakah*, above note 33 at para 11.

when assessing a remedy under section 24 of the *Charter* if a violation of section 8 is made out.

At this stage, we highlight three general points related to how one might conceptualize a *legal* right to privacy.

First, the Supreme Court has recognized three broad zones of privacy that operate as "useful analytical tools"[75] for identifying the alleged privacy interest at hand. There is *privacy of the person*, which "protects bodily integrity, and in particular the right not to have our bodies touched or explored to disclose objects or matters we wish to conceal."[76] There is *territorial privacy*, which covers a "hierarchy" of places from, *inter alia*, a dwelling house, a hotel, a commercial space, a car, a school, and even a prison.[77] Finally, there is *informational privacy*, with at least three sub-dimensions, namely secrecy,[78] control (in Westin's sense),[79] and anonymity.[80] In assessing the strength of an informational privacy claim, the Court occasionally draws on another analytical device, namely whether it relates a

> biographical core of personal information which individuals in a free and democratic society would wish to maintain and control from dissemination to the state[,] which include[s] information which tends to reveal intimate details of the lifestyle and personal choices of the individual.[81]

Second, the Court has emphasized that the assessment of an objectively reasonable expectation of privacy is a *normative*, not a descriptive, exercise.[82] The mere risk of intrusion does not of itself defeat one's reasonable expectation of privacy.[83] The question is "not what risks the claimant has taken, but which risks should be imposed on him in a free and democratic society."[84] The ultimate normative question is one of

---

75 *Tessling*, above note 18 at para 24.

76 *Ibid* at para 21.

77 *Ibid* at para 22.

78 *Spencer*, above note 16 at para 38.

79 *Ibid.*

80 *Ibid* at para 38.

81 *R v Plant*, [1993] 3 SCR 281 at 293 [*Plant*].

82 *Reeves*, above note 33 at para 41; *Spencer*, above note 16 at para 68; *Tessling*, above note 18 at para 42.

83 *Reeves*, above note 33 at para 41; *Marakah*, above note 33 at para 41; *R v Wong*, [1990] 3 SCR 36 at 45 [*Wong*]. There has, however, been occasional backsliding, see Steve Coughlan, *Criminal Procedure*, 4th ed (Toronto: Irwin Law, 2020) at 89. We will return to this point in Chapter 4.

84 *Reeves*, above note 33.

balancing the individual's privacy interest, objectively assessed, against the state's interest in law enforcement.[85]

Finally, the Supreme Court has recognized that in conducting this balancing it is essential to reflect on the values underpinning the right to privacy in order to assess the strength of the claim and the impact of the intrusion. Privacy rights exist on a spectrum. Broadly speaking, the core values the Court identifies are dignity, integrity, and autonomy.[86] Balancing these personal interests against state interests is an exercise "laden with value judgments" and should be assessed from the "perspective of the reasonable and informed person who is concerned about the long-term consequences of government action for the protection of privacy."[87]

C. WHY DOES PRIVACY MATTER?

There is an extensive literature exploring the values underpinning the right to privacy.[88] These values are varied, multifarious, and overlapping.[89] For the purpose of presentation, they may usefully be grouped under two broad headings: the deontological and the consequentialist. The former refers to the intrinsic values of privacy, foregrounding human dignity, autonomy, integrity, and personhood. The latter focuses on the functional value to individuals and to society when privacy is respected, and the harms that may result when privacy is violated.

---

85 See, for example, *Hunter*, above note 9 at 160 (Dickson CJ, balancing of privacy against state interest in law enforcement as part of the test for a reasonable expectation of privacy); *Plant*, above note 81 at 293 (Sopinka J, factors that allow for a contextual balancing of privacy and its underlying values of dignity and autonomy with effective law enforcement); *Schreiber v Canada (Attorney General)*, [1998] 1 SCR 841 at para 58 (Lamer CJ, dissenting, but not on this point) [*Schreiber*]; but see *Tessling*, above note 18 at paras 17–18, and 64 (Binnie J, for the Court: balancing must be struck between privacy and societal demands of safety and law enforcement in the context of s 8; relevance of the seriousness of the crime under investigation should be assessed when determining whether the search was reasonable).

86 See for example *Plant*, above note 81 at 293.

87 *R v Patrick*, 2009 SCC 17 at para 14.

88 For a detailed discussion, from which some of the below is drawn, see Hunt, "Conceptualizing Privacy," above note 14.

89 See David Feldman, "Privacy-Related Rights and Their Social Value" in Peter Birks, ed, *Privacy and Loyalty* (Oxford: Oxford University Press, 1997) at 21 [Feldman, "Privacy-Related Rights"], noting that "[a]ny attempt to identify a *single* interest at the core of privacy is doomed to failure, because privacy derives its weight and importance from its capacity to foster the conditions for a wide range of . . . aspects of human flourishing" [emphasis in original].

1) Deontological Values: Dignity, Autonomy, and Personhood

Scholars have long argued that violations of privacy constitute affronts to human dignity. Dignity here is typically used in the Kantian sense.[90] As Megan Richardson has observed, this harks back to the earliest writings on privacy from Warren and Brandeis, who employ Kant's "dignitarian rhetoric" of the individual's "inviolate personality" as the "moral basis" for their conception of the right to be let alone.[91] For Kant, dignity requires that each individual be treated as an end in themself, rather than as a means to furthering some other end. There is thus a *prima facie* ethical injunction against using people:

> [M]an ... [as a] rational being, exists as an end in himself and not merely as a means to be arbitrarily used by this or that will. He must in all his actions, whether directed to himself or to other rational beings, always be regarded at the same time as an end .... Persons are, therefore, not merely subjective ends, whose existence as an effect of our actions has a value for us; but such beings are objective ends, i.e., exist as ends in themselves.[92]

Disregarding an individual's expectations of privacy treats them as a mere instrument in pursuit of other objectives, violating this imperative.[93] Moreover, as Jeffrey Rosen has argued, in the context of surveillance, the intrusion itself undermines dignity because it necessarily "transforms the self from *subject to object*."[94] Stanley Benn explained why this may be "insulting," in Kantian terms:

---

90 For example, see Benn, "Privacy, Freedom, and Respect," above note 19 at 6–26; Fried, "Privacy," above note 27 at 477–78; Elizabeth L. Beardsley, "Privacy: Autonomy and Selective Disclosure" in J. Roland Pennock & John W. Chapman, eds, *Nomos XIII: Privacy* (New York: Atherton Press, 1971) at 64–70.

91 Richardson, *Advanced Introduction*, above note 37 at 18; see also Bloustein, "Privacy," above note 19 at 971 and 1003.

92 N.A. Moreham, "Why Is Privacy Important? Privacy, Dignity and Development of the New Zealand Breach of Privacy Tort" in J. Finn & S. Todd, eds, *Law, Liberty, Legislation: Essays in Honour of John Burrows QC* (Wellington: LexisNexis NZ, 2008) at 235, citing Immanuel Kant, *Grounding for the Metaphysics of Morals; with On a Supposed Right to Lie Because of Philanthropic Concerns*, 3d ed translated by James W. Ellington (Indianapolis: Hackett, 1993) at 35–36.

93 Moreham *ibid* at 235–36; Fried, "Privacy," above note 27 at 478–79; Gross, "Privacy and Autonomy," above note 27 at 178.

94 Jeffrey Rosen, "The Purposes of Privacy: A Response" (2001) 89:6 *Georgetown Law Journal* 2117 at 2124 [Rosen, "Purposes"].

> [It treats] people as objects or specimens . . . and not as subjects with sensibilities, ends, and aspirations of their own, morally responsible for their own decisions, and capable, as mere specimens are not, of reciprocal relations with the observer . . . [Surveillance] show[s] less than a proper regard for human dignity.[95]

Echoes of this transgression on the individual's inviolate personality are evident in *Aubry v Editions Vice Versa inc*[96] in which the Supreme Court found a violation of privacy protected under the *Quebec Charter of Rights and Freedoms,*[97] where a journalist photographed a woman without consent while she was sitting on the steps of a public fountain.[98] Despite the anodyne nature of the photograph, the Court determined "moral prejudice" was established:

> [TRANSLATION] each time a photographer invades someone's privacy or serves it up to the public. The camera lens captures a human moment at its most intense, and the snapshot "defiles" that moment. The privileged instant of personal life becomes "this object image offered to the curiosity of the greatest number." A person surprised in his or her private life by a roving photographer is stripped of his or her transcendency and human dignity, since he or she is reduced to the status of a "spectacle" for others . . . . This "indecency of the image" deprives those photographed of their most secret substance.[99]

The implications for human dignity and physical integrity are obviously even more pronounced where the invasion of privacy involves physical touching or close examination of the body, the most extreme versions for law enforcement being cavity or strip searches.[100] As the Supreme Court of Canada recognized in *R v Golden*, these "constitute the ultimate affront to human dignity."[101] Importantly, the Court has occasionally referenced the values of dignity and integrity in the context of section 8 *Charter* claims involving territorial and informational privacy as well.[102]

---

95 Benn, "Privacy, Freedom, and Respect," above note 19 at 6–7; Gavison, "Privacy," above note 26 at 255.

96 [1998] 1 SCR 591 [*Aubry*].

97 CQLR c C-12, s 5, affording a "right to respect" for "private life."

98 *Aubry*, above note 96.

99 *Ibid* at para 69. The above is taken from Hunt, "Voyeurism," above note 70.

100 See Andrea Slane, "From Scanning to Sexting: The Scope of Protection of Dignity-Based Privacy in Canadian Child Pornography Law" (2010) 48 *Osgoode Hall Law Journal* 543 at 553.

101 *R v Golden*, 2001 SCC 83 at para 76.

102 *Schreiber*, above note 85 at para 19 (search of bank records); *Plant*, above note 81 at 293 (perimeter search of residence; search of electricity records).

Human dignity is closely related to personal autonomy, another key value said to underpin the right to privacy.[103] Autonomy refers to each individual's capacity to be self-determining, in the sense of being free to "live their life in accordance with their own particular ideas of the individual good."[104] Personal autonomy is manifested daily by individuals when they choose how to behave or present themselves depending on different contexts (professional, social, family, and so on). As Westin explained:

> Every individual lives behind a mask in this manner; indeed, the first etymological meaning of the word "person" was "mask," indicating both the conscious and the expressive presentation of the self to a social audience.[105]

In the case of covert or secret surveillance, the individual is necessarily deprived of the opportunity to make informed decisions about how to manage self-presentation to a known audience, to deploy what Gross referred to as "editorial efforts."[106] As Benn explained, secret watching is therefore "objectionable because it deliberately deceives a person about his world, thwarting, for reasons that *cannot* be his reasons, his attempts to make a rational choice" about self-presentation.[107] If information is gleaned and subsequently disclosed, the consequences to the individual can be harmful, as Westin explained:

> If the mask is torn off and the individual's real self is bared to a world in which everyone else still wears his mask and believes in masked performances, the individual can be seared by the hot light of selective, forced disclosure.[108]

Surveillance which is known or suspected, as opposed to covert, also has serious implications for personal autonomy. Empirical sociological work has shown convincingly that people behave differently if they know they are being watched. Even suspecting one is being monitored tends to stifle individuality and produces conformity.[109] This is a phenomenon known

---

103 Westin, *Privacy and Freedom*, above note 31 at 35–37.

104 Beate Rössler, *The Value of Privacy*, translated by R.D.V. Glasgow (Cambridge: Polity, 2005) at 43; and see Gavison, "Privacy," above note 26 at 449.

105 Westin, *Privacy and Freedom*, above note 31 at 36.

106 Gross, "Privacy and Autonomy," above note 27 at 172–74.

107 Benn, "Privacy, Freedom, and Respect," above note 19 at 10–11; and see Jeffrey H. Reiman, "Privacy, Intimacy, and Personhood" (1976) 6:1 *Philosophy & Public Affairs* 26 at 36–39 [Reiman, "Privacy, Intimacy"].

108 Westin, *Privacy and Freedom*, above note 31 at 36–37; and see Hamish Stewart, "Normative Foundations for Reasonable Expectations of Privacy" (2011) 54 *Supreme Court Law Review* 335 at 344.

109 See Richards, *Why Privacy Matters*, above note 15 at 127–28 and 136–38.

as the Panoptic effect,[110] which is usefully explored further in the context of personhood, another value animating the right to privacy.

Drawing on the work of prominent sociologist Erving Goffman,[111] Reiman has argued that the formation and expression of individuality and personhood depend on the person regarding themself as an independent moral agent with the exclusive right to shape their own destiny.[112] In Reiman's view, "privacy is a precondition of personhood" because through its observance, coded in social norms of etiquette—what Goffman termed rules of deference and demeanour[113]—society communicates to the individual that their existence is their own, as an independent moral agent who is part of but also distinct from the collective.[114] The opposite occurs where surveillance is widespread, and privacy virtually non-existent, such as in prisons. Here we see the "mortification of the self;" the individual's sense of identity is killed off, their moral autonomy eviscerated, and their behaviour tends to conformity.[115] Edward Bloustein has argued along the same lines, positing that personhood, which encompasses one's "independence, dignity and integrity" as an autonomous individual is what Warren and Brandeis had in mind when they said invasions of privacy cause "spiritual" harm to one's "inviolate personality."[116] Bloustein's vivid elucidation of the point is worth quoting in full:

> The man who is compelled to live every minute of his life among others and whose every need, thought, desire, fancy or gratification is subject to public scrutiny, has been *deprived of his individuality* and human dignity. . . . His opinions, being public, tend never to be different; his aspirations, being known, tend always to be conventionally accepted ones; his feelings, being openly exhibited, tend to lose their quality of unique personal warmth and to become the feelings of every man. Such a being, although sentient, is fungible; he is not an individual.[117]

---

110 Daniel J. Solove, "A Taxonomy of Privacy" (2006) 154:3 *University of Pennsylvania Law Review* 477 at 495 [Solove, "Taxonomy"].

111 Erving Goffman, *Asylums: Essays on the Social Situation of Mental Patients and Other Inmates* (New York: Anchor Books, 1961) [Goffman, *Asylums*].

112 Reiman, "Privacy, Intimacy," above note 107 at 39.

113 Goffman, *Asylums*, above note 111.

114 Reiman, "Privacy, Intimacy," above note 107 at 39 & 40–44.

115 *Ibid* at 40–41, citing Goffman, *Asylums*, above note 111 at 23–25; and see Solove, "Taxonomy," above note 110 at 495.

116 Bloustein, "Privacy," above note 19 at 971.

117 *Ibid* at 1003 [emphasis in original].

2) Functional Values

Scholars have long argued that privacy is important functionally as well. One theme concerns the idea of sanctuary. As Sidney Jourard, a psychologist, recognized, privacy allows people to be "off-stage," where they can "simply be, rather than be respectable."[118] This is important for mental health,[119] or, as Benn put it starkly, a precondition to remaining "sane."[120] It is also linked to the deontological values of *autonomy* and *personhood*, discussed above. As to the former, having space free from social pressures to conform is critical for fostering individuality,[121] authenticity, and identity;[122] and regarding the latter, one needs separation from the collective in order to develop as a "psychologically and socially distinct person."[123]

Another theme links privacy to individual human flourishing. Being off-stage allows for self-reflection. As Westin observed, this has a "major moral dimension," because it is "primarily in periods of privacy" that one takes "inventory of ongoing conduct" and can measure behaviour against one's ideals.[124] Privacy also provides space for concentration, experimentation, and creativity.[125] By providing space for free-thinking and belief, for the testing and refinement of ideas free from public scrutiny, privacy is essential to fostering genuine free expression.[126]

---

118 Sidney Jourard, "Some Psychological Aspects of Privacy" (1966) 31:2 *Law & Contemporary Problems* 307 at 310–11 [Jourard, "Psychological Aspects"]; and see Benn, "Privacy, Freedom, and Respect," above note 19 at 24–25; Lisa M. Austin, "Privacy and the Question of Technology" (2003) 22 *Law & Philosophy* 119 at 147.

119 Jourard, "Psychological Aspects," above note 118; see also Milton R Konvitz, "Privacy and the Law: A Philosophical Prelude" (1966) 31:2 *Law & Contemporary Problems* 272 at 277; Gavison, "Privacy," above note 26 at 447.

120 Benn, "Privacy, Freedom, and Respect," above note 19 at 24–25; *R v Dyment*, [1988] 2 SCR 417 at para 17 [*Dyment*], "privacy is essential for the well-being of the individual."

121 Paul A. Freund, "Privacy: One Concept or Many" in J. Roland Pennock & John W. Chapman, eds, *Nomos XIII: Privacy* (New York: Atherton Press, 1971) at 195; Fried, "Privacy," above note 27 at 483–84; Thomas Nagel, "Concealment and Exposure" (1998) 27 *Philosophy & Public Affairs* 3 at 19; Westin, *Privacy and Freedom*, above note 31 at 36–37.

122 See Richards, *Why Privacy Matters*, above note 15 at 113–19.

123 Arnold Simmel, "Privacy Is Not an Isolated Freedom" in J. Roland Pennock & John W. Chapman, eds, *Nomos XIII: Privacy* (New York: Atherton Press, 1971) at 73; Rosen, "Purposes," above note 94 at 2124.

124 Westin, *Privacy and Freedom*, above note 31 at 40.

125 Gavison, "Privacy," above note 26 at 447; Edward J. Bloustein, "Privacy Is Dear at Any Price: A Response to Professor Posner's Economic Theory" (1978) 12:3 *Georgia Law Review* 429 at 453; Gross, "Privacy and Autonomy," above note 27 at 176.

126 Eric Barendt, "Privacy and Freedom of Speech" in Andrew T. Kenyon & Megan Richardson, eds, *New Dimensions in Privacy Law: International and Comparative Perspectives* (Cambridge: Cambridge University Press, 2006) at 23–30.

Privacy is functionally important also because it facilitates the formation and maintenance of relationships with others.[127] Simply stated, privacy provides the necessary "shield for intimate relationships,"[128] because, as Fried noted, it is through the voluntary and selective sharing of intimacies between individuals, while excluding others, that close relationships are formed.[129] Such relationships are essential for human flourishing, and closely tied to the concept of personhood as well. As Fried explained: "To respect, love, trust, feel affection for others and to regard ourselves as the objects of love, trust and affection is at the heart of our notion of ourselves as persons among persons."[130]

Moreover, by facilitating selective disclosure, privacy enables the individual to maintain the variety of different roles they occupy in society.[131] Each of these roles may differ depending on social conventions of propriety, and on their desire to conform to them.[132] Of course, forced disclosures of private thoughts or activities from one context or role to another can be damaging to one's relationships and potentially destroy the bonds of intimacy.[133]

Last, but certainly not least, scholars have argued that privacy is essential for democracy. To the extent that a society tolerates *invasions* of privacy, it fails to respect its members as individuals, and departs from its commitment to humanity and civility.[134] This point is not merely symbolic. The principles of dignity and autonomy are at the very core of the liberal political tradition that forms the basis of Western society.[135] Westin recognized that all totalitarian regimes—whether far left or right—rely on widespread surveillance of citizens and are openly hostile to individual privacy.[136] The reasons, of course, are obvious: privacy facilitates individuality and autonomy, and nurtures the "development of political ideas and expression," making it, in the words of Richards, an "essential source of political power for citizens against the state."[137]

---

127 See generally Beatte Roessler & Dorota Mokrosinska, *Social Dimensions of Privacy* (Cambridge: Cambridge University Press, 2015).

128 Gavison, "Privacy," above note 26 at 447.

129 Fried, "Privacy," above note 27 at 482–84.

130 *Ibid* at 484–86.

131 Richards, *Why Privacy Matters*, above note 15 at 120–23.

132 James Rachels, "Why Privacy Is Important" (1975) 4:4 *Philosophy & Public Affairs* 323 at 327.

133 Fried, "Privacy," above note 27 at 482–85.

134 Edward Shils, "Privacy: Its Constitution and Vicissitudes" (1966) 31:2 *Law & Contemporary Problems* 281 at 306.

135 See Feldman, "Privacy-Related Rights," above note 89 at 27.

136 Westin, *Privacy and Freedom*, above note 31 at 25.

137 Richards, *Why Privacy Matters*, above note 15 at 132.

Surveillance, as we have seen, stifles autonomy and tends to produce conformity in thought and behaviour. It is, in short, a "fundamental means of social control."[138]

The Supreme Court of Canada has often recognized the democratic value of privacy. For example, in *R v Dyment*, an early case interpreting section 8 of the *Charter*, the Court stated succinctly: "society has come to realize that privacy is at the heart of liberty in a modern state."[139] In *R v Wong*, it further opined: "the notion that the agencies of the state should be at liberty to train hidden cameras on members of society wherever and whenever they wish is fundamentally irreconcilable with what we perceive to be acceptable behaviour on the part of government."[140] In *Alberta (Information and Privacy Commissioner) v United Food and Commercial Workers, Local 401*, the Court held: "the importance of the protection of privacy in a vibrant democracy cannot be overstated," because "[d]emocracy depends on an autonomous, self-actualized citizenry that is free to formulate and express unconventional views. If invasions of privacy inhibit individuality and produce conformity, democracy itself suffers."[141]

138 Westin, *Privacy and Freedom*, above note 31 at 62.

139 *Dyment*, above note 120 at 427, and "[t]he restraints imposed on government to pry into the lives of the citizen go to the essence of a democratic state."

140 *Wong*, above note 83.

141 *Alberta (Information and Privacy Commissioner) v United Food and Commercial Workers, Local 401*, 2013 SCC 62 at para 22, quoting Hunt, "Conceptualizing Privacy," above note 14.

CHAPTER 2

AN OVERVIEW OF SECTION 8

A. INTRODUCTION

The text of section 8 of the *Charter* reads: "Everyone has the right to be secure against unreasonable search or seizure."[1] It raises three issues that are helpful to think about separately. What constitutes a search or seizure for purposes of section 8? Who can carry out a search that engages section 8? And what is an "unreasonable" search? Briefly, a search or seizure is anything done for an investigative purpose by a state actor that interferes with a space or thing over which a person has a reasonable expectation of privacy. The search or seizure will be reasonable if it is authorized by law, the law is reasonable, and the search or seizure is conducted in a reasonable manner.

To understand this summary, we need to know the answer to a few more basic questions: what is a reasonable expectation of privacy? Who is a state actor? What sort of actions amount to a search or seizure? When is a search or seizure authorized by a reasonable law? And when is it reasonably conducted?

In the rest of this chapter, we sketch out the answers to these questions and explore them in more detail in the rest of the book. To begin with, however, we turn to the cases where the Supreme Court first articulated the main ideas that have come to animate section 8: *Hunter v Southam*

1 *Canadian Charter of Rights and Freedoms*, Part I of the *Constitution Act, 1982*, being Schedule B to the *Canada Act 1982* (UK), 1982, c 11 [*Charter*].

Inc and *R v Collins*.[2] Among the Court's many important holdings on search and seizure, these two cases still furnish the basic contours of the constitutional right to privacy in Canada. Yet they each offer a distinct set of answers to the question of what constitutes a reasonable search or seizure, and how the two decisions fit together can lead to confusion.

B. *HUNTER, COLLINS,* AND REASONABLE SEARCH

1) *Hunter v Southam Inc*

Hunter is the single most important case on section 8. It lays out the basic groundwork for the Court's approach to search and seizure. It is, for this reason, worth discussing in detail.

The case involved an investigation of the Southam newspaper chain for anti-competitive practices under the *Combines Investigation Act* (*CIA*), an earlier version of what is now the *Competition Act*.[3] Hunter, the director of the Combines Investigations Branch, exercised a power under the *CIA* to authorize a search of the offices of the *Edmonton Journal*, a division of Southam, for evidence of a criminal offence under the Act.[4]

---

2 *Hunter et al v Southam Inc*, [1984] 2 SCR 145 [*Hunter*] and *R v Collins*, [1987] 1 SCR 265 [*Collins*].

3 *Combines Investigation Act*, RSC 1970, c C-23 [*CIA*]; *Competition Act*, RSC 1985, c C-34.

4 The Court does not explicitly characterize as criminal the offences in the Act that could be investigated using the search powers at issue. But this can be inferred by context. The warrant in *Hunter* that investigators served on the *Edmonton Journal* identified the offences, in ss 33 and 34(1)(c) of the *CIA*, of knowingly assisting in the formation of a monopoly and selling products "unreasonably low" with a view to "eliminating a competitor." Each was an indictable offence with a penalty of up to two years imprisonment. Other offence provisions in the Act, to which the powers of search and seizure at issue applied, included misrepresentation in s 36, which allowed for up to five years in prison. The powers at issue thus applied to prosecutions for *criminal* as opposed to regulatory offences. Justice Prowse, at the Court of Appeal for Alberta in this case, saw the powers in the *CIA* in this light, holding that the *Criminal Code*'s warrant provisions "constitute the minimal prerequisites for reasonable searches and seizures in connection with the investigation of any criminal offence, including possible violations of the *Combines Investigation Act*," cited at 152 of *Hunter*, above note 2. Later, when addressing the correct standard to apply to the search powers in this case, Dickson J, as he then was, writes: "The state's interest in detecting and preventing *crime* begins to prevail over the individual's interest in being left alone at the point where credibly-based probability replaces suspicion," at 167–68 [emphasis added]. However, in later decisions, members of the Court expressed the view that Dickson J in *Hunter* was crafting a

The *CIA* provided that where the director simply believed that a place contained evidence, he could authorize agents of the branch to enter it and search and seize anything of relevance.[5] A further provision stipulated that another person had to "certify" the director's authorization, a person from the Restrictive Trade Practices Commission, the larger body of which the branch formed a part.[6] Certification involved nothing more than confirmation that the investigation was in progress. The authority to search and seize under the *CIA* was sweeping.[7]

After agents conducted the search and seized documents, Southam sought an interim injunction, arguing that the law at issue was contrary to section 8. The search may have been authorized by law, but the law itself was unreasonable. Southam failed at trial but succeeded at the Alberta Court of Appeal.[8] Appealing to the Supreme Court, the commission conceded that the *CIA* contained a more permissive warrant scheme than the one found under the *Criminal Code* (requiring probable grounds).[9] But it argued that the *CIA* still authorized a reasonable search because competition offences are more difficult to investigate and prove than other criminal offences.[10] The government was thus urging the Court to read the *Charter* restrictively and to be deferential as to the possible scope of a "reasonable search." Justice Dickson, as he then was, writing for the Court, preferred a different approach. Invoking a long common law history of interpreting constitutional documents in a broad and generous fashion, he held that the *Charter* is "a purposive

---

set of standards for a search power meant to apply in the criminal context, despite the *CIA* being essentially a regulatory statute. See L'Heureux-Dubé J's opinion in *Comité paritaire de l'industrie de la chemise v Potash; Comité paritaire de l'industrie de la chemise v Sélection Milton*, [1994] 2 SCR 406 at 444–45 [*Comité*], noting that "[t]he fact that the [*CIA*] was not limited to regulated industries meant that the strict requirements generally found in criminal law were applied to it, even though the purposes of the Act were administrative." See also La Forest J's decision in *Thomson Newspapers Ltd v Canada (Director of Investigation and Research, Restrictive Trade Practices Commission)*, [1990] 1 SCR 425 at 519–21 [*Thomson Newspapers*].

5 *CIA*, above note 3, s 10(1).

6 *Ibid*, s 10(3).

7 Justice Dickson, *Hunter*, above note 2 at 150, notes: "The authorization has a breathtaking sweep; it is tantamount to a licence to roam at large on the premises of Southam Inc. at the stated address 'and elsewhere in Canada'."

8 *Southam Inc v Canada (Combines Investigation, Director)*, 1983 ABCA 32.

9 Citing an earlier equivalent to the warrant power in s 487 of the *Criminal Code*, RSC 1985, c C-46 [*Criminal Code* or *Code*].

10 *Hunter* above note 2; as Dickson J summarizes the submission, at 154, competition offences entail "less basis for certainty and specificity, both as to the commission of an offence and as to the existence of specific physical evidence in relation to such offence."

document," the purpose of which is "to guarantee and to protect" the rights it entrenches.[11] It is meant to "constrain governmental action inconsistent with those rights;" it is not "an authorization for governmental action."[12]

If the *Charter* is a "purposive document," to discern the meaning of "reasonable search" the Court had to define "the purpose underlying s. 8" or "delineate the nature of the interests it is meant to protect."[13] Historically, rights to be secure against unreasonable search and seizure were rooted in property and trespass law.[14] Yet, the wording of section 8 provides no such limitation, enshrining instead "a broad and general right to be secure from unreasonable search and seizure."[15] To discern what this entails, Dickson J cited with approval Stewart J's opinion of the US Supreme Court in *Katz v United States*,[16] in which the majority held "the Fourth Amendment protects people, not places" thus expanding the scope of search protections well beyond property.[17] As Harlan J had held in *Katz* in relation to the Fourth Amendment, Dickson J held that section 8 seeks to protect not things or places but an individual's interest in a "reasonable expectation of privacy."[18] Intriguingly, Dickson J also asserted that "[l]ike the Supreme Court of the United States, I would be wary of foreclosing the possibility that the right to be secure against unreasonable search and seizure might protect interests beyond the right of privacy, but for purposes of the present appeal I am satisfied that its protections go at least that far."[19] It would be many years before the Court would revisit this passage and pursue the opening it creates by considering other interests — a thread we pick up in later chapters.[20]

From the first part of *Hunter*, then, we glean that section 8 guarantees a broad and general right to be secure against unreasonable search

---

11 *Ibid* at 156.

12 *Ibid*.

13 *Ibid* at 157.

14 *Ibid*, citing *Entick v Carrington*, [1765] EWHC KB J98.

15 *Hunter*, above note 2 at 158.

16 389 US 347 (1967) [*Katz*].

17 *Hunter*, above note 2 at 159. *Katz* involved the use of eavesdropping technology by the FBI, without a warrant, while the accused was speaking in a phone booth, thus raising the question of whether Fourth Amendment protections extended to the conversation.

18 *Ibid*. Justice Dickson adopted the phrase "reasonable expectation of privacy" from Prowse J's use of it in *Hunter* at the Alberta Court of Appeal; but its original source is Harlan J's concurring opinion in *Katz*, above note 16. For more on the origins of the concept, see Chapter 4, Section A(1).

19 *Hunter*, above note 2 at 159.

20 See the discussion in Chapter 4, Section C(1) and Section C(4)(f) of the Court's recognition, in *R v Spencer*, 2014 SCC 43 [*Spencer*], of an interest in anonymity.

and seizure, which at least includes a right of privacy from unjustified state intrusion. The remainder of the decision deals with the issue of when a law authorizing a search is reasonable. Justice Dickson prefaces the discussion by asserting an important principle often neglected in later decisions of the Court on section 8. If the purpose of the section is to protect people from "unjustified state intrusions upon their privacy," it requires "a means of preventing unjustified searches before they happen, not simply of determining, after the fact, whether they ought to have occurred in the first place."[21] This has been done by requiring a warrant, or a form of prior authorization.[22] However, Dickson J concedes that "it may not be reasonable in every instance" to insist on one—a point we return to below.[23] Where feasible, a warrant is a "precondition" for a valid search or seizure, or, adopting Stewart J's language in *Katz*, Dickson J held: "a warrantless search is *prima facie* 'unreasonable'."[24] The party seeking to justify a warrantless search bears the onus of rebutting the presumption of unreasonableness.[25]

The search power in the *Combines Investigation Act* provided for prior authorization but was unreasonable in two respects. In order for any warrant scheme to be "meaningful," the person authorizing the search needs to be able to assess the evidence, and whether the standard has been met, in a neutral and impartial manner.[26] They need not be a judge but must be capable of "acting judicially."[27] Under the *CIA*, the director of investigations authorized the search, but they played an investigatory and prosecutorial role; and the member of the commission tasked with "certifying" the authorization lacked independence because the commission itself acted as "investigator and judge with respect to breaches of the Act."[28] Neither was neutral nor independent enough to act judicially, rendering the search power here unreasonable on this ground alone.

The scheme under the Act was also deficient for allowing a warrant on essentially no grounds. A purposive interpretation of section 8 requires a sufficiently rigorous standard for granting a warrant so as to prevent unjustified searches from taking place. For guidance on the appropriate standard in conventional criminal cases, Dickson J looked to *Entick v Carrington*'s "strong reason to believe" and to the Fourth

21 *Hunter*, above note 2 at 160.
22 *Ibid*.
23 *Ibid* at 161.
24 *Ibid*.
25 *Ibid*.
26 *Ibid* at 162.
27 *Ibid*.
28 *Ibid* at 163.

Amendment's "probable cause" as precedent. Both capture the notion that "[t]he state's interest in detecting and preventing crime begins to prevail over the individual's interest in being left alone at the point where credibly-based probability replaces suspicion."[29] In the normal course, he held, the minimum standard for reasonable search is one requiring a warrant, issued independently, on reasonable and probable grounds to believe "an offence has been committed and that there is evidence to be found at the place of the search."[30] The power at issue in the *Combines Investigation Act* allowed a search on the mere possibility that evidence would be found. This was a further basis on which to find the power unreasonable and in violation of section 8.

Hunter is commonly cited for the proposition that a warrantless search is *prima facie* unreasonable, or presumptively unreasonable, shifting the burden to the Crown to prove a warrantless search reasonable. The case does not address other ways the Crown might establish this, but by pointing at such a possibility, it implies that a search might be reasonable in reliance on other authority—for example, exigent circumstances or valid consent. However, *Hunter* does address a larger and equally important question: when might a *law* authorizing a search be reasonable (or allow for a reasonable search) if it does not require a warrant on probable grounds?

Justice Dickson addresses this point in two key passages. Together, they set out a framework the Court would later adopt for assessing when a search law is reasonable. Early in the decision, Dickson J held that the "limitation on the right guaranteed by s. 8 . . . indicates that an assessment must be made as to whether *in a particular situation* the public's interest in being left alone by government must give way to the government's interest in intruding on the individual's privacy in order to advance its goals, notably those of law enforcement."[31] *Hunter* itself holds that, in the normal course, a law strikes the right balance between state and personal interests when it requires a warrant on probable grounds. Expanding on this, Dickson J held:

> History has confirmed the appropriateness of this requirement as the threshold for subordinating the expectation of privacy to the needs of law enforcement. [However,] [w]here the state's interest is not simply law enforcement as, for instance, where state security is involved, or where the individual's interest is not simply his expectation of privacy as, for instance, when the search threatens his bodily integrity, the

---

29 *Ibid* at 167.

30 *Ibid* at 168.

31 *Ibid* at 159–60 [emphasis added].

> relevant standard might well be a different one. That is not the situation in the present case.[32]

More broadly, Dickson J suggested here that what will constitute a "reasonable search or seizure" under section 8 could not be decided once and for all. It will depend on context. As Charron J would later put it, deciding on the reasonableness of a law under section 8 is "a function of both the importance of the state objective and the degree of impact on the individual's privacy interest."[33] In some cases, where the state interest in search is high and the personal interest in privacy is low—at the border, for example—a reasonable search could be warrantless.[34] Conversely, where a person's privacy interest is heightened—for example, in a strip search or a device search on arrest—something more than "probable grounds to believe evidence will be found" may be necessary to render it reasonable, such as a measure of urgency or expediency.[35] A reasonable search—and a reasonable search law—is one that strikes a reasonable balance between state and individual interests in the context at issue.

A few years after *Hunter*, in *R v Simmons*,[36] Dickson CJ had cause to revisit the idea of reasonableness under section 8 being situation specific and added an important qualification. "While a determination of reasonableness must depend to some degree on the circumstances in which a search is performed" he wrote, "the safeguards articulated in *Hunter v. Southam Inc.* should not be lightly rejected":[37]

> Although *Hunter* did not purport to set down immutable pre-conditions for validity applicable to all searches, the Court arrived at the three minimum prior authorization requirements only after examining the values s. 8 is meant to protect. Foremost among these values is the interest in preventing unjustified searches before they occur. This is a basic value regardless of situational constraints. In light of the importance of preventing unjustified searches, departures from the *Hunter v. Southam Inc.* standards that will be considered reasonable will be exceedingly rare.[38]

---

32 *Ibid* at 167–68.

33 *R v Rodgers*, 2006 SCC 15 at para 27.

34 *R v Simmons*, [1988] 2 SCR 495 [*Simmons*].

35 See *R v Golden*, 2001 SCC 83 [*Golden*] and *R v Fearon*, 2014 SCC 77 [*Fearon*], requiring a measure of urgency in addition to the grounds for arrest. Both are discussed further in Chapter 6, Section D(4).

36 *Simmons*, above note 34.

37 *Ibid* at 527.

38 *Ibid.*

In ways to be seen in later chapters of this book, in the decades that followed, the Court has not held true to this principle. Judges have often invoked the importance of "preventing unjustified searches before they occur," but have also condoned a raft of departures from the *Hunter* standards. They did not turn out to be rare. And at least a few of these lower standards have drawn criticism as to their effectiveness in preventing unjustified searches before they occur—though the possibility of reassessing and revising them remains open to courts in the future.

To return to *Hunter* itself, at the end of the case, Dickson J declined to address section 1, but cast doubt on "what further balancing of interests, if any, may be contemplated by s. 1, beyond that envisaged by s. 8."[39] The Court has since rarely gone on to address a section 8 violation in much detail under section 1, given that it would not survive the minimal impairment part of the test for section 1 under *R v Oakes*.[40] Lower courts have, on occasion, proceeded to consider violations of section 8 under section 1, but *Hunter* suggests that the appropriate place to consider balance and proportionality is under section 8 itself.[41]

2) *R v Collins*

Three years after *Hunter*, the Supreme Court in *R v Collins* offered a different answer to the question of what constitutes a reasonable search under section 8—which can give rise to confusion about how it relates to *Hunter*. The facts in *Collins* are brief and less important than the new test that emerges. But they lend a sense of what prompted a new and broader test, and how it operates.

An officer, acting on a belief that the accused was a heroin dealer, found her seated in a pub and suddenly tackled her to the floor while seizing her by the throat to prevent her from swallowing potential evidence.[42]

39 *Hunter*, above note 2 at 169–70.

40 *R v Oakes*, [1986] 1 SCR 103. See also *Lavallee, Rackel & Heintz v Canada (Attorney General)*; *White, Ottenheimer & Baker v Canada (Attorney General)*; *R v Fink*, 2002 SCC 61, noting at para 46: "if, as here, the violation of s. 8 is found to consist of an unjustifiable impairment of the privacy interest protected by that section, everything else aside, it is difficult to conceive that the infringement could survive the minimal impairment part of the *Oakes* test." Similar comments are made in *R v Grant*, [1993] 3 SCR 223 at 241 and *Canada (Attorney General) v Chambre des notaires du Québec*, 2016 SCC 20 at paras 89–91.

41 A recent example can be found in *R v Canfield*, 2020 ABCA 383, holding that search powers under the *Customs Act*, RSC 1985, c 1 (2nd Supp) as applied to electronic devices violate s 8 of the *Charter* and are not reasonable under s 1. But in this case, the court proceeded to a s 1 analysis after declining to decide what the correct balance of interests calls for under s 8 itself.

42 *Collins*, above note 2 at 270–71.

The officer conceded the force he used was "considerable."[43] At issue for the Court was whether the search was authorized by law—whether the officer had grounds to believe he was likely to find narcotics on the accused—and if so, whether he "carried out the search in a manner that made the search unreasonable."[44] This latter question was a new consideration under section 8. It raised the possibility that a search could be authorized by a reasonable law, as contemplated in *Hunter*, but still be unreasonable under section 8 because of the manner in which it was carried out.

Under the *Narcotic Control Act*, the officer had authority to search the accused if he had reasonable grounds to believe she was committing an offence under the Act.[45] Whether he had reasonable grounds was unclear. He relied in part on hearsay evidence, and the trial judge mistakenly refused to consider that evidence in assessing whether the officer had reasonable grounds.[46] Justice Lamer, as he then was, noted that this was done in error but left for a retrial the issue of whether the officer did have reasonable grounds.[47] For the purpose of the appeal, he assumed the officer did not. Was the search reasonable under section 8 if the officer lacked grounds?

Justice Lamer picked up where *Hunter* had left off, by noting that a warrantless search is *prima facie* unreasonable, shifting the burden to the Crown to establish it was reasonable on a balance of probabilities.[48] Then, almost in passing, Lamer J set out what has become the general test for section 8: "A search will be reasonable if it is authorized by law, if the law itself is reasonable and if the manner in which the search was carried out is reasonable."[49] This test has been invoked in countless section 8 cases since *Collins*.

By setting out this test, Lamer J implied that *Hunter* offered an answer to the first two prongs of the test—in the context of the normal conventional criminal case. Looking back at *Hunter* from the vantage of the *Collins* test, we see that in the normal course, a reasonable search in a criminal case—e.g., the search of an office or a residence—would require a warrant on probable grounds. But in other contexts, a reasonable search might involve something more or less onerous for police.

43 *Ibid* at 271.

44 *Ibid* at 278.

45 *Narcotic Control Act*, RSC 1970, c N-1, s 10(1).

46 *Collins*, above note 2 at 273.

47 *Ibid*, noting at 279 that the Court had decided reasonable grounds could be based on hearsay in *Eccles v Bourque*, [1975] 2 SCR 739.

48 *Collins*, above note 2 at 277–78.

49 *Ibid* at 278.

More broadly, a reasonable search, as articulated in *Hunter*, is one that conforms to a law that strikes an appropriate balance between the state's interest in the search and the individual's interest in privacy. And lastly, Lamer J added a new requirement: a search must also be reasonably conducted.

In *Collins* itself, police relied on section 10 of the (now replaced) *Narcotic Control Act*, which allowed for warrantless searches in drug investigations on reasonable grounds. Justice Lamer noted the appellant took no issue with whether it constituted a reasonable search law. But since, on the record, the officer lacked reasonable grounds, the search was "unreasonable because unlawful [unauthorized] and carried out with unnecessary violence."[50] It failed both the first and third parts of the *Collins* test.

Collins sets out three ways a search or seizure can be unreasonable under section 8, and it also illustrates how each of them might occur. Before moving on to other elements of section 8, it may help to address how *Collins* and *Hunter* tend to be applied in practice.

3) *Hunter* and *Collins* in Practice: Challenging a Search

A person may challenge a search or seizure as unreasonable under section 8 in a number of ways that draw directly on *Hunter* and *Collins*.

First, given the holding in *Hunter* that the purpose of section 8 is to protect a person's reasonable expectation of privacy in a place or thing, a person must first establish they have "standing" to challenge a search or seizure under section 8 by establishing that they had a reasonable privacy interest in the thing or place searched or seized. We expand on this point further below and in Chapter 4. Once a claimant has standing, the court turns to the question of whether the search or seizure was reasonable.

Where police have carried out a search or seizure under a warrant, following *Hunter*, the court will presume the search or seizure was valid and the party challenging this bears the onus of proving otherwise.[51] There are a number of ways to do this. One is to argue that the warrant was issued unlawfully—i.e., it required probable grounds to believe an offence had occurred and evidence would be found in the place to be searched, and the application for the warrant (the "information to obtain") did not meet this test. Another possibility is to argue that a search was not carried out in accordance with the terms of the warrant,

---

50 *Ibid* at 279.

51 *Ibid* at 277–78; applying this reasoning, see *R v James*, 2019 ONSC 4131 at para 26 and *R v Marogy*, 2020 ONCJ 416 at para 18.

or the warrant itself allowed for a search that was inconsistent with the statutory provisions for granting the warrant. We explore these challenges to searches with a warrant in Chapter 5. A party might concede that the warrant was valid but argue that the law authorizing the issuing of the warrant was an unreasonable law—something typically done when the law at issue is relatively new (the topic of Chapter 7). A party might concede that a search was authorized under a reasonable law, but argue it was carried out in an unreasonable manner (the topic of Chapter 8). Finally, a person might concede that a seizure was valid but argue that provisions for post-seizure reporting or the return of items were not complied with, rendering the seizure unreasonable (addressed in Chapter 3).

What if a search or seizure was carried out without a warrant? In this case, following *Hunter*, a court will presume the search or seizure to be unreasonable, shifting the onus to the Crown to establish all three prongs of the *Collins* test, including, first, whether the search was authorized by law. Usually police rely on a specific authority and the Crown argues the police met the requirements for exercising that authority. Often, however, police believe they have lawful authority to search or seize under one law or another—or even pursuant to a warrant they assume is valid—but, for whatever reason, they turn out to be mistaken. The Crown is still free to establish the search was authorized by some other law. So long as the conduct of state agents satisfies the requirements of one authority or another, the search will be authorized by law.

We explore in chapters 5 and 6 the wide range of possible sources of law—in statutes and common law—that authorize police and other state agents to carry out a search or seizure. In general terms, there are three forms of authority: powers pursuant to a warrant, warrantless powers, and consent. Briefly, valid consent requires that police inform a person of the reason for the search and the person's right to refuse.[52] Statutes contain myriad powers to search or seize with a warrant, pertaining to everything from breath, blood, bodily impressions, DNA, wiretapping and surveillance, device data, data transmission, and firearms, among others. There is even a "general warrant," in provision in section 487.01 of the *Criminal Code*, which allows a court to authorize police to use "any device or investigative technique or procedure or do any thing described in the warrant that would, if not authorized, constitute an unreasonable search or seizure."[53]

Not all warrant powers require probable grounds to believe evidence of an offence will be found. Some warrants can be issued on reasonable

52 *R v Borden*, [1994] 3 SCR 145 at 162; *R v Wills* (1992), 7 OR (3d) 337 at para 44 (CA). Consent is explored further in Chapter 6, Section D(1).

53 *Criminal Code*, above note 9.

suspicion, where they contemplate less intrusive searches (e.g., breath samples at roadside) or where the state has a pressing interest in a search and a person has a lesser privacy interest (e.g., strip search at the border).[54] Statutes also provide for powers to carry out a warrantless search and seizure, such as in exigent circumstances or situations where there is a high state interest and a low privacy interest (e.g., carrying goods over the border, being searched on entry to a prison).[55] Finally, a host of powers can be found at common law, setting out things police may do "ancillary" to their duties to keep the peace and enforce the law, including search without a warrant on arrest or detention, in exigent circumstances, or using sniffer dogs—among others.[56]

A search or seizure that was not authorized by law would be unreasonable and would violate section 8. If it was authorized by law, the court would continue with the *Collins* test.

The second part of the *Collins* test addresses whether a law authorizing a search or seizure is reasonable. In most cases, the court will only touch on this briefly, before moving on. It plays an important role in two situations. One is when Parliament or a provincial legislature introduces a law authorizing a new form of search or seizure, and soon after a person challenges whether it is reasonable. An example of this can be found in *R v SAB*,[57] where the accused challenged *Criminal Code* provisions for obtaining a DNA warrant as an unreasonable law.[58] The Court found the law to be reasonable for striking an appropriate balance between a pressing state interest in obtaining highly accurate DNA evidence and an individual's right to dignity and physical integrity. The warrant requires probable grounds, and the process for obtaining a sample is minimally intrusive.

A second kind of case in which courts engage the second part of the *Collins* test are cases where they do so implicitly. This happens when courts recognize new search powers at common law. In the process of crafting reasonable limits on the power, the court implies that it constitutes a reasonable search law. For example, in *R v Mann*,[59] the Supreme Court recognized a police power to carry out a brief pat-down search incident to an investigative detention. A person's privacy should give way to an officer's safety concerns where the officer has reasonable grounds

54 These examples are explored in more detail in Chapter 6.

55 See Chapter 6, Section A(7) and Chapter 6, Section B(3).

56 See Chapter 6, Section D.

57 2003 SCC 60 at paras 43–52.

58 *Criminal Code*, above note 9, ss 487.04–487.09.

59 2004 SCC 52.

to believe safety is at issue and where the pat-down search is brief.[60] Another example can be found in *R v Fearon*,[61] where the Court crafted a test for when police are authorized to search a cellphone incident to arrest. In the normal course, police with grounds to arrest a person can search them without requiring additional grounds for the search.[62] But to search a phone, police need to satisfy a further set of conditions—given the higher privacy interest we have in electronic devices relative to our pockets or immediate surroundings.[63] We look at more examples of both kinds of cases on reasonable search laws—and why they were found reasonable—in Chapter 7.

Finally, in every search or seizure case—with or without a warrant—the court needs to consider the third part of the *Collins* test (assuming the Crown satisfies the first two parts). Whether police carried out the search or seizure in a reasonable manner will depend on the facts of a case, but caselaw provides guidance on various fronts, including search on arrest, strip searches, dynamic entry warrant executions, and computer searches. The general principle emerging from these cases is that a search should be "no more intrusive than is reasonably necessary to achieve its objectives."[64] Courts expect state agents to be minimally invasive and avoid undue embarrassment, humiliation, or destruction of property. For example, police should conduct strip searches in the field (as opposed to the police station) only in exigent circumstances, where there is reason to believe important evidence would otherwise be lost or safety is at issue.[65] They should be carried out, if practicable, by a person of the same gender; a person should first be given a chance to remove secreted items on their own; cavity searches should be done, if possible, with the assistance of a medical professional.[66] In computer searches pursuant to a warrant, when police realize they have "no reason to search a particular program or file on the device" they must avoid doing so.[67] When searching a phone on arrest, police should not search "the entire contents" of the device, and they must take "detailed notes" of what they examined.[68] We explore these and other examples in more detail in Chapter 8.

60 *Ibid* at paras 37 and 43.

61 *Fearon*, above note 35.

62 *Cloutier v Langlois*, [1990] 1 SCR 158.

63 We explore the test in *Fearon* in Chapter 6, Section D(4)(a).

64 *R v Vu*, 2013 SCC 60 at para 22 [*Vu*].

65 *Golden*, above note 35.

66 *Ibid* at para 102.

67 *Vu*, above note 64 at para 61.

68 *Fearon*, above note 35 at paras 78 and 82.

We note a point of procedure here. Often, police will take a series of steps to gather evidence in the course of an investigation. Two or three of them may amount to a search. Police will use the fruits of one search to obtain information or grounds that they then use to obtain a warrant for (or exercise powers in) a subsequent search. This in turn might provide police with grounds for obtaining a further warrant and carrying out a further search. When courts review the validity of these searches under section 8, they proceed chronologically. An accused will typically challenge the validity of the search that occurs earliest in time. If the court finds that police violated their rights under section 8 in obtaining information or evidence in the first search, the court will exclude that information when assessing whether police had sufficient grounds in the next search. In other words, the court does not stop after concluding the first search was unreasonable and conduct an assessment under section 24(2) in order to exclude the fruits of the first search when considering the validity of the second search. A finding that an earlier search was unreasonable can thus create a domino effect, resulting in a holding that a series of searches were unreasonable.[69]

For example, in *R v Evans*, police carried out an unreasonable search knocking on the door to sniff odours emanating from within a home and used this to obtain a warrant to search it.[70] The initial (sniff) search was unreasonable; the grounds obtained from the search had to be excised from the grounds for obtaining the warrant; the warrant was invalid, rendering the second search (of the home) unreasonable.

In the rest of this chapter, we turn to matters that play a preliminary role in the section 8 analysis. When is section 8 engaged? We gleaned from *Hunter* that the purpose of section 8 is to protect a reasonable expectation of privacy. This means that if police search or seize something over which there is no reasonable expectation of privacy, section 8 is not engaged. If there is a reasonable expectation of privacy to any degree, then section 8 is engaged.[71] Some commentators suggest that

---

69 A question arises, in cases involving two or more accused, whether a finding that person A's rights were breached in an early part of an investigation should result in the excision of information obtained as a result of the breach from an application for a warrant later executed against persons A and B. Caselaw is divided on this question, with some courts holding that the poisoned fruit should only be excised from the warrant application in relation to person A and other courts holding that it should be excised from the warrant application in relation to both person A and person B. For a summary of caselaw on point across Canada, see *R v Kang*, 2020 BCSC 1151. We discuss the process of challenging warrants in more detail in Chapter 5, Section C.

70 *R v Evans*, [1996] 1 SCR 8 [*Evans*].

71 *R v Cole*, 2012 SCC 53 at para 9.

whether a search has taken place under section 8 can be reduced to the question of whether there was a reasonable expectation of privacy in the place or thing searched. This is true in the sense that without such an expectation, section 8 is not engaged. Yet one can have a reasonable expectation of privacy over something and police conduct in relation to it might not amount to a search or seizure (because their actions did not interfere with a person's privacy or were not intended to do so, or were not carried out for an investigative purpose—points explored further below and in Chapter 3). It is important to keep these issues in mind as separate and distinct. Establishing a breach of section 8 requires both privacy interest and an interference for an investigative purpose. It also requires a third thing—assumed but not addressed in *Hunter* or *Collins*. The search or seizure must be conducted by a state agent to engage section 8, by virtue of the fact that the *Charter* applies only to actions of the state.[72] We address who can be a "state agent" under section 8 below (and in more detail in Chapter 3).

C. WHEN IS SECTION 8 ENGAGED?

1) Reasonable Expectation of Privacy

This is a large topic. A good portion of the Supreme Court's decisions on section 8 deal with whether a claimant had a reasonable expectation of privacy in a given situation. Our aim here is only to introduce the concept. Chapter 4 explores it in depth. We highlight three ideas that emerge from the caselaw. A reasonable expectation of privacy is normative, contextual, and a matter of degree.

In a pair of early cases, *R v Duarte* and *R v Wong*,[73] the Court held that whether a person has a reasonable expectation of privacy in a given situation should not depend on the risk of state interference stemming from the unlawful use they might be making of a place or thing. It should depend on whether members of a "free and democratic society" would expect to be left alone from state intrusion in a place or thing *of that nature*.[74] For example, the accused in *Wong* had used a hotel room to run a gambling operation. The majority held that he had a reasonable expectation of privacy in the room because members of a free society

72 *Charter*, above note 1, s 32; *RWDSU v Dolphin Delivery Ltd*, [1986] 2 SCR 573 [*Dolphin Delivery*].

73 *R v Duarte*, [1990] 1 SCR 30, 65 DLR (4th) 240 [*Duarte*]; *R v Wong*, [1990] 3 SCR 36 [*Wong*].

74 *Wong*, *ibid* at 45–46.

would expect to enjoy privacy from the state when staying in a hotel room. Similarly, whether we have a heightened or lower expectation of privacy in a given place or thing—in a home, for example, or at the border—depends not on what a given person might expect but what we might assume is a common societal expectation. As the Court held in *Tessling*, "[e]xpectation of privacy is a normative rather than a descriptive standard."[75]

The analysis of a reasonable expectation of privacy is also context sensitive. The Court has distinguished three general forms of privacy: personal, territorial, and informational, giving rise to a hierarchy in terms of the degree of privacy we expect in each context.[76] Bodily searches are potentially the most invasive, followed by searches of intimate spaces within our homes and, to a lesser degree, places such as offices or vehicles.[77] Searches that involve our personal information can also be exceedingly intrusive given how much can be gleaned about our lives from our data.[78] We have a high expectation of privacy over information that touches on a "biographical core of personal information" that "tends to reveal intimate details of [our] lifestyle and personal choices."[79]

Over time, the Court has fashioned a general test for a reasonable expectation of privacy that asks whether in the totality of the circumstances the expectation was reasonable.[80] It uses four criteria to guide this inquiry: "What was the subject matter of the alleged search? Did the claimant have a direct interest in the subject matter? Did the claimant have a subjective expectation of privacy in the subject matter? If so, was the claimant's subjective expectation of privacy objectively reasonable?"[81]

When assessing the subject matter of the search, courts are concerned not with the particular item or place searched or seized but with what it discloses or interferes with.[82] Searching messages on a phone involves more than just seizing a phone and reading texts; it entails an intrusion into a private (chat) room.[83] Analogously, when they seize a computer, police not only "deprive individuals of control over intimate

---

75 *R v Tessling*, 2004 SCC 67 at para 42.

76 *Ibid* at paras 21–24; *R v Dyment*, [1988] 2 SCR 417 at 428–30 and 438 [*Dyment*].

77 See, e.g., *R v Pohoretsky*, [1987] 1 SCR 945, with Lamer J, as he then was, noting at 949 that "a violation of the sanctity of a person's body is much more serious than that of his office or even of his home."

78 *Fearon*, above note 35; *Vu*, above note 64.

79 *R v Plant*, [1993] 3 SCR 281 at 293 [*Plant*].

80 *R v Marakah*, 2017 SCC 59 at para 11 [*Marakah*].

81 *Ibid* [numbers omitted]; *R v Spencer*, above note 20 at para 18.

82 *Vancouver (City) v Ward*, 2010 SCC 27 at para 65; *Marakah*, above note 80 at para 15.

83 *Marakah*, above note 80 at para 28.

data," they also preserve it, making it "subject to potential future state inspection."[84]

Control, ownership, and possession are relevant to whether a claimant has a subjective expectation of privacy, and whether that expectation is objectively reasonable. But neither control nor ownership nor possession of a space or thing are decisive.[85] We can have a reasonable privacy interest in a friend's apartment we spend time in,[86] a friend's car we ride along in,[87] or even a text we send them that police later find on their phone.[88] In each case, whether we have a reasonable expectation of privacy in something we do not own, possess, or control will depend on why we thought it reasonable to expect to be left alone from state intrusion, and whether, from a normative perspective, it was a belief others would share in a free society.

The "totality" test helps us determine whether we have a reasonable expectation of privacy. If we do to any degree, and the search or seizure was carried out by a state agent for an investigative purpose, section 8 is engaged. But how high or low an expectation of privacy we have becomes important at later stages of a constitutional challenge to a search. As noted earlier, courts take the degree of privacy into account when assessing whether a law authorizing a search is reasonable and whether police conducted a search reasonably. Courts also do so when assessing a remedy under section 24 of the *Charter* if a violation of section 8 is made out (the topic of Chapter 9).

For these purposes, a body of caselaw dealing with different situations offers us a guide as to when a search or seizure is more or less invasive of our privacy. Taking a breath sample is less invasive than a blood sample or DNA swab.[89] More invasive still are the steps that police take to record our words or images through surveillance tools, when they search an electronic device, or carry out a strip search.[90] We also have

---

84 *R v Reeves*, 2018 SCC 56 at para 30.

85 *Marakah*, above note 80; *R v Edwards*, [1996] 1 SCR 128.

86 *R v Edwards*, *ibid*, finding in that case that the accused did not, but recognizing the possibility that he might have had the facts been different.

87 *R v Belnavis*, [1997] 3 SCR 341.

88 *Marakah*, above note 80.

89 *Goodwin v British Columbia (Superintendent of Motor Vehicles)*, 2015 SCC 46 at para 65, noting that "a roadside ASD test is far less intrusive than many other searches or seizures that may be performed for law enforcement purposes, such as the blood sample at issue in *Dyment*, above note 76, or a DNA swab, which contains deeply personal information: *R. v. S.A.B.*, 2003 SCC 60, [2003] 2 S.C.R. 678, at para. 48."

90 *Duarte*, above note 73 at 43–45; *Vu*, above note 64 at paras 40–45; *Golden*, above note 35 at para 89.

high or low privacy expectations in different settings. We have some but not much privacy over our bodies and goods at the border;[91] high school students have some but not a high degree of privacy in their persons, bags, and lockers at school;[92] businesses subject to inspections should expect a lower degree of privacy in their workplaces.[93]

Finally, it is important to be clear about when we do not have a reasonable expectation of privacy. Generally, we do not have privacy over things we do in public—though we can still expect not to be individually surveilled by the state without authorization.[94] We do not have a reasonable expectation in things we abandon. Depending on where we place our garbage, once we make clear that we intend for it to be taken away, it is no longer private, since we have little idea of what happens to it once collected.[95] The *Charter* does not protect us from "tattletales." We cannot reasonably expect that people we share secrets with will not tell the police. If they do, we cannot rely on their lack of discretion as a shield from law enforcement.[96]

2) What Is a Search or Seizure Under Section 8?

In *R v Evans*, Sopinka J held that a "search" under section 8 occurs where "a person's reasonable expectations of privacy are somehow diminished by an investigatory technique."[97] In other cases, a search involves conduct amounting to an "invasion of a reasonable expectation of privacy."[98] In *R v Kang-Brown*, a search is described as an "investigative technique" that reveals something about the inner content of a place or thing over which we have a reasonable expectation of privacy.[99]

There are many cases on specific actions that constitute a search under section 8, which we explore in Chapter 3. To take just a few examples, in *Evans* police suspected the accused was running a marijuana

91 *Simmons*, above note 34 at 516–17.

92 *R v M(MR)*, [1998] 3 SCR 393 at paras 31–34.

93 *Comité*, above note 4; *R v McKinlay Transport Ltd*, [1990] 1 SCR 267 [*McKinlay*].

94 *R v Wise*, [1992] 1 SCR 527 at 558 [*Wise*] and *R v Spencer*, above note 20 at paras 43–44.

95 *R v Patrick*, 2009 SCC 17 at para 55. However, we do have a privacy interest in discarded bodily samples when in custody (see, e.g., *R v Stillman*, [1997] 1 SCR 607 at paras 59–64).

96 *Duarte*, above note 73 at 51–52. A person to whom we text a secret who brings a copy of the text message to police is a different issue, dealt with in Chapter 3, Section E(3).

97 *Evans*, above note 70 at para 11.

98 *Wise*, above note 94 at 533; *R v AM*, 2008 SCC 19 at para 8 [*AM*].

99 *R v Kang-Brown*, 2008 SCC 18 at para 58 [*Kang-Brown*].

grow operation in his home and knocked on the door with the intention of sniffing for the scent of marijuana.[100] Police had carried out a search because their action exceeded the scope of the implied permission to knock at the door and intruded upon a "reasonable expectation of privacy in the approach to [the] home."[101] Police carried out a search when they used sniffer dogs to detect the contents of bags passengers were carrying at a bus station and a student's backpack in a high school.[102] In *R v MacDonald*, police responding to a noise complaint pushed open the accused's door when they noticed he had an object hidden behind his leg.[103] Pushing open the door to get a better look amounted to a search because it "constituted an intrusion upon Mr. MacDonald's reasonable privacy interest in his dwelling."[104] Police carry out a search whenever they conduct electronic surveillance.[105]

Turning to the concept of a "seizure," La Forest J's concurring opinion in *R v Dyment* sets out a widely cited definition: "the essence of a seizure under s. 8 is the taking of a thing from a person by a public authority without that person's consent."[106] A seizure need not involve taking something from a person directly—police conduct a seizure under section 8 when they receive an item from a third party.[107] For example, in *Dyment*, a doctor took a vial of blood from an accused after a car accident for medical purposes, learned the accused had been drinking, then gave the sample to police. The majority held that police had "seized" the sample because the accused had retained a privacy interest in it when the officer received it. However, not every case that involves a transfer of evidence to a state agent will constitute a seizure. As La Forest J held in *Dyment*: "If I were to draw the line between a seizure and a mere finding of evidence, I would draw it logically and purposefully at the point at which it can reasonably be said that the individual had ceased to have a privacy interest in the subject-matter allegedly seized."[108]

100 *Evans*, above note 70.
101 *Ibid* at para 14.
102 *Kang-Brown*, above note 99; *AM*, above note 98.
103 *R v MacDonald*, 2014 SCC 3.
104 *Ibid* at para 27.
105 *Duarte*, above note 73 at 42.
106 *Dyment*, above note 76 at 431.
107 *R v Colarusso*, [1994] 1 SCR 20 at 58.
108 *Dyment*, above note 76 at 435.

Another action recognized as a seizure is an order to produce documents over which a person has a privacy interest, such as therapeutic records, business records, or financial documents.[109] By contrast, demanding a licence and insurance on a vehicle stop does not amount to search because it does not involve "an intrusion on a reasonable expectation of privacy."[110] We canvass more examples of seizures in Chapter 3.

3) Who Can Carry It Out?

Section 32 of the *Charter*, along with the Court's interpretation of that section, limit the application of the *Charter* to actions of the state or agents of the state.[111] Police or investigators who carry out searches on behalf of a government agency clearly engage section 8 because they act under the substantial control of government and pursuant to powers set out in legislation. Civilians or non-government agents can also qualify as "state agents" under section 8 in two ways. One is to perform a government function or act pursuant to a power set out in a statute[112]— for example, when carrying out a citizen's arrest.[113] More commonly, a person becomes a state agent where they act at the behest or direction of police or another state actor.[114]

In *R v Buhay*, security guards at a bus station opened a locker on the suspicion that it contained illicit drugs. After finding drugs, they put them back in the locker and notified police.[115] The Court held that although guards are regulated under legislation, they were not exercising a statutory power in opening the locker. As Arbour J held, "the proper question is whether the security guards would have searched the contents of locker 135 but for the intervention of the police."[116]

Caselaw explored in Chapter 3 canvasses other situations where courts have had to decide whether a person is a state agent for the purposes of section 8.

---

109 *R v Mills*, [1999] 3 SCR 668 at para 77; *Thomson Newspapers*, above note 4; *McKinlay*, above note 93.

110 *R v Hufsky*, [1988] 1 SCR 621 at 638, 84 NR 365.

111 *Dolphin Delivery*, above note 72; *McKinney v University of Guelph*, [1990] 3 SCR 229 at 261.

112 *Eldridge v British Columbia (Attorney General)*, [1997] 3 SCR 624; *R v Buhay*, 2003 SCC 30 at para 25 [*Buhay*].

113 *R v Lerke*, 1986 ABCA 15.

114 *R v Broyles*, [1991] 3 SCR 595 at 608; *Buhay*, above note 112 at para 25.

115 *Buhay*, *ibid*.

116 *Ibid* at para 29.

D. REMEDIES FOR VIOLATING SECTION 8

To round out our conceptual overview of section 8, we conclude with the question of remedies. The *Charter* contemplates three consequences for a violation of section 8. A party may ask the court to strike down or declare invalid a law that authorizes an unreasonable search or seizure on the basis that it constitutes an unreasonable limit on the right under section 1 of the *Charter*. A party might invoke section 24(1) of the *Charter*, which allows the court to grant any remedy it "considers appropriate and just in the circumstances," including compensation or a judicial stay of proceedings. Yet the most common remedy sought for an unreasonable search or seizure is to have evidence excluded under section 24(2) of the *Charter.* (Remedies under both section 24(1) and 24(2) are the topic of Chapter 9.)

Briefly, section 24(2) provides that where the court concludes that evidence was obtained in a manner that infringed a *Charter* right, "the evidence shall be excluded if it is established that, having regard to all circumstances, the admission of it in the proceedings would bring the administration of justice into disrepute." In *R v Grant*, the Court held that "[t]he inquiry is objective" and is concerned with whether "a reasonable person, informed of all relevant circumstances and the values underlying the *Charter*, would conclude that the admission of the evidence would bring the administration of justice into disrepute."[117] When asking this question, courts should consider the "long-term" impact of condoning the police conduct at issue by admitting the evidence.[118] And the focus is "societal" and "not aimed at punishing the police or providing compensation to the accused."[119] To help guide courts in deciding whether to admit evidence, judges could consider three "lines of inquiry": "(1) the seriousness of the *Charter*-infringing state conduct (admission may send the message the justice system condones serious state misconduct), (2) the impact of the breach on the *Charter*-protected interests of the accused (admission may send the message that individual rights count for little), and (3) society's interest in the adjudication of the case on its merits."[120]

When assessing the seriousness of the state conduct in the case of a section 8 breach, courts consider police conduct in the course of a search or seizure. Did officers fail to put their minds to whether a warrant was necessary through negligence or inadvertence; did they misjudge

117 *R v Grant*, 2009 SCC 32 at para 68 [*Grant*].

118 *Ibid.*

119 *Ibid* at para 70.

120 *Ibid* at para 71.

whether they had reasonable grounds to believe there were exigent circumstances permitting a warrantless search? Or was the conduct more serious: was it part of a pattern of ignoring *Charter* rights, or was the search itself heavy-handed or excessively forceful?

When assessing the impact of the breach on "*Charter* protected interests," courts are concerned with interests section 8 is meant to protect: dignity, integrity, and autonomy.[121] The higher the expectation of privacy in the space or thing unlawfully searched or seized, the more serious the impact on those interests.[122] On the third line of inquiry, the court asks whether the "truth-seeking function of the criminal trial process would be better served by admission of the evidence, or by its exclusion."[123] Where the evidence is tangible and reliable—a piece of physical evidence directly implicating the accused—and where it is the only or a crucial piece of evidence for the prosecution, this will favour admission. The three lines need to be "balanced" qualitatively and the overall question of potential disrepute to the administration of justice considered in the totality of the circumstances.[124]

---

121 *Plant*, above note 79 at 292.

122 *Grant*, above note 117 at para 78.

123 *Ibid* at para 79.

124 *Ibid* at paras 85–86.

CHAPTER 3

WHAT IS A SEARCH OR SEIZURE?

A. INTRODUCTION: WHEN IS SECTION 8 ENGAGED?

Section 8 of the *Charter* protects "a right to be secure against unreasonable search or seizure" and it will apply to a given case only if three things are true.[1] The person carrying out the search or seizure must be a state actor or a person acting as their agent. The action they take must amount to an investigative step or be carried out for an investigative purpose.[2] And the action must amount to a taking or interfering with something in which a claimant has a reasonable expectation of privacy.[3]

1 *Canadian Charter of Rights and Freedoms*, Part I of the *Constitution Act, 1982*, being Schedule B to the *Canada Act 1982* (UK), 1982, c 11 [*Charter*].

2 In most cases, this is implied or assumed. Examples of cases where it becomes an issue include *R v Evans*, [1996] 1 SCR 8 [*Evans*] and *R v Colarusso*, [1994] 1 SCR 20 [*Colarusso*], both discussed further below.

3 In *Quebec (Attorney General) v 9147-0732 Québec inc*, 2020 SCC 32, Abella J noted, at para 128, that

> [o]nly ss. 8 and 11(b) within the ss. 7 to 14 grouping [in the *Charter*] have been found by this Court to apply to corporations. In *Hunter* [*v Southam Inc*], the Court accepted, without discussion or explanation, that the s. 8 right to be secure against unreasonable search or seizure could apply to corporations. Subsequently, in *Thomson Newspapers Ltd. v. Canada (Director of Investigation and Research, Restrictive Trade Practices Commission)*, [1990] 1 SCR 425, at pp. 521–22, La Forest J. noted that an unlawful search or seizure could have a significant impact on the privacy rights of individuals within a corporation.

If so, the police or other state actor have "engaged" a claimant's rights under section 8. The engagement continues beyond the time when a state agent has collected evidence and extends throughout the period the evidence is held in state hands. A failure on the part of police or other state agent to return, protect, or in some cases destroy the evidence in a reasonable manner may amount to an unreasonable search or seizure, even if the initial collection took place months or even years before.

Our focus in this chapter is on the elements of the first two of the three necessary ingredients for engaging section 8. We deal first with when a person or entity is a state actor or agent. We turn in the remainder of the chapter to what actions constitute a search or seizure; what post-collection events continue to affect the reasonableness of a search or seizure; and the question of standing. We devote the next chapter to a "reasonable expectation of privacy."

B. WHEN IS A SEARCH CONDUCTED BY A STATE ENTITY OR ACTOR?

Section 32 of the *Charter* limits the application of the rights it protects to the actions of the federal and provincial governments of Canada and matters within their respective authority.[4] It does not apply to private actors.[5] When does a person or an entity fall into either group?

1) When the *Charter* Applies

The Supreme Court has held that the *Charter* can apply to an actor or entity in one of two ways. If they are part of government or they are an entity over which the government exercises "substantial control"[6] or "routine or regular control,"[7] the *Charter* will apply to all of the activities of that entity.[8] The *Charter* will also apply if an actor or entity imple-

---

4 This includes municipalities, their acts, and laws: *Godbout v Longueuil (City)*, [1997] 3 SCR 844.

5 *RWDSU v Dolphin Delivery Ltd*, [1986] 2 SCR 573; *Vriend v Alberta*, [1998] 1 SCR 493.

6 *Greater Vancouver Transportation Authority v Canadian Federation of Students — British Columbia Component*, [2009] 2 SCR 295 at para 16. On what substantial control may constitute, see *Douglas/Kwantlen Faculty Association v Douglas College*, [1990] 3 SCR 570, and *McKinney v University of Guelph*, [1990] 3 SCR 229.

7 *Stoffman v Vancouver General Hospital*, [1990] 3 SCR 483 at 513–14, distinguishing "routine or regular control" (where the *Charter* does apply) from "ultimate or extraordinary" control (where it does not).

8 *Eldridge v British Columbia (Attorney General)*, [1997] 3 SCR 624 at para 44.

ments a "specific statutory scheme or a government program," in which case the *Charter* will apply only in relation to those acts and not private ones.[9] In the context of section 8, in addition to police, actors that are clearly part of government or entities over which government exerts substantial control might include anything from city bylaw officers, investigators for regulatory agencies, public transit security officers, or employees at public hospitals.

The *Charter* applies only to government *in* Canada or to an entity within its authority.[10] When police work with foreign agencies, the *Charter* does not apply to actions undertaken by those agencies, even where they act at the behest of Canadian officials, if the foreign agency is governed by foreign law.[11] Where Canadian police investigating in a foreign territory work with local police, the *Charter* will not apply unless that country consents to the enforcement of Canadian law in that jurisdiction.[12] However, while evidence may not have been *obtained* outside Canada in a manner that violated a *Charter* right, its admission in a trial in Canada may violate the right to a fair trial protected in section 11(d) of the *Charter* and be excluded under section 24(1).[13]

2) When a Person Acts as a State Agent

A private actor can become an agent of the state in one of two ways: if they carry out a governmental purpose or if they act at the direction of or in coordination with a state actor.[14] In the case of other private actors, such as store security guards or citizens providing evidence to police, the question in each case is whether in relaying or providing the evidence to a state actor they would have done what they did "but for" some positive, initiating act by the state actor.

R v Broyles is the leading decision on when a person acts as an agent for law enforcement for *Charter* purposes.[15] In that case, police arranged with a friend of the accused to visit him in custody wearing a wiretap and

---

9 *Ibid.*

10 *Schreiber v Canada (Attorney General)*, [1998] 1 SCR 841 [*Schreiber*].

11 *Ibid* at paras 33–34; see also *R v Terry*, [1996] 2 SCR 207.

12 *R v Hape*, [2007] 2 SCR 292 at paras 102–6.

13 *R v Harrer*, [1995] 3 SCR 562.

14 In *R v Lerke*, 1986 ABCA 15, the court held s 8 to apply to a person carrying out a citizen's arrest, since they were carrying out a government function. The court in *R v AMJ*, 1999 BCCA 366 held a contrary view. We credit Edward Greenspan et al, *Martin's Annual Criminal Code* (Toronto: Carswell, 2022) for these sources.

15 *R v Broyles*, [1991] 3 SCR 595. The case was framed as a violation of the right to silence, recognized under s 7 of the *Charter*, and makes no mention of s 8 but is cited extensively in search and seizure cases.

captured incriminating statements. Justice Iacobucci held that "[o]nly if the relationship between the informer and the state is such that the exchange between the informer and the accused is materially different from what it would have been had there been no such relationship should the informer be considered a state agent for the purposes of the exchange."[16] More succinctly, the general test for whether someone is an agent asks: "would the exchange between the accused and the informer have taken place, in the form and manner in which it did take place, but for the intervention of the state or its agents?"[17] In this case, it was clear that the conversation itself would not have taken place without the "intervention" of the officer. By contrast, had police approached a cellmate afterwards to elicit information, it would not have had an effect on the conversation itself.

A clear example of an agency relationship arising on the basis of police direction can be found in *R v Pohoretsky*.[18] Arriving at the scene of a car accident, an officer noticed a case of beer and advised another officer to attend the hospital to get a sample from the accused. The second officer asked the attending doctor to take a blood sample and she did so, when she had neither the accused's consent nor any medical need to take the sample.

In *R v M(MR)*, a vice principal, suspecting that a student possessed marijuana, called police and invited an officer to be present in his office as he searched the student.[19] Upon finding a bag of marijuana, he handed it to the officer who proceeded with an arrest. For the majority, the fact that there was some "cooperation" between the vice principal and police—what the trial judge had described as an "agreed strategy"—was not in itself enough to meet the test in *Broyles*. Justice Cory held that the search would have taken place here "in the form and manner in which it did," i.e., in a materially similar way, had police not been involved. The primary motive for the search was not to assist police but to enforce school rules.[20] Justice Major, in dissent, deferred to the trial judge's finding that the vice principal had acted as an agent by construing police involvement here as more than mere cooperation. The officer instructed the vice principal on how to conduct the search. The school policy of calling the police when a student was found in possession of drugs also made a school official in those cases "a *de facto* agent of the police."[21]

---

16 *Ibid* at 608.
17 *Ibid.*
18 [1987] 1 SCR 945.
19 *R v M(MR)*, [1998] 3 SCR 393.
20 *Ibid* at para 29.
21 *Ibid* at paras 78–79.

C. WHAT ACTS CONSTITUTE A SEARCH?

In *R v Evans*, Sopinka J held that state actors conduct a "search" for the purposes of section 8 where "a person's reasonable expectations of privacy are somehow diminished by an investigatory technique" or where "state examinations constitute an intrusion upon some reasonable privacy interest."[22]

In *Evans* police knocked at the door of the accused's home in a deliberate effort to "get a whif [*sic*] or a smell" of marijuana emanating from it to obtain grounds for a warrant to search it for a suspected grow operation.[23] The majority held that the implied invitation to knock that applies in residential contexts (for "convenient communications") does not extend to police carrying out an investigation.[24] Police visited the house with an investigative purpose and intruded on the accused's privacy. Detecting odours at the door amounted to a search.

Applying the test in *Evans*, the Supreme Court has held a variety of different actions to constitute a search under section 8. Police conduct a search when they inspect something;[25] when they carry out a wiretap or surreptitiously record a conversation;[26] when they install a tracking device on a vehicle;[27] when they ask an internet service provider to give them the subscriber information associated with an internet protocol address;[28] when they use a sniffer dog to detect odours emanating from bags at bus depots, airport terminals, or schools;[29] when they conduct a bedpan vigil (usually done at the border);[30] when they take bodily samples such as hair or teeth impressions;[31] when they push open the front door of a residence to get a better look at what is in a person's hand;[32] when they enter a workplace to conduct a regulatory inspection;[33] and when they find an item reported stolen and proceed to review documents found inside it.[34] More broadly, in *R v Spencer*, the Court held that

22 *Evans*, above note 2 at para 11.

23 *Ibid* at para 16.

24 *Ibid* at paras 15–16.

25 *R v Cole*, 2012 SCC 53 at para 34 [*Cole*].

26 *R v Duarte*, [1990] 1 SCR 30 [*Duarte*].

27 *R v Wise*, [1992] 1 SCR 527.

28 *R v Spencer*, 2014 SCC 43 at para 66 [*Spencer*].

29 *R v Kang-Brown*, 2008 SCC 18; *R v AM*, 2008 SCC 19.

30 *R v Monney*, [1999] 1 SCR 652.

31 *R v Stillman*, [1997] 1 SCR 607 [*Stillman*].

32 *R v MacDonald*, 2014 SCC 3.

33 *Comité paritaire de l'industrie de la chemise v Potash*, [1994] 2 SCR 406 [*Comité*].

34 *R v Law*, 2002 SCC 10, dealing with police finding a safe and searching documents found within it.

"[w]here a police officer requests disclosure of information relating to a suspect from a third party, whether there is a search depends on whether, in light of the totality of the circumstances, the suspect has a reasonable expectation of privacy in that information."[35]

In some cases, the Court has described an action as both a search and a seizure. For example, in *Duarte*, La Forest J speaks of "surreptitious electronic surveillance of the individual by an agency of the state" without a warrant as "an unreasonable search or seizure under s. 8."[36] In *R v Saeed,* the Court describes obtaining a penile swab as both a search and a seizure.[37] In terms of whether section 8 is engaged, nothing appears to turn on the difference, since, as La Forest J affirmed in *R v Dyment*, section 8 protects against "searches *or* seizures."[38]

The Supreme Court has also made important rulings on what is not a search. Police or other state agents do not conduct a search when they only converse with someone, rather than also surreptitiously recording the conversation.[39] Police did not conduct a search by installing a recording device to measure power flowing into a residence suspected of drug production for three reasons: the electricity authority's regulations provided notice of possible cooperation with police; the information did not intrude upon a privacy interest (did not reveal anything "intimate" or relevant to the inhabitant's "biographical core"); and the consumption data was not meant to be confidential.[40] Police did not carry out a search when they used "Forward Looking Infra-Red" technology to detect heat patterns radiating from a building, since the state of the technology at the time could not produce information that would uncover intimate details or core biographical data about the people inside.[41] Police do not carry out a search in demanding a driver's licence and insurance at roadside, given a lack of privacy in the information.[42] Police do not conduct a search when they collect garbage left at the curb (but on a person's property), because it is abandoned and no longer retains a privacy interest.[43]

---

35 *Spencer*, above note 28 at para 67, Cromwell J writing for the Court.

36 *Duarte*, above note 26 at 42.

37 *R v Saeed*, 2016 SCC 24; see, e.g., paras 19–20.

38 *R v Dyment*, [1988] 2 SCR 417 at 431 [emphasis in original] [*Dyment*]. The Court has held that distinct considerations arise in the case of a seizure: *R v Reeves*, 2018 SCC 56 at para 30 [*Reeves*]—a point discussed further below.

39 *Duarte*, above note 26; see also *R v Fliss*, 2002 SCC 16, where Arbour J, at para 12, held: "a conversation with an informer, or a police officer, is not a search and seizure. Only the recording of such conversation is."

40 *R v Gomboc*, 2010 SCC 55, quoting here from para 36.

41 *R v Tessling*, 2004 SCC 67.

42 *R v Hufsky*, [1988] 1 SCR 621.

43 *R v Patrick*, 2009 SCC 17 [*Patrick*].

And police did not conduct a search when they disclosed information obtained from a lawful wiretap to American authorities, because this is more properly understood as a post-search use of the information, engaging different protections.[44]

In *R v Mills*, five members of the Supreme Court held that no search had taken place when an undercover officer, posing as a fourteen-year-old female, emailed and texted with the accused in a child luring case and used "screen capture" software to record the exchange for use in the prosecution.[45] The trial judge held the conversation to be private and that using screen-capturing tools to record the messages was a form of wiretapping (or an "interception" under the *Criminal Code*), requiring a warrant.[46] In separate opinions, Brown J (along with Abella and Gascon JJ) and Karakatsanis J (joined by Wagner CJ) held that the conversation in this case was no different from any other a person might have with an undercover officer. It was not transformed by taking place in writing. Retaining the written record of it (or taking screenshots) did not constitute a wiretap. As Brown J put it, "if Mills had sent a letter or passed a note to an undercover officer, s. 8 would not require the officer to get a warrant prior to reading it."[47] Justice Brown went further than Karakatsanis J in finding the accused could not have had an objectively reasonable expectation of privacy with a young person he did not know. Justice Martin held that the accused did retain a privacy interest in the conversation, despite involving a young person, since this issue should not turn on with whom one happens to be speaking. Police carried out an interception by producing a record of the conversation in part because they did so using a program or device separate from the software or platform in which the conversation had taken place. She had thus likened the situation to an undercover officer or informant wearing a recording device—something the Court in *Duarte* had held police require a warrant to do so.[48] She also held it to be an interception in light of the purpose of the wiretap provisions in protecting the expectation that no permanent recording of a communication between a person and a state agent would be surreptitiously acquired by the state without a warrant. Justice Moldaver held that both Brown and Karakatsanis JJ's reasons were "sound in law" and formed a basis to dismiss the appeal.[49]

---

44 *Wakeling v United States of America*, 2014 SCC 72.

45 *R v Mills*, 2019 SCC 22 [*Mills*].

46 *Criminal Code*, RSC 1985, c C-46 [*Criminal Code* or *Code*].

47 *Mills*, above note 45 at para 45.

48 *Ibid* at para 139.

49 On one reading of *Mills*, Moldaver J's endorsement of Brown J's reasons renders that opinion the majority holding.

In *Re X*, the Federal Court of Canada considered whether the use by the Canadian Security Intelligence Service of what is called "Stingray technology" constitutes a search.[50] This involves the use of a "cellular site simulator" to capture International Mobile Subscriber Identity numbers and International Mobile Equipment Identity numbers of a cellphone or other electronic device. Stingray devices capture these device identifiers by mimicking a cell tower in its reception and transmission of signals to a target's devices, thus enabling agents to track a target's movement and communication data. Using Stingray technology to obtain data in this way constitutes a search because, together with other information agents may possess, it permits state officials to form a "profile" about a target, including "core biographic personal information."[51]

D. WHAT ACTS CONSTITUTE A SEIZURE?

In *Dyment*, La Forest J held that "the essence of a seizure under s. 8 is the taking of a thing from a person by a public authority without that person's consent."[52] In *Thomson Newspapers Ltd v Canada (Director of Investigation and Research, Restrictive Trade Practices Commission)*, Wilson J defined a seizure as "the taking hold by a public authority of a thing belonging to a person against that person's will."[53] Neither definition states that in order to engage section 8, the thing that state actors take from a person must be something over which they have a reasonable expectation of privacy. The Court makes this clear elsewhere in each case, finding in *Dyment* that taking a blood sample engaged section 8 because the accused retained a privacy interest in it, and finding in *Thomson Newspapers* that documents ordered to be disclosed were private. Justice Fish makes the connection to privacy explicit in *Cole*: "a taking is a seizure, where a person has a reasonable privacy interest in the object or subject matter of the state action and the information to which it gives access."[54]

50 *Re X*, 2017 FC 1047.

51 *Ibid* at para 6.

52 *Dyment*, above note 38 at 431.

53 [1990] 1 SCR 425 at 493 [*Thomson Newspapers*].

54 *Cole*, above note 25 at para 34. For further examples, see the discussion of a continuing privacy interest in bodily samples in *Colarusso*, above note 2, and in *Stillman*, above note 31. By contrast, seizing garbage in *Patrick*, above note 43, did not constitute a seizure that engages s 8 because of a lack of privacy in it when left at the curb for pick up. All three cases are canvassed further below.

The Supreme Court has held that state agents carry out a seizure under section 8 in various situations, including when they exercise powers under regulatory legislation to demand the production of documents;[55] when, in the course of a regulatory inspection, they exercise a statutory power to make copies of documents;[56] when they obtain bodily samples, such as hair or teeth impressions, or those found on discarded tissue from a person in custody;[57] and when they obtain a DNA sample.[58] An order for the production of documents under the *Code*'s third-party records regime in sexual offence cases constitutes a seizure.[59] Special warrants of seizure for chattels under the "proceeds of crime" provisions of the *Code* involve a seizure, as do the "restraint order" provisions that freeze real property or money in a bank account from being transferred.[60] And, as noted above, the Court has described an "interception" or wiretap under Part VI of the *Criminal Code* as a seizure (as well as a search).[61]

By contrast, police do not carry out a seizure under section 8 when they pick up garbage at the curb, since it is abandoned and its collection does not intrude upon a reasonable privacy interest.[62] The federal Crown did not conduct a seizure when officials wrote Swiss authorities to request bank records, since this only constituted a request to seize the records, not a seizure in itself.[63] A requirement in a collective agreement (in a federally regulated workplace) for the employer to provide the union periodically the names and addresses of members of a bargaining unit did not constitute a seizure under section 8, since members could reasonably expect the information would be used in this way.[64]

---

55 *Thomson Newspapers*, above note 53; *R v McKinlay Transport Ltd*, [1990] 1 SCR 627; *British Columbia Securities Commission v Branch*, [1995] 2 SCR 3; *Canada (Attorney General) v Chambre des notaires du Québec*, 2016 SCC 20.

56 *Comité*, above note 33.

57 *Stillman*, above note 31.

58 *R v SAB*, 2003 SCC 60.

59 *R v Mills*, [1999] 3 SCR 668.

60 *Quebec (Attorney General) v Laroche*, 2002 SCC 72 [*Laroche*], LeBel J for the majority noting at para 54:

> [G]iven that a restraint order is intended to supplement seizures that are taking place contemporaneously, and that they place property under the control of the justice system that might otherwise have eluded it, whether for the purpose of a criminal investigation or for the punishment of crimes that fall within Part XII.2 of the *Criminal Code*, such an order must be characterized as a seizure within the meaning of s. 8 of the *Charter*.

61 *Duarte*, above note 26.

62 *Patrick*, above note 43.

63 *Schreiber*, above note 10.

64 *Bernard v Canada (Attorney General)*, 2014 SCC 13.

E. WHEN TRANSFER OR RECEIPT AMOUNTS TO A SEARCH OR SEIZURE

1) State Actor Gives Item to Police

In *Dyment*, *Colarusso*, and *Cole*, the Supreme Court held that a state actor who acquires evidence lawfully can give rise to a seizure under section 8 when they transfer the item to police and police take it from them for an investigative purpose.[65] The Court takes what can be called a principled approach in these cases by assuming the primary question is whether the item an agent turns over to police is one in which an accused still has a privacy interest against the state. In each of these cases, the Court found that the accused did retain a privacy interest in the item and that police conducted a seizure when receiving it. Police also carried out an unreasonable search in each case when they proceeded to analyze or make investigative use of the item without being authorized by law.

In *Dyment*, a doctor took a vial of blood from an accused for medical purposes, after a car accident and without his knowledge. Discovering the accused had been drinking, the doctor turned over the sample to police.[66] In concurring opinions, the majority held that the officer's receipt of the samples constituted a "seizure," for the reasons La Forest J set out. Whether the officer's receipt of the sample amounted to a seizure did not turn, for La Forest J, on whether the doctor volunteered or the officer asked for the sample. Evidence of the conversation between the two was unclear.[67] For La Forest J, the matter turned on whether a privacy interest persisted. "If I were to draw the line between a seizure and a mere finding of evidence," he wrote, "I would draw it logically and purposefully at the point at which it can reasonably be said that the individual had ceased to have a privacy interest in the subject-matter allegedly seized."[68]

The officer's receipt of the sample became a seizure in *Dyment* not because the doctor chose to make a different use of it, but because the accused retained a privacy interest in the sample when the officer received it.[69] A further element assumed in La Forest J's discussion but not made overt was the officer's intention to use the sample for an

65 *Dyment*, above note 38; *Colarusso*, above note 2; and *Cole*, above note 25.

66 *Dyment*, above note 38.

67 *Ibid* at 434.

68 *Ibid* at 435.

69 As La Forest J puts it, *ibid*, "the sample was surrounded by an aura of privacy meriting *Charter* protection."

investigative purpose.[70] Given the heightened privacy interest in the body, a seizure without a warrant was unreasonable.[71] Justice MacIntyre, in dissent, declined to construe the officer's receipt of the sample as a seizure, employing an approach that has reappeared in recent caselaw (discussed further, below). Any breach of privacy here was due to the doctor and thereafter—MacIntyre J is silent on this point—the privacy interest had essentially lapsed.[72] The officer was under a duty to make use of "real evidence" and there was nothing improper in his doing so.[73]

Colarusso also involved police obtaining blood evidence from another state agent, but the acts constituting a seizure are different from those in *Dyment*.[74] Following a motor vehicle accident involving a fatality in which alcohol was suspected, hospital staff took a blood sample and, with an officer's assistance, a urine sample. The trial judge held that the accused had consented to the samples being taken "for medical purposes."[75] Pursuant to powers in the *Coroners Act*, the coroner obtained the blood and urine samples from the lab technician and turned them over to a police officer at the hospital for storage at a forensic lab for later analysis.[76] The Crown called a forensic toxicologist who had analyzed the samples at the lab at the coroner's request, to assist in the latter's investigation under the Act. The toxicologist's blood-alcohol readings from the samples formed a basis for the accused's conviction. In a 5:4 decision, a majority of the Supreme Court affirmed the trial judge's finding that when the officer assisted in obtaining the urine sample, he was not conducting a seizure, but merely assisting hospital staff. However, after the coroner had arrived, because the accused retained a privacy interest in the sample, what followed amounted to an unreasonable seizure in two ways. The officer carried out a seizure when he received the samples from the coroner for storage at a forensic lab because they were then available for a prosecutorial purpose, the officer intended "from the outset" to use

70 This assumption runs through the discussion at 431–32 *ibid*, i.e., in discovering alcohol in the sample, the doctor gave it to the officer as potential evidence of an offence, and the officer accepted it to potentially use for that purpose.

71 *Ibid* at 438; as La Forest J notes, at 422, the incident predates the inclusion in the *Criminal Code* of a power to demand a blood sample on probable grounds to believe the accused has driven while impaired (s 238(3) at the time).

72 *Ibid* at 442: "If there was a wrongful seizure, it was made by the doctor and there is no evidence which would implicate the police officer."

73 *Ibid*.

74 *Dyment*, above note 38; *Colarusso*, above note 2.

75 *Colarusso*, above note 2 at 30.

76 *Ibid* at 30–31, discussing s 16(2)(c) and (5) of the *Coroners Act*, RSO 1980, c 93.

them for that purpose, and did so without a warrant.[77] Alternatively, the coroner's seizure from hospital staff became unreasonable by his making the samples available to police and failing to confine his use of them to the (non-criminal) purposes set out in the *Coroners Act*.[78]

The minority in *Colarusso* held that the coroner's initial seizure from hospital staff was the only authority the Crown needed to make lawful use of the sample for the purpose of a prosecution. Police delivering the samples to the lab did not amount to a seizure, since they were "essentially acting as a courier."[79] There was no *taking* by police. The coroner's involvement of police as a courier, the storage of the samples at the forensic lab, and their analysis by the toxicologist were all authorized under the *Coroners Act* and well within the scope of his inquiry. The fact that the inquiry happened to produce evidence relevant to the criminal case is unfortunate for the accused but did not make any part of it a prosecutorial seizure.[80] Dissenting judges saw "no difference, as far as the police actions are concerned, between this case and one in which the Crown subpoenas a hospital lab technician to give evidence that came into existence during *bona fide* medical procedures and is relevant to a criminal proceeding."[81]

The complicating factor in *Colarusso* is that the steps taken by the officer and the lab technician were consistent with two forensic purposes, both a criminal and a coroner's investigation. The dispute between the majority and minority is framed as one turning on the limits of the accused's consent. Another way to approach the facts is to suggest that the accused's consent was not fully informed. Had he known that taking a sample "for medical purposes" might include some use by the coroner, he may not have consented. The larger point, however, is that both the majority and minority agree on the central issue: was the blood sample private? Did the accused's initial consent permit the state to do what it did here? The two sides disagree on the answer, but they each agree that whether there was a seizure under section 8 turns not on who gave what

77 *Ibid* at 58–59. At 60, La Forest J also describes police as having independently seized the samples: "Given the effective control by the police over the samples held by another agent of the state, I would conclude that the police seized the blood sample from the appellant independently of the coroner's seizure (although the police seizure was obviously facilitated by the actions of the coroner)."

78 *Ibid* at 58 and 62–65.

79 *Ibid* at 42.

80 The opinion, authored by all four members of the minority (Lamer CJ, Cory and Major JJ, and McLachlin J, as she then was), considered at 44–45 whether calling the analyst to testify constituted a "seizure by the Crown," but did not decide the issue.

81 *Ibid* at 42.

to whom, but on the validity and scope of the initial consent—which is another way of asking: did he retain some measure of privacy?[82]

In *Cole*, a technician in a high school discovered nude pictures of a student on a teacher's board-issued laptop and reported them to the principal, who gave the laptop to police.[83] Without obtaining a warrant, police examined the content of the device and made a mirror image of its hard drive. Cole was charged with possession of child pornography. The Supreme Court held that in taking custody of the laptop for more than a brief period of time (to obtain a warrant) and examining its contents without a warrant, police had carried out an unreasonable search and seizure.[84]

Cole had retained a privacy interest in the content of the items given to police due in part to the understanding that teachers would make some personal use of their school-owned laptops.[85] School officials may have been authorized to seize the computer under a statutory duty to "maintain a safe school environment," but this did not provide *police* authority for their warrantless seizure or examination.[86] Justice Fish likened the transfer of items from school officials to police here to the situation in *Colarusso*, where state agents had seized samples for one legitimate purpose but then used them for another, citing La Forest J in that case for the point that:

> The state cannot, however, have it both ways; it cannot be argued that the coroner's seizure is reasonable because it is independent of the criminal law enforcement arm of the state while the state is at the same time attempting to introduce into criminal proceedings the very evidence seized by the coroner.[87]

---

82 A contrast can be drawn here with the facts in *Laroche*, above note 60, which the Supreme Court distinguished from those in *Colarusso* in holding, at paras 82–84, that when regulators turned over to police evidence obtained when the owner of a garage disclosed information required under a regulatory scheme intended to oversee the sale and repair of vehicles, they did not carry out a seizure since the owner did not have a reasonable expectation of privacy in the information disclosed to regulators—no privacy in relation to the state in general. The implication here was that it would not have been reasonable to assume that irregularities involving potential criminal activity would not be shared with police.

83 *Cole*, above note 25.

84 *Ibid*. In separate reasons, Abella J agreed with the majority on s 8, but contrary to the majority would have excluded the evidence under s 24(2).

85 *Ibid* at para 72.

86 *Ibid* at para 28.

87 *Ibid* at 68, citing *Colarusso* above note 2 at 62–63.

Here the principal had seized the laptop for "administrative purposes" on grounds lower than those in a criminal seizure, and that seizure was reasonable precisely because it did not contemplate criminal consequences.[88]

Relevant to our discussion here is how Fish J describes the handover and initial conduct of police upon receipt of the laptop. He makes clear that school officials were "legally entitled to inform the police of its discovery of contraband on the laptop."[89] Had they done so, this "would doubtless have permitted the police to obtain a warrant to search the computer for the contraband." But, "receipt of the computer from the school board did not afford the police *warrantless access* to the personal information contained within it. This information remained subject, at all relevant times, to Mr. Cole's reasonable and *subsisting* expectation of privacy." This raises the question of whether merely *taking custody* of the laptop constituted a seizure under section 8. Justice Fish writes:

> The police may well have been authorized to take physical control of the laptop and CD *temporarily, and for the limited purpose of safeguarding potential evidence of a crime until a search warrant could be obtained.* However, that is not what occurred here. Quite the contrary: The police seized the laptop and CD *in order to search their contents for evidence of a crime* without the consent of Mr. Cole, and without prior judicial authorization.[90]

Justice Fish's assertion that police were temporarily authorized to hold the computer "until a search warrant could be obtained" implies that police had to obtain a warrant because merely receiving it and choosing to hold onto it constituted a seizure under section 8. He provided no source for the temporary authority to hold the item while obtaining a warrant. His treatment of the issue here is too brief to infer that he was positing a new power to seize at common law. A further possible source of authority to apply here is the plain view power in section 489(2) of the *Code*, which permits officers in the execution of their duties (in this case, receiving a report) to seize an item they reasonably believe will afford evidence of an offence.[91]

If police carried out a seizure in receiving the laptop from school officials in *Cole*, could they rely on the school board's consent to search the laptop—since the board owned it? The Court said no: a third party may

88 *Cole*, above note 25 at paras 67–71.

89 *Ibid* at para 73.

90 *Ibid* at para 65 [emphasis in original].

91 *Criminal Code*, above note 46. However, relying on this power would permit more than a *temporary* seizure and therefore may not have been what Fish J had in mind.

not waive another person's privacy interest.[92] In the American version of the doctrine, Fish J notes, third-party consent is valid on the basis that an individual assumes a risk when sharing information with that party that they might disclose it to police.[93] The Supreme Court of Canada rejected the risk analysis in *Duarte* and *Wong* as a basis for deciding whether a person retains a privacy interest in a place or thing.[94] Third-party consent also fails to satisfy Canadian law on valid consent. As Fish J held:

> For consent to be valid, it must be both voluntary and informed. The adoption of a doctrine of third party consent in this country would imply that the police could interfere with an individual's privacy interests on the basis of a consent that is *not* voluntarily given by the rights holder, and *not* necessarily based on sufficient information in his or her hands to make a meaningful choice.[95]

As in *Dyment* and *Colarusso*, police receipt of evidence from a third party in *Cole* amounted to a seizure not because of who gave police the item but because the accused retained a privacy interest in it. Cole retained an interest because the third party's shared interest and consent did not vitiate his interest or relieve police of the obligation of obtaining his consent or other authority to interfere with his privacy.

Steven Penney, commenting on *Cole*, noted that although the Court rejected the third-party consent doctrine here, courts before and since *Cole* have permitted a form of it framed in a different way: "rather than saying that the third party waived the accused's section 8 rights, they have instead asked whether the third party had an independent authority to consent to the search."[96] In some cases, where an accused shares with a third party a privacy interest in a space—for example, over the common space in a shared apartment—one party's consent can authorize police entry. Justice LaForme, for the Ontario Court of Appeal in *Reeves* encapsulated the principle informing these cases in holding:

> [N]ormatively, it would not be reasonable for one resident to expect that the other co-resident could never invite an agent of the state into the residence. In fact, one could reasonably expect that the other might

92 *Cole*, above note 25 at paras 74–77

93 *Ibid* at para 76, Fish J citing *United States v Matlock*, 415 US 164 (1974); *Illinois v Rodriguez*, 497 US 177 (1990); *United States v Ziegler*, 474 F3d 1184.

94 *Duarte*, above note 26 at 47–48, and *R v Wong*, [1990] 3 SCR 36 at 45 [*Wong*].

95 *Cole*, above note 25 at para 78.

96 Steven Penney, "Consent Searches for Electronic Text Communications: Escaping the Zero-Sum Trap" (2018) 56:1 *Alberta Law Review* 1 at 9 [Penney, "Zero Sum"].

> have a legitimate interest in consenting to entry by law enforcement into common spaces from time to time.[97]

As Professor Penney notes, courts have applied this reasoning to various co-residents, including spouses and parents[98] and those in multi-unit buildings.[99] Could similar reasoning apply to a computer with two or more users? If the laptop in *Cole* had been shared with another teacher who turned it in, Penney asks, might the Court have found their consent sufficient authority to seize and possibly search some portion of it?[100] Would this depend on whether or how their personal data were commingled, i.e., the presence or absence of separate user accounts, passwords, etc.?[101]

In the next section, we follow *Reeves* on appeal to the Supreme Court of Canada, where the majority declined to decide whether a spouse can consent to police entry to a home—leaving uncertain the Court's position on whether a party with a shared interest can provide an independent form of authority to enter a private space, as contemplated by LaForme JA in the court below.[102] However, the Court did address the question in relation to a computer, holding that a spouse who consented to police seizure of a computer she co-owned with her husband did *not* authorize police to seize it.[103] Notably, neither the majority nor dissenting opinions at the Supreme Court in *Reeves* factored in the nature of the commingling of shared interests in the computer. Nothing appeared to turn on whether Reeves had a separate user account, password protection, or what portion of the data was searched. The majority tacitly treated the spouse's consent to seize the computer as analogous to her consenting to search something more like a shared bedroom than a common space like a kitchen or living room.

---

97 *R v Reeves*, 2017 ONCA 365 at para 48 [*Reeves* ONCA], cited in Penney, *ibid*. See also *R v Clarke*, 2017 BCCA 453, holding at paras 55 and 64 that the appellant and the primary occupant had "overlapping" privacy interests in "the common areas of the house" and that the latter had "the authority to consent to police entry" into those spaces but not to search a "tarp-covered pile of property" in the garage where both had agreed he would keep some of his personal possessions.

98 Among the examples Penney cites are, on spousal consent: *R v T (RMJ)*, 2014 MBCA 36; *Reeves* ONCA, *ibid*; and *R v Parsons*, 2017 NLCA 64; with parental consent: *R v Rai*, 1998 CanLII 4630 (BCSC); *R v W (JP)*, 21 WCB (2d) 339 (BC Prov Ct (Youth Ct)); and *R v Wagner* (1994), 40 BCAC 70.

99 *R v Redd*, 2013 BCSC 2071.

100 Penney, "Zero Sum," above note 96 at 11.

101 *Ibid*.

102 *Reeves*, above note 38.

103 *Ibid* at paras 40–55.

2) Police Request or Take the Item from a Third Party

The Supreme Court has applied a similar principled approach to cases where police request or take an item from a third party. In each case, the question is not whether police did or did not know the content of the container or device, but whether the accused retained a reasonable expectation of privacy in the item at issue.

R v Buhay may be the best illustration of what we are calling the Court's principled approach.[104] The accused rented a locker in a bus depot, and security guards detected an odour of marijuana emanating from it. An agent for Greyhound opened the locker and guards found a duffle bag inside containing marijuana. The guards placed it back inside, locked the locker, and called police. They directed police to the locker; officers smelled marijuana emanating from it; the Greyhound agent opened the locker and an officer seized the bag. Justice Arbour, for a unanimous Court, affirmed the findings of the courts below that in their initial search, the security guards were not state agents since they acted independently from police. Calling police was a voluntary act, not evidence of their carrying out a governmental function.[105] But when a guard opened the locker and the officer reached in to remove the bag, police conducted a seizure under section 8. In a passage that captures the core of the decision, Arbour J held:

> In this case, it cannot reasonably be said that the appellant had ceased to have a privacy interest in the contents of his locker. The subsequent conduct of the police should be considered a seizure within the meaning of s. 8. I see no basis for holding that a person's reasonable expectation of privacy as to the contents of a rented and locked bus depot locker is destroyed merely because a private individual (such as a security guard) invades that privacy by investigating the contents of the locker. The intervention of the security guards does not relieve the police from the *Hunter* requirement of prior judicial authorization before seizing contraband uncovered by security guards. To conclude otherwise would amount to a "circumvention of the warrant requirement."[106]

Despite a third party directly leading police to the locker and police knowing its contents, the accused retained a privacy interest in it against the state.

In *Spencer*, the Court held that when police asked a third party for information pertaining to the accused, police carried out a search

---

104 *R v Buhay*, 2003 SCC 30 [*Buhay*].

105 *Ibid* at paras 30–31.

106 *Ibid* at para 34.

because the accused had a privacy interest in the information. Police had asked the accused's internet service provider, Shaw, for the subscriber information attached to an internet protocol address implicated in a child pornography offence.[107] The Ontario Court of Appeal had dealt with similar facts in *R v Ward*, holding that "[t]he [officer's] request, coupled with the voluntary co-operation with the request by the third party holder of the information, may or may not be a search or seizure depending on whether a claimant can establish a reasonable expectation of privacy in the information as against the state."[108] The court in that case found the accused had no privacy interest in his subscriber information. The Supreme Court in *Spencer* held that a person does retain a privacy interest in this information, despite the allowance for voluntary disclosure of it in the *Personal Information Protection and Electronic Documents Act*.[109] Justice Cromwell, for the Court, framed the entire decision around the assertion that whether Spencer's rights under section 8 were engaged depended on whether he had a privacy expectation in the information at issue. "If he did," Cromwell J asserted without elaboration, "then obtaining that information was a search."[110] Since the police had no authority for requesting the private information at issue, their request, receipt, and use of it violated section 8. In *R v Marakah*, police obtained text messages authored by the accused by seizing and searching the recipient's phone without authority.[111] The majority of the Court held that a sender can, in some cases, retain a reasonable privacy interest in messages they send despite not having control over them in the recipient's hands. Chief Justice McLachlin held that "[t]o accept the risk that a co-conversationalist could disclose an electronic conversation is not to accept the risk of a different order that the state will intrude upon an electronic conversation absent such disclosure."[112] A sender does not have full control once they hit send, but they do exercise "meaningful control over the information they send by text message by making choices about how, when, and to whom they disclose the information."[113] For Moldaver and Côté JJ in dissent, a sender's "total absence of control" over a message in a recipient's hands renders any expectation of privacy

---

107 *R v Spencer*, above note 28.

108 *R v Ward*, 2012 ONCA 660 at para 50. The Saskatchewan Court of Appeal applies the same reasoning to similar facts in *R v Trapp*, 2011 SKCA 143 at paras 18–19.

109 *Spencer*, above note 28; *Personal Information Protection and Electronic Documents Act*, SC 2000, c 5.

110 *Spencer*, *ibid* at para 16.

111 *R v Marakah*, 2017 SCC 59 [*Marakah*], discussed further in Chapter 4.

112 *Ibid* at para 40, citing *Duarte*, above note 26 at 44.

113 *Marakah*, above note 111 at para 39.

on the part of a sender unreasonable.[114] The Court in *Marakah* was not addressing whether police conduct a search or seizure when a party to the exchange turns it over to police. It dealt in this case with police *taking* the recipient's phone without their consent. The chief justice did, however, comment on the implications of the majority's holding (about continuing privacy in a sent message) for the consensual disclosure of text messages to police, a point canvassed further below. Suffice it to note here that the Court's approach in this case to deciding whether police conducted a search against the accused in obtaining his texts from a recipient's phone turned—as it has in all the Court's earlier cases on police acquisition of evidence—on whether the accused retained a privacy interest in the item at issue.

The Court maintained a similar focus on the question of a persisting privacy interest in *Reeves*, a case involving police taking an item with a civilian third party's consent.[115] Reeves's spouse found child pornography on the home computer she shared with him and reported this to police. An officer met with her at the family home and, with the spouse's consent, took the computer and held it for four months without a warrant and without reporting the seizure (as required under section 489.1 of the *Criminal Code*). All members of the Supreme Court agreed that the spouse's consent did not serve to waive Reeves's privacy interest in the computer against law enforcement, and that when police took it, this constituted a warrantless seizure that violated section 8.[116] The holding turned on the majority's affirmation of three propositions: from *Marakah*, the notion that shared control over an item is not fatal to the finding that Reeves retained a privacy interest;[117] the point from *Cole* that a co-possessor of a privacy interest cannot waive the accused's privacy interest, because the risk of third-party disclosure does not vitiate the need for first-party consent;[118] and that the heightened privacy interest that computers attract calls for heightened protections—either a warrant or valid consent from each privacy holder.[119]

114 *Ibid* at para 133.
115 *Reeves*, above note 38.
116 *Ibid* at paras 27–58.
117 *Ibid* at paras 37–39.
118 *Ibid* at paras 40–55.
119 *Ibid* at paras 34–35, Karakatsanis J quoting *R v Morelli*, 2010 SCC 8 at para 105 [*Morelli*]: "[c]omputers often contain our most intimate correspondence. They contain the details of our financial, medical, and personal situations. They even reveal our specific interests, likes, and propensities." Justice Karakatsanis also notes that "[c]omputers act as portals—providing access to information stored in many different locations," citing *R v Vu*, 2013 SCC 60 at para 44; *R v Fearon*, 2014 SCC 77 at paras 131–32; computers also "contain information that is

The Crown in *Reeves* sought to distinguish *Cole* by arguing that "Reeves' spouse had an equal and overlapping privacy interest in the computer."[120] Whereas in *Cole*, the school owned the computer but Cole was its only user. The Court of Appeal accepted this distinction, holding that "[i]t was not reasonable for Reeves to expect [his spouse] would not be able to consent to . . . the taking of the shared computer."[121] But for Karakatsanis J, on behalf of the majority, "[e]ffectively, these arguments mean either that Reeves had *no* reasonable expectation of privacy in the computer when it was taken by the police, or that his spouse's consent operated to waive Reeves' *Charter* rights."[122] Reeves's spouse's consent could only nullify his interest on a form of the risk analysis dismissed in relation to surreptitious surveillance in *Duarte* and in relation to text messages seized from a recipient in *Marakah*.[123]

On why the police act of taking and holding the computer engaged Reeves's section 8 rights, Karakatsanis J held:

> [W]hile the privacy interests engaged by a seizure may be different from those engaged by a search, Reeves' informational privacy interests in the computer data were still implicated by the seizure of the computer. When police seize a computer, they not only deprive individuals of *control* over intimate data in which they have a reasonable expectation of privacy, they also ensure that such data remains *preserved* and thus subject to potential future state inspection.[124]

She added that police here were "not after the physical device (to collect fingerprints on it, for example), but rather sought to preserve and permit access to the data it contained."[125] As noted earlier, the finding entailed a disagreement with the Ontario Court of Appeal, which had held that seizing the computer did not interfere with Reeves's privacy interest. And, once again, the holding did not turn on the nature of the commingling of information on the device—i.e., whether or not Reeves

---

automatically generated, often unbeknownst to the user" (citing *Vu* at para 42); and they "retain information that the user may think has been deleted" (citing *Vu* at para 43). Finally, at para 35 of *Reeves*: "The unique and heightened privacy interests in personal computer data clearly warrant strong protection, such that specific, prior judicial authorization is presumptively required to seize a personal computer from a home."

120 *Reeves*, above note 38 at para 40.

121 *Reeves* ONCA, above note 97 at para 62.

122 *Reeves*, above note 38 at para 40.

123 *Duarte*, above note 26 and *Marakah*, above note 111, cited at para 42 in *Reeves*, above note 38.

124 *Reeves*, above note 38 at para 30.

125 *Ibid* at para 31.

had a separate user account or which files were searched. How far the ruling in *Reeves* extends to cases involving persons with shared interests in a space or item is a point we return to in the next section.

3) Civilian Brings Item to Police

Civilians often report suspected crimes to police and describe pieces of evidence they have seen, including the content of private containers, bags, or devices belonging to the accused. Police receipt of a *description* of this evidence is not a search or seizure.[126] The Supreme Court in *Buhay*, *Cole*, and *Reeves* suggests a rationale for this: in receiving a mere description, police do nothing on their part to interfere with a suspect's privacy.[127] Are things different when civilians bring police the item directly and police take custody of it or proceed to examine it? Do police conduct a seizure merely by receiving it or a search by perusing, even briefly?

The Supreme Court of Canada has yet to decide this issue directly, but it has addressed the question in *obiter*. In *Marakah*, the majority held that a recipient may retain a privacy interest in a text message police obtain from a recipient's device.[128] In that case, police had seized the phone from the recipient and searched it without the recipient's consent. Considering what police should do in the case of a voluntary disclosure by a recipient, McLachlin CJ wrote:

> Assuming that s. 8 is engaged when police access text messages volunteered by a third party . . . , a breach can be avoided if the police obtain a warrant prior to accessing the text messages. As stated in *Cole*, "[t]he school board was . . . legally entitled to inform the police of its discovery of contraband on the laptop" and "[t]his would doubtless have permitted the police to obtain a warrant to search the computer for the contraband" (para. 73). Similarly, victims of cyber abuse are legally entitled to inform the police, which will typically permit the police to obtain a warrant. The police officers will be aware that *they should not look at the text messages in question prior to obtaining a warrant.*[129]

---

126 See, e.g., *R v Molyneaux*, 2020 PECA 2, involving a third party's report of incriminating contents of the accused's cellphone; finding at para 54 that the accused had a "direct interest in the subject matter of his cell phone, [but had] no direct interest in [the complainant's] memory of what she saw or in the freedom she has to tell whomsoever she pleases."

127 *Buhay*, above note 104; *Cole*, above note 25; *Reeves*, above note 38.

128 *Marakah*, above note 111.

129 *Ibid* at para 50 [emphasis added], citing *Cole*, above note 25.

The chief justice's assertion that an officer should not look at the text before obtaining a warrant implies that even looking at the item would constitute a search. Receiving the item from the victim, rather than police asking for or taking it, *did not change the analysis*. The primary question here was whether the accused retained a privacy interest in the chat.

Chief Justice McLachlin offered no rationale for her view. She did not explain why a police officer who meets with a civilian must avoid looking at a printed copy of a chat she had with a potential suspect without first obtaining a warrant. If, as she pointed out, a civilian's report will "typically permit the police to obtain a warrant," why insist on the officer taking that step? What extra measure of protection does this provide to potentially innocent suspects? Put another way, what mischief on the part of the state does it avoid?

The Court has confronted this issue in various cases where the step of obtaining a warrant may seem like a formality. For example, in *Duarte*, the Court held that even where police have one party's consent to conduct a wiretap (i.e., an informant's consent), they still need to obtain a warrant.[130] In *Spencer*, the Court held that police need authority to carry out a search before asking an internet service provider for a user's subscriber information, despite the fact that privacy law permits a service provider to make disclosures to law enforcement.[131] The Court reasons in these cases that even if in most instances police will easily obtain a warrant or have probable grounds for a search, the requirement to establish grounds holds the state to a certain standard that helps to avoid casual or unnecessary intrusions into our privacy. We need not be concerned that the state may be reading our texts or looking at our photos on the basis of a civilian report about possible illicit content in them, unless the report is credible, the officer's belief in the probability of an offence having occurred is reasonable, and an independent third party confirms this. The high privacy interest in these items makes a search of the items on anything less than a warrant unreasonable.[132]

Chief Justice McLachlin's comments in *Marakah* about police needing a warrant before looking at evidence a third party volunteers were *obiter* because the police in that case seized the recipient's phone without consent. We anticipate that the Supreme Court will hear a case in the near future that deals with the issue directly, settling the question of whether a third party bringing police evidence engages a suspect's rights

130 *Duarte*, above note 26.

131 *Spencer*, above note 28.

132 The Court applies this reasoning in *Duarte*, above note 26 (to wiretaps); in *Marakah*, above note 111 (to text messages); and in *Reeves*, above note 38, *Cole*, above note 25, and *Morelli*, above note 119 (to computers).

under section 8 when police receive and review it. We expect the Court will take an approach consistent with McLachlin CJ's *obiter* in *Marakah*, which follows the Court's principled approached discussed in the previous two sections above. In *Dyment*, *Collarusso*, *Buhay*, *Cole*, *Spencer*, and *Reeves*, the Court held that when police take or receive evidence, they engage a person's rights under section 8 not because of who gave them the item, or how they came into possession of it, but on the principled basis that *taking possession and examining it interfered with a reasonable expectation of privacy.*

The Supreme Court will likely have to decide the issue soon given how contentious it has become in lower courts. More cases are emerging that involve complainants or third parties bringing police evidence in the form of texts, email, or photos containing information that possibly engages a suspect's privacy. A number of recent trial and appellate decisions we turn to in this section have held that when a third party brings police an item over which a suspect retains a privacy interest, police do not conduct a seizure when they take custody of it or a search when they proceed to look at or analyze it. Courts have arrived at these positions for different reasons.

In some cases, the court recognizes that the accused may have a privacy interest in the item at issue, but holds that a third party's voluntary disclosure of it to police (or a screenshot of it) meant that police had done nothing on their part amounting to a *taking* of the item or an *interference with* the suspect's interest.[133] In some cases, the recipient's consent authorizes police action.[134] A third body of cases is consistent with the Supreme Court's principled approach in taking the primary question to be whether the accused retained a reasonable expectation of privacy in the messages at issue or what is depicted in a screenshot or found on a device.[135] A brief look at some of these cases shows how peculiarities in the evidence, or in how police obtain it, can lead to confusion.

In *R v King*, the accused's wife, suspecting him of infidelity, obtained his password, accessed his devices, and discovered what she believed was

133 *R v King*, 2021 ABCA 271 [*King* ABCA]; in *Estrella Llaneza c R*, 2019 QCCQ 3012 the court held the sender had no privacy in the sent messages turned over, but also held at para 29 that having been given the phone by the recipient, extracting the messages, and reading them, "police did not take anything from the accused." See also *R v Amdurski*, 2022 ONSC 1338 [*Amdurski*] and *R v AK*, 2022 ABQB 503 [*AK*], discussed further below.

134 *R v Orlandis-Habsburgo*, 2017 ONCA 649, in *obiter* [*Orlandis-Habsburgo*]; *R v Lowrey*, 2016 ABPC 131 [*Lowrey*]; *R v Phagura*, 2019 BCSC 1638 [*Phagura*]—all discussed further below.

135 Among other cases discussed below are *R v King*, 2019 ABPC 236 [*King* ABPC] and *R v Morgan*, 2020 ONCA 279 [*Morgan*].

child pornography.[136] She took screenshots of some of the images on his devices and saved the screenshots to a USB drive. She described to police the images she saw and gave the USB drive to the officer. The officer in turn examined the screenshots on the disk and used the information to obtain a warrant to seize and search King's devices. The trial judge held the accused had a privacy interest in the screenshots the officer reviewed on the USB drive since the subject matter of the search was not the drive or the screenshots themselves, but, in effect, the glimpse they afforded inside King's devices. Looking at the screenshots, the officer could see "how [the accused] organized his desktop computer, including the backdrop or 'wallpaper', the placement and titles of folders, the titles of images and videos, and the presence of other non-illicit information."[137] All of this revealed "personal information about Mr. King," rendering the officer's act of viewing the screenshots a form of search. Following *Reeves*, the court held that King's wife could not consent to the search on his behalf and that it was unreasonable under section 8.[138]

The Alberta Court of Appeal treated the pictures the wife had saved on the USB drive as a further form of her *describing* or reporting the alleged offence.[139] Justice Slater held that "[t]he examination of the USB flash drive by the police was not an examination of any thing or place that belonged to or that was under the control of the appellant."[140] The holding rests on the assumption that what the officer did in this case is substantially different from what police did in *Buhay*.[141] In *Buhay*, police looked inside a private locker. In *King*, police looked not inside the husband's computer directly, but at a photo depicting a direct view of the inside of it. Does that make for a meaningful difference? The trial judge's assessment in *King* is more plausible: i.e., the officer did more than merely look at a picture of a picture (or several such pictures). He looked at the *content* of the picture within a picture. The officer had a substantial view of the content inside the accused's computer. The difference this makes can be easily illustrated by considering what would happen if the screenshots the wife provided to police depicted not pornographic images on King's computer, but an email, text exchange, or journal entry. Clearly in that case, the officer proceeding to *read* these items would be doing more than "receiving a report."

---

136 *King* ABPC, above note 135.

137 *Ibid* at para 24.

138 *Ibid* at para 38, citing *Reeves*, above note 38 at para 62.

139 *King* ABCA, above note 133.

140 *Ibid* at para 18.

141 *Buhay*, above note 104.

King has since been cited in a later appellate decision for the proposition that "where information is brought to the police by an independent third party acting on its own initiative, and where the police merely receive and review it, there has been no search or seizure by the state which engages s. 8."[142] Trial courts have applied similar logic. In *R v Bear-Knight*,[143] the court found the accused did not have a privacy expectation in the screenshot of a Facebook message the complainant brought to police. Regardless of this, police receipt of the item from a third party presenting it to them voluntarily meant that this could not be a search or seizure under section 8 or, if it was, the party's consent sufficed to authorize police to conduct it.[144] In *Lowrey*, a mother and her fourteen-year-old daughter brought police the printout of a conversation the daughter had with the accused on Facebook.[145] The court held that despite the accused's "marginal expectation of privacy" in it, the daughter's consent was "sufficient to authorize the search undertaken" by the officer.[146] In *Amdurski*, the court held: "[t]here was no seizure by the police because the text messages were voluntarily turned over to the police by a concerned parent."[147] In *Phagura*, the complainant consented to police taking photos of a text exchange on her phone that she had with the accused.[148] The court found the accused had lacked a reasonable privacy interest in the messages, but proceeded to address whether the complainant's consent provided sufficient authority for the search.[149] Since the complainant and the accused had "an overlapping interest" in the exchange, it was not reasonable for the accused "to think or expect that Ms. M.K. would not be able to consent to provide such information

142 *AK*, above note 133 at para 34, involving screenshots of social media communications taken by an undercover US law enforcement agent and police in Canada receiving and reviewing the screenshots without a warrant.

143 2021 SKQB 258.

144 *Ibid* at para 52, noting that the "complainant's actions in taking the screenshot, which the evidence suggests she voluntarily gave to the investigating officer, did not reflect surreptitious state action;" and at para 53:

> [T]he complainant had every right to provide the police with the screenshot of the message she received. When she did so, she expressly consented to the police taking possession of it. In this context, there is some absurdity in the notion that the police should be expected to obtain a warrant to collect evidence in the lawful possession of a person who wishes, freely and voluntarily, to provide the evidence to the police without a warrant.

145 *Lowrey*, above note 134.

146 *Ibid* at paras 83–85.

147 *Amdurski*, above note 133 at para 4.

148 *Phagura*, above note 134.

149 *Ibid* at paras 56–57.

to the police."[150] Her consent was "valid and sufficient for the police to obtain copies" of the exchange.[151]

There is certainly an appeal to the reasoning in these cases, arising from a sense of not wanting to needlessly impede civilians reporting a crime or police investigating it in good faith. An often-cited expression of this reasoning is found in a passage in the Ontario Court of Appeal decision in *Orlandis-Habsburgo*.[152] In this case, an electricity company, Horizon, volunteered suspicious consumption data to police. Reviewing it gave police grounds for a warrant. The accused argued that police receipt and review of the data constituted an unreasonable search and seizure. The trial judge held the accused lacked an objectively reasonable privacy interest in the data.[153] The Court of Appeal overturned this ruling, finding the accused did have a reasonable interest.[154] However, police did not seize or search the data on receipt of it from Horizon because the company had a working arrangement with police from the outset, rendering Horizon a state agent.[155] Justice Doherty went on to consider, in *obiter*, what would have happened if Horizon were independent. Company officials could describe the suspicious data to police, which police could then include in an affidavit for a warrant. Why, then, should things be different if an independent Horizon were to give police a copy of the data itself (as occurred here)?[156] Justice Doherty asserted:

> I have considerable difficulty with the submission that s. 8 is engaged if the police look at information in which an accused has a legitimate privacy interest, even if that information is brought to the police by an independent third party acting on its own initiative. On that approach, s. 8 would be engaged if a "whistleblower" took confidential documents belonging to her employer to the police to demonstrate the employer's criminal activity. Must the police refuse to look at the documents to avoid violating the employer's s. 8 rights?[157]

This captures an intuitive sense in which it would seem pointlessly formalistic to require a warrant to permit an officer to read a document when they already know what it contains. Yet this is essentially what happened in *Buhay*, *Cole*, and *Reeves*, where police already knew what

150 *Ibid* at para 62.
151 *Ibid*.
152 *Orlandis-Habsburgo*, above note 134.
153 *Ibid* at para 8, summarizing the holding at trial.
154 *Ibid* at para 111.
155 *Ibid* at para 35.
156 *Ibid* at para 33.
157 *Ibid* at para 34.

the locker, laptop, or home computer contained.[158] Despite this, in each case the Court held that a third party's disclosure of the content did not negate the accused's privacy in it against the state.

The answer in these cases—along with McLachlin CJ's *obiter* in *Marakah*—to Doherty JA's question "must the police refuse to look?" is: yes. The broader explanation for why (canvassed earlier and found in a host of Supreme Court decisions from *Hunter* to *Reeves*) is, in short, the high privacy interest in digital evidence can best be protected by holding police to certain standards before searching. This avoids unnecessary violations of privacy and affords everyone the assurance that there are effective safeguards against casual state intrusion.[159]

A third group of cases applies this reasoning and is consistent with the Supreme Court's principled approach. Whether police carry out a search or seizure turns in these cases not on whether a third party volunteered the evidence, but on whether the accused retained a privacy interest in it. A good example can be found in *R v Morgan*, where the accused was held not to have a privacy interest in messages he sent a woman he met only the night before and in texts he had sent to her mother's phone.[160] In *R v KA*, the court held that messages sent by two alleged pimps and human traffickers with their alleged "sex worker and slave" were not messages in which the accused had an objectively reasonable privacy interest, given the exploitive and tenuous nature of the relationships involved.[161]

Applying similar reasoning, other courts have come to the opposite conclusion—the accused did retain a privacy interest in the evidence

---

158 *Buhay*, above note 104; *Cole* above note 25; *Reeves*, above note 38.

159 The main holding in *Orlandis-Habsburgo*, above note 134, is consistent with this line of reasoning. The police investigation began, Doherty JA held at para 36, when Horizon began observing suspicious patterns. Since the accused retained a privacy interest in the data, Horizon's use of it in coordination with police rendered it a search requiring authority, at para 116. Police lacked authority, rendering the search unreasonable, at paras 118–19.

160 *Morgan*, above note 135.

161 *R v KA and ASA*, 2022 ONSC 1241 [*KA and ASA*], using these terms to describe the figures involved. For a further example involving a tenuous and exploitive relationship see *Amdurski*, above note 133. By contrast, in *R v Craig*, 2016 BCCA 154, a child luring case, the court held that the accused retained a reasonable privacy interest in messages he sent to an underage girl. The court arrived at this conclusion (overturning the trial judge on point) by placing an emphasis not on the exploitive nature of the relationship but on the private nature of what he disclosed in the messages. Justice Bennett, at para 139, held: "Not only were the messages personal but they exposed highly intimate details of Mr. Craig's lifestyle and personal choices. In his discussions with E.V., he is flirtatious, discloses aspects of his sexuality, sexual history, drug use, and arranges to provide liquor to underage persons."

turned over, resulting in a finding that the warrantless search of the evidence was unreasonable. One example can be found in the trial decision in *King*, noted earlier, involving police examination of screenshots.[162] Another can be found in *R v CM*, where the court held that the accused retained a privacy interest in messages sent to his former stepdaughter, which she gave to police.[163] The finding was based in part on the accused having known the recipient for a long time and standing in "a quasi-parental role towards her."[164] In *R v Devic*, a person responding to a Craigslist advertisement posted by a member of "Creep Catchers" retained a privacy interest despite not knowing their anonymous interlocutor.[165] In *R v Rafferty*, a father brought police his son's phone following his son's death from a drug overdose.[166] Police found messages on it incriminating the accused, believed to be the sender, in drug trafficking. Applying *Marakah*, the court held the accused retained a privacy interest in the messages, giving rise to a search when police read them following the father's disclosure of the phone.

The disparity in approach among lower courts to civilian disclosure of evidence will likely continue until the Supreme Court decides a case directly on point. When it does, we expect the Court will focus on whether the accused retained a privacy interest in the item at issue against the state. In the case of texts or emails, this will involve asking whether the complainant's shared privacy interest in the message could provide police authority to seize and search based on the complainant's consent alone. How the Court will decide this question will depend, in turn, on how it decides to expand or distinguish its earlier rulings in *Cole* and *Reeves*.[167] In those cases, the Court held that a party with a shared interest in a computer cannot provide police authority to search on the basis of their consent alone. Does this extend to anything over which there is a shared interest? Or only computers? Or things *like* a computer? Chief Justice McLachlin's *obiter* in *Marakah* suggests the possibility that the Court might decide that text exchanges should not be approached differently from the computer seized in *Reeves*. As noted above, even a victim of "cyber abuse" turning over a chat to police would not, in McLachlin CJ's view, authorize police to read the texts without a warrant.[168] This would

162 *King* ABPC, above note 135.
163 *R v CM*, 2022 ONCJ 372.
164 *Ibid* at para 37.
165 *R v Devic*, 2018 BCPC 318.
166 *R v Rafferty*, 2018 ONCJ 881.
167 *Cole*, above note 25; *Reeves*, above note 38.
168 *Marakah*, above note 111 at para 50.

imply that the shared interest in a private chat is not materially different from a shared interest in a computer.

We suggest that the question of whether civilian disclosure to police constitutes a search or seizure should remain focused on whether the accused retains a privacy interest in the item at issue against the state. The Supreme Court should apply the four-part test in *Spencer* and *Marakah* for deciding whether an accused retains a reasonable expectation of privacy in an item.[169] In the case of an email or a text a complaint turned over to police, this would entail asking whether a reasonable person in the position of the accused might have accepted as reasonable the form of disclosure made in that case to the state if it were presented to them as a hypothetical. Examples can be found in the caselaw. Can a male in an exploitive relationship with an adolescent female reasonably expect her not to reveal to parents or police communications that urge her to engage in criminal activity?[170] This is not tantamount to asking whether there was a *risk* the other person might do so in the sense of an unexpected betrayal, an approach the Court rejected in *Marakah*. Taking a case-by-case approach to whether an exchange is private may appear to run contrary to the Court's earlier jurisprudence affirming a normative and content-neutral approach to assessing reasonable expectation of privacy.[171] Setting that debate aside, however, the point here is that concerns about the absurdity of police needing a warrant before reading a text message a civilian brings them belong in the assessment of whether the accused

169 *Ibid*; *Spencer*, above note 28.

170 This was essentially the question in *Amdurski*, above note 133, where the court found that the accused did not have a reasonable expectation of privacy in texts sent to the complainant in light of his knowledge that she was under the age of consent and he communicated with her to arrange sex for money. In *R v Patterson*, 2018 ONSC 4467, a case involving child luring of a fifteen-year-old boy, the court held at para 26:

> A reasonable person in Mr. Patterson's position would foresee the possibility that the victim's parents could be monitoring his Facebook activities. Or that the victim might disclose the conversations to a trusted friend. Or that the victim might mistakenly leave his Facebook page open on the family computer where the communications could be discovered by a parent or sibling.

The question in *KA and ASA*, above note 161 at para 63, was whether "alleged pimps and human traffickers" had a reasonable privacy interest in "text messages with their alleged sex worker and slave." The court found that they did not have a reasonable interest.

171 *Duarte*, above note 26 at 47–48, and *Wong*, above note 94 at 45; see also Martin J's opinion in *Mills*, above note 45 at paras 113–14 taking issue with Brown J's opinion in this case that "it is not reasonable for an adult to expect privacy when communicating with a vulnerable child who is a stranger." Justice Martin contends "this position reintroduces the 'loss of control due to risk of disclosure' analysis that this Court recently rejected in *Marakah*."

retained a reasonable privacy interest in the communication—and not, if they did have an interest, whether receipt constituted a search or seizure.

A further issue that remains unresolved in the Supreme Court's jurisprudence is whether police receiving a description or report from a third party about the incriminating content of a piece of evidence (the printout of a chat, an email) authorizes police to take custody of it—to seize it—when the party volunteers it. Chief Justice McLachlin's *dicta* in *Marakah* and the Court's holding in *Cole* assume that, when a civilian has described the incriminating content of an item, police are authorized to receive and take custody of it briefly, until a warrant can be obtained. Yet neither opinion provides a source of authority for this temporary seizure.[172] In the absence of discussion on this point, neither case should be read as authority for the recognition of a new common law power of temporary seizure. In *Reeves*, the majority held that the officer was not authorized to *take* the computer where the co-owner, Reeves's wife, told police it contained evidence of an offence. This was due in part to the finding that even taking the computer, rather than also searching it, amounted to a non-trivial interference with the accused's privacy interest.[173] It was due also to the fact that the officer in *Reeves* testified to not believing he had reasonable grounds to seize the computer under the "plain view" provisions of the *Criminal Code*.[174] A reading of the three cases would imply, then, that an officer receiving a report of incriminating information contained in the item would need authority to seize it, even temporarily, and a warrant before searching it.

A possible source of authority for a temporary seizure can be found in the plain view powers of the *Criminal Code*.[175] Section 489(2) of the *Code* permits officers in the execution of their duties (which would include receiving a report) to seize an item they reasonably believe will afford evidence of an offence. *Cole* and *Reeves* suggest that police would either have to satisfy the test in section 489(2) (i.e., have reasonable grounds) or point to some other authority (e.g., exigent circumstances) to avoid a finding that agreeing to keep custody of the item violates section 8.[176]

---

172 As noted earlier, in *Cole*, above note 25, the school board provided police with a teacher's school-issued laptop and reported its illicit contents. Justice Fish, at para 65, assumed without elaborating that police might have had temporary authority to "seize" or take custody of the laptop for the period it would take to obtain a warrant.

173 *Reeves*, above note 38 at para 30.

174 *Ibid* at para 21, considering the plain view power in s 489(2) of the *Criminal Code*, above note 46.

175 *Criminal Code*, above note 46.

176 An imminent and serious threat would give rise to exigent circumstances, authorizing police to search without a warrant, under s 487.11 of the *Criminal Code*, *ibid*.

Lastly, we raise a question about what the Court's holdings in *Cole*, *Marakah*, and *Reeves* might mean for cases where a civilian surreptitiously records a conversation and turns it over to police.[177] If an accused may retain a privacy interest in a text conversation in the sender's hands, might they also retain a privacy interest against the state in a conversation an interlocutor surreptitiously records? And if that person brings the recording to police, do police carry out a seizure upon receiving it or a search if they listen to it? At least one trial court has applied the reasoning in *Cole*, *Marakah*, and *Reeves* to find that the accused retained a reasonable privacy interest in a surreptitious recording a civilian brought them, and police violated section 8 by listening to it without a warrant.[178]

In *R v Vey*, the person who made the surreptitious recording was not a party to the conversation, and thus making it was illegal.[179] She had suspected her husband of having an affair and left an iPod under the dining room table, which captured her husband's conversation with the other woman when they were alone in the house. They spoke about killing the other woman's spouse. When the wife who made the secret recording brought it to police, an officer advised that police had to take it from her, which the court found to be a seizure.[180] The accused couple retained a privacy interest in the recording, because it was an intimate conversation while they were alone in the house and they did not consent to it being recorded.[181] Police needed a warrant to seize and search (listen to) it.[182]

We suggest that police also engage section 8 in a more common scenario: a civilian makes a recording lawfully (or not contrary to the *Criminal Code*) and volunteers it to police (rather than an officer demanding it).[183] Following *Marakah*, an accused would have a reasonable expectation of privacy in the subject matter of a surreptitious recording—the conversation itself—given its confidential or private nature.[184] Provin-

177 *Cole* above note 25; *Marakah*, above note 111; *Reeves*, above note 38. For a more detailed treatment of this topic, see Robert Diab, "Surreptitious Recordings by Civilians in Criminal Trials: Challenging Their Admissibility at Common Law and Under the *Charter*" (2023) *Canadian Criminal Law Review* (forthcoming) [Diab].

178 *R v Vey*, 2019 SKQB 135 [*Vey*].

179 Section 184(1) of the *Criminal Code*, above note 46, makes it an offence to record a conversation to which one is not a party and lacks the consent of any party.

180 *Vey*, above note 178 at para 125.

181 *Ibid* at paras 126–28.

182 *Ibid* at para 152.

183 Section 184(2)(a) of the *Criminal Code*, above note 46, sets out as an exception to the offence in s 184(1), the situation in which a person records a conversation to which he or she is a party or where he or she has one party's consent. Making a secret recording might still be a tort under provincial law or at common law. For more on this, see Diab, above note 177.

184 *Marakah*, above note 111.

cial privacy law and criminal cases in which recordings are tendered (recognizing a prejudice to the accused) would support the finding that this expectation is objectively reasonable.[185] *Marakah* also holds that an accused would not lose his privacy interest due to a lack of control over the recording in the complainant's hands.[186] If so, transfer of it to police or Crown would render it a search or seizure for similar reasons set out in *Dyment*, *Colarusso*, and *Cole*.[187] In those cases, police had engaged section 8 when they took custody of a private item for an investigative purpose.

If police receipt of a surreptitious recording engages section 8, what difference would it make to insist that police need a warrant to retain the recording at length and listen to it? We believe there are two important ways this would protect people's privacy against casual or unnecessary state intrusion. Justice Karakatsanis noted in *Reeves* that a police seizure not only deprives a person of control over private data on a device, but it also ensures the preservation of the data for future state inspection.[188] This is true of a surreptitious recording. State possession of it deprives a person of control over the fate and possible dissemination of it. Insisting police obtain a warrant here would mean that police would have to report the seizure of a recording to a justice and comply with post-seizure requirements in the *Criminal Code*, including the provisions for returning or destroying the evidence in the event of a stay or after the proceeding has ended.[189]

Justice Karakatsanis also provided a broader rationale in *Reeves* that also applies here. The requirement that police obtain a warrant to render a search presumptively reasonable "more accurately accords with the expectations of privacy Canadians attach to their use of personal home computers and encourages more predictable policing."[190] As the Court held in *Hunter v Southam Inc*, predictable policing and protecting privacy

---

185 Manitoba, Saskatchewan, and Newfoundland and Labrador's privacy legislation explicitly stipulates that surreptitious recording without lawful authority is *prima facie* evidence of a violation of the tort of privacy and actionable *per se*: *Privacy Act*, RSS 1978, c P-24 (Saskatchewan); *The Privacy Act*, CCSM c P125 (Manitoba); *Privacy Act*, RSNL 1990, c P-22 (Newfoundland and Labrador). See also earlier cases applying a common law test for admission of secret recordings in *R v GJ*, 2012 ONSC 5413; *R v Iyer*, 2015 ABQB 577; *R v Parsons*, 2017 NLTD(G) 160.

186 *Marakah*, above note 111 at para 40.

187 *Dyment*, above note 38; *Colarusso*, above note 2; *Cole*, above note 25.

188 *Reeves*, above note 38 at para 30.

189 *Criminal Code*, above note 46, ss 489.1 and 490, discussed in the next section below.

190 *Reeves*, above note 38 at para 35.

are both supported in turn by clear rules and objective standards that help to avoid unreasonable searches before they occur.[191]

F. POST-COLLECTION EVENTS IN WHICH A SEARCH OR SEIZURE CONTINUES

Section 8 might continue to be engaged long after an initial search or seizure has taken place—extending throughout the period of police custody of an item or storage in a database, to include the returning, sharing, or final destruction of the item. In practical terms, police contend most frequently with sections 487, 489.1, and 490 of the *Criminal Code*, which require them to bring to a justice anything seized, to document what they have seized, and to eventually return the items when certain conditions are met.[192] Interception or wiretap provisions in Part VI of the *Code* contain requirements to eventually report to a target the fact that a wiretap has taken place and rules around the disclosure, sealing, and destruction of wiretap evidence.[193] The *Code* makes it an offence to use information obtained from a wiretap or from a seizure pursuant to a DNA warrant for anything other than a narrow set of purposes.[194] Breaching any of these rules may constitute a violation of section 8 on the basis that the search or seizure did not *continue* to be authorized by law or did not continue to be conducted in a reasonable manner.[195]

---

191 In *Hunter v Southam Inc*, [1984] 2 SCR 145, Dickson J, as he then was, noted at 160 that the purpose of s 8 is,

> to protect individuals from unjustified state intrusions upon their privacy. That purpose requires a means of *preventing* unjustified searches before they happen, not simply of determining, after the fact, whether they ought to have occurred in the first place. This, in my view, can only be accomplished by a system of *prior authorization*, not one of subsequent validation [emphasis in original].

192 The provisions are discussed in detail in Chapter 5, Section B(5).

193 See ss 196(1), 193(2) & (3), and 187(1.5) the *Criminal Code*, above note 46, further discussed in Chapter 6, Section A(2)(d).

194 The wiretap disclosure offence is set out in s 193(1) of the *Criminal Code*, above note 46, with exceptions in s 193(2); the DNA disclosure offence is set out in ss 487.05(1)(b), 487.08(1) & 487.08(2) of the *Code*.

195 See, e.g., *Reeves*, above note 38 at paras 63–65, noting the failure to comply with the reporting requirements in s 489.1 and the detention limits in s 490(2) of the *Criminal Code* as distinct violations of s 8 of the *Charter*.

G. STANDING

We began this chapter by noting that a claimant or an accused's rights under section 8 are engaged when three things are true: a state actor conducts what amounts to a search or seizure of a thing over which the person has a reasonable expectation of privacy (REP). We devote Chapter 4 to REP but highlight here an aspect of REP referred to as "standing."

In some cases, it is not clear whether a claimant or accused has standing to argue a violation of section 8 because they have a less immediate connection to the thing searched. For example, police search (or discover or receive) another person's device containing an exchange of text messages with the accused and seek to use it as evidence against the accused. Another common example involves police searching another person's house and finding stolen property, guns, or drugs in a room they believe to be rented or used by the accused. The Supreme Court in *R v Jones* held:

> [C]ounsel for a s. 8 applicant may ask the court to assume as true for s. 8 purposes any fact that the Crown has alleged or will allege in the prosecution against him. In other words, where the alleged Crown facts, if taken to be true, would establish certain elements of the applicant's s. 8 claim, he or she need not tender additional evidence probative of those facts in order to make out those same elements. Although the entirety of the facts and the Crown theory may not be apparent at the time of the *voir dire*, the court may infer it from the nature of the charges. Alternatively, the court may encourage prosecutors to be forthright in regards to their theory.[196]

If the Crown's position that guns they found when searching C's house belonged to A, who is now on trial before the court, A may rely on the Crown's theory that the guns belong to A in a *voir dire* in which A argues the guns were obtained in violation of *her* rights under section 8. Justice Côté describes this as an exception to the rule that the applicant bears the burden on a *Charter* application (where, ordinarily under section 8, the applicant would bear the initial burden of establishing they have an REP in the thing searched or seized).[197] The Court held in *Jones* that the accused could rely on the Crown's theory that he was the author of text messages sent to another person and stored in (and seized from) that person's internet account.

---

196 *R v Jones*, 2017 SCC 60 at para 32.
197 *Ibid* at para 33.

One virtue of the *Jones* rule about standing is that if the claimant or accused is not successful in their section 8 application on the *voir dire* and the evidence is admitted, they are still free to argue at trial that the evidence does not clearly establish the items (guns, drugs) searched or seized were theirs. As Côté J notes, if defence counsel relies on the Crown's theory in the *voir dire* to suggest the item belonged to the accused, defence counsel would be "ethically barred" from arguing at trial the item belonged to someone else. Counsel could, however, argue that the Crown has not met its burden of proving possession, control, authorship, etc., beyond a reasonable doubt.[198]

To be clear, then, evidence is often obtained in the course of searching person A's home, car, person, or text messages that is then used either as grounds for obtaining a warrant against person B or as evidence in a trial against B. In either case, B may only challenge police acquisition of the evidence (or the use of information gleaned from it in an application for a warrant against B) if B had an REP in the initial search of A's home, car, text exchange, etc. It is not uncommon in drug cases, for example, for the Crown to rely on a sequence of searches with a warrant involving person C, with each search uncovering new information or evidence used to obtain a further warrant against C. In these cases, the accused, C, has standing under section 8 to go as far back in the chain as they are in a position to assert that they had an REP in the thing searched (or information gathered) or the Crown's theory is that they did.

A final point to highlight here that will arise again in the following chapter: abandonment. In a number of cases, an accused in hot pursuit or immediately upon being stopped by police is alleged to toss away a gun or a bag of drugs or some other piece of incriminating evidence—and police find the item in close proximity. In a prosecution for possession or trafficking, the Crown's theory will be that the item belonged to the accused. This would give the accused standing to challenge the admissibility of the item under sections 8 and 24(2). However, a body of caselaw—predating *Jones*—holds that in these circumstances, the accused has abandoned any privacy interest in the gun, drugs, or other item, precluding them from relying on section 8.[199] In practical terms, this debate likely now unfolds in most if not all cases as a debate held in the course of a *voir dire* on section 8. The question of abandonment is highly fact-dependent and whether it applies must be assessed case-by-case.

---

198 *Ibid* at para 24.

199 See, e.g., *R v LB*, 2007 ONCA 596; *R v Nesbeth*, 2008 ONCA 579; *R v Plummer*, 2011 ONCA 350.

CHAPTER 4

WHAT IS A REASONABLE EXPECTATION OF PRIVACY?

A. INTRODUCTION

In this chapter, we examine the Supreme Court of Canada's approach to assessing whether a person has a reasonable expectation of privacy (REP) in a place or thing for the purposes of section 8 of the *Charter*.[1] We do so by explaining the foundational principles that guide courts in their REP inquiry, highlighting the Court's normative approach to the issue, and exploring how the Court has dealt in general terms with the concepts of risk, control, and standing as they relate to the REP inquiry. We also look in some detail at the Court's four step framework for assessing whether an REP arises. But to begin, we briefly address the origin of the concept of an REP and highlight a few basic points about how courts apply the concept in practice.

1) Origin of the Concept

As we noted in Chapter 2, the Supreme Court in *Hunter v Southam* held that the purpose of section 8 is to protect a "reasonable expectation of privacy."[2] In doing so, Dickson J, as he then was, adopted the phrase

1 *Canadian Charter of Rights and Freedoms*, Part I of the *Constitution Act, 1982*, being Schedule B to the *Canada Act 1982* (UK), 1982, c 11 [*Charter*].

2 *Hunter et al v Southam Inc*, [1984] 2 SCR 145 at 159 [*Hunter*].

from Prowse J's use of it in *Hunter* at the Alberta Court of Appeal.[3] But it first entered legal discourse in 1967, in Harlan J's concurring opinion for the US Supreme Court in *Katz v United States*—or, more precisely, in oral argument.[4] Prior to *Katz*, that Court had interpreted the protections of the Fourth Amendment to apply only to intrusions upon physical property.[5] The Court held in *Olmstead v United States* (1928) that state agents could conduct a warrantless wiretap of the accused's phone lines, since it did not involve trespass or other intrusions on his property.[6] This led to a series of cases holding that state agents do not engage Fourth Amendment protections even on a person's property, so long as the agent did not trespass.[7] However, as technology of electronic surveillance continued to evolve into the 1960s, Congress and the courts began to debate and reassess earlier assumptions about the propriety of warrantless surveillance powers.[8]

These developments culminated in the US Supreme Court's decision in *Katz*.[9] The accused in *Katz* was engaged in illegal bet-making from a phone booth that state agents were surveilling without a warrant, using a device on the outside of the booth.[10] In a concurring opinion, Harlan J radically reconfigured Fourth Amendment protections by holding that they applied not to property or places but to situations in which a person held a reasonable expectation of privacy.[11] The phrase, which had not appeared in briefs submitted to the Court, was first used by counsel Harvey Schneider in oral argument.[12] As Peter Winn writes,

---

3 *Southam Inc v Canada (Combines Investigation, Director)*, 1983 ABCA 32 at para 13.

4 *Katz v United States*, 389 US 347 (1967) [*Katz*]; Peter Winn, "*Katz* and the Origins of the Reasonable Expectation of Privacy Test" (2016) 40 *McGeorge Law Review* 1 at 9 [Winn].

5 The Fourth Amendment states: "The right of the people to be secure in their persons, houses, papers, and effects, against unreasonable searches and seizures, shall not be violated, and no Warrants shall issue, but upon probable cause, supported by Oath or affirmation, and particularly describing the place to be searched, and the persons or things to be seized." (US Const Amend IV.)

6 *Olmstead v United States*, 277 US 438 at 465–66 (1928).

7 *Hoffa v United States*, 385 US 293 (1966); *Lewis v United States*, 385 US 206 (1966), cited in Monu Bedi, "Facebook and Interpersonal Privacy: Why the Third Party Doctrine Should Not Apply" (2013) 54:1 *Boston College Law Review* 1 at 9 [Bedi].

8 Winn, above note 4 at 2–4, discussing *Berger v New York*, 388 US 41 (1967) and bills before Congress that year.

9 *Katz*, above note 4.

10 *Ibid* at 348, 352–53, 354 n14, and 356, cited in Bedi, above note 7 at 10.

11 *Katz*, above note 4, Stewart J at 347 holding "the Fourth Amendment protects people, not places" and explicitly overturning the "trespass doctrine" at 353; Harlan J, concurring, holding at 361–62, that the Amendment protects "reasonable expectations of privacy."

12 Winn, above note 4 at 9.

> even today, more than forty years later, when we listen to the recording of the argument, now available for the first time on the Internet, one cannot help but sense the electricity in the air as he presented the test for the first time to the public. The justices seized on the test like children with a new toy, ran through various hypothetical fact situations, and then tested it against common intuitions of privacy norms.[13]

As Winn explains, "the test gave courts more flexibility to protect a broader concept of human dignity at a time when information technology had outstripped what property rights alone could protect."[14] Adopting the phrase in *Katz*, Harlan J articulated a new two-part test for the Fourth Amendment to apply: "first that a person have exhibited an actual (subjective) expectation of privacy and, second, that the expectation be one that society is prepared to recognize as 'reasonable.'"[15] The phone booth here may have been publicly accessible, Harlan J held, but once Katz had stepped inside and closed the door, it became "a temporarily private place, whose momentary occupant's expectations of freedom from intrusion . . . [were] reasonable."[16]

2) Practical Application of REP

Turning back to the *Charter*, a person claiming that a state actor has violated section 8 has the burden of establishing, on a balance of probabilities, that they had an REP in a place or thing searched or seized.[17] The burden arises from the Supreme Court's holding in *Hunter* that the purpose of section 8 is to protect an REP and that section 8 is not engaged unless a claimant can establish an REP in the place or thing searched or seized.[18] Once a person establishes they had an REP in the place or

13 *Ibid.*

14 *Ibid.*

15 *Katz*, above note 4 at 361.

16 *Ibid.*

17 See the discussion of burdens on a s 8 application in *R v Collins*, [1987] 1 SCR 265 at 277–78, though in this case, the Court assumed—without discussion—the accused had a privacy interest in the object of the search (her body).

18 *Hunter*, above note 2 at 159, Dickson J holding that "[t]he guarantee of security from unreasonable search and seizure only protects a reasonable expectation [of privacy]." Interpreting this passage in *Schreiber v Canada (Attorney General)*, [1998] 1 SCR 841 at para 18, Lamer CJ held that "s. 8 would only be implicated if the individual who was claiming a *Charter* breach could show that he or she had a reasonable expectation of privacy in the place searched or the material seized. If no such expectation exists, there can be no *Charter* breach, as s. 8 only protects people, not places or things." See also Iacobucci J (dissenting but not on this point) at para 49: "the preventative/prophylactic guarantees and measures which

item at issue, the burden shifts to the Crown to establish, on a balance of probabilities, the search or seizure was reasonable.[19]

A key point to keep in mind at the outset is that in many cases, the court assumes or finds that what police have searched or seized is private, without engaging in much, if any, analysis or applying a specific test. Examples of this include cases involving the search of a person on arrest or the search of a person's home pursuant to a warrant. A trial court will often simply cite a Supreme Court case for the general proposition that we have a reasonable privacy interest in our bodies, cars, computers, or homes and move on to address whether the search was reasonable.

Cases that engage in a more detailed analysis of whether the accused had an REP in the place or item at issue are cases that present the court with a novel situation or circumstances that give rise to a debate about whether the accused had a reasonable privacy interest against the state. This might arise in any number of ways, as illustrated by the cases in this chapter, though, in a general sense, the cases tend to involve novel investigative techniques or evidence obtained from an accused indirectly: for example, from a third party, when possibly abandoned, or where the accused shared or did not own or possess the space or item at issue.

Even where there may be some debate as to whether a person had a reasonable privacy interest against the state in a place or item searched, the Supreme Court has recently provided another means of circumventing a more detailed analysis of an REP. In *R v Jones*, the Court held that "an accused mounting a s. 8 claim may ask the court to assume as true any fact that the Crown has alleged or will allege in the prosecution against him in lieu of tendering evidence probative of those same facts in the *voir dire*."[20] In other words, if the Crown seeks to tender into evidence a gun seized from a bedroom in a home with an unknown occupant, on the theory that the accused occupied the room and possessed the gun, they need not establish these facts in the course of a challenge to the search or seizure under section 8. They can ask the court to assume, for the purpose of the *Charter* challenge, that the room and the gun belonged to her.[21] In some cases, adopting the Crown's theory will result in an REP being obvious—as in the example involving the bedroom. In

are at the heart of s. 8 are not engaged until a reasonable expectation of privacy in the information sought has been recognized."

19 For more detail, see the overview of s 8 in Chapter 2.

20 *R v Jones*, 2017 SCC 60 at para 9 [*Jones*].

21 Justice Côté, writing for the majority in *Jones*, *ibid*, added at para 24 that counsel for the accused would be free to argue at trial that the Crown had not proved possession beyond a reasonable doubt, but would be "ethically barred" from arguing that the room or gun belonged to someone else.

other cases, relying on the rule in *Jones* may only establish a subjective expectation of privacy, but not whether it was objectively reasonable. This is common where police obtain a copy of a text exchange and the Crown alleges the accused was the sender of incriminating messages. The court must decide in these cases whether he retained an objectively reasonable privacy interest in those messages.[22]

When a court does endeavour to engage in a more detailed analysis of whether a person had an REP in a space or an item, the analysis often ultimately depends on the court deciding a normative question—a central idea in this chapter. By "normative," we mean that a court asks not whether the accused intended the space or item to remain private, but whether in a broader sense, reasonable members of society considering the space or item, in a generic sense, would expect that it should remain free from state intrusion. A good example can be found in *R v Wong*.[23] The Supreme Court in that case held that whether the accused had a reasonable privacy interest in a hotel room he rented did not depend on the (unlawful) use he made of it or whether there was a risk of state intrusion in the circumstances. It turned on the broader normative question of whether members of "a free and democratic society" would expect to enjoy privacy from the state when staying in a hotel room.[24]

We also emphasize, at the outset, that the REP analysis has two dimensions, which Professor Coughlan helpfully refers to as a "threshold" and a "scale."[25] These should be kept distinct.[26] Section 8 is engaged if one *has* an REP in a thing searched. It does not matter how much. The threshold question is whether a person's expectation of privacy was or was not *reasonable*. The result is binary: one has an REP or one does not.[27] If the claimant does not establish an REP, section 8 is not engaged; and there has not been a "search" or "seizure" within the meaning of the *Charter*. If the claimant does have an REP, section 8 is engaged—so long as the two other necessary elements for a search or seizure are present

22 This is the scenario in *Jones* itself. For further examples, see the discussion of whether and when police receiving a text from a recipient constitutes a search or seizure in Chapter 3, Section E(3).

23 *R v Wong*, [1990] 3 SCR 36 [*Wong*].

24 *Ibid* at 44–45.

25 Steve Coughlan, *Criminal Procedure*, 4th ed (Toronto: Irwin Law, 2020) at 81 [Coughlan].

26 See *R v Edwards*, [1996] 1 SCR 128 at para 45 [*Edwards*]: "As a general rule, two distinct inquires must be made .... First, has the accused a reasonable expectation of privacy. Second, [if yes], was the search ... conducted reasonably."

27 A diminished expectation of privacy is still a reasonable one at this threshold stage: *R v Cole*, 2012 SCC 53 at para 9 [*Cole*].

(i.e., a state actor carried out an investigative technique or a taking that interfered with the claimant's REP).[28]

Although the REP question is binary, in the sense that it yields a "yes" or "no" answer, this does not mean that all privacy interests recognized under section 8 are of equal weight. To the contrary, the Supreme Court has recognized privacy rights exist on a spectrum, meaning a privacy interest can be weak but nevertheless attract a legal REP. *R v Cole* illustrates the point.[29] The accused, Cole, was a teacher who had used his work issued laptop to store child pornography. Applying the totality of circumstances test (discussed below), the Supreme Court held that while some factors weighed in favour of an REP and others militated against it, overall, Cole had a diminished but nevertheless reasonable expectation of privacy and the search had engaged section 8.[30]

The second question identified above is one of scale. Assuming the court has found an REP in a place or thing, it must then decide whether the search was reasonable. Broadly speaking, courts here evaluate the relative strength of the privacy interest at hand and seek to balance it against the state's interest in law enforcement. The Supreme Court has held that core values underpinning our privacy interests include dignity, integrity, and autonomy.[31] Simply stated, the stronger the privacy interest at the threshold stage, the greater the justification required to interfere with it at the scale stage. As Charron J put it, reasonableness here is "a function of both the importance of the state objective and the degree of impact on the individual's privacy interest."[32] Because this second question involves balancing, it means the relative strength or weakness of the privacy interest assessed at the first "threshold" stage will affect the assessment of whether section 8 has been infringed at the second "scale"

---

28 See the discussion of these elements in Chapter 3, Section A.

29 *Cole*, above note 27.

30 *Ibid* at para 9, and at para 58 the Court summarized:

> The nature of the information in issue heavily favours recognition of a constitutionally protected privacy interest. Mr. Cole's personal use of his work-issued laptop generated information that is meaningful, intimate, and organically connected to his biographical core. Pulling in the other direction, of course, are the ownership of the laptop by the school board, the workplace policies and practices, and the technology in place at the school.

31 See for example *R v Plant*, [1993] 3 SCR 281 at 292–93 [*Plant*]; and see Chapter 1, Section C(1), for discussion of these values.

32 *R v Rodgers*, 2006 SCC 15 at para 27.

stage.[33] The question of whether a search or seizure was reasonable is shaped by three further inquiries, which are the focus of later chapters.[34]

B. FOUNDATIONAL PRINCIPLES

1) Normative Not Descriptive Standard

The Supreme Court of Canada has emphasized repeatedly that the section 8 analysis involves a normative standard. This has a number of dimensions relating to the threshold aspect of the REP test.[35] The normative standard is often used in contrast to a descriptive one.[36] The normative approach is concerned with whether the claimant *ought* to expect privacy; whereas a descriptive standard is concerned with whether they expected privacy in fact. The distinction is vital because if an REP was judged entirely on the basis of a descriptive standard, there would be a danger of erosion, as the more privacy was invaded empirically, the less reasonable it would be to expect it in the future. This conjures images of George Orwell's *1984*, where one might conclude that nobody could reasonably expect privacy anywhere because everyone knew Big Brother was always watching.[37] As Binnie J cautioned in *R v Patrick*, a "government that increases its snooping on the lives of citizens, and thereby makes them suspicious and reduces their expectation of privacy, will not thereby succeed in unilaterally reducing their constitutional entitlement to privacy protection."[38]

---

33 Note that the strength of the privacy interest is relevant in a third way as well. Assuming s 8 has been violated, courts must consider whether to exclude the evidence obtained under s 24(2) of the *Charter*. The strength or weakness of the privacy interest affects this analysis: see *Cole*, above note 27 at paras 91–92 and 97.

34 Chapter 5 (Searches and Seizures Authorized by Law 1: Standard Warrant); Chapter 6 (Searches and Seizures Authorized by Law 2: Other Authority); Chapter 7 (When Is a Search Law Reasonable?); Chapter 8 (When Is a Search Reasonably Conducted?).

35 See generally Hamish Stewart, "Normative Foundations for Reasonable Expectations of Privacy" (2011) 54:12 *Supreme Court Law Review* 335 [Stewart, "Normative Foundations"]; Lisa Austin, "Information Sharing and the 'Reasonable Ambiguities' of Section 8 of the Charter" (2007) 57 *University of Toronto Law Journal* 499 [Austin]; E. Patton-Simpson, "Privacy and the Reasonable Paranoid: The Protection of Privacy in Public Places" (2000) 50:3 *University of Toronto Law Journal* 305 [Patton-Simpson].

36 *R v Tessling*, 2004 SCC 67 at para 42 [*Tessling*].

37 *Ibid*; George Orwell, *1984* (London: Penguin, 1949).

38 *R v Patrick*, 2009 SCC 17 at para 14 [*Patrick*].

2) Normative Standard Operates Against the State

The normative standard is really a question of legal entitlement: *should* privacy be protected in the totality of circumstances? Assessing this requires courts to keep a number of other considerations in mind. Crucially, there is a relational dimension to the inquiry. Insofar as section 8 is concerned, reasonable expectations of privacy do not operate in the air, against the world, or among individuals; rather, they operate as between individuals and the state. Recall that if the answer to the binary threshold REP inquiry is "no," then section 8 is simply not engaged. Agents of the state would, in such cases, be free to deploy the investigative technique without the need to justify it.[39] Because of this, courts should reflect carefully in each case on the implications of arriving at a negative answer to the threshold binary question. As Binnie J wrote in *Patrick*, the "privacy analysis is laden with value judgments which are made from the independent perspective of the reasonable and informed person who is concerned about the long-term consequences of government action for the protection of privacy."[40] This analysis compels attention to the values underpinning privacy—principally dignity, autonomy, and integrity—as well as the potential impacts on the same should the state be free to deploy the investigative technique at its sole discretion.[41] It should also beg fundamental questions about freedom and democratic norms. As La Forest J observed in *R v Dyment*, "society has come to realize that privacy is at the heart of liberty in a modern state .... The restraints imposed on government to pry into the lives of the citizen go to the essence of [democracy]."[42] In *R v Wong*,[43] La Forest J emphasized that section 8 "must be interpreted as providing a continuing framework for the legitimate exercise of government power"[44] and this involves consideration of "whether giving [judicial] sanction to the particular form of unauthorized surveillance in question would see the amount of privacy and freedom remaining to citizens diminished to a compass inconsistent with the aims of a free and open society."[45]

39 Coughlan, above note 25 at 88.

40 *Patrick*, above note 38 at para 14.

41 *Tessling*, above note 36 at para 25, citing *Plant*, above note 31 at 293. See Chapter 1 for a discussion of these underlying values.

42 *R v Dyment*, [1988] 2 SCR 417 at 427–428 [*Dyment*]; and see *Wong*, above note 23 at 47 referring to unrestrained surveillance as "fundamentally irreconcilable with what we perceive to be acceptable behaviour on the part of government."

43 *Wong*, above note 23.

44 *Ibid* at 44.

45 *Ibid* at para 46; and see *R v Reeves*, 2018 SCC 56 at para 28 [*Reeves*].

Finally, the prophylactic function of section 8 should not be forgotten. In *Hunter v Southam*,[46] the Supreme Court of Canada's first decision interpreting section 8, Dickson J emphasized that the "purpose" of section 8 is to protect people from "unjustified state intrusions upon their privacy . . . before they happen, not simply . . . determining, after the fact, whether they ought to have occurred in the first place."[47] Professor Coughlan has argued, and we agree, that the threshold analysis ought therefore to be relatively "easy to meet," so that infringements can be deterred before they arise, while also giving courts the ability to evaluate competing interests, at the second balancing or scale stage, should this be necessary.[48]

3) Normative Standard and Risk, Control, and Standing

Foregrounding the relational aspect of the normative REP inquiry, as a standard operating against the state, is vital for yet another reason: it frames how courts should approach the related notions of risk, control, and standing. As explained below, the mere fact that another individual can access one's property, person, or information should not carry undue weight when resolving the question as to whether that person has an REP *vis-à-vis* the state. As Professor Stewart has observed, if this were so, "the consequences for privacy would be disastrous."[49] Privacy rights would shrink wherever there is a risk of intrusion by others; and the state could then point to such empirical vulnerability of intrusion to justify its own surveillance. As La Forest J observed in *R v Duarte*,[50] in such a state "there would be no meaningful residuum of our right to live our lives free from surveillance."[51]

Regarding risk, American courts have adopted a third-party doctrine, which provides that individuals do not have an REP in relation to information they have disclosed to another person. The reasoning is that by sharing information, the claimant assumes the risk of subsequent disclosure, and thereby forfeits their privacy interest.[52] The Supreme Court

---

46 *Hunter*, above note 2.

47 *Ibid* at 160.

48 Coughlan, above note 25 at 83; see also at 88.

49 Hamish Stewart, "Reasonable Expectations of Privacy as Rights," in C.D.L. Hunt & R. Diab, eds, *The Last Frontier: Digital Privacy and the Charter* (Toronto: Thomson Reuters, 2021) 34 at 46 [Stewart, "Reasonable Expectations"].

50 [1990] 1 SCR 30 [*Duarte*].

51 *Ibid* at 44.

52 See Nader Hassan et al, *Search and Seizure* (Toronto: Emond Montgomery, 2021) at 29–30 [Hassan], citing *United States v Miller*, 425 US 435 (1976); *United States v Jacobsen*, 104 S Ct 1654 (1984).

of Canada has rejected such categorical thinking, preferring instead to analyze the matter contextually, in the totality of circumstances. An early illustration comes from *Duarte*, in which the Court found a violation of section 8 in relation to a conversation between the accused and a police informant who was wearing a secret recording device.[53] The Court distinguished between the risk one assumes when speaking to another person that they may later divulge the information, which "no set of laws could immunize us from," and the risk of surreptitious electronic surveillance by the state. These risks, the Court concluded, are of a "different order"; the former is a risk we run when living in a free society, but the latter, normatively, is not:

> A society which exposed us, at the whim of the state, to the risk of having a permanent electronic recording made of our words every time we opened our mouths might be superbly equipped to fight crime, but would be one in which privacy no longer had any meaning . . . . It is unacceptable in a free society that the agencies of the state be free to use this technology at their sole discretion. The threat this would pose to privacy is wholly unacceptable.[54]

This distinction is evident in recent Supreme Court judgments as well. In *R v Spencer*, the police had become aware, through a publicly available file-sharing site, that child pornography sites were being accessed from an internet protocol (IP) address in Saskatoon, but they did not know to which specific person or physical address this IP related. They requested Shaw, the local internet service provider, to inform them of the subscriber information for that IP, and Shaw complied with this request. Justice Cromwell, for the Court, determined that, in the totality of circumstances, an REP was established because the "disclosure of this information will often amount to the identification of a user with intimate or sensitive activities being carried out online, usually on the understanding that these activities would be anonymous."[55] Drawing on

53 *Duarte*, above note 50.

54 *Ibid* at 44–45; and see *Wong*, above note 23, where La Forest J, for the majority, held at 48:

> [T]here is an important difference between the risk that our activities may be observed by other persons, and the risk that agents of the state, in the absence of prior authorization, will permanently record those activities on videotape, a distinction that may in certain circumstances have constitutional implications. To fail to recognize this distinction is to blind oneself to the fact that the threat to privacy inherent in subjecting ourselves to the ordinary observations of others pales by comparison with the threat to privacy posed by allowing the state to make permanent electronic records of our words or activities.

55 *R v Spencer*, 2014 SCC 43 at para 66 [*Spencer*].

Duarte, Cromwell J specifically rejected the argument that by sharing his IP address with the service provider, Shaw, the accused thereby forfeited an REP in this information *vis-à-vis* the state.[56] The question of risk is important also in cases where the accused has exposed their activities to public view. In *R v Wong*,[57] La Forest J, for the majority, determined that an REP existed in circumstances where the accused was surreptitiously video-recorded by police while operating an illegal betting parlor in his hotel room. He specifically rejected the Ontario Court of Appeal's decision in that case, which found no REP on the basis that by opening his hotel room to the public, the accused had "court[ed] observation by the other persons in the room, [thereby] effectively relinquish[ing] any right to maintain a reasonable expectation of freedom from the much more intrusive invasion of privacy constituted by surreptitious video surveillance on the part of the state."[58] As in *Duarte*, such reasoning fails to distinguish between the risk one runs when appearing in public (or inviting the public into an otherwise private place) that they may be observed, with the far more insidious risk of unrestricted electronic surveillance by the state. Simply stated, "[w]e must be prepared to live with the first risk, but, in a free and open society, need not tolerate the specter of the second."[59]

Related to this idea of the assumption of risk is the notion of control. Put broadly, the argument has been advanced that it is not reasonable for an individual to have a legally recognized REP in relation to activities or information to which others have ready access. As with risk, the Supreme Court has rejected such a categorical approach, preferring instead to assess such arguments in the totality of circumstances. *R v Marakah* illustrates the point.[60] The police searched W's smartphone and discovered text messages incriminating him as well as his accomplice M who had sent the messages. The issue on appeal, as it related to M, was whether M could have an REP in relation to messages he had sent to W that were seized from W's smartphone. A majority of the Court answered this question in the affirmative, stating: a "person does not lose control of information for the purposes of s. 8 simply because another person possesses it or can access it."[61] Once again, approaching the issue normatively and from a relational perspective led the majority to conclude that despite the "technological reality" that text messages once sent no

56 *Ibid*; *Duarte*, above note 50.

57 *Wong*, above note 23.

58 *Ibid* at 49.

59 *Ibid* at 51.

60 *R v Marakah*, 2017 SCC 59 [*Marakah*].

61 *Ibid* at para 41.

longer remain in the exclusive control of the sender, "he or she may yet reasonably expect that information to remain safe from state scrutiny."[62] Simply stated, "control is not dispositive, but only one factor to be considered in the totality of the circumstances."[63] Similar reasoning was followed in *R v Cole*.[64] A school computer technician found pornographic images stored on a teacher's work issued laptop. These were turned over to police without a warrant. The Supreme Court determined, unanimously, that the teacher had an REP in relation to these computer files, even though he lacked the ability—both physically and legally—to control access to them by the school, which retained ownership of the computer throughout.[65] *R v Reeves* is apposite as well.[66] The accused shared a home computer with his spouse. Upon discovering child pornography on the computer, the spouse alerted police and consented to the seizure of the device. The issue on appeal was whether the accused had an REP in relation to the computer. Once again, the answer, contextually, was "yes." While control is relevant, a "lack of control is not fatal to finding a reasonable expectation of privacy."[67] The relational nature of the inquiry assessed normatively buttressed the majority's finding that "while it is reasonable to ask citizens to bear the risk that a co-user of their shared computer may access their data on it, and even perhaps discuss this data with the police, it is not reasonable to ask them to bear the risk that the co-user could consent to the police *taking* this computer."[68]

Sometimes arguments about control overlap with the question of standing. If the item searched is not within the accused's possession, but

---

62 *Ibid.*

63 *Ibid* at para 44. Contrast the majority's approach with the dissenting reasons of Moldaver J, who determined that M did not have an REP in relation to the sent text messages. For him, control was the "crucial" factor (para 117), and "a person's expectation of privacy in informational subject matter that falls under another person's exclusive control cannot be reasonable in a society that values the freedom of individuals to share information" (para 129). For criticism, see Simon Stern, "Textual Privacy and Mobile Information" (2018) 55 *Osgoode Hall Law Journal* 398; Hamish Stewart, "Reasonable Expectations," above note 49 at 46.

64 *Cole*, above note 27.

65 *Ibid* at paras 50–58.

66 *Reeves*, above note 45.

67 *Ibid* at para 38.

68 *Ibid* at para 43; at para 44:

> I cannot accept that, by choosing to share our computers with friends and family, we are required to give up our *Charter* protection from state interference in our private lives. We are not required to accept that our friends and family can unilaterally authorize police to take things that we share. The decision to share with others does not come at such a high price in a free and democratic society.

rather in someone else's possession, a question may arise as to whether the *accused* has been searched at all. If not, they have no standing to argue their section 8 rights were infringed. Indeed, this was the basis for the Ontario Court of Appeal's decision in *R v Marakah*, which concluded the complainant did not have standing to challenge the search of text messages he had sent that were located on another person's smartphone.[69] As we just saw, a majority of the Supreme Court disagreed, holding that the claimant had an REP in relation to these text messages, and hence did have standing to challenge their admissibility.[70] This was a defensible position, given the inherently private nature of communications by text, which are capable of revealing "personal and core biographical information about the participants in the conversation."[71]

In other circumstances, however, courts have struggled with the question of standing, falling back into a control-type analysis. This has been especially true in cases involving territorial privacy. In *R v Edwards* the police searched an apartment rented by the accused's girlfriend, discovered drugs on the premises they believed belonged to the accused, and charged him with possession for the purposes of trafficking.[72] He was convicted at trial. A majority of the Supreme Court determined that the accused did not have an REP in relation to the place searched or the drugs seized. As to the former, he was simply a "privileged guest"[73] who lacked authority to regulate access.[74] Regarding the drugs, he could not demonstrate a subjective expectation of privacy because he denied they were his.[75] Because the accused could not establish an REP, it followed that "no personal right" of his was "affected by the police conduct at the apartment," and hence he had no standing to challenge the admissibility of the evidence under the *Charter*.[76]

The majority in *R v Belnavis* followed similar reasoning.[77] The police stopped a car for speeding. One woman was driving, a teenager was in the passenger seat, and a third woman, Lawrence, was in the back seat. The officer noticed several garbage bags in the back seat, which were

69 *R v Marakah*, 2016 ONCA 542.

70 *Marakah*, above note 60 at para 13.

71 *Ibid* at paras 33–37.

72 *Edwards*, above note 26.

73 *Ibid* at para 47.

74 *Ibid* at para 49.

75 *Ibid* at para 44. The majority acknowledged that it may be possible to establish an REP in goods seized, but here it felt constrained by the trial record where the accused denied they were his. He only acknowledged the drugs were his at the Supreme Court of Canada.

76 *Ibid* at para 51.

77 *R v Belnavis*, [1997] 3 SCR 341 [*Belnavis*].

open and full of clothing with the tags still attached. When asked who owned the bags, Lawrence replied that each passenger owned one, but did not specify which bag belonged to each individual. Ultimately, it was determined that they contained stolen property and Lawrence was charged with possession of the same. The issue on appeal to the Supreme Court, as it related to Lawrence, was whether she had an REP in relation to the vehicle and the bags. Following *Edwards*, a majority determined she did not.[78] She was a mere passenger. She did not own the vehicle, could not control access to it, and there was no evidence of a history or special relationship between her and the driver that would afford her "some special access to or privilege in regard to the vehicle."[79] Regarding the bags themselves, no REP was established because Lawrence did not identify which bag belonged to her, and there was nothing indicating ownership on them. In the majority's view, a "garbage bag is very different from a suitcase with initials displayed or a kit bag with a name on it. A green garbage bag offers no hints that it has a particular owner."[80] Although the language of standing was not explicitly employed, the implication is the same as *Edwards*: without a demonstrated REP, Lawrence could not claim *her Charter rights* were violated.[81]

It is worth pausing to note that in both *Edwards* and *Belnavis*, La Forest J penned pointed dissents that foregrounded the normative underpinnings of section 8. In *Edwards*, he wrote:

> [T]he protection accorded by s. 8 is not in its terms limited to searches of premises over which an accused has a personal right to privacy in the sense of some direct control or property. Rather the provision is intended to afford protection to all of us to be secure against intrusion by the state or its agents by unreasonable searches or seizures, and is not solely for the protection of criminals even though the most effective remedy will inevitably protect the criminal as the price of liberty for all. . . .

---

78 *Edwards*, above note 26.

79 *Belnavis*, above note 77 at para 22. Note that the majority, at para 23, did suggest that there could be special circumstances giving a passenger an REP in relation to a vehicle's contents, such as:

> For example, in many cases there would be little difference in the expectation of privacy for the owner-operator of a car and that of his or her spouse. Similarly, if two people were travelling together on an extended journey and were sharing driving responsibilities and expenses, each would be likely to have an equal expectation of privacy in the vehicle.

80 *Ibid* at para 24.

81 *Ibid* at para 25.

> Moreover, s. 8 does not merely prohibit unreasonable searches or seizures, but also guarantees to everyone the right to be *secure* against such unjustified state action. . . .
>
> It is a public right, enjoyed by all of us. It is important for everyone, not only an accused, that police (or what is even more dangerous for the public, other agents of the state) do not break into private premises without warrant.[82]

Justice La Forest echoed these concerns in *Belnavis*, where he criticized the majority's approach to privacy "by reference to legalistic property concepts" rather than by "reference to what the citizen should expect in a free a democratic society."[83] In his view:

> These property concepts go some way towards protection of the driver or owner, but the passenger is not equally protected. In this case the majority's approach virtually eviscerates the right of a wide range of passengers in an automobile to be left alone by the police, and allows the police to importune even those considered to retain some element of privacy. I find the approach wholly inappropriate in a free society and quite simply disturbing in its general implications.[84]

Although the Supreme Court is now differently constituted in its entirety compared to when *Edwards* and *Belnavis* were decided, similar divisions arguably persist. This can be seen in *R v Le*.[85] Five young men were in the private backyard of a housing co-operative, "hanging out" and talking. The accused was one of the invited guests on the property. Police entered the backyard, trespassing without consent of the owner, and began questioning the men. The accused fled and was subsequently arrested for possession of drugs and a firearm. He was convicted at trial. At the Supreme Court of Canada, the accused challenged the admissibility of this physical evidence found on his person on the basis of sections 8 and 9 of the *Charter*. Justices Brown and Martin, for the majority of three, proceeded to dispose of the appeal on the latter basis,[86] holding that Le had been arbitrarily detained and excluded the evidence under section 24(2) of the *Charter*.

Importantly, for the present discussion, Brown and Martin JJ took the opportunity to comment in *obiter* on section 8, noting that the majority did "not wish to be seen as endorsing the analysis tentatively

---

82 *Edwards*, above note 26 at para 59 [citations omitted, emphasis in original].

83 *Belnavis*, above note 77 at para 50.

84 *Ibid* [citations omitted].

85 *R v Le*, 2019 SCC 34 [*Le*].

86 *Ibid* at paras 5, 133, and 166 (Brown and Martin JJ wrote for themselves and Karakatsanis J).

put forward" by Moldaver J in his dissenting reasons.[87] Justice Moldaver agreed with the majority reasons in the Ontario Court of Appeal, which, relying on *Edwards* and *Belnavis*, determined that the accused, as an invited guest, could not establish an REP in the circumstances of the case.[88] In a passage cited and endorsed by Moldaver J, a majority of the court below had observed that "[o]ne cannot realistically talk about a reasonable expectation of privacy in respect of real property without talking about an ability to control, in some way, those who can enter upon, or remain on, the property."[89] The accused's lack of legal or *de facto* control in the circumstances drove its conclusion that no REP existed.[90] Justices Brown and Martin were critical of this approach, stating that the analysis should not "proceed with the assumption that a categorical factor, like control, will have a dominating impact on whether a person has a reasonable expectation of privacy."[91] Instead, courts must focus on the underlying normative question, namely "whether a privacy claim ought to be recognized as beyond state intrusion absent constitutional justification if Canadian society is to remain a free, democratic and open society."[92] In their view, "a case can be made that invited guests can, in some circumstances, have reasonable expectations of privacy in their host's property."[93]

C. PRINCIPLES GUIDING THE FOUR STEP REP INQUIRY

In assessing the threshold REP question, the Supreme Court has endorsed the following four step inquiry:

1) What was the subject matter of the evidence obtained by the police?

---

87 *Ibid* at para 135.

88 *Ibid* at para 226. The majority characterized Moldaver J's reasons as "express[ing] doubt about whether Mr. Le had standing to challenge the search as an invited guest on the property of another individual" at para 135.

89 *Ibid* at para 199, Moldaver J quoting *R v Le*, 2018 ONCA 56 at para 52 [*Le* ONCA].

90 *Le*, above note 85 at para 199, Moldaver J quoting *Le* ONCA, *ibid* at para 53.

91 *Le*, above note 85 at para 136.

92 *Ibid* [citations omitted].

93 *Ibid* at para 137. Commentators have argued that Karakatsanis J's reasons in *Reeves*, above note 45, finding that an REP can exist in shared property, was not intended to be confined to personal computers, but rather extends to shared spaces more generally, with the effect that the position in *Edwards*, above note 26, has arguably been "superseded" and should be approached with "caution" at least concerning co-occupants and co-users of shared spaces: Hassan, above note 52 at 49.

2) Does the claimant have a direct interest in the subject matter?
3) Did the claimant have a subjective expectation of privacy in the subject matter?
4) Was the subjective expectation of privacy objectively reasonable?[94]

The above test must be applied flexibly in the "totality of circumstances."[95] The contours of this analysis are shaped by a variety of considerations, especially concerning the fourth question, above, in relation to which the courts have identified various factors. These will be discussed at the end of Section C of this chapter. At this stage, it is important to note that such factors are not intended to be exhaustive,[96] and, as we shall see, each factor may be more or less important depending on the particular context. The Court in *Spencer* observed that the "fact that these considerations must be looked at in the 'totality of the circumstances' underlines the point that they are often interrelated, that they must be adapted to the circumstances of the particular case" and analyzed "as a whole."[97] As we saw above in *Cole*, where these considerations pull in different directions, a diminished but nevertheless reasonable expectation of privacy may be established.

1) The Subject Matter of the Search

Characterizing the subject matter at issue is an important undertaking that often influences the outcome of the REP analysis.[98] When doing so, it is helpful to ask: *what were the police really after*?[99] In *R v Patrick*,[100] which concerned a police search of the claimant's trash bag left on the curb outside of his home, the Crown argued the subject matter was simply "garbage." Justice Binnie, for the majority, cautioned against such "oversimplification," which he said "misses (or assumes away) the point in issue":

> Residential waste includes an enormous amount of personal information about what is going on in our homes, including a lot of DNA on household tissues, highly personal records (e.g., love letters, overdue

94 See *Tessling*, above note 36 at para 19; *Marakah*, above note 60 at para 11.

95 *Edwards*, above note 26 at para 45; *Tessling*, above note 36 at para 19; *R v Mills*, 2019 SCC 22 at para 13 [*Mills*] ("this Court has also consistently maintained that examining the totality of the circumstances entails an evaluation of all aspects of privacy").

96 *Edwards*, above note 26 at para 46; *Cole*, above note 27 at para 45.

97 *Spencer*, above note 55 at para 17.

98 *Ibid* at para 35.

99 *Marakah*, above note 60 at para 15.

100 *Patrick*, above note 38.

> bills and tax returns) and hidden vices (pill bottles, syringes, sexual paraphernalia, etc.). . . . [A] garbage bag may more accurately be described as a bag of "information" whose contents, viewed in their entirety, paint a fairly accurate and complete picture of the householder's activities and lifestyle. Many of us may not wish to disclose these things to the public generally or to the police in particular.[101]

A proper characterization of the subject matter requires "examining the connection between the police investigative technique and the privacy interest at stake."[102] The subject matter "must be defined functionally, not in terms of physical acts, physical space, or modalities of transmission" but rather "by reference to the nature of the privacy interests potentially compromised by the state action."[103] This requires taking a holistic approach, which considers "not only the nature of the precise information," but also the "nature of the information that it reveals."[104]

The Supreme Court of Canada has recognized three zones of privacy that operate as "useful analytical tools" for identifying the privacy interest allegedly implicated by the investigative technique at issue.[105] There is *privacy of the person*, which "protects bodily integrity, and in particular the right not to have our bodies touched or explored to disclose objects or matters we wish to conceal."[106] There is *territorial privacy*, which covers a "hierarchy" of places from, *inter alia*, a dwelling house, a hotel, a commercial space, a car, a school, and even a prison.[107] Finally, there is *informational privacy*, with at least three sub-dimensions, namely secrecy,[108] control,[109] and anonymity.[110] In assessing the strength of an informational privacy claim, the Court occasionally draws on another analytical device, namely whether it relates to a "biographical core of personal information which individuals in a free and democratic society would wish to maintain and control from dissemination to the state" and this includes "information which tends to reveal intimate details of the lifestyle and personal choices of the individual."[111] The closer the information lies to the biographical core, the more likely it is to attract

101 *Ibid* at para 30.
102 *Spencer*, above note 55 at para 26.
103 *Marakah*, above note 60 at paras 14–15 [citations omitted]; *Reeves*, above note 45 at para 29.
104 *Marakah*, above note 60 at para 15.
105 *Tessling*, above note 36 at para 24.
106 *Ibid* at para 21.
107 *Ibid* at para 22.
108 *Spencer*, above note 55 at para 38.
109 *Ibid* at para 40.
110 *Ibid* at para 38.
111 *Plant*, above note 31 at 293; *Marakah*, above note 60 at para 31.

an REP,[112] although an REP can exist in non-biographical information.[113] In assessing whether information relates to the biographical core, it is important to focus not simply on the content of the information itself, but more broadly on its potential to reveal other personal information.[114] These broad zones of privacy are not mutually exclusive and hence may overlap, but attention to each is important as they may raise distinct considerations, depending on context.[115]

The Court's approach to identifying the subject matter may be usefully illustrated by way of some examples arising in what might fairly be described as hard cases. As noted above, in *Spencer*, police in a case involving possession of child pornography sought the subscriber information attached to an IP address from an internet service provider.[116] Justice Cromwell, for the unanimous Court, noted that while identifying the subject matter was often straightforward, in other instances, such as in *Spencer* itself, the matter was difficult, as reflected in the divergent views taken in the courts below.[117] The Crown's position was that the subject matter was simply a name, address, and telephone number matching a publicly available IP address. The trial judge, and one member of the Saskatchewan Court of Appeal, agreed.[118] On this view, the information was anodyne and did not touch upon Spencer's biographical core. Spencer's position, which was reflected in the majority's reasons in the Saskatchewan Court of Appeal, was that it was more than simply mundane subscriber information, because it had the potential to reveal other information touching upon his personal lifestyle choices.[119] Justice Cromwell agreed, emphasizing the importance of assessing not just the "precise information sought, but also . . . the nature of the information that it reveals."[120] In his view, the subject matter of the search was the "identity of a subscriber whose Internet connection is linked to particular, monitored Internet activity."[121] Accessing this information allowed the police to link together the identified individual and the personal information he provided anonymously. The Court recognized that anonymity

---

112 *Cole*, above note 27 at para 46.
113 *R v AM*, 2008 SCC 19 at para 68 [*AM*].
114 *Marakah*, above note 60 at para 32; and see *Elementary Teachers Federation of Ontario v York Regional District School Board*, 2022 ONCA 476 at para 56 [*Elementary Teachers*].
115 *Spencer*, above note 55 at para 36; *Tessling*, above note 36 at para 24.
116 *Spencer*, above note 55.
117 *Ibid* at paras 23–25.
118 See *ibid* at paras 24–25.
119 *Ibid* at para 25.
120 *Ibid* at para 26.
121 *Ibid* at para 33.

is an aspect of informational privacy, which was "particularly important" in the context of internet usage.[122] This search trenched on a strong privacy interest, because once identified with a particular individual, the IP address is "capable of revealing" much about that individual, "including the individual's online activity in the home."[123]

Marakah concerned whether the claimant had an REP in relation to text messages he had sent, and hence no longer controlled, which the police obtained by searching the recipient's smartphone.[124] Chief Justice McLachlin, writing for the majority, determined that he did. She cautioned about taking a technical view of the subject matter by focusing narrowly on the location of the information, or whether the text message was sent, received, or transmitted, which may vary between devices and change with technological developments.[125] The police, in her view, were not after copies of the files, or the smartphone itself. Rather, taking a functional view, in "harmony with the need to take a broad, purposive approach to privacy protection," she determined it was the "electronic conversation between two or more people that law enforcement seeks to access."[126] Owing to the inherently private medium of text messaging, and the *potential* for these conversations to reveal details of one's personal and lifestyle choices, this information was determined to engage the claimant's biographical core, even if the actual information conveyed in the text messages was anodyne.[127]

The importance of considering the tendency of ostensibly mundane information to support inferences relating to other more personal information is illustrated also in cases involving external examinations of houses to detect unusual electricity patterns suggestive of drug production. In an early case, *R v Plant*,[128] a majority of the Court determined

122 *Ibid* at para 45; for a discussion of this aspect of the decision, see C. Hunt & M. Rankin, "*R v Spencer*: Anonymity, the Rule of Law, and the Shrivelling of the Biographical Core" (2015) 61:1 *McGill Law Journal* 193.

123 *Spencer*, above note 55 at para 32, quoting with approval from Cameron JA's reasons in *R v Trapp*, 2011 SKCA 143 at para 35. A similar debate about the subject matter of the search in relation to a police request for a person's IP address is currently unfolding. In *R v Bykovets*, 2022 ABCA 208, the Alberta Court of Appeal upheld the trial decision finding no REP in an IP address on the basis that the subject matter of the search was the IP address itself and not information police might obtain once in possession of the address. At the time of this writing, the Supreme Court of Canada has heard submissions in *Bykovets* and has yet to render its decision.

124 *Marakah*, above note 60.

125 *Ibid* at para 19.

126 *Ibid*.

127 *Ibid* at paras 32–35.

128 *Plant*, above note 31.

that the accused did not have an REP in relation to computer records revealing his home's electricity consumption, which the police obtained on suspicion the accused was operating a grow operation. The records revealed total energy consumption of the home that could be compared to that of several neighbours. Justice Sopinka commented that "in fostering the underlying values of dignity, integrity and autonomy, it is fitting that s. 8 of the *Charter* should seek to protect a biographical core of personal information which individuals in a free and democratic society would wish to maintain and control from dissemination to the state."[129] In his view, the impugned electricity records failed to meet this standard, as they showed nothing more than patterns of consumption, and did not reveal "intimate details of the appellant's life since electricity consumption reveals very little about the personal lifestyle or private decisions of the occupant of the residence."[130]

In *R v Tessling*, a unanimous Supreme Court came to the same conclusion. The police, suspecting a grow operation, deployed a forward looking infra-red (FLIR) device to scan the exterior of the accused's home from an airplane.[131] The FLIR device was able to detect heat emanations from each room, rather than overall electricity consumption as in *Plant*, and hence could be regarded as comparatively more intrusive. Indeed, Abella JA (as she then was), in the Ontario Court of Appeal, determined that an REP was established on the basis the FLIR technology enabled police to draw inferences about activities in the home.[132] Nevertheless, Binnie J, for the Court, determined that the accused did not have an REP in the circumstances. This determination was driven, in large part, by his characterization of the subject matter of the search, and its limited potential impact on privacy. In his view, the subject matter of the search was "externally obtained information [heat emanations] about the home."[133] The technology was still relatively crude and could not itself detect the source of the heat or the nature of the activity that created it.[134] While heat emanations could support the inference that a grow operation existed, they could also support other inferences about activities in the home, and FLIR was not useful in distinguishing between them. Because the heat emanations offered "no insight" into the personal or lifestyle choices of the accused, it did not touch a "biographical core

129 *Ibid* at 293.
130 *Ibid*.
131 *Tessling*, above note 36.
132 *R v Tessling* (2003) 63 OR (3d) 1 at paras 61 and 65 (CA).
133 *Tessling*, above note 36 at para 54.
134 *Ibid* at para 53.

of personal information," and hence its disclosure in his view "scarcely affect[ed]" the accused's dignity, autonomy, and integrity.[135]

R v Gomboc, issued seventeen years after *Plant*, also involved a grow operation. The police requested a utility company to install a digital recording ammeter (DRA), which measured electricity patterns flowing into the accused's residence.[136] A majority of the Supreme Court determined that the accused did not have an REP in the circumstances. As with *Plant* and *Tessling*, the result was driven largely by the majority's framing of the subject matter of the search. Justice Deschamps, writing for herself and a majority of three other justices, emphasized that the data revealed by the DRA and its potential for supporting other inferences about activities in the home were "central" to the case.[137] In her view, the electrical data revealed very limited information. It revealed total electricity consumption, and the cycles of usage, but did not reveal which devices were consuming electricity. At most the DRA could support the inference of a possible grow operation, by revealing a pattern of electricity usage consistent with grow cycles, but revealed nothing else about the activities in the home.[138] As the DRA did not engage the biographical core of personal information, and therefore had minimal impacts on the accused's privacy interests, it was determined that no REP arose.[139] Notably, several other justices disagreed, and would have found the DRA did attract an REP, but for other considerations in the case.[140] In terms of the subject matter of the search, these justices distinguished *Tessling* (in which the heat pattern information from FLIR was "meaningless"), noting that the DRA data provided in *Gomboc* enabled a "strong inference" about the presence of a grow operation, which, being information located inside of a home, should be considered private.[141]

---

135 *Ibid* at para 63.

136 *R v Gomboc*, 2010 SCC 55 [*Gomboc*].

137 *Ibid* at para 14.

138 *Ibid* at paras 14–15.

139 *Ibid* at paras 35–39.

140 In *Gomboc*, above note 136, Abella J (writing for herself and LeBel and Binnie JJ), concurred in the result, but wrote separately, finding that the DRA technique would likely have attracted an REP but for the statutory framework that enabled the utility to share this information with police, which the accused could have opted out of, but did not. We discuss this issue of the impact of regulations on the REP analysis further below.

141 *Ibid*. Justice Abella (for herself and LeBel and Binnie JJ) at paras 80–81, and see para 57; and see the reasons of McLachlin CJ and Fish J, dissenting, who would have found an REP, for the reasons given by Abella J, emphasizing that the DRA yields strong inferences about the probable existence of a grow operation inside the home, and the individual's connection to such probable criminal activity is biographical core information, at para 130.

Interestingly, in *R v Orlandis-Habsburgo*,[142] Doherty JA, for a unanimous Ontario Court of Appeal, revisited the question of whether electricity consumption data attracted an REP. In his view, the data obtained in this case could not be "meaningfully distinguished" from that in *Gomboc*,[143] and hence it would be a "stretch to suggest that the inferences available from that data would reveal 'biographical core' information about the residents of the home."[144] Nevertheless, relying on *Spencer*, and in particular its emphasis that in defining the subject matter of the search the court must look beyond the specific information obtained and consider its potential to reveal other inferences about personal information,[145] and also that claims to informational privacy are not limited to the biographical core,[146] Doherty JA determined that an REP was established:

> The subject matter of the search includes both the raw data and the inferences that can be drawn from that data about the activity in the residence. In the same way that the subscriber information in *Spencer* permitted a strong inference as to certain internet activity at a given point in time, the energy consumption data supplied [in this case] permitted a strong inference as to a certain ongoing activity [a grow operation] within the residence.[147]

Justice Doherty's REP analysis is consistent also with a pair of earlier Supreme Court decisions concerning the use of sniffer dogs to detect drugs. In *R v Kang-Brown*,[148] and its companion case *R v AM*,[149] the Court determined unanimously that section 8 was engaged by the use of such dogs, because of the significance and quality of the information obtained about concealed contents.[150] In the words of Deschamps and Rothstein JJ:

> The dog's positive indication allowed for a strong, immediate and direct inference to be made about the contents of the appellant's bag, and this involved a certain intrusion on informational privacy . . . [including]

142 2017 ONCA 649 [*Orlandis-Habsburgo*].

143 *Ibid* at para 57.

144 *Ibid* at para 79.

145 *Ibid* at para 66.

146 *Ibid* at para 79.

147 *Ibid* at para 75.

148 2008 SCC 18 [*Kang-Brown*].

149 *AM*, above note 113.

150 *Kang-Brown*, above note 148 at para 58 (McLachlin CJ and Binnie J); and see paras 1 and 17 (Lebel, Fish, Abella, and Charron JJ); para 175 (Deschamps and Rothstein JJ); para 227 (Bastarache J).

> intimate personal details about an accused, such as his or her having come into contact with a controlled substance either as a drug trafficker, an illegal drug user or a legal drug user (such as a user of marijuana for medicinal purposes), or by being in the company of drug users. The very personal nature of this information suggests that the appellant had an objectively reasonable expectation of privacy.[151]

2) The Claimant's Interest in the Subject Matter

Typically, once the court has identified the subject matter of the search, the claimant's direct interest in it is obvious. In assessing this aspect of the test, the following principles should be borne in mind. First, the Supreme Court has long recognized a principle of neutrality, which is to say that the social merit, or lawfulness, of the activity or evidence discovered is irrelevant to the question of whether the claimant can show a constitutional interest in it. In *R v Wong*, the police installed a hidden surveillance camera in a hotel room registered to the accused, on suspicion he was operating an illegal betting parlour. The Alberta Court of Appeal determined no REP existed, partly on the basis that the very activities recorded were unlawful.[152] A majority of the Supreme Court of Canada disagreed. Justice La Forest, writing for the majority of five, determined that the criminal nature of the activity surveilled cannot be relied on to invalidate an REP, because, if that were permissible, it could lead to a system of "subsequent validation for searches," as police could in theory surveil anyone they wished and then point to any illegal activity they happened to discover to justify the initial intrusion *post hoc*.[153] Such an approach is contrary to the foundational purpose of section 8 recognized in *Hunter*, namely to *prevent* unauthorized searches *before* they happen.[154] As a consequence of the principle of neutrality, "the fruits of a search cannot be used to justify an unreasonable privacy violation."[155]

Although this principle of neutrality has been repeatedly affirmed by the Court,[156] there has arguably been a recent backsliding. In *R v Mills* a police officer posed online as a fourteen-year-old girl ("Leann") with the intention of catching internet child lurers.[157] Over a period of

151 *Ibid* at para 175.

152 *Wong*, above note 23, noting CA's finding here.

153 *Ibid* at 50.

154 *Ibid*; *Hunter*, above note 2.

155 *Marakah*, above note 60 at para 48.

156 *Patrick*, above note 38 at para 32, Binnie J; *AM*, above note 113 at paras 70–73, Binnie J; *Spencer*, above note 55 at para 36, Cromwell J for the Court; *ibid* at para 48, McLachlin CJ; *R v JJ*, 2022 SCC 28 at para 48, Moldaver J.

157 *Mills*, above note 95.

two months, the accused sent messages to the undercover officer via Facebook and email. He was subsequently arrested and charged with child luring. Mills argued that he had an REP in relation to the internet messages he had sent to the "child." A majority of the Supreme Court disagreed. Justice Brown, writing for himself and two other justices, determined that, normatively speaking, the relationship between the accused and "Leann" was not "worthy" of section 8 protection from state intrusion.[158] He offered two reasons. First, he emphasized the importance of preventing the sexual exploitation of children, who were increasingly vulnerable in the internet era.[159] Second, because of the investigatory technique deployed—the creation of a fake "Leann" who would receive messages from others—the police knew, from the outset, of the relationship between the accused and the officer. Accordingly, in Brown J's view, unlike *Wong*,[160] *Marakah*,[161] and *Duarte*,[162] there was no danger of intruding on a potentially private conversation between individuals whose relationship was unknown to police.[163] Taken together, Brown J framed the *ratio* as follows:

> The proposition that I advance is . . . that Mills cannot establish an objectively reasonable expectation of privacy in these particular circumstances, where he conversed with *a child* online who was *a stranger* to him and, *most importantly*, where the police knew this when they created her.[164]

Justice Karakatsanis (writing for herself and Wagner CJ) concurred in the result, but for different reasons. In her view, no REP was established, and hence section 8 was not engaged, because, normatively speaking, it is "not reasonable to expect that your messages will be kept private from the intended recipient (even if the intended recipient is an undercover officer)."[165] This was not a case, in her view, like *Duarte*, where police surreptitiously recorded an oral conversation between the accused and an undercover officer, which would attract an REP. Rather,

158 *Ibid* at para 26.

159 *Ibid* at para 23.

160 *Wong*, above note 23 (REP existed where police surreptitiously recorded a conversation between the accused in a hotel room and others visiting there to gamble illegally).

161 *Marakah*, above note 60 (REP existed where police obtained contents of text messages from the recipient's smartphone sent by the accused to that person).

162 *Duarte*, above note 50 (REP existed where police surreptitiously recorded a conversation between the accused and a police informant).

163 *Mills*, above note 95 at paras 27–29.

164 *Ibid* at para 30 [emphasis in original].

165 *Ibid* at para 36.

it was analogous to a direct conversation between the accused and the undercover officer herself, which the Court in *Duarte* recognized does not engage section 8.[166] Justice Moldaver concurred with the "sound," though different, reasons offered by both Brown and Karakatsanis JJ[167] to form a plurality of six justices.

Justice Martin offered a strong dissent in *Mills*. In her view, Brown J's approach represented an unwarranted departure from the Court's principle of neutrality and courted the danger identified in *Hunter* of permitting unregulated state surveillance of certain undesirable activities subject only to after the fact justification.[168] According to Martin J:

> [T]he position that "adults cannot reasonably expect privacy online with children they do not know" shifts the analysis from a "reasonable" expectation of privacy to a "legitimate" expectation of privacy. The view that some relationships are *a priori* criminal and therefore do not *legitimately* attract an expectation of privacy both assumes criminality where there may be none, and assumes that there can be no reasonable privacy interests in illegal communications. Both of these assumptions are incorrect.[169]

The different sets of majority reasons in *Mills* raise a number of policy concerns. If Brown J's reasons relating to the nature of the relationship between an adult and a child not known to them being not worthy of constitutional protection are highlighted, it poses a challenge, recognized by Martin J, to the Court's longstanding principle of neutrality. Should this proposition be extended to other contexts, there is, moreover, a danger of "carving out privacy-free zones for particular relationships,"[170] which could then be justified after the fact on the basis that illegal activities were discovered. A preferable reading of *Mills*, in our view, is a narrow one, concentrating on the overlap between the reasons offered by Brown and Karakatsanis JJ, which emphasized that there was no danger of the police intruding on a private conversation between two non-state actors, since one party to the messages was in fact an undercover officer. While this avoids the main criticism levelled by Martin J, above, it does nevertheless raise the unsettling prospect of state fishing expeditions, where undercover officers pose as ordinary individuals for the purposes

166 *Ibid* at paras 42, 44.

167 *Ibid* at para 66.

168 *Ibid* at paras 117–25.

169 *Ibid* at para 123.

170 Stewart, "Reasonable Expectations," above note 49 at 51–52, quoting and agreeing with Martin J in *Mills*, *ibid* at para 130.

of recording one's online communications,[171] which arguably is not consistent with what people expect in a free and democratic society.[172]

A second issue that may arise in relation to the accused's interest in the subject matter of the search concerns the question of standing. Although not expressly stated as such, finding a lack of standing could be conceptualized as a finding that the accused lacked a direct interest in the subject matter of the search. As discussed above,[173] the Supreme Court has determined that an individual could not claim an REP in relation to bags left at another person's apartment where he was simply a privileged guest (*Edwards*),[174] or by an individual whose bags were searched while she was a passenger in another's vehicle (*Belnavis*).[175] These results were influenced by how the subject matter of the search was framed. In *Edwards*, the accused claimed a territorial privacy interest in his girlfriend's apartment. Once the Court determined that, as a mere guest, he had no REP in the apartment, he was unable to show any direct interest in the bags that were searched on the property. *Belnavis* followed similar reasoning. The accused, as a mere passenger in another's vehicle, could not show a privacy interest in the search of the car itself.[176]

Had the individuals in *Edwards* and *Belnavis* clearly identified the items that were searched as belonging to them, their direct interest in the same would presumably be uncontroversial, and the problem could be avoided. This approach, however, places the accused in a bind, insofar as one aspect of their defence is to deny the *actus reus* of the criminal charges by denying the bags belonged to them.[177] Fortunately, the Supreme Court has recently overcome this problem. The details are explained immediately below, when assessing the third step of the inquiry: the individual's subjective expectation of privacy.

---

171 See Michelle Biddulph, "The Privacy Paradox: *Marakah*, *Mills*, and the Diminished Protections of Section 8" (2020) 43:5 *Manitoba Law Journal* 161 at 192–93.

172 It has been argued that the legality of the police deploying the investigative technique in *Mills*, above note 95 in the future is debatable in light of the Court's recent jurisprudence on entrapment in *R v Ahmad*, 2020 SCC 11; see Biddulph, *ibid* at n 110.

173 See Section B(3).

174 *Edwards*, above note 26.

175 *Belnavis*, above note 77.

176 Note this conceptual difficulty did not arise in *Le*, above note 85, because the police, though entering onto property (thereby raising issues of territorial privacy) happened to search the body of the accused himself, hence clearly engaging an interest in personal privacy in which his direct interest is obvious.

177 *Edwards*, above note 26 at para 44; *Belnavis*, above note 77 at para 24.

3) Subjective Expectation of Privacy

In *R v Jones*,[178] the accused was convicted at trial of drug trafficking. The central evidence against him concerned various text messages the police obtained from a Telus account associated with his co-accused. He challenged the admissibility of the text messages but led no evidence of his authorship of the same. The trial judge determined, and the Ontario Court of Appeal affirmed, that in these circumstances he could not establish a subjective expectation of privacy in the text messages or a direct interest in them. Following *Edwards*, he was determined to lack standing to challenge their admissibility.[179] The Supreme Court disagreed. Justice Côté, for the majority, determined that, for the purposes of challenging the admissibility of evidence on the basis of section 8, the accused may rely on the Crown's theory to presume, or otherwise infer from other facts it alleged, that the accused had a subjective expectation of privacy in support of his *Charter* application without the need to offer additional probative evidence on *voir dire*.[180] Applying this approach, Côté J concluded that, as the presumed author of the impugned text messages, Jones had a subjective expectation of privacy and a direct interest in the same, following *Marakah*.

More generally, the subjective expectation requirement, while said to be an "important" factor,[181] has never been a "high hurdle."[182] There is a danger, recognized by Binnie J in *Tessling*, that overemphasizing this factor could lead to the self-erosion of privacy rights, as increases in state snooping could effectively reduce subjective expectations of privacy to nil.[183] As Côté J explained in *Jones*, "a *Charter* claimant's subjective belief that Big Brother is watching should not, through the workings of s. 8, be permitted to become a self-fulfilling prophecy."[184] Such an approach would not be consistent with the normative underpinnings of the REP framework.[185]

In light of these decisions, one might question whether demonstrating a subjective expectation of privacy remains a legal requirement to engage section 8.[186] While the Supreme Court has identified it as

178 *Jones*, above note 20.
179 *Ibid* at paras 6 & 7.
180 *Ibid* at paras 9, 21, and 33.
181 *Tessling*, above note 36 at para 42.
182 *Patrick*, above note 38 at para 37.
183 *Tessling*, above note 36 at para 42.
184 *Jones*, above note 20 at para 21.
185 *Ibid* at para 20.
186 Coughlan, above note 25 at 94–95.

a discrete requirement in its totality of circumstance test,[187] there are instances in which the Court has been prepared to assume it, without much argument, based on the nature of the information itself,[188] or its location,[189] or now, as we just saw in *Jones*, based on the Crown's theory. In *Tessling*, Binnie J cautioned the "absence" of a subjective expectation "should not be used too quickly to undermine the protection afforded by s. 8 to the values of a free and democratic society"[190] and the Ontario Court of Appeal has apparently gone further, stating a subjective expectation of privacy "cannot be a prerequisite to a finding of a reasonable expectation of privacy."[191]

4) Objective Reasonableness: A Multifactorial Analysis

The objective reasonableness of the claimant's expectation of privacy is often the "major battleground" for section 8.[192] Over the years, the Court has identified a variety of factors that are to be applied in the "totality of circumstances."[193] These factors are "of substance, not of form."[194] While each individual marker speaks to an empirical fact that may or may not exist in the circumstances of the case, the overall analysis is "normative rather than simply descriptive."[195] Thus, while "sensitive to the factual context," the REP inquiry "is inevitably 'laden with value judgments which are made from the independent perspective of the reasonable and informed person who is concerned about the long-term consequences of

187 *Tessling*, above note 36 at para 32.

188 *Cole*, above note 27 at para 43 (subjective expectation of privacy assumed in contents of a laptop based on the fact the claimant used it to access the internet).

189 *Patrick*, above note 38 at para 37 (subjective expectation assumed where information relates to activities in the home); and see *Gomboc*, above note 136 at para 57.

190 *Tessling*, above note 36 at para 42.

191 *Orlandis-Habsburgo*, above note 142 at para 44.

192 *Tessling*, above note 36 at para 43.

193 *Cole*, above note 27 at para 40.

194 *Ibid.*

195 *Spencer*, above note 55 at para 18. See Coughlan, above note 25 at 89, noting that although the various REP considerations listed by the Court are "fundamentally factual ones," the ultimate conclusion requires a "normative assessment" about the subject's legal "entitlement." For a discussion of this point, noting a tendency for courts to occasionally slip into an empirical analysis and lose sight of the underlying normative values of s 8, see Stewart, "Normative Foundations," above note 35; Austin, above note 35. For a defence of the importance of imbedding social norms and empirical practices into the broader normative inquiry, see Avner Levin, "Ought from Is: Towards Truly Reasonable Expectations of Privacy," in C.D.L. Hunt & R. Diab, eds, *The Last Frontier: Digital Privacy and the Charter* (Toronto: Thomson Reuters, 2021) 59, especially at 78–88.

government action for the protection of privacy'."[196] These consequences entail judicial reflection on the instrumental importance of privacy to preserving freedom and democratic norms, as well as on the deontological values of dignity, integrity, and autonomy that underpin the right to privacy.[197] The REP factors are not intended to be exhaustive,[198] must be tailored to the circumstance of each particular case,[199] and vary in importance depending on context.

The Supreme Court has organized and presented these factors differently over the years. The seminal case, *Edwards*, concerned a claim to territorial privacy; the issue was whether the claimant had an REP in drugs found in his girlfriend's apartment.[200] Justice Cory listed the following considerations for this type of claim:

> (i) presence at the time of the search; (ii) possession or control of the property or place searched; (iii) ownership of the property or place; (iv) historical use of the property or item; (v) the ability to regulate access, including the right to admit or exclude others from the place; (vi) the existence of a subjective expectation of privacy; and (vii) the objective reasonableness of the expectation.[201]

Subsequently, in *Tessling*, where the investigative technique (forward looking infra-red device (or FLIR)) deployed by the police captured heat emanations from a home to support the inference of a marijuana grow operation, both informational and territorial privacy interests were at issue.[202] Justice Binnie reorganized the *Edwards* factors into four lines of inquiry, which are reflected in the structure of this chapter (the first three of which we have already explored above):

1) What was the subject matter of the search?
2) Did the accused have a direct interest in the same?
3) Did the accused have a subjective expectation of privacy?; and
4) Was the expectation of privacy objectively reasonable in the circumstances?[203]

In relation to this fourth question, Binnie J listed the following considerations:

---

196 *Spencer*, above note 55 at para 18 [citations omitted].
197 For elucidation, see Chapter 1.
198 *Cole*, above note 27 at para 45.
199 *Tessling*, above note 36 at para 31.
200 Ultimately, he did not.
201 *Edwards*, above note 26 at para 45, often referred to as the "Edwards Factors."
202 Ultimately, no REP was established.
203 *Tessling*, above note 36 at para 32.

a. the place where the alleged "search" occurred;
b. whether the subject matter was in public view;
c. whether the subject matter had been abandoned;
d. whether the information was already in the hands of third parties; if so, was it subject to an obligation of confidentiality?
e. whether the police technique was intrusive in relation to the privacy interest;
f. whether the use of surveillance technology was itself objectively unreasonable;
g. whether the [investigative technique] exposed any intimate details of the respondent's lifestyle, or information of a biographical nature.[204]

Subsequently, in *Patrick*, the Court had to consider whether the claimant had an REP in relation to the contents of a garbage bag left on the curbside outside his home, which was searched by police. Justice Binnie recognized that personal, territorial, and informational privacy interests may overlap, identified the latter two zones as relevant to the instant case, and deployed the same four part structure developed in *Tessling*, while adding the additional consideration under the final step of whether the "police trespass[ed] on the appellant's property and, if so, what [was] the impact of such a finding on the privacy analysis?"[205]

In recent cases concerning informational privacy claims, the Court has continued to apply the four lines of inquiry developed in *Tessling*.[206] In *Cole*, in which the Court determined a teacher had an REP in relation to the information stored on his work issued laptop, which was discovered by a school technician and handed over to the police, Fish J, for the majority, also considered the fact that schoolboard policies existed warning teachers that information stored on work computers may be monitored by administrators.[207] The existence of similar policies (whether derived from contractual relationships or other legislation) that ostensibly permit a third party to share the claimant's information with the police have been important contextual factors in other informational privacy claims as well,[208] which we discuss further below.

---

204 *Ibid.*

205 *Patrick*, above note 38 at para 27.

206 *Cole*, above note 27 at para 40; *Spencer*, above note 55 at para 18; *Marakah*, above note 60 at para 11.

207 *Cole*, above note 27 at para 55. This factor weighed against an REP, but ultimately, at para 58, an REP was found to exist based largely on the informational content and medium of a computer touching on the claimant's biographical core.

208 *Gomboc*, above note 136 at paras 31–32; *Spencer*, above note 55 at paras 54–67.

In the remaining part of this chapter, we elaborate on various factors just identified as they relate to the fourth line of the modern inquiry for establishing an objectively reasonable expectation of privacy.

a) Intrusiveness to Privacy Interests

The intrusiveness of the investigative technique should be assessed in relation to its impact on the values underpinning privacy.[209] Broadly speaking, the core values the Court identifies are dignity, integrity, and autonomy.[210] We elucidate these values in Chapter 1, Section C(1). Here we briefly explore jurisprudence relating to relative intrusiveness following the Supreme Court's three broad "zones" of privacy, namely personal, territorial, and informational. Again, we note that these "zones" are not mutually exclusive categories, but simply analytical tools. Overlap between the zones frequently occurs.[211] At the outset, it is worthwhile highlighting an early observation by La Forest J, which later courts have often neglected. In *R v Evans*, the police suspected an illegal marijuana grow operation and knocked on the accused's door in order to get a "sniff."[212] Justice La Forest cautioned against placing too much emphasis on the ostensible non-intrusiveness of this technique, noting that "the seemingly minor intrusion here would almost inevitably lead, and in fact did lead, to a more intrusive search."[213] In our view, courts would do well to keep this observation in mind, lest the protections afforded by section 8 erode over time where the intrusion, analyzed in isolation, may appear relatively anodyne. Nevertheless, and despite this caution, the Court has taken the position that the "lack of intrusiveness is a factor" in the REP assessment.[214]

i) *Personal Privacy*

Personal privacy, it should be recalled, has been described by the Court as protecting "bodily integrity, and in particular the right not to have our bodies touched or explored to disclose objects or matters we wish to conceal."[215] Interferences with bodily integrity invariably engage a threshold REP. Strip searches, for example, are "inherently humiliating and degrading regardless of the manner in which they are carried out and thus constitute significant injury to an individual's intangible

---

209 *Tessling*, above note 36 at para 54.
210 See for example *Plant*, above note 31 at 293.
211 *Spencer*, above note 55 at para 36; *Tessling*, above note 36 at para 24.
212 *R v Evans*, [1996] 1 SCR 8 [*Evans*].
213 *Ibid* at para 3.
214 *Tessling*, above note 36 at para 50.
215 *Ibid* at para 21.

interests."[216] Frisk or pat-down searches, which are routinely conducted on detention or arrest, also engage a reasonable privacy interest.[217] Persons in prison do not have a reasonable privacy interest in surveillance or frisk searches routinely carried out for security,[218] but courts have held that surveillance of a cell in police lockup that captures the use of a toilet violates an REP.[219] The Supreme Court has determined that students have an REP in the contents of their pockets and bags while at school (and possibly also their lockers), though this is generally diminished by their knowledge that school authorities may search their personal effects for prohibited items as part of maintaining a safe school environment.[220]

Personal privacy is seriously implicated where the state takes samples of bodily substances. The state cannot avoid the application of section 8 where it receives such samples from doctors who have taken these for medical purposes.[221] As explained below,[222] where the subject, who is not in police custody, abandons their DNA, by voluntarily discarding a cigarette butt, tissue, chewing gum, or the like, the police may "ordinarily" seize and test this evidence without violating an REP.[223] However, abandonment will not be found where the accused discards such items when they are in police custody,[224] or arguably if the subject is under constant police surveillance at the material time.[225]

---

216 *Vancouver (City) v Ward*, 2010 SCC 27 at para 64; and see *R v Golden*, 2001 SCC 83.

217 See *R v Mann*, 2004 SCC 52, setting out a test for search incident to "investigative detention"; see also *Cloutier v Langlois*, [1990] 1 SCR 158, affirming a police power to search incident to arrest, including the inside of a detainee's pockets (though not framed as a s 8 inquiry). See further discussion of these powers in Chapter 6, Section D(4)(a).

218 *Weatherall v Canada (Attorney General)*, [1993] 2 SCR 872 at 877.

219 *R v Mok*, 2015 ONCA 608; *R v Alfreds*, 2020 ABPC 32; *R v Andre*, 2018 ABPC 261; and *R v Dean*, 2017 ABPC 37.

220 *R v M(MR)*, [1998] 3 SCR 393 at paras 33–34 (affirming an REP in pockets and recognizing a possible REP in lockers); *AM*, above note 113 (affirming an REP in a backpack); and see *R v Jarvis*, 2019 SCC 10 [*Jarvis*], discussing criminal voyeurism, but drawing on s 8 *Charter* principles, and finding students have an REP not to be surreptitiously filmed at school by their teacher even if no REP exists in relation to the incidental capture of their image by closed circuit TV cameras.

221 *Dyment*, above note 42; *R v Colarusso*, [1994] 1 SCR 20, discussed in Chapter 3, Section E(1).

222 See Section C(4)(c).

223 *R v Stillman*, [1997] 1 SCR 607 at para 62 [*Stillman*].

224 *Ibid* at para 59.

225 *D'amico c R*, 2019 QCCA 77 at para 110 (Vauclair JA) [*D'amico*].

ii) *Territorial Privacy*

Regarding *territorial privacy*, the common law has long recognized the sanctity of the home as attracting a very high privacy interest. As far back as 1604, the King's Bench in *Semayne's Case* declared that "the house of everyone is to him his castle and fortress."[226] Physical intrusions into the home continue to engage a very strong privacy interest in the *Charter* era. In *R v Silveira*,[227] which involved police conducting a warrantless search of a home, the Court noted:

> The home is the one place where persons can expect to talk freely, to dress as they wish and, within the bounds of the law, to live as they wish. The unauthorized presence of agents of the state in a home is the ultimate invasion of privacy. It is the denial of one of the fundamental rights of individuals living in a free and democratic society.[228]

Trespassing onto property, in order to conduct a "perimeter search" of a dwelling to detect illegal activities within (such as drug production), violates the subject's REP in territorial privacy.[229] Reaching across the outer edge of the subject's property line, but without physically stepping onto land, probably constitutes a trespass but has been held to only peripherally engage the subject's interest in territorial privacy.[230] Police have an implied licence to enter onto property and approach a dwelling to communicate with the owner.[231] Where the police have a different purpose in mind, as in *Evans* where they approached in order to get a "sniff" of the home, the "implied conditions of that licence have effectively been breached, and the person carrying out the unauthorized activity approaches the dwelling as an intruder," thereby trenching on

---

226 *Semayne's Case* (1604), 77 ER 194; and see *Entick v Carrington*, [1765] EWHC KB J98, where Lord Camden held that "our law holds the property of every man so sacred, that no man can set his foot upon his neighbour's close without his leave."

227 [1995] 2 SCR 297.

228 *Ibid* at para 148; and see *Tessling*, above note 36 at para 38, "it may be presumed unless the contrary is shown in a particular case that information about what happens inside the home is regarded by the occupants as private."

229 *R v Wiley*, [1993] 3 SCR 263; and see *R v Kokesch*, [1990] 3 SCR 3; *R v Grant*, [1993] 3 SCR 223.

230 *Patrick*, above note 38 at para 45. But note in this case, which involved reaching onto property to collect garbage, the intrusion was framed as implicating informational privacy, as the police were really after the informational contents of the sealed bag of information. This was highly intrusive as it had the potential to reveal much about the subject, but no REP was ultimately established due to the abandonment principle, discussed in detail further below.

231 *Evans*, above note 212.

an REP.[232] As discussed below,[233] the Court has determined that a mere guest on another's property, without the ability to control access, does not have a territorial REP,[234] although more recent decisions suggest this proposition should not be taken as categorical.[235]

An REP in relation to territorial privacy can exist outside of one's residential property. The Court has analogized the privacy of a hotel room to that of a home, recognizing a strong REP therein.[236] It has recognized an REP in relation to a storage locker rented for a twenty-four hour period at a bus terminal.[237] An REP exists in relation to one's vehicle, whether that be a personal car[238] or the sleeping compartment of a commercial truck cab,[239] though it is diminished due to the highly regulated nature of this subject matter. As discussed below,[240] the Court has determined that a mere guest in another's vehicle, without the ability to control access to it, lacks a territorial REP,[241] although arguably this decision must be revisited in light of recent caselaw.[242] The Court has held that employees have an REP in their personal activities conducted in the workplace, though these must be assessed in light of the totality of circumstances, and will often be diminished based on the existence of any contractual policies in the workplace and other operational realities pertaining thereto.[243]

---

232 *Ibid* at para 15.

233 See Section C(4)(h).

234 *Edwards*, above note 26.

235 *Le*, above note 85, Brown and Martin JJ holding for the majority at para 137: "We are of the view that a case can be made that invited guests can, in some circumstances, have reasonable expectations of privacy in their host's property. The determination of when, and to what extent, these guests have a reasonable expectation of privacy will be fact and context specific."

236 *Wong*, above note 23.

237 *R v Buhay*, 2003 SCC 30 [*Buhay*].

238 *R v Mellenthin*, [1992] 3 SCR 615; and see *R v Mackenzie*, 2013 SCC 50 at para 31 (motor vehicles "are places in which individuals have a reasonable but 'reduced' expectation of privacy"), which is analogous to a bus terminal or a school, citing *Kang-Brown*, above note 148 and *R v AM*, above note 113.

239 *R v Nolet*, 2010 SCC 24 [*Nolet*].

240 See Section C(4)(h).

241 *Belnavis*, above note 77.

242 *Le*, above note 85, Brown and Martin JJ holding for the majority at para 136: "it may still be objectively reasonable for a guest present on private property to expect that the state will not enter uninvited."

243 *Cole*, above note 27 at paras 52–54; and see below discussion, in Section C(4)(d).

iii) Informational Privacy

Regarding *informational privacy*, assessing the intrusiveness of a purported "search" requires consideration not simply of the content of the information itself, but also its potential to reveal other personal information.[244] Informational privacy encompasses at least three subdimensions, namely secrecy,[245] control,[246] and anonymity.[247] Information that is secret, or entrusted to another in confidence, will typically attract a strong privacy interest.[248] Control refers to the claim of individuals to "determine for themselves when, how, and to what extent information about them is communicated to others."[249] Because it is premised on the principle that "all information about a person is in a fundamental way his own, for him to communicate or retain for himself as he sees fit,"[250] the subject's interest in control will often persist even though they have shared this information with others.[251] Accordingly, as discussed at the outset of this chapter,[252] the Court has been prepared to recognize that a person retains an REP in relation to text messages they sent that were obtained by police from a different person's smartphone.[253]Anonymity was recently recognized in *Spencer* as another aspect of informational privacy, which is particularly important in the context of internet usage.[254] Information may be communicated, with an intent that it be publicly available, but the subject maintains an interest in being anonymous, which is to say in not being "identified" as the "person providing it."[255] In *Spencer* itself, the Court held that the accused had an REP in the subscriber information attached to his IP address, because this enabled police to link his computer use to illegal online activities. Another dimension of privacy as anonymity, recognized in *R v Wise*,[256] concerns one's interest, when

---

244 *Marakah*, above note 60 at para 32; and see *Elementary Teachers*, above note 114 at para 56.

245 *Spencer*, above note 55 at para 38.

246 *Ibid*.

247 *Ibid*.

248 *Ibid* at para 39, citing *McInerney v MacDonald*, [1992] 2 SCR 138; and see *Cole*, above note 27 at para 46 (the more "confidential the information, the more willing reasonable and informed Canadians will be to recognize the existence of a constitutionally protected privacy interest").

249 *Spencer*, above note 55 at para 40.

250 *Ibid*.

251 *Ibid*.

252 See Section B(3) and see further below the discussion in Section C(4)(h).

253 *Marakah*, above note 60.

254 *Spencer*, above note 55 at para 45.

255 *Ibid* at para 42.

256 [1992] 1 SCR 527 at 558 [*Wise*]; and see *Spencer*, above note 55 at para 44.

moving about in public places, to be free from personal identification and extensive surveillance by the state.

In assessing the strength of an informational privacy claim, the Court often considers whether the subject matter falls within a "biographical core of personal information."[257] The closer the information lies to the biographical core, the more likely it is to attract an REP,[258] as such information engages the claimant's interests in the values underpinning section 8, namely dignity, integrity, and autonomy.[259] The "biographical core" is discussed in more detail immediately below, under a separate heading, given the Court's tendency to list it as a discrete factor to be assessed in the totality of circumstances.[260] Before turning to that discussion, it is important to first briefly highlight the special place computers occupy in the jurisprudence pertaining to informational privacy.

In *R v Morelli*,[261] Fish J, for a majority of the Supreme Court, succinctly explained the extremely strong privacy interest inherent in personal computers. His words are worth quoting in full:

> It is difficult to imagine a search more intrusive, extensive, or invasive of one's privacy than the search and seizure of a personal computer.
>
> First, police officers enter your home, take possession of your computer, and carry it off for examination in a place unknown and inaccessible to you. There, without supervision or constraint, they scour the entire contents of your hard drive: your emails sent and received; accompanying attachments; your personal notes and correspondence; your meetings and appointments; your medical and financial records; and all other saved documents that you have downloaded, copied, scanned, or created. The police scrutinize as well the electronic roadmap of your cybernetic peregrinations, where you have been and what you appear to have seen on the Internet — generally by design, but sometimes by accident.[262]

Justice Cromwell, for the Court, further elaborated on the special privacy of computers in *R v Vu*,[263] emphasizing (1) "computers store immense amounts of information";[264] (2) much of which is "automatically generated, often unbeknownst to the user," which enables "investigators

257 *Plant*, above note 31 at 293; *Marakah*, above note 60 at para 31.
258 *Cole*, above note 27 at para 46.
259 *Ibid* at para 45.
260 *Tessling*, above note 36.
261 2010 SCC 8 [*Morelli*].
262 *Ibid* at paras 2–3; and see *Cole*, above note 27 at paras 47–48 for elaboration.
263 2013 SCC 60 [*Vu*].
264 *Ibid* at para 41.

to access intimate details about a user's interests, habits, and identity, drawing on a record that the user created unwittingly";[265] (3) this digital record often persists, unbeknownst to the user, despite their attempts to delete it;[266] and (4) when connected to the internet, computers transcend their physical location, operating as "portals to an almost infinite amount of information that is shared between different users and is stored almost anywhere in the world."[267] Given the technological capabilities of modern smartphones, it should be no surprise that these are treated substantively the same as computers insofar as one's profound privacy interest therein is concerned.[268]

b) Biographical Core Information

As just mentioned, in assessing the strength of an informational privacy claim, courts often consider whether the information at issue relates to a "biographical core of personal information" that individuals in a "free and democratic society would wish to maintain and control from dissemination to the state," which includes information tending to reveal "intimate details of the lifestyle and personal choices of the individual."[269] The closer the information lies to the biographical core, the more likely it is to attract an REP.[270] Importantly, however, an REP can still exist in non-biographical information.[271]

Two principal issues arise in relation to this analytical device. First, how is it to be assessed? Second, what is its proper role in the overall totality of circumstances test? The Supreme Court's approach has evolved in relation to both of these issues over the years.

When assessing whether information falls within the biographical core, recent decisions have emphasized that the focus is not simply on the precise information obtained, but also more broadly on its "potential" to support other inferences.[272] Sometimes, the inherently private nature of the item searched means there is a potential for other inferences of an intimate nature to be drawn. In *Marakah*, for example, McLachlin CJ, for the majority, determined that the accused had an REP in relation to text messages he had sent to a friend that were discovered by police when searching the recipient's smartphone.[273] According to the chief justice,

265 *Ibid* at para 42.
266 *Ibid* at para 43.
267 *Ibid* at para 44.
268 *Ibid* at para 38.
269 *Plant*, above note 31 at 293; *Marakah*, above note 60 at para 31.
270 *Cole*, above note 27 at para 46.
271 *AM*, above note 113 at para 68.
272 *Marakah*, above note 60 at para 32.
273 *Ibid*.

for purposes of section 8, the text conversation *itself* is analogous to an "opaque and sealed bag of information,"[274] and individuals have an "acute privacy interest in the *fact* of their electronic communications,"[275] which can be readily inferred from the reality that people "may be inclined to discuss personal matters in electronic conversations precisely because they understand that they are private."[276] Because a search of the smartphone "*may* betray information which tends to reveal intimate details of the lifestyle and personal choices of the individual," the participants in the conversation have an REP "in its contents, whatever [those contents] may be."[277] Similar reasoning supported the majority's determination in *Cole* that a teacher had an REP in relation to the contents of his work issued laptop, regardless of the content actually discovered. This was because computers used for personal use, "regardless of where they are found or to whom they belong," can be expected to contain the "details of our financial, medical, and personal situations" and, when connected to the internet, to "reveal our specific interests, likes, and propensities, recording in the browsing history and cache files the information we seek out and read, watch, or listen to on the Internet."[278] Searching a personal computer thus has the *potential* to reveal information falling at the "very heart of the biographical core" protected by section 8 of the *Charter*.[279] Recently, in *Elementary Teachers Federation of Ontario v York Regional District School Board*,[280] the Ontario Court of Appeal found an REP in relation to a private, password protected blog operated by two school teachers, which they accidentally left open at work. The school principal had discovered the blog and used the information to discipline them. The Court held that, due to the form in which the communications were held, whether the blog contained intimate details about the teachers "is not relevant" to whether their "communications should be protected." It was, "in essence, their diary" and they were "entitled to record their private thoughts — including complaints about co-workers and supervisors — for their own purposes and to expect that those thoughts would remain private."[281]

Focusing, as these decisions do, on the investigative technique's *potential* for revealing personal information certainly resonates with the

274 *Ibid.*
275 *Ibid* at para 33 [emphasis in original].
276 *Ibid* at para 34.
277 *Ibid* at para 32 [emphasis added]; and see *Vu*, above note 263.
278 *Cole*, above note 27 at para 47; and see also *Spencer*, above note 55 at para 47.
279 *Cole*, above note 27 at para 48.
280 *Elementary Teachers*, above note 114.
281 *Ibid* at para 56.

privacy concerns animating section 8, including its underlying values of dignity, integrity, and autonomy. Nevertheless, there is a danger, which manifested in earlier decisions, to conclude that if no such inferences can be drawn from ostensibly mundane information, the information falls outside the biographical core and is not worthy of constitutional protection. As explained above, when discussing the "subject matter of the search," the majority reasons in *Plant* found no REP in relation to computer records revealing electricity consumption patterns in the home, which suggested illegal drug production, on the basis they did not reveal "intimate details of the appellant's life since electricity consumption reveals very little about the personal lifestyle or private decisions of the occupant of the residence."[282] Likewise, in *Tessling*, the Court found no REP where the police trained FLIR technology on a home to detect unusual heat patterns suggestive of a grow operation.[283] The "biographical core" was not engaged because the heat emanations offered "no insight" into the personal or lifestyle choices of the rights claimant.[284] The majority in *Gomboc* likewise found no REP in relation to information obtained from a digital device that monitored and recorded electricity consumption in the home, revealing patterns of usage consistent with a grow operation.[285] Since it did not reveal anything else about activities within the home, the Court held the information did not touch on the biographical core.[286] Recall that *Gomboc* featured strong dissenting reasons.[287]

More recent judicial developments cast doubt on the majority's narrow approach to the biographical core in *Plant*, *Tessling*, and *Gomboc*. Insofar as these earlier decisions seemed to require that some meaningful information about the accused be gleaned *in addition to the illegal activity in question*, they appear to have been overtaken by subsequent decisions. In *Kang-Brown*, the unanimous Court found an REP in circumstances where the police used a sniffer dog to detect the presence of drugs in a backpack.[288] Justices Deschamps and Rothstein emphasized that this

282 *Plant*, above note 31 at 293.

283 *Tessling*, above note 36.

284 *Ibid* at para 63.

285 *Gomboc*, above note 136.

286 *Ibid* at paras 14–15.

287 *Ibid*, Abella J (for herself and LeBel and Binnie JJ), at paras 80–81, and see para 57; and see the reasons of McLachlin CJ and Fish J, dissenting, who would have found an REP, for the reasons given by Abella J, emphasizing that the DRA yields strong inferences about the probable existence of a grow operation inside the home, and the individual's connection to such probable criminal activity is biographical core information.

288 *Kang-Brown*, above note 148; and see the companion case *AM*, above note 113.

technique enabled a "strong, immediate and direct inference to be made" about the "contents of the bag," and this had the potential to reveal "intimate personal details" about the accused, including his "coming into contact with a controlled substance" potentially as a "drug trafficker."[289] This same reasoning should apply equally to *Plant*, *Tessling*, and *Gomboc*, for in each of those cases the investigative technique utilized by the police also enabled strong inferences about whether illegal grow operations were operating inside the residences.[290] If potentially being a drug trafficker qualifies as an intimate personal detail, as it did in *Kang-Brown*, then operating an illegal grow operation, in *Plant*, *Tessling*, and *Gomboc*, surely does so as well.[291] Indeed, in all of these cases, what the police were *really after* was evidence of illegal drug activity, and in each case the technique deployed enabled the state to penetrate a barrier (walls, a backpack) and draw that specific inference. Interestingly, the Ontario Court of Appeal recently found an REP in electricity consumption data in circumstances that could not be "meaningfully distinguished" from those in *Gomboc*,[292] on the basis that it revealed a strong inference about the presence of an illegal grow operation inside the accused's home, but otherwise did not reveal anything else about other activities therein.[293]

These recent decisions are welcome developments if we recall the relational aspect of the normative REP inquiry. Section 8 does not protect an abstract right to privacy *per se*; rather, it confers a right to be free from unreasonable searches or seizures by the state.[294] As Binnie J wrote in *Patrick*, the "privacy analysis is laden with value judgments which are made from the independent perspective of the reasonable and informed person who is concerned about the long-term consequences of government action for the protection of privacy."[295] The material question, from this perspective, is not whether the information itself is intimate or highly personal, but whether we are prepared to tolerate state snooping into our homes, or bags, without prior authorization or other authority.[296]

As to the second question identified above—the proper role of the biographical core in the overall REP analysis—here too we see judicial evolution. While the concept featured prominently in Sopinka J's reasons in *Plant*, there was no express suggestion in that case that information

289 *Kang-Brown*, above note 148 at para 175.

290 See *Spencer*, above note 55 at para 47.

291 Indeed, see McLachlin CJ's dissenting reasons in *Gomboc*, above note 136 at para 130.

292 *Orlandis-Habsburgo*, above note 142 at para 57.

293 *Ibid* at para 75; and see *Spencer*, above note 55 at para 27.

294 See the discussion of when s 8 is engaged in Chapter 3, Section A.

295 *Patrick*, above note 38 at para 14.

296 See generally Stewart, "Normative Foundations," above note 35 and Austin, above note 35.

must fall within the biographical core to merit constitutional protection. The concept, it seems, was intended to be one factor among many, albeit an important one.[297] Subsequently, in *R v AM*, Binnie J stated that, as a matter of principle, the "biographical core" is simply an "analytical tool," and that it was never intended to be "conclusive of the analysis of information privacy."[298]

Nevertheless, other decisions have suggested a more definitive role for the biographical core, casting it as something of a constitutional threshold that must be crossed before section 8 is engaged. For example, in *Patrick*, a case involving a police search of garbage outside of a home, Binnie J emphasized that the information found in the garbage fell within the biographical core information, suggesting that the biographical core was a prerequisite to engaging section 8.[299] In *Tessling*, Binnie J presented the biographical core as simply one factor among many to be assessed in the totality of circumstances,[300] but his application of that test suggested otherwise. Justice Binnie's conclusion that the appellant's subjective expectation of privacy was objectively unreasonable was driven almost entirely by his determination that the information at issue (heat emanations from his home, detected by police using an infrared camera) did "not touch on 'a biographical core of personal information'."[301] As such, according to Binnie J, the appellant failed to cross what he called the "constitutional threshold" required to engage section 8.[302]

Similarly, in *Gomboc*, Deschamps J for the majority held that the "central issue" in the section 8 analysis was whether the information at issue (electricity records) "disclose[d] intimate details of the lifestyle and personal choices of the individual that form part of the biographical core

297 Justice Sopinka called for a contextual approach applying multiple factors, including the nature of the information, the relationship to any party claiming confidentiality, the place the information was gathered, and the manner in which it was gathered. The biographical core was simply one factor (see *Plant*, above note 31 at 293).

298 *AM*, above note 113 at para 68. Recently, in *Elementary Teachers*, above note 114 at para 55, the unanimous Ontario Court of Appeal stated that the "Biographical core information is merely a type of information—one factor that may be considered in determining whether, as a normative matter, a reasonable expectation of privacy exists. It is not a prerequisite for that finding."

299 *Patrick*, above note 38 at paras 31,40.

300 *Tessling*, above note 36 at para 31.

301 *Ibid* at para 62.

302 *Ibid*; and see also Ian Kerr & Jena McGill, "Emanations, Snoop Dogs and Reasonable Expectations of Privacy" (2007) 52:3 *Criminal Law Quarterly* 392 at 412–14 [Kerr & McGill]; Jane Bailey, "Framed by Section 8: Constitutional Protection of Privacy in Canada" (2008) 50:3 *Canadian Journal of Criminology & Criminal Justice* 279 at 295.

data protected by the *Charter*'s guarantee of informational privacy."[303] She concluded that police had not engaged section 8 in obtaining the electricity records, because they were meaningless and incapable of revealing any intimate activities inside the home. Importantly, Deschamps J based her decision on the similar findings of Sopinka J in *Plant* and Binnie J in *Tessling*, interpreting both cases as requiring that information be meaningful, in the sense of revealing something "intimate," before section 8 of the *Charter* could be engaged.[304] Scholars have debated the role of the biographical core ever since.[305]

In our view, treating the biographical core, as *AM* does, as simply one non-determinative factor among many has both principled and practical advantages over treating it as a threshold of sorts. Regarding it as a threshold question poses something of a false dichotomy. Put simply, "meaningfulness" is not a binary characteristic, but rather a continuous spectrum in which all information is at least somewhat "meaningful."[306] A further problem is that a binary approach causes courts to analyze information in isolation, asking whether it *alone* is intimate, biographical, or capable *itself* of revealing meaningful insights into the individual's private life.[307] This approach has the potential of shrinking the scope of section 8 considerably because "*information can always be reduced to smaller and smaller bits of data*, which, through the reductive process, eventually no longer reveal biographical core information."[308]

Treating the biographical core as simply one factor among many—as opposed to a prerequisite to engaging section 8—frees courts from having to come to a firm conclusion as to whether or not such meaningful inferences can be drawn. Accordingly, if the arguments are evenly matched on this question, courts can reach a neutral conclusion (characterizing the information as somewhat meaningful[309]) and then move on to the other *Tessling* factors to decide whether an individual has a

303 *Gomboc*, above note 136 at para 35.

304 *Ibid* at para 38.

305 See Stuart Hargreaves, "*R. v. Gomboc*: Considering the Proper Role of the 'Biographic Core' in a Section 8 Informational Privacy Analysis" (2012) 59:1 *Criminal Law Quarterly* 86 at 100; Mathew Johnson, "Privacy in the Balance: Novel Search Technologies, Reasonable Expectations, and Recalibrating Section 8" (2012) 58: 3 & 4 *Criminal Law Quarterly* 442 at 491 (noting the Court's recent cases seemed to turn on whether the information was "meaningful" in the sense of being intimate or biographical).

306 Johnson, *ibid*.

307 For a discussion of this trend, see: Kerr & McGill, above note 302 at 414–16; Johnson, above note 305 at 491–92.

308 Kerr & McGill, above note 302 at 414–15 (emphasis in the original).

309 Johnson, above note 305 at 491.

constitutionally protected privacy interest. This approach is more in keeping with the decidedly multifactorial analysis refined in *Tessling*, making it desirable from a precedential standpoint. It also frees courts from having to draw artificial lines based upon a false dichotomy of meaningfulness, which may facilitate clearer decision making in the future. This has a real practical appeal in the context of novel search technologies, for in these cases answering the meaningfulness inquiry in a "yes or no" manner is notoriously difficult.[310]

c) Abandonment

Abandonment was central to the majority's reasons in *Patrick*.[311] The police, suspecting an illegal ecstasy lab, collected garbage bags from bins located just inside the property line of the accused. This required reaching into the airspace over the property line, though not physically stepping onto the property itself. The bags contained assorted drug-making paraphernalia, chemical residues, and receipts for suspicious chemicals.[312] Justice Binnie, for the majority, determined that, but for the issue of abandonment, the totality of circumstances favoured an REP.[313] The nature of the information concealed in the bags engaged the accused's biographical core, in terms of informational privacy, as it permitted inferences into his lifestyle;[314] and while there was no physical trespass onto property, territorial privacy was also engaged "peripherally"[315] by reaching into his property's airspace. Nevertheless, Binnie J determined that the accused had abandoned his privacy interest. Abandonment, according to Binnie J, is a question of fact,[316] which calls for an assessment of whether the claimant has "acted in relation to the subject matter of his privacy claim in such a manner as to lead a reasonable and independent observer to conclude that his continued assertion of a privacy interest is unreasonable in the totality of the circumstances."[317] The focus here is on

310 For a discussion, see Renee M. Pomerance, "Redefining Privacy in the Face of New Technologies: Data Mining and the Threat to 'Inviolate Personality'" (2005) 9:3 *Canadian Criminal Law Review* 273. In *Spencer*, above note 55, ascertaining the meaningfulness of the accused's IP address and whether it engaged his biographical core was the central issue dividing lower courts: see *ibid* at paras 24–25.

311 *Patrick*, above note 38.

312 *Ibid* at para 3.

313 *Ibid* at para 40.

314 *Ibid* at para 71.

315 *Ibid* at paras 44–45. Regarding territorial privacy, Binnie J observed "it seems obvious that the police could not with impunity position a cherry picker in the laneway behind the appellant's house and, without 'setting foot' on the property, grab various objects off the appellant's lawn and porch for inspection."

316 *Ibid* at para 25.

317 *Ibid*.

the claimant's conduct, not that of police, garbage collectors, or passersby who may have collected the bags.[318] According to Binnie J, by placing the bags in garbage bins for collection by the municipal authorities, the claimant "had done everything required to rid himself of the contents, including whatever private information was embedded therein," which was "inconsistent with the continued assertion of a constitutionally protected privacy interest."[319]

Whatever the merits of this ultimate conclusion, there is a tension in Binnie J's approach. While abandonment is framed expressly as a question of fact, the application of the doctrine clearly calls for a normative conclusion. Indeed, as Binnie J himself recognized, abandonment is really a matter of drawing a "reasonable cut-off point,"[320] and this in turn must be informed by balancing (1) "societal interests in protecting individual dignity, integrity, and autonomy with effective law enforcement"; (2) "whether an accused has conducted himself in a manner that is inconsistent with the *reasonable* continued assertion of a privacy interest"; and (3) the "long-term consequences for the due protection of privacy interests in our society."[321] Despite calling for such *normative* balancing, his reasons are driven almost entirely by the *fact* that the claimant had placed garbage bags out for collection, which he determined was simply inconsistent with a continued privacy interest. Justice Binnie did not address the long-term consequences of permitting such state actions, which he held to trench on the claimant's biographical core. Nor does it appear that he considered other REP factors, which militated in favour of an REP. Simply stated, abandonment itself exerted a dominating influence on the decision, apparently overwhelming other considerations, and operating in practice not so much as a factor, but as a threshold of sorts. This appears inconsistent with the totality of circumstances test.[322]

A second difficulty here is that, in our view, Binnie J drew insufficient attention in *Patrick* to the relational aspect of the REP inquiry. There is a

---

318 *Ibid* at para 54.

319 *Ibid* at para 2; see also para 64.

320 *Ibid* at para 54.

321 *Ibid* at para 20.

322 Justices Brown and Martin, in *Le*, above note 85, cautioned against treating one factor as virtually determinative of the REP inquiry. They noted the REP analysis should not "proceed with the assumption that a categorical factor, like control, will have a dominating impact on whether a person has a reasonable expectation of privacy." Instead, courts must focus on the underlying normative question, namely "whether a privacy claim ought to be recognized as beyond state intrusion absent constitutional justification if Canadian society is to remain a free, democratic and open society," at para 136. These comments about control in *Le* would appear to bite at Binnie J's approach to abandonment in *Patrick*, above note 38.

difference, from the perspective of the ordinary rights claimant, between an intention to abandon an item to garbage collectors and an intention to hand this information over to the state, given the importance of privacy to liberty and democracy, and the spectre of permitting unfettered state scrutiny of refuse, without any prior justification. Notably, Abella J, in her concurring reasons, was sensitive to these other issues. She was concerned that a finding of abandonment would give the state unfettered access to what is often deeply personal information about the individual's lifestyle.[323] She was also skeptical about equating an intention to abandon garbage to the municipal waste disposal authorities with an intention to permit police access to the same.[324] And she was concerned that the majority was elevating abandonment above other factors in the overall REP analysis.[325] In her view, which we respectfully share, the appropriate conclusion was that the accused had a diminished but nevertheless reasonable expectation of privacy in the circumstances of the case, thereby engaging section 8.[326]

Prior to *Patrick*, the Supreme Court briefly discussed the principle of abandonment in *R v Law*.[327] The claimant had his safe stolen from his place of business and reported it to police. The police eventually located the safe in a field, where it was found open. It contained various business documents that another officer, suspecting tax fraud, photocopied and forwarded to Revenue Canada. Justice Bastarache, for the Court, stated that "the mere fact that the police recover lost or stolen property is insufficient to support an inference that the owner voluntarily relinquished his expectation of privacy in the item."[328] He found an REP in the contents of the safe on the basis that the claimant did not voluntarily discard the private information and "one would have expected the stolen property to remain private following its recovery, as it was before its theft."[329] The decision foregrounds the claimant's volition in discarding the item searched as the key issue underpinning abandonment.

Lower courts have found abandonment in a variety of other contexts. For example, where individuals are living in an apartment, they abandon garbage when they toss it into a common receptacle inside the building,

---

323 *Ibid* at para 80.

324 *Ibid* at paras 88–89.

325 *Ibid* at paras 85 and 89.

326 *Ibid* at para 90. She ultimately concluded that despite an REP, the police were entitled to search the bags because they had ample evidence to believe a crime had been committed, at para 91.

327 2002 SCC 10.

328 *Ibid* at para 17.

329 *Ibid* at para 18.

where it is commingled with other refuse.[330] An accused abandoned a firearm when, in the course of a search, he threw it out a window and onto a neighbour's yard.[331] In another case, the accused, when confronted by police in the stairwell of his ninth floor apartment building, abandoned his bag when he threw it down the stairs.[332] An accused fleeing a vehicle that police were searching was found to abandon a gun he had left behind.[333] A court has also found abandonment in a case where police confronted an accused on school property, causing him to walk toward the officer, leaving the bag behind, and when asked who the bag belonged to, replied "I don't know."[334] Abandonment has featured also in cases before the Ontario Court of Appeal involving police impounding and searching vehicles under the *Highway Traffic Act*,[335] which permits this in cases of "abandoned" vehicles.[336]

Abandonment remains an important issue in cases involving discarded objects searched for DNA. *Stillman* raised the question of whether a suspect, who was in police custody at the station, had an REP in relation to a Kleenex he had used and discarded in the station's bathroom, which the police retrieved and tested for DNA without his knowledge or consent.[337] A majority of the Supreme Court answered this question in the affirmative. Importantly, the decision turned very much on the fact the accused was in police custody for several days and had indicated through his lawyer that he did not consent to provide any bodily samples for DNA testing. The majority reasoned that given his lengthy detention, it was inevitable that he would blow his nose, use the bathroom, eat with a spoon, or the like during his detention. Permitting the police to obtain DNA from such sources would render his expressed decision not to consent meaningless.[338] In relation to those not in police custody, however, the majority stated in *obiter* and by way of general guidance

330 *Express Transaction Services Inc v Canada (Attorney General)*, 2012 QCCA 1093.

331 *R v Stevens*, 2012 ONCA 307.

332 *R v Nesbeth*, 2008 ONCA 579 at para 22.

333 *R v Plummer*, 2011 ONCA 350.

334 *R v LB*, 2007 ONCA 596 at paras 69–70.

335 RSO 1990, c H 8.

336 Contrast *R v Ellis*, 2016 ONCA 598 (abandonment of vehicle found where suspect parked his car and walked away from the vehicle left on another's private driveway where it could not legally remain, thus evidencing factual intent to distance himself from it) with *R v Dunkley*, 2016 ONCA 597 (no abandonment of vehicle where suspect parked it at a commercial gas station, not knowing he was being followed by police, and then fled police on foot; no clear and unambiguous intent to abandon it could be inferred from his parking of it).

337 *Stillman*, above note 223.

338 *Ibid* at para 59.

that was a "different situation" and the "police may ordinarily collect and test" a discarded "kleenex or cigarette butt . . . without any concern about consent."[339]

Post-*Stillman*, appellate decisions have found abandonment to occur where the accused, not in police custody, leaves a glass and straw at a restaurant,[340] discards a tissue in a motel room obtained by police after the claimant checked out,[341] and in relation to chewing gum which the claimant spit into a cup, as part of a ruse concocted by undercover police to trick him into believing that he was participating in a gum tasting survey.[342] More recently, however, two members of the Quebec Court of Appeal questioned whether the broad *obiter* proposition in *Stillman*, which apparently permits DNA searches of discarded items by those not in police custody, should still be followed. The case, *Damico c R*,[343] involved an undercover operation, in which the police, who had the claimant under constant surveillance, tricked him into believing he was attending a business meeting and later collected a cup he used for DNA testing without his knowledge. In a nuanced decision, Vauclair J held that, at a minimum, *Stillman* should be read narrowly, noting the broad *obiter* proposition in that case that police may collect such evidence from those not in custody was couched by the word "ordinarily."[344] In his view, this made room for the qualification that the proposition only extends to those who are at complete liberty when they discard items, and should not include those who are under police surveillance at the material time and are tricked by police into discarding items as part of a ruse. In such circumstances, there is little difference, from the perspective of the claimant's volition, between one in this situation and one who is formally detained, as in *Stillman*.[345] More broadly, Vauclair J also doubted whether a sensible inference could be drawn that a person who discards a cup has also intended to abandon the DNA located thereon.[346] DNA attracts a high privacy interest, and "one abandons 'it' everywhere, all the time without even giving the slightest thought to it. It is 'the inevitable consequence of the normal functioning of the human body'."[347]

---

339 *Ibid* at para 62.

340 *Usereau c R*, 2010 QCCA 894.

341 *R v Love*, 1995 ABCA 448.

342 *R v D(W)*, 2009 ABCA 179.

343 *D'amico*, above note 225.

344 *Ibid* at para 114.

345 *Ibid* at para 110. In both cases, the police are deliberately affording themselves the opportunity to collect DNA, rather than simply gathering what they find by happenstance.

346 *Ibid* at para 99.

347 *Ibid*.

Simply stated, an intention to abandon a cup or a tissue should not be equated with an intention to abandon one's DNA. With respect, this strikes us as an obvious and sensible distinction, especially if we recall again the relational aspect of the normative REP inquiry. A choice to throw away a tissue should not be equated automatically with a decision to abandon one's DNA to the state for subsequent testing. Justice Ruel agreed that, insofar as abandonment is concerned, the court must distinguish between voluntarily discarding a cup and the DNA contained thereon,[348] but nevertheless determined that in the totality of circumstances no REP was established.[349] Justice Thibault, for her part, determined that the DNA had been abandoned, following the guidance from *Patrick* and *Stillman*.[350] In our view, given the principled divisions in this case, further guidance from the Supreme Court of Canada is warranted. Unfortunately, the Court denied leave to appeal as of right in this case.[351]

d) Impact of Regulations, Policies, and Contracts

The existence of regulations or contractual provisions pertaining to the claimant's information have been important considerations affecting the REP analysis in a variety of contexts over the years. An early decision, *British Columbia Securities Commission v Branch*,[352] raised the issue of whether individuals had an REP in relation to business records they were ordered to surrender to the Securities Commission pursuant to its statutory powers of investigation. The Court determined that only a "limited" expectation of privacy existed in such materials, because "in a highly regulated industry, such as the securities market, the individual is aware, and accepts, justifiable state intrusions. All those who enter into this market know or are deemed to know the rules of the game."[353] The same reasoning was followed in *R v Nolet*,[354] this time in relation to whether a commercial truck driver had an REP in the sleeping quarters of his truck, which contained a duffle bag that the police searched after a traffic stop. Justice Binnie, for the Court, was prepared to presume a subjective expectation of privacy that was objectively reasonable in relation to the sleeping quarters, on the basis that it functioned essentially as a "mobile

---

348 *Ibid* at paras 352 and 362.

349 *Ibid* at paras 366–85.

350 *Ibid* at para 317.

351 *R v D'Amico*, 2019 SCC 23, holding at para 3 that "Vauclair J.A.'s disagreement does not go to the result and is better characterized as a concurring opinion or an opinion concurring in the result."

352 [1995] 2 SCR 3.

353 *Ibid* at paras 63–64.

354 Above note 239.

home."[355] Nevertheless, he was quick to add that this expectation of privacy was "necessarily low" because commercial trucking was a highly regulated industry and the driver "would be well aware of the possibility of mandatory inspections and searches, whether for documents or for potential violation of any one of the countless obligations imposed by the regulatory scheme."[356]

The relevance and impact of regulations on the REP inquiry became more contentious in *R v Gomboc*.[357] The police requested a utility company, Enmax, to install a digital recording ammeter (DRA), which measured electricity patterns from the accused's residence, on suspicion there was a grow operation. A central issue in the case, which divided the Supreme Court into three groups, concerned the impact on the claimant's REP of a *Code of Conduct Regulation* enacted pursuant to provincial legislation,[358] which permitted the utility to disclose customer information "to a peace officer for the purpose of investigating an offence if the disclosure is not contrary to the express request of the customer."[359] Gomboc did not request Enmax to keep his information confidential. Justice Deschamps, writing for herself and three other justices, held that the relationship between Enmax and its customers was "highly significant"[360] and it weighed "heavily against giving the asserted expectation of privacy constitutional recognition"[361] primarily because the *Code of Regulation* provided "express notice" to customers that there may be voluntary cooperation between Enmax and the police; and, further, individuals should expect, in the highly regulated energy sector, that utilities would handle information according to the rules established in that sector.[362] Despite Deschamps J's emphasis on the importance of the *Regulation*, she was careful not to allow it to determine the result, preferring to treat it as one factor among many in the totality of circumstances.[363] Justice Abella, concurring in the result, thought the *Regulation* was itself "determinative" that there was no REP,[364] as it was "clear and unambigu-

355 *Ibid* at para 31.
356 *Ibid*.
357 *Gomboc*, above note 136.
358 *Ibid* at para 31, referring to the *Electric Utilities Act*, SA 2003, c E-5.1.
359 *Ibid*.
360 *Ibid*.
361 *Ibid* at para 33.
362 *Ibid* at para 32.
363 *Ibid*. As discussed above, Deschamps J determined ultimately that no REP existed, owing largely to the fact that the DRA was not seen to engage the claimant's biographical core, given the limited information it yielded about activities within the home.
364 *Ibid* at para 95.

ous" in its terms regardless of whether the claimant himself knew of its existence.[365] Chief Justice McLachlin and Fish J dissented. In their view, an REP was established, in the totality of circumstances, and the existence of the *Regulation* did not militate against this conclusion, primarily because it was obscure and not something an ordinary customer would know existed, or, even if they did, would not expect that it authorized the utility to take the intrusive measure of installing a DRA device to their home and share that information with police.[366]

In *Spencer* the Court was called on to consider the extent to which the contractual and statutory framework governing the provision of internet services affected Spencer's reasonable expectation of privacy in the subscriber information attached to his IP address.[367] Police obtained this information from Shaw, the internet service provider, and used it to link Spencer to illegal activity online. As concerned the contractual framework, Cromwell J emphasized that courts must "proceed with caution"[368] when considering general contracts of adhesion, for these are not individually negotiated and the consumer may not have read them. Nevertheless, he held that the existence of the contract should have some impact on a claimant's privacy interests, because "[a] reasonable [Internet] user would be aware that the use of the service would be governed by certain terms and conditions, and those terms and conditions were readily accessible through Shaw's website."[369] The Court then analyzed three sets of interrelated — and ambiguous — contractual provisions and concluded that, taken together, they were "confusing and equivocal in terms of their impact on a user's reasonable expectation of privacy"[370] and, as such, did not in these circumstances militate against an REP.

The Court then turned to examine provisions of the *Personal Information Protection and Electronic Documents Act*,[371] observing at the outset that it was "not much more illuminating" than the contractual terms of the IP service agreement.[372] *PIPEDA* imposed various substantive obligations on private sector organizations for the safe handling and

---

365 *Ibid* at para 94. Recently, in *Alberta (Justice and Solicitor General) v Bassett*, 2022 ABCA 280 at para 39, the unanimous Alberta Court of Appeal applied *Gomboc*, above note 136, in factually similar circumstances and concluded that "at a minimum, where a customer had not asked that their customer information not be shared with police, there was no reasonable expectation of privacy."

366 *Gomboc*, above note 136 at paras 139–40.

367 *Spencer*, above note 55.

368 *Ibid* at para 54.

369 *Ibid* at para 57.

370 *Ibid* at para 60.

371 SC 2000, c 5 [*PIPEDA*].

372 *Spencer*, above note 55 at para 60.

non-disclosure of personal information. However, section 7(3)(c.1)(ii) permitted organizations to disclose personal information without the data subject's knowledge or consent to government institutions pursuant to the latter's written declaration that it has "lawful authority" to acquire this information.[373] The Crown argued that this provision rendered Spencer's expectation of privacy objectively unreasonable. The Court disagreed. It held that this provision simply "lead[s] us in a circle" because "the issue is whether there was such lawful authority which in turn depends in part on whether there was a reasonable expectation of privacy with respect to the subscriber information."[374] But perhaps more importantly, the Court concluded that, instead of militating against an expectation of privacy, *PIPEDA* actually supported it. This was because the protection of privacy is *PIPEDA*'s *raison d'être*, and it would therefore be "reasonable for an Internet user to expect that a simple request by police would not trigger an obligation to disclose personal information."[375] Having reached this conclusion, the Court determined that, in the totality of circumstances, Spencer had a reasonable expectation of privacy in his subscriber information, and that a police request that Shaw voluntarily disclose this information amounted to a "search" under section 8 of the *Charter*.[376]

In *R v Cole*,[377] the Supreme Court found that a teacher had an REP in the information stored on his work issued laptop computer. A school technician, conducting routine maintenance, discovered images of nude students, copied the hard drive, passed it on to the principal who in turn gave it to the police, who then inspected the contents without first obtaining a warrant. The Court determined that while ownership of the laptop was "relevant," it was not "determinative."[378] What was more "significant" was the *context* in which the teacher had placed information on the employer owned laptop, which in turn required the court to consider the "policies, practices, and customs" of the workplace in which the computer was being used.[379] On the one hand, teachers had been informed that incidental personal use of computers was permitted; but on the other, the school board's policy and procedures manual asserted ownership over not only the hardware but also the data stored on it, in the following terms: "Information technology systems and all data and

373 *Ibid*, citing *PIPEDA*, above note 371, s 7(3)(c.1).

374 *Spencer*, above note 55 at paras 61–62.

375 *Ibid* at para 62.

376 *Ibid* at para 74.

377 *Cole*, above note 27.

378 *Ibid* at para 51.

379 *Ibid* at para 52.

messages generated on or handled by board equipment are considered to be the property of [the board], and are not the property of users of the information technology."[380] Moreover, the principal had reminded teachers annually that this policy applied to them and that they should not assume files stored on network computers would be private.[381] In this context, the Court concluded that Cole had a diminished but nevertheless reasonable expectation of privacy in the files.[382]

What does *Cole* mean for privacy in work issued laptops and phones? There is no categorical answer. Whether a person has an REP in a work issued device will depend on the facts of the case. It will turn in part on how a court defines the "subject matter of the search," along with the implied or explicit terms or conditions of the agreement between an employer and employee as to the intended use of the device. In *Elementary Teachers Federation of Ontario v York Regional District School Board*,[383] discussed above, the Ontario Court of Appeal assessed a teacher had an REP in a chat log the principal discovered on her laptop. The court held that the subject matter of search was not the data contained on the school issued device, but the chat log situated in the Cloud.[384] Since the log was password protected and restricted to a small group of teachers, it gave rise to a reasonable privacy interest.[385] This was not diminished by the fact that the teacher had failed to close the laptop, log out, or put it asleep.[386]

e) Seriousness of the Offence Being Investigated

In *Plant*, Sopinka J noted that the seriousness of the offence being investigated was a factor to be considered in the "balance" when determining whether section 8 was engaged.[387] In *Tessling*, Binnie J, for the Court, observed that this should not be a relevant consideration for assessing whether an REP arose. Rather, it was a factor better considered at the second stage of the section 8 inquiry, where, assuming an REP was established, the issue is whether the search was reasonable.[388] In our view, this

---

380 *Ibid* at para 50.
381 *Ibid* at para 55.
382 *Ibid* at para 58.
383 See text, above note 114.
384 *Ibid* at para 50.
385 *Ibid* at para 51.
386 *Ibid*.
387 *Plant*, above note 31 at 295.
388 *Tessling*, above note 36 at para 64. The seriousness of the underlying offence becomes relevant also under s 24(2) of the *Charter*, if, in light of a s 8 violation, the accused challenges the admissibility of evidence: see *Tessling*, above note 36 at para 64; *Spencer*, above note 55 at para 79.

is a sensible point. Given the principle of neutrality, discussed above,[389] the seriousness of the crime should not affect the threshold REP inquiry. Moreover, considering this at the REP stage courts the danger of the state double dipping, relying on the seriousness of the crime to discount the REP, and then doing so again to justify the search as being reasonable. Such an approach threatens to erode the deterrent function of section 8.

f) Subject Matter Exposed to Public View

The relevance of exposure to public view divided the Supreme Court of Canada in *Wong*.[390] The case involved the police installing a surreptitious video-recording device inside a hotel room rented by the accused, on suspicion that he was operating an illegal betting parlour. The Ontario Court of Appeal determined that no REP was "possible" because the accused had invited many strangers into the room by circulating pamphlet invitations to attend these gaming sessions within the community.[391] Justice La Forest, writing for himself and four other justices,[392] categorically rejected this analysis, stating that he could not "attach any importance" to these circumstances, for there was no "logical nexus between these factors, and the conclusion that the police should have been free to videotape the proceedings in the hotel room at their sole discretion."[393] Following *Duarte*, he determined that "it would be an error to equate the risk of having one's words overheard [by other individuals] with the risk of having the state, at its sole discretion, make a permanent electronic recording of those words."[394] This was especially true where the location of the subject matter, a hotel room, was in his view similar to a home, and hence the activities therein naturally attracted a high privacy interest. Yet at least part of La Forest J's assessment of REP in this case turned on his finding that "while the appellant had rented a room in an establishment to which selected members of the public had access, he had seen to it that activities in the room were conducted behind locked doors and drawn drapes."[395] By contrast, for Lamer CJ, writing for himself and McLachlin J (as she then was) in dissent, the room may have been closed during the session, but it had become, in essence, a public place. The accused had distributed the invitations so

389 See Section C(2) and see *Wong*, above note 23 at 50.

390 *Wong*, above note 23.

391 *Ibid* at 49–50.

392 *Ibid* at 51. Justices Dickson, L'Heureux-Dube, and Sopinka agreed with La Forest J; Wilson J dissented in the result, due to the s 24(2) analysis, but expressly agreed with La Forest J's reasons on the approach to and existence of an REP.

393 *Ibid.*

394 *Ibid.*

395 *Ibid* at 49.

"indiscriminately," by circulating pamphlets at various restaurants and bars, that it amounted to an "invitation" to the "public at large." [396] The accused simply could not reasonably expect that strangers, "including the police," would not be present, which was fatal to establishing an REP in the circumstances.

The central difficulty, in our view, with Lamer CJ's minority approach in *Wong* lies in his failure to carefully measure the scope of the invitation issued against the impugned state conduct when assessing its impact on the accused's REP. Following *Duarte*, even if it is fair to say that by issuing a broad invitation, the accused took the risk that undercover officers may attend and observe his activities (and use what was learned to then obtain a warrant for further surveillance), the accused had not assumed the risk that police would surreptitiously record his activities without prior authorization. Notably, the facts in *Wong* did not involve an undercover officer attending the activity in question, but rather the installation of a secret recording device in advance of the gaming session at issue. We agree with the majority that even if the room had been converted to a public place, no one would have reasonably expected that this would entail being surreptitiously recorded by the state. This seems a more plausible reflection of what a member of the public might reasonably have expected in attending such an event.

The impact of exposing the subject matter of the search to public view, subsequent to a public invitation of sorts, arose also in *R v Evans*.[397] The police, acting on a tip, suspected the accused was growing marijuana in his house. They knocked on the front door and upon the accused opening it smelled marijuana and arrested him. Justice Sopinka, for the majority, observed that a person cannot have an REP in circumstances where they have authorized the conduct in question.[398] In assessing this, he noted the longstanding common law rule that occupants of a dwelling house impliedly invite, and grant permission to, members of the public, including the police, to approach the door and knock.[399] Importantly, he further observed that "if one views the invitation to knock as a *waiver* of the occupier's expectation of privacy in the approach to his or her home, it becomes necessary to determine the terms of that waiver."[400] The scope of this invitation is informed by its purpose, which is to facilitate "convenient communication" with occupants of the house.[401] Where the

396 *Ibid* at 63.
397 *Evans*, above note 212.
398 *Ibid* at para 5.
399 *Ibid* at para 6.
400 *Ibid* at para 7 [emphasis in original].
401 *Ibid* at para 8.

police have a different purpose in mind, in this case to collect evidence of suspected illegal activity occurring inside the home, the "implied conditions of that license have effectively been breached, and the person carrying out the unauthorized activity approaches the dwelling as an intruder."[402] Given that the police had the subsidiary purpose of getting a "whiff" of marijuana and were not merely knocking to communicate with the accused, they exceeded the scope of the implied invitation, thus intruding on the accused's REP in "the approach to the door of his . . . dwelling."[403] Interestingly, Sopinka J in *Evans* made two other observations that are relevant to our criticism of Lamer CJ's reasoning in *Wong*, immediately above. First, he drew support for his approach in *Evans* by analogizing to *Duarte*. The latter case, he reasoned, involved an implied invitation between the accused and the undercover officer to engage in a private conversation, but the scope of that invitation could not be extended to "authorize an activity with a different purpose, namely, the surreptitious recording of what was said."[404] Second, he reasoned that if the police in *Evans* could rely on the theory of implied licence to knock on doors, even though their purpose in doing so was motivated by a desire to find evidence of illegal activity (as the dissent found), this raised the "Orwellian" spectre that law enforcement could target high crime neighbourhoods under the ruse of communicating with occupants when in fact they were conducting "spot checks" for illegal activity.[405] As La Forest J wrote in his concurring reasons in *Evans*, "[o]ur society simply cannot accept police wandering about or 'sniffing' around our homes."[406] In our view, these observations apply to *Wong* as well. Inviting the public into one's hotel room may have entailed police being present to investigate, but not an invitation to have them install recording devices in that room. Such an approach is fundamentally irreconcilable with what people expect in a free and open society.

A different set of facts raised the issue of 'public view' in *R v Wise*.[407] The police surreptitiously installed a radio transponder "beeper" in the backseat of the accused's car, in order to assist them with visual surveillance of the accused, moving about the city, which they were already undertaking. The device was relatively crude. It revealed the car's approximate location, but it was not capable of pinpointing the vehicle with any degree of precision. Justice Cory, writing for himself and three

402 *Ibid*.

403 *Ibid* at para 6.

404 *Ibid* at para 11.

405 *Ibid* at para 13.

406 *Ibid* at para 3.

407 *Wise*, above note 256.

other justices, determined that the accused had an REP in relation to the installation itself, which involved an illegal trespass, and also in relation to the monitoring of the accused's location using the device. Ultimately, however, they decided to admit the evidence under section 24(2), influenced by their determination that the intrusion at issue was relatively minimal, as the responder was crude and because individuals have a reduced expectation of privacy in vehicles due to the highly regulated nature of the activity. Justice La Forest, dissenting, agreed the accused had an REP, but he would have excluded the evidence under section 24(2). Justice La Forest's reasons in relation to the existence of an REP were illuminating, and they foreshadowed later developments in *Spencer*[408] by contemplating anonymity as an important privacy interest underpinning section 8. Quoting from an American law review article, he endorsed the view that "in a variety of public contexts, we may expect to be casually observed, but may justifiably be outraged by intensive scrutiny. In these public acts we do not expect to be personally identified and subject to extensive surveillance, but seek to merge into the 'situational landscape'."[409] The beeper in question was not capable of recording any private conversations, and hence was distinguishable in its degree of intrusiveness from *Duarte* and *Wong*. Nevertheless, it compromised the subject's interest in moving about anonymously in public and allowed the state to deploy these devices at whim, raising the Orwellian policy concerns identified in *Duarte* and *Wong*.[410] Commenting on these, La Forest J wrote:

> I must confess to finding it absolutely outrageous that in a free society the police or other agents of the state should have it within their power, at their sole discretion and on the basis of mere suspicion, to attach a beeper on a person's car that permits them to follow his or her movements night and day for extended periods.[411]

The Crown's position, in response, was to urge the Court to follow American law, where there is simply no expectation of privacy when a person ventures into public, as their movements are easily observable by

---

408 *Spencer*, above note 55.

409 *Wise*, above note 256, quoting Melvin Gutterman in his article "A Formulation of the Value and Means Models of the Fourth Amendment in the Age of Technologically Enhanced Surveillance" (1988) 39 *Syracuse Law Review* 647 at 706.

410 *Wise*, above note 256 at 557, "George Orwell in his classic dystopian novel *1984* paints a grim picture of a society whose citizens had every reason to expect that their *every movement* was subject to electronic video surveillance. The contrast with the expectations of privacy in a free society such as our own could not be more striking." [Emphasis in original.]

411 *Ibid* at 558.

passersby.[412] Justice La Forest rejected this submission, on the basis that, first, it falls back into a "risk analysis" of a type the Supreme Court of Canada had rejected in *Duarte* and *Wong*; and second, because it fails to distinguish between the relative intrusiveness between being observed by others (including the police) and being constantly surveilled, surreptitiously, with technology that creates a permanent electronic recording. Pulling these threads together, La Forest J concluded that

> it is constitutionally unacceptable that the state should be allowed to rest a justification for the unauthorized electronic surveillance of a given person on the mere fact that that person had been in a situation where he could be the object of scrutiny on the part of private individuals. To sanction state intrusions on this basis is to blind oneself to the fact that the threat to privacy inherent in courting the ordinary observations of other members of society pales by comparison with the threat to privacy posed by allowing the state to electronically monitor our every movement.[413]

The concept of privacy as anonymity in *Wise* would serve as an important precedent two decades later, in an unexpected application to cyberspace.

In *Spencer*, Cromwell J, for the unanimous Court, explicitly recognized anonymity as an important dimension of informational privacy protected by section 8.[414] Justice Cromwell endorsed La Forest J's REP analysis in *Wise*, noting that individuals may retain a constitutionally protected privacy interest even when venturing out in public. This principle, according to Cromwell J, extended also to public acts carried out online.[415] Citing renowned privacy theorist Alan Westin, he reasoned that individuals may participate in online activities, and their communications may be accessible to "millions of people," but the subject retains an interest in not being identified as the author.[416] In his view, Spencer had an REP in relation to the subscriber information attached to his internet protocol address (i.e., his name and home address). By requesting and obtaining this, police were able to connect him to specific activity online, compromising his interest in remaining anonymous. Tracking his movements online in this way engaged a "high level of informational privacy,"[417] given that online activities potentially reveal a great deal about the individual, and hence touch on a biographical core of

412 *Ibid* at 561, citing *United States v Knotts*, 460 US 276 (1983).
413 *Ibid* at para 564.
414 *Spencer*, above note 55 at para 41.
415 *Ibid* at para 45.
416 *Ibid*.
417 *Ibid* at para 51.

information that a person would reasonably expect to be kept secret from the state.

It may be instructive, albeit not binding, to note that the Supreme Court has found privacy invasions in relation to intrusions occurring in public places in cases involving claims outside section 8 of the *Charter*.[418] In *Aubry v Editions Vice Versa Inc*,[419] the Supreme Court found a violation of privacy protected under the *Quebec Charter of Rights and Freedoms*,[420] where a journalist photographed a woman without consent while she was sitting on the steps of a public fountain. Despite the anodyne nature of the photograph, which was taken while the subject was in plain view of passersby, the Court determined "moral prejudice" was established

> each time a photographer invades someone's privacy or serves it up to the public. The camera lens captures a human moment at its most intense, and the snapshot "defiles" that moment. The privileged instant of personal life becomes "this object image offered to the curiosity of the greatest number." A person surprised in his or her private life by a roving photographer is stripped of his or her transcendency and human dignity, since he or she is reduced to the status of a "spectacle" for others. . . . This "indecency of the image" deprives those photographed of their most secret substance.[421]

The Supreme Court has noted the affront to dignity occasioned by unauthorized photography outside of Quebec as well. Consider *Alberta (Information and Privacy Commissioner) v United Food and Commercial Workers, 401*,[422] which involved complaints by individuals photographed while in plain view outdoors by a union when they were crossing a picket line. The Court held that Alberta's *Personal Information Protection Act*,[423] like all legislation with the primary purpose of protecting privacy, is "quasi-constitutional in nature,"[424] because privacy is "intimately connected to individual autonomy [and] dignity,"[425] values which were engaged by the unauthorized photography in question.

---

418 For a discussion of privacy in public, see Patton-Simpson, above note 35; and D. Lai, "Public Video Surveillance by the State: Policy, Privacy Legislation, and the Charter" (2007) 45:1 *Alberta Law Review* 43.

419 [1998] 1 SCR 591 [*Aubry*].

420 RSQ c C-12, s 5, affording a "right to respect" for "private life."

421 *Aubry*, above note 419 at para 69.

422 2013 SCC 62 [*Alberta (Information and Privacy Commissioner)*].

423 SA 2003, c P-6.5.

424 *Alberta (Information and Privacy Commissioner)*, above note 422 at para 22.

425 *Ibid*. For a detailed discussion, see C. Hunt, "The Future of Privacy: The Conflict with Free Expression" (2015) 43:4 *The Advocates' Quarterly* 391; see also *Douez v Facebook, Inc*, 2017 SCC 33, in which the Court held that British Columbia's

Finally, in *R v Jarvis*,[426] the Supreme Court determined that a school teacher was guilty of criminal voyeurism where he surreptitiously filmed the breasts of female students with a hidden pen camera as they moved about in plain view in populated areas of their school. The offence requires, among other things, that the victim be in "circumstances that give rise to a reasonable expectation of privacy."[427] Chief Justice Wagner, for a majority of six justices, determined that Parliament must have intended that existing jurisprudence interpreting section 8 of the *Charter* would inform the meaning of this criminal provision,[428] because, despite the different contexts, both section 8 of the *Charter* and section 162(1) of the *Criminal Code* are aimed at protecting individual privacy.[429] Taking guidance from the *Charter* jurisprudence, he held, first, that the assessment must be "contextual," taking into account the "totality of circumstances."[430] These circumstances must be informed by "fundamental shared ideals about privacy," "our everyday experiences,"[431] and a "common sense understanding of the concept."[432] Second, privacy cannot be understood as an "all or nothing" concept.[433] A person may be in circumstances where they cannot expect "complete privacy," such as a public place, but that does not mean they automatically forfeit or waive all reasonable expectations of privacy.[434] Relatedly, courts should not employ a "risk analysis" when assessing an REP, which is to say "reducing the inquiry to whether the person put themselves at risk of intrusion" as the controlling factor.[435] Third, the REP inquiry contemplates a "normative rather than a descriptive standard."[436] Whether an expectation of privacy is reasonable should be guided by the values underpinning that right (namely, dignity, autonomy, and the personal integrity of the individual),[437] and by a consideration of the "norms of

Privacy Act, RSBC 1996, c 373 (which creates a statutory privacy tort) was quasi-constitutional because of the importance of privacy "and its role in protecting one's physical and moral autonomy," at para 59, "play an essential role in a free and democratic society and embody key Canadian values" at para 58.

426 *Jarvis*, above note 220.

427 *Criminal Code*, RSC 1985, c C-46, s 162(1).

428 *Jarvis*, above note 220 at para 56.

429 *Ibid* at para 59.

430 *Ibid* at para 60.

431 *Ibid* at para 59.

432 *Ibid* at para 60.

433 *Ibid* at para 61.

434 *Ibid*.

435 *Ibid* at para 68.

436 *Ibid*.

437 *Ibid* at paras 65–68.

conduct in our society."[438] Applying these principles to the facts, Wagner CJ determined the students did have an REP at the material times. While a school is not a traditionally private place, and students should expect to be casually observed by others or even recorded incidentally by security cameras while in common areas, but social norms are such that students would not expect to be surreptitiously recorded for a sexual purpose by their teacher as they were in *Jarvis*.[439]

g) Shared Spaces

Lower courts have grappled with whether a reasonable expectation of privacy exists in the common spaces of condominiums. While a series of earlier trial decisions in Ontario answered this question in the negative,[440] the Ontario Court of Appeal has recently held that a person can have an REP in such circumstances, but its strength will vary depending on how many people are expected to use the area in question. Courts have found a "low" expectation of privacy in busy garages and elevator lobbies, for example, and a stronger expectation in less travelled parts of the building, especially in hallways leading up to the subject's front door.[441] Where the intrusion relates to CCTV footage, as opposed to undercover police observations inside such common areas, the REP analysis depends on whether residents are aware of the presence of cameras.[442] Courts in British Columbia have found an REP in the information obtained from CCTV cameras and fob access records that recorded the occupants' comings and goings inside common areas of their condominiums.[443] The British Columbia Court of Appeal found an REP in the lobby of a condominium where the subject was observed, but not recorded, by undercover officers who had been admitted to the building under a general warrant.[444]

438 *Ibid* at para 68.

439 *Ibid* at paras 73, 76, 89 & 90. For a detailed discussion of this decision, see C. Hunt, "Voyeurism and the Charter: A Comment on the Supreme Court of Canada's Privacy Principles in *R v Jarvis*" in C.D.L. Hunt & R. Diab, eds, *The Last Frontier: Digital Privacy and the Charter* (Toronto: Thomson Reuters, 2021).

440 *R v Brewster*, 2016 ONSC 8038; *R v Zekarias*, 2018 ONSC 4752.

441 *R v Yu*, 2019 ONCA 942 at paras 82–84 [*Yu*]; and see discussion at paras 70–74; and see *R v White*, 2015 ONCA 508.

442 *Yu*, above note 441 at para 85, holding that if they were unaware of closed-circuit cameras, an REP exists.

443 See *R v Latimer*, 2020 BCSC 488; *R v Kim*, 2020 BCSC 1064; *R v Kang*, 2020 BCSC 1474; *R v Biring*, 2021 BCSC 2654.

444 *R v Pipping*, 2020 BCCA 104.

h) Ownership or Control

Ownership, and its relationship to control, can be usefully discussed in the context of *physical locations*, *chattels*, and pure *information*, depending on the nature of the alleged search, so long as it is borne in mind that sharp divisions do not exist between categories, and hence overlap sometimes occurs.

i) Physical Locations

As discussed above,[445] these factors featured prominently in the early cases of *Edwards* and *Belnavis* with respect to the physical locations of the searches at issue. The accused in *Edwards* could not establish an REP in relation to drugs seized in his girlfriend's apartment, as he was not the owner, or leaser, of the apartment, did not contribute money to rent, and lacked authority to regulate access to the space.[446] Similarly, in *Belnavis*, a majority determined that the accused, who was a passenger in another's vehicle at the time of the search, had no REP in relation to bags of stolen property located in the car. She did not own the vehicle, could not control access to it, and there was no evidence of a history or special relationship between her and the driver that would afford her "some special access to or privilege in regard to the vehicle."[447]

Edwards and *Belnavis* must now be read in light of more recent decisions. As concerns the question of ownership, or control, of the *physical location* of the search, Brown and Martin JJ, for the majority in *Le*, recently emphasized, albeit in *obiter*, that the analysis should not "proceed with the assumption that a categorical factor, like control, will have a dominating impact on whether a person has a reasonable expectation of privacy."[448] Instead, courts must focus on the underlying normative question, namely "whether a privacy claim ought to be recognized as beyond state intrusion absent constitutional justification if Canadian society is to remain a free, democratic and open society."[449] In their view, "a case can be made that invited guests can, in some circumstances, have

445 See Section B(3).

446 *Edwards*, above note 26 at paras 46–49.

447 *Belnavis*, above note 77 at para 22. Note that the majority did suggest, at para 23, that there could be special circumstances giving a passenger an REP in relation to a vehicle's contents, such as:

> For example, in many cases there would be little difference in the expectation of privacy for the owner-operator of a car and that of his or her spouse. Similarly, if two people were travelling together on an extended journey and were sharing driving responsibilities and expenses, each would be likely to have an equal expectation of privacy in the vehicle.

448 *Le*, above note 85 at para 136.

449 *Ibid* at para 136 [citations omitted].

reasonable expectations of privacy in their host's property."[450] The case involved a police search of the accused who was in the backyard of a friend's house, and the clear implication from the majority's discussion in *Le* is that an REP would likely have arisen had it been necessary to decide the question.[451]

The relevance of ownership and control of real property was recently discussed in the Ontario Court of Appeal decision in *R v Chow*.[452] The accused owned an apartment which he rented to a stranger for a ten-day period. He was charged with criminal voyeurism after the renter discovered a secret camera hidden inside an alarm clock located in the apartment. Justice Huscroft, writing for the court, overturned the trial judge's finding that police violated the accused's REP when the renter permitted them to enter the apartment. Contrary to the court below, Huscroft JA determined that although the accused owned the apartment, retained keys to it, and could regulate access, he did not have either a subjective or an objectively reasonable expectation of privacy in the apartment during the ten-day period it was rented and lived in by the victim, who was a stranger to him.[453] In the circumstances, it was the renter who had a privacy interest in the apartment, not the owner. This finding might be debated.[454] However, in terms of future guidance, Huscroft JA observed:

> I do not say an owner's expectation of privacy can never be objectively reasonable once property has been rented to a third party. An objectively reasonable expectation of privacy may exist in a variety of rental contexts. It may exist, for example, where accommodation is shared or where the property rented is a home that includes personal effects. In

---

450 *Ibid* at para 137.

451 Note that Moldaver J, in dissent, at para 199, took a different view, agreeing with the court below that no REP was possible, following *Edwards*, above note 26 and *Belnavis*, above note 77, because the accused was simply a guest with no ability to control access to the backyard in question. Commentators have argued that Karakatsanis J's reasons in *Reeves*, above note 45, finding that an REP can exist in shared property, were not intended to be confined to personal computers, but rather extend to shared spaces more generally, with the effect that the position in *Edwards*, above note 26 has arguably been "superseded" and should be approached with "caution," at least concerning co-occupants and co-users of shared spaces: Hassan, above note 52 at 49.

452 *R v Chow*, 2022 ONCA 555 [*Chow*].

453 *Ibid* at paras 27–43.

454 We note there were three separate views on REP in this case: the trial judge finding that the owner had an REP and the renter could not authorize police to enter; the summary appeal court judge holding that the owner had an REP in the space and the renter could authorize police to enter but not search; and the Court of Appeal holding the owner had no REP.

> these contexts, an accused's dignity, integrity, and autonomy interests may be more readily apparent. It is impossible to be prescriptive given the normative nature of the concept.[455]

A final case to consider applying similar logic is *R v Buhay*.[456] The question in this case was whether the accused had an REP in relation to the contents of a locker he had rented for a twenty-four-hour period at a bus terminal, but after it had been opened and searched by terminal security guards. Justice Arbour, for the unanimous Supreme Court, answered this question in the affirmative, noting that Buhay had control of the locker by virtue of renting it and possessing a key. The fact that this control was not exclusive, as the bus company maintained ownership of the locker and also had access to it with a master key, did not "remove" his normative entitlement to an REP.[457]

ii) Chattels

As concerns *ownership of a chattel*, in *Edwards* the Supreme Court held that the accused could not establish an REP in relation to bags containing drugs, located in his girlfriend's apartment, due in part to the fact that he denied they were his.[458] Likewise, in *Belnavis*, the accused could not establish an REP in relation to garbage bags of stolen property located inside a car she was travelling in as a passenger, because she did not identify which belonged to her, and there was nothing indicating ownership on them. In the majority's view, a "garbage bag is very different from a suitcase with initials displayed or a kit bag with a name on it. A green garbage bag offers no hints that it has a particular owner."[459] In our view, these holdings must be revisited, as they appear to have been overtaken by the Supreme Court's decision in *Jones*[460] insofar as that case established that the accused can rely on the Crown's theory that an item belonged to the accused to raise a presumption to that effect.[461] While technically this proposition related only to the accused's establishment of a subjective expectation of privacy and a direct interest in the item in question, there is no reason in principle why it should not also be

455 *Chow*, above note 452 at para 37.
456 *Buhay*, above note 237.
457 *Ibid* at para 22.
458 *Edwards*, above note 26 at para 44.
459 *Belnavis*, above note 77 at para 24.
460 *Jones*, above note 20.
461 *Ibid* at paras 9, 21, and 33. This follows naturally from Côté J's reasons, which broadly permit relying on the Crown's theory to establish that the chattel in question belonged to the accused.

extended to other elements of the section 8 inquiry on *voir dire*, including ownership or control under the REP analysis.[462]

Sometimes, however, the Crown submits that the accused lacked exclusive ownership or control of a chattel and did not therefore have an REP. *Jones* would be of little assistance in such cases. Nevertheless, recent decisions reveal a tendency of the Court to approach such arguments in a nuanced manner, not as an all or nothing proposition. In *Cole*, for example, the Supreme Court determined that the accused, a school teacher, had an REP in relation to the contents of his work issued and work owned laptop computer.[463] Despite his lack of legal ownership, and lack of exclusive practical control of the laptop, due to school policies that permitted the school technician to access the laptop's contents, which the accused was aware of, he did have an REP in the data on the device, and school officials (and later police) interfered with this when they examined it. This decision was driven largely by the fact that computers can be expected to contain highly personal information and therefore engage the claimant's biographical core.[464] Yet, in the course of the decision, the Court also emphasized that while "the ownership of property is a relevant consideration, it is not determinative," and it should not "carry undue weight within the contextual analysis."[465]

The Court takes a similar approach to ownership in *Reeves*.[466] The accused shared a home computer with his spouse. Upon discovering child pornography on the computer, the spouse alerted police and consented to the seizure of the device. The issue on appeal was whether the accused had an REP in relation to the computer and whether his wife's consent to the seizure provided police authority to interfere with it. Once again, the answer, contextually, was that he did have an REP and her consent could not provide authority to seize the device or serve to waive his REP. Justice Karakatsanis, for the majority, held that while both control and ownership are relevant, a "lack of control is not fatal to finding a reasonable expectation of privacy,"[467] nor is a lack of ownership "determinative."[468] The relational nature of the inquiry assessed normatively buttressed the majority's finding that

> while it is reasonable to ask citizens to bear the risk that a co-user of their shared computer may access their data on it, and even perhaps

462 See *R v Labelle*, 2019 ONCA 557 at para 31.
463 *Cole*, above note 27.
464 *Ibid* at paras 48–49, discussing *Morelli*, above note 261.
465 *Ibid* at para 51.
466 *Reeves*, above note 45.
467 *Ibid* at para 38.
468 *Ibid* at para 39.

discuss this data with the police, it is not reasonable to ask them to bear the risk that the co-user could consent to the police *taking* this computer.[469]

iii) Information

Finally, where the subject matter of the claim is characterized as purely *informational*, arguments around one's lack of control have little weight in recent jurisprudence for negating the subject's REP.[470] *Marakah*, discussed above, illustrates the point. The police searched W's smartphone and discovered text messages that incriminated him as well as his accomplice M who had sent the messages. The issue on appeal was whether M could have an REP in relation to messages he had sent to W that were located on W's smartphone. A majority of the Court answered this question in the affirmative, stating: a "person does not lose control of information for the purposes of s. 8 simply because another person possesses it or can access it."[471] Once again, approaching the issue normatively and from a relational perspective led the majority to conclude that despite the "technological reality" that text messages once sent no longer remain in the exclusive control of the sender, and hence there is a risk the recipient may voluntarily disclose their contents, "he or she may yet reasonably expect that information to remain safe from state scrutiny."[472] Simply stated, "control is not dispositive, but only one factor to be considered in the totality of the circumstances."[473]

The majority's holding in *Marakah* is consistent in relation to control with the Court's unanimous decision in *Spencer*, discussed above.[474]

469 *Ibid* at para 43 and at para 44:

> I cannot accept that, by choosing to share our computers with friends and family, we are required to give up our *Charter* protection from state interference in our private lives. We are not required to accept that our friends and family can unilaterally authorize police to take things that we share. The decision to share with others does not come at such a high price in a free and democratic society.

470 There was, of course, a strong informational privacy aspect in cases like *Cole*, above note 27 (contents of a laptop in possession of the accused but owned by the school) and *Reeves*, *ibid.* (contents of a shared computer).

471 *Marakah*, above note 60 at para 41.

472 *Ibid.*

473 *Ibid* at para 44. Contrast the majority's approach with the dissenting reasons of Moldaver J, who determined that M did not have an REP in relation to the sent text messages. For him, control was the "crucial" factor, at para 117, and "a person's expectation of privacy in informational subject matter that falls under another person's exclusive control cannot be reasonable in a society that values the freedom of individuals to share information" (at para 129).

474 *Spencer*, above note 55.

The Court in *Spencer* had no trouble finding the accused had an REP in the subscriber information linked to his IP address, which linked him to online activity in which he was reasonably entitled to maintain anonymity, despite the fact this information was in the hands of a third party (Shaw, the ISP provider) and hence not in his control.[475]

Having said this, the majority's approach in *Mills*,[476] discussed above,[477] while not explicitly premised on the notion of control, does have a practical impact on the existence of an REP in electronic communications no longer in one's exclusive possession, at least in circumstances factually analogous to *Mills*. There, a police officer posed online as a fourteen-year-old girl ("Leann") with the intention of catching internet child lurers. Over a period of two months, the accused sent messages to the undercover officer via Facebook and email. He was subsequently arrested and charged with child luring. Mills argued that he had an REP in relation to the internet messages he had sent to the "child." A majority of the Court disagreed. Justice Karakatsanis, writing for herself and Wagner CJ, determined that Mills had no REP in the messages, and hence section 8 was not engaged, because, normatively speaking, it is "not reasonable to expect that your messages will be kept private from the intended recipient (even if the intended recipient is an undercover officer)."[478] Justice Brown, writing for himself and Abella and Gascon JJ, determined Mills had no REP here in part because there was no danger of intruding on a potentially private conversation between individuals whose relationship was unknown to police.[479] This was because, due to the investigatory technique deployed—the creation of a fake "Leann" (who was an undercover officer) who received messages from the accused—the police knew, from the outset, of the relationship between the accused and the officer. Justice Moldaver agreed with both of these views.[480] The implication appears to be, at a minimum, that one does not have an REP in direct communications with an undercover officer

---

475 *Ibid*; and see *Jones*, above note 20 at para 45, "the sender of a text message retains a reasonable expectation of privacy in records of text messages stored in a service provider's infrastructure notwithstanding that he relinquished direct control over those messages."

476 *Mills*, above note 95.

477 See Section C(2).

478 *Mills*, above note 95 at para 36.

479 *Ibid* at paras 27–29.

480 *Ibid* at para 66.

(not a new point).[481] As discussed above,[482] Martin J in *Mills* offered a number of criticisms of the approach taken by Brown J in that case. Of relevance to the current discussion, she characterized his reasons as reintroducing a type of risk analysis by implication, wherein a "loss of control due to risk of disclosure" drives the conclusion that no REP can exist.[483] This, Martin J wrote, derived from Brown J's observation that it is "not reasonable for an adult to expect privacy when communicating with a vulnerable child who is a stranger because hoping that a complete stranger will keep one's communications private is a 'gamble'."[484]

Insofar as control remains a factor in the REP analysis, there is a danger that it may exert an influence on the analysis in a manner verging on a type of risk analysis identified by Martin J above.[485]

481 See, e.g., *R v Fliss*, 2002 SCC 16, distinguishing between an officer's testimony of what the accused said to him (over which the accused had no REP) and the transcript of a recording of it (in which he did have an REP).

482 See Section C(2).

483 *Mills*, above note 95 at para 114.

484 *Ibid* at para 114, referring to Brown J's reasons at paras 22–23.

485 See Pierre-Luc Deziel, "Clarifying the Role of 'Control' in Section 8 Jurisprudence," in C.D.L. Hunt & R. Diab, eds, *The Last Frontier: Digital Privacy and the Charter* (Toronto: Thomson Reuters, 2021) 89 at 117.

CHAPTER 5

SEARCHES AND SEIZURES AUTHORIZED BY LAW 1: STANDARD WARRANT

In earlier chapters, we highlighted two important facets of section 8 of the *Charter*.[1] A state actor does not engage a person's right to be "secure against unreasonable search or seizure" unless that person has a reasonable expectation of privacy in the place or thing searched or seized. If they do, the Crown must prove the search or seizure was reasonable. To do this, the Crown must satisfy a court that the search or seizure was authorized by law, the law is reasonable, and the search or seizure was carried out in a reasonable manner.[2] In this chapter and the next, we canvass law that authorizes police or other state actors to conduct a search or seizure.

There are many sources and a wide range of them. Federal and provincial statutes set out powers to search or seize with and without a warrant, and common law authorizes a host of further powers for search and seizure with and without a warrant. Some of the powers are quite intricate. Books for practitioners contain entire chapters on specific kinds of warrants.[3] We aim in the next two chapters to provide a comprehensive yet concise survey of the various powers available.

---

1 *Canadian Charter of Rights and Freedoms*, Part I of the *Constitution Act, 1982*, being Schedule B to the *Canada Act 1982* (UK), 1982, c 11 [*Charter*].

2 *R v Collins*, [1987] 1 SCR 265 at 278 [*Collins*].

3 See, e.g., Scott C. Hutchinson et al, *Search and Seizure Law in Canada* (Toronto: Thomson Reuters, 2022); James A. Fontana & David Keeshan, *The Law of Search and Seizure in Canada*, 12th ed (Toronto: LexisNexis Canada, 2021); and Nader Hasan et al, *Search and Seizure* (Toronto: Emond, 2021).

Our focus in this chapter is on how one applies for a warrant (by submitting an "information to obtain"), the general rules on issuing and executing a warrant, followed by reporting and other post-seizure requirements. We conclude the chapter with a discussion of how to challenge a warranted search. We illustrate all of this by devoting this chapter to one of the most commonly used search powers in criminal investigations: the "standard" warrant under section 487 of the *Criminal Code*.[4] (We save for the next chapter other statutory powers and ancillary police powers at common law.)

Most of the powers we canvass in this chapter and the next involve the use of one of two standards: reasonable probability or reasonable suspicion. Both chapters assume a knowledge of these standards. We address them briefly here at the outset, before moving on to warrants.

A. REASONABLE PROBABILITY VERSUS SUSPICION

We saw, in Chapter 2, in *Hunter v Southam Inc*,[5] that police cannot carry out searches on a whim or a hunch about a crime having been committed or evidence being found in the place they wish to search. In order to avoid abuses of police power, we ask the police to demonstrate a level of certainty about the facts before they decide to search or arrest, or do something invasive or forceful. How much certainty police need depends on the situation and power they exercise. Levels of certainty fall within a spectrum: from a hunch to absolute certainty. A hunch or mere suspicion is a belief that something might be the case, a mere possibility. A "reasonable suspicion" is a belief that something is reasonably possible—more than hypothetical but less than a likelihood.[6] A "reasonable probability" is a belief that something is likely to be the case.[7] It has often been equated with the civil standard of something being "more likely

4 *Criminal Code of Canada*, RSC 1985, c C-46 [*Criminal Code* or *Code*]. The standard warrant in s 487 is not to be confused with the "general warrant" in s 487.01 of the *Code*, discussed in Chapter 6. General warrants permit police to employ investigative techniques or "do any thing" not authorized under other warrant provisions.

5 *Hunter et al v Southam Inc*, [1984] 2 SCR 145 [*Hunter*].

6 *R v Chehil*, 2013 SCC 49 at para 27 [*Chehil*]: "while reasonable grounds to suspect and reasonable and probable grounds to believe are similar in that they both must be grounded in objective facts, reasonable suspicion is a lower standard, as it engages the reasonable possibility, rather than probability, of crime."

7 *Hunter*, above note 5 at 167; *Chehil*, *ibid*.

than not" or a "balance of probabilities," though the Supreme Court has not endorsed this equation.[8]

In the context of arrest, the Court has held that the standard of "reasonable and probable grounds," which requires a belief in the "reasonable probability of [a] crime," "exists when "there is an objective basis for the belief which is based on compelling and credible information."[9] The standard does not require evidence amounting to a *prima facie* case (evidence sufficient for a conviction in the absence of a contrary explanation or other evidence)[10] and is lower than proof beyond a reasonable doubt.[11] In *R v Beaver*, where the Court was divided 5:4, the majority ended a dispute among lower courts as to whether "reasonable probability," in the context of arrest, is tantamount to "more likely than not" in holding that police do *not* need to "establish that the offence was committed on a balance of probabilities."[12] In a vigorous dissent, Martin J held that "[r]easonable grounds is a high threshold that is met at the point where credibly based probability replaces suspicion," suggesting that if the standard is not equated with "more likely than not," it should not entail much less.[13]

Standards differ depending on the situation. In the case of less invasive searches, such as a breath sample at roadside or the use of a sniffer dog at a bus station, the law permits police to search or seize on the lower standard of a reasonable suspicion (i.e., that a suspect has alcohol in their body, that people in a given area might be carrying illicit substances in their bags). For more invasive searches, such as a breathalyzer test at the police station or the search of a home with a warrant, the law requires the higher standard of a reasonable probability (i.e., a belief the suspect was likely driving while impaired, or that an offence has been committed and evidence will likely be found in the home).

The courts use different phrases to refer to the same standard. The Supreme Court has confirmed that in the context of section 8, "reasonable belief," "reasonable grounds to believe," and "reasonable and probable grounds" are synonymous with "reasonable probability."[14] Statutes

---

8 Steven Penney, "Standards of Suspicion" (2017) 65 *Criminal Law Quarterly* 23 at 31.

9 *R v Beaver*, 2022 SCC 54 at para 72 [*Beaver*], citing *Mugesera v Canada (Minister of Citizenship and Immigration)*, 2005 SCC 40 at para 114 [*Mugesera*].

10 *Beaver*, *ibid*, citing *R v Storrey*, [1990] 1 SCR 241 at 251 [*Storrey*] and *R v Shepherd*, 2009 SCC 35 at para 17 [*Shepherd*].

11 *Storrey*, *ibid* at 250.

12 *Beaver*, above note 9 at para 72, citing *Mugesera*, above note 9 at para 114.

13 *Beaver*, *ibid* at para 167.

14 *R v Debot*, [1989] 2 SCR 1140 at 1166 [*Debot*]; *Baron v Canada*, [1993] 1 SCR 416 at 446–47 [*Baron*]; *R v Wiley*, [1993] 3 SCR 263. "Reasonable grounds to believe" is equated with a belief that something is probable or likely throughout criminal

have adopted this shorthand way of referring to the standard, often using "reasonable grounds to believe" to signify what courts have confirmed is "reasonable and probable grounds" in the provision at issue. (We adopt this shorthand throughout this chapter and the next; where we describe a power as requiring "reasonable grounds to believe" or "reasonable grounds," this can be taken to mean a belief that something is "reasonably probable.") Similarly, the Supreme Court and many statutes use the phrase "reasonable grounds to suspect" to refer to reasonable suspicion.[15]

The Court's decision in *R v Storrey*,[16] a case involving arrest, sheds light on what is meant by "reasonable" in these standards, and the reasoning in this case has been applied in the search context. An officer must subjectively or personally hold the requisite grounds, but they must also be "justified from an objective point of view."[17] This means that "a reasonable person placed in the position of the officer must be able to conclude that there were indeed reasonable and probable grounds for the arrest."[18] The reasonable person shares the officer's knowledge, training, and experience.[19] Evidence based on the training and experience "should not be uncritically accepted, but neither should it be approached with 'undue scepticism.'"[20] Courts should respect that "the exercise of police powers is not a "scientific or metaphysical exercise," but one that calls for application of "[c]ommon sense, flexibility, and practical everyday experience."[21] Police cannot rely on evidence they discover after an arrest to justify their grounds for arrest.[22]

---

law and also in other areas of the law. The Supreme Court in *Mugesera*, above note 9, interpreting provisions of an earlier version of the current *Immigration and Refugee Protection Act*, SC 2001, c 27, dealing with the exclusion of suspected war criminals from Canada, held, at para 114, that "reasonable grounds to believe" in those provisions of the Act required "something more than mere suspicion, but less than the standard applicable in civil matters of proof on the balance of probabilities."

15 *Chehil*, above note 6; *R v Kang-Brown*, 2008 SCC 18.

16 *Storrey*, above note 10.

17 *Ibid* at 251. See *R v Caslake*, [1998] 1 SCR 51 [*Caslake*] for an example applying the subjective and objective requirements in the context of reasonable grounds under s 8. Note that where an officer directs another officer to conduct an arrest, only the directing officer needs to have subjective and objectively reasonable grounds: *Beaver*, above note 9 at para 72, citing *Debot*, above note 14, at 1166–67.

18 *Storrey*, above note 10 at 251.

19 *Ibid* at 250–51; *Beaver*, above note 9 at para 72.

20 *Beaver*, above note 9 at para 72, citing *R v MacKenzie*, 2013 SCC 50 at paras 64–65 [*MacKenzie*].

21 *Beaver*, *ibid*, citing *R v Canary*, 2018 ONCA 304 at para 22.

22 *Beaver*, *ibid*, citing *R v Biron*, [1976] 2 SCR 56 at 72.

When assessing whether grounds are met, police and courts on review can take a wide range of information into account, including what would be hearsay.[23] In *R v MacKenzie*, a case involving the reasonable suspicion standard in the search context, the Court held that officer training and experience can inform both subjective and objective facets, in which case, the question is whether the reasonable person in the position of the officer would share the belief at issue.[24] However, where an officer's grounds for arrest are based on a mistake of law (i.e., where an officer assumes that facts before them amount to something that turns out not to be an offence), regardless of how reasonable the mistake may have been, the arrest is invalid.[25] This would presumably also apply to reasonable grounds under section 8. Whether the reasonable grounds standard has been met in a given case is a question of law and will be assessed on review on the standard of correctness.[26]

In *R v Garofoli*, the Court set out guidelines for when tips by informants can form probable grounds in the search context.[27] Statements from an informant can contribute to grounds, but "evidence of a tip from an informer, by itself, is insufficient to establish reasonable and probable grounds."[28] To assess the reliability of the tip, police and reviewing courts should consider "the totality of the circumstances," including the "degree of detail" a tip contains; the informant's source of knowledge; and indicia of the informer's reliability such as past performance or confirmation from other sources.[29] Police and courts may not rely on the results of the search after the fact as evidence of the tip's reliability.[30]

More broadly, whether police had a reasonable and probable belief or a reasonable suspicion depends on the "totality of the circumstances."[31] Elaborating upon this in *R v Chehil*, Karakatsanis J writes:

---

23 *Eccles v Bourque*, [1975] 2 SCR 739 [*Eccles*]; *Collins*, above note 2; *R v Garofoli*, [1990] 2 SCR 1421 [*Garofoli*].

24 *MacKenzie*, above note 20 at para 64.

25 *R v Tim*, 2022 SCC 12.

26 *Beaver*, above note 9 at paras 73, 167; *Shepherd*, above note 10 at para 20; *R v MacKenzie*, above note 20 at para 54. Justice Jamal in *Beaver*, at para 73, draws a helpful distinction between the trial judge's findings of fact with respect to the "existence of reasonable and probable grounds" (i.e., beliefs the officer may or may not have held, facts known, etc.) and whether "the facts as found by the trial judge amount to reasonable and probable grounds." The judge's factual findings are reviewable "only for palpable and overriding error."

27 *Garofoli*, above note 23.

28 *Ibid* at 1456.

29 *Ibid* at 1457.

30 *Ibid.*

31 *Chehil*, above note 6 at para 29; *R v Mann*, 2004 SCC 52 para 34 [*Mann*]; *Storrey*, above note 10 at 251.

> The inquiry must consider the constellation of objectively discernible facts that are said to give the investigating officer reasonable cause to suspect that an individual is involved in the type of criminal activity under investigation. This inquiry must be fact-based, flexible, and grounded in common sense and practical, everyday experience.[32]

The assessment should also include "[e]xculpatory, neutral, or equivocal information."[33] In the context of detention and arrest, reasonable suspicion or belief must also be individualized rather than vague and general—an officer must have grounds to suspect or believe the suspect in question is implicated in an offence.[34] In the search context, a similar specificity is required depending on the power at issue. In *Chehil*, the Court upheld the validity of a search using sniffer dogs in relation to a specific passenger getting off a bus, about whom police had various pieces of information suggesting a real possibility that he was a drug courier. Below, we canvass the requirements for a warrant that include a reasonable probability that evidence will be found of a specific offence in a particular place, connected to a specific person.

B. A GENERAL INTRODUCTION TO WARRANTS

A good place to begin the topic of warrants is Major J's dicta in *CanadianOxy Chemicals Ltd v Canada (AG)* about their general nature:[35]

> The purpose of s. 487(1) [or warrants more broadly] is to allow the investigators to unearth and preserve as much relevant evidence as possible. To ensure that the authorities are able to perform their appointed functions properly they should be able to locate, examine and preserve all the evidence relevant to events which may have given rise to criminal liability. It is not the role of the police to investigate and decide whether the essential elements of an offence are made out—that decision is the role of the courts. The function of the police, and other peace officers, is to investigate incidents which might be criminal, make a conscientious and informed decision as to whether charges should be laid, and then present the full and unadulterated facts to the prosecutorial authorities.[36]

32 *Chehil*, above note 6 at para 29.

33 *Ibid* at para 33.

34 *Ibid* at para 30; *Mann*, above note 31 at para 34.

35 *CanadianOxy Chemicals Ltd v Canada (AG)*, [1999] 1 SCR 743 [*CanadianOxy*].

36 *Ibid* at para 22.

Warrants are investigative tools. They submit the process of gathering evidence to the rule of law. They are premised on the scale being tipped from suspicion to probability of a crime having been committed and the likelihood of evidence relating to it being found in a given place or thing. These are the broader principles. But much about the legality of a search turns on the details. To appreciate how and where these arise, it may help to briefly address how warrants are obtained.

1) Applying for a Warrant (the Information to Obtain)

Police or other state agents apply for a warrant by preparing a document called an Information to Obtain a Search Warrant (ITO) or an equivalent to this.[37] The ITO is an affidavit, typically authored by a police officer with first-hand knowledge of the facts of an investigation. The officer or affiant may be referred to in the ITO as the "informant." The ITO consists of a detailed narrative explaining how the informant has come to believe on reasonable grounds that an offence has been committed and evidence of it is to be found in the place to be searched—and it specifies what they expect to find there.[38] After swearing or affirming the affidavit, police submit it to a justice on an *ex parte* basis (we note exceptions below). The receiving justice reviews the ITO, impartially, to decide whether it does establish reasonable grounds to believe an offence has been committed and evidence is to be found in a given place—or meets other requirements of the statutory provision allowing for the warrant. The justice either issues the warrant or declines to do so. The review process can take anywhere from a few days to a few minutes (but is usually done in relatively short order). The warrant itself is issued in a

37 Commonly used warrant provisions will stipulate who may apply for them; s 487 refers to a "peace officer or a public officer," both of which are defined terms in s 2 of the *Code*, above note 4. "Peace officers" include police and customs officers, among others; "public officers" include "any officer while the officer is engaged in enforcing the laws of Canada relating to revenue, customs, excise, trade or navigation." By contrast to warrants under s 487, general warrants in s 487.01 are limited to "peace officers." See also Steve Coughlan & Alex Gorlewski, *The Anatomy of Criminal Procedure: A Visual Guide to the Law* (Toronto: Irwin Law, 2019) at 43.

38 Warrant provisions may also be issued on the basis of a belief that an offence *will* be committed. As discussed below, s 487 of the *Code* authorizes a warrant in various cases; one is a belief that evidence will be found in a place that is "intended to be used for the purpose of committing any offence against the person for which a person may be arrested without warrant." Other warrants discussed in Chapter 6 can be authorized on a belief that an offence has been committed or will be committed (including tracking and transmission data warrants in ss 492.1 and 492.2 and "general warrants" in s 487.01). (See also Coughlan & Gorlewski, *ibid* at 42.)

prescribed form, with content it must include.[39] It is typically addressed to peace officers in the jurisdiction in which it is sought or, in some cases, a named officer; it summarizes the grounds for believing an offence has been committed and describes the things to be searched for and the place to be searched; it stipulates hours within which the search may occur; it authorizes the entry to a place and search for the items; and it states the requirement to bring items seized before a justice or to provide them with a report on them.

We highlight a few more specific points.

When drafting the ITO, the affiant or informant has a duty to make "full and frank disclosure of material facts."[40] As Fish J held in *R v Morelli*,[41] "a police officer—indeed, any informant—must be particularly careful not to 'pick and choose' among the relevant facts in order to achieve the desired outcome. The informant's obligation is to present all material facts, favourable or not."[42] An affiant or informant can rely on hearsay to establish reasonable grounds in an ITO.[43] They can also cite confidential or anonymous sources to establish reasonable grounds, but a tip by itself would be insufficient.[44] An affiant or informant must be careful not to include information that might reveal the identity of a confidential source, but the ITO still must establish probable grounds. Where it relies on a confidential source to a large extent, the ITO must include enough information to establish the source's reliability—by noting the detail and precision of their information, corroboration with other sources, and the affiant's knowledge or past experience with that source.[45] Also, the information on which an affiant or informant relies in an ITO to establish probable grounds must have been gathered lawfully. If it turns out that material observations in the ITO were obtained in violation of the *Charter*, they will be excised or removed from consideration on a challenge to the validity of the warrant after the fact.[46]

---

39 The general structure of an ITO for a warrant under s 487 of the *Criminal Code* is set out in Form 1 found in the appendix to the *Code*, above note 4.

40 *R v Araujo*, 2000 SCC 65 [*Araujo*].

41 2010 SCC 8 at para 2 [*Morelli*].

42 *Ibid* at para 58.

43 *Garofoli*, above note 23 at 1456; *Eccles*, above note 23 at 745–46, making the point in relation to grounds for arrest.

44 *Garofoli*, above note 23 at 1456; *R v Leipert*, [1997] 1 SCR 281 [*Leipert*].

45 *Garofoli*, above note 23 at 1455–56.

46 We explore the process for challenging the validity of a warrant further below, in Section C of this chapter.

For most warrants, including section 487 of the *Code*, the "justice" issuing the warrant is a justice of the peace or a provincial court judge.[47] Some warrants may only be issued by a superior court judge, others by a judge of either the provincial or superior court.[48] The Supreme Court in *Araujo* encouraged justices reviewing a warrant to take an active role in assessing whether grounds are met:

> The judge should not view himself or herself as a mere rubber stamp, but should take a close look at the material submitted by the applicant. He or she should not be reluctant to ask questions from the applicant, to discuss or to require more information or to narrow down the authorization requested if it seems too wide or too vague.[49]

A justice may provide reasons for refusing to grant the warrant, and a party may reapply.[50] A justice who includes reasons for refusing a warrant should not be seen advising an applicant on what to include the next time around. Doing so could raise questions about impartiality.[51]

A final point to note here pertains to discretion. Warrant provisions in the *Criminal Code* or other statute usually state that a justice or a judge "*may* issue a warrant" where reasonable grounds are established or other conditions are met.[52] The Supreme Court in *Baron v Canada* found a warrant provision in the *Income Tax Act* to be unreasonable because it *required* that a warrant be issued if reasonable grounds were established.[53] Leaving no residual discretion to refuse a warrant compromises a judge's ability to act judicially in seeking to strike an appropriate balance between individual and state interests in a particular case by "empower[ing] the judge to consider all the circumstances."[54] A court must retain this discretion since "[n]o set of criteria will always be determinative or sufficient to override the right of the individual to privacy."[55]

---

47 A "justice" is defined in s 2 of the *Criminal Code*, above note 4, to mean "a justice of the peace or a provincial court judge." However, as Coughlan & Gorlewski note, above note 37 at 41, in some provinces, superior court judges are given powers of provincial court judges under provincial law, authorizing them to issue these warrants.

48 See, e.g., the general warrant provisions, in s 487.01 of the *Code*, discussed in Chapter 6, Section A(1).

49 *Araujo*, above note 40 at para 29.

50 *R v Gray* (1993), 85 Man R (2d) 211 (CA).

51 *R v Krist* (1998), 113 BCAC 176 (CA).

52 For example, s 487 of the *Code* states that a justice "may at any time issue a warrant" where conditions in the section are met.

53 *Baron*, above note 14, considering the *Income Tax Act*, SC 1970-71-72, c 63.

54 *Ibid* at 437.

55 *Ibid*.

Judges need "a sufficient degree of flexibility . . . in order that justice be done to the respective interests involved."

This residual discretion is not, however, a basis for challenging a warrant. For reasons to be explored further below, this has to do with the test for reviewing whether a warrant was lawfully issued. The question for the court on review is not whether a warrant should have been issued (i.e., whether the reviewing judge themself would have issued it) but whether there was "reliable evidence that might reasonably be believed on the basis of which the authorization could have issued."[56] In practical terms, it would be difficult to persuade a court on review that despite finding that grounds or conditions were met, the warrant still *could not have been issued*. As a result, there is no body of cases in which a reviewing court overturns a warrant on the view that the issuing justice should have exercised the discretion not to issue it. A judge being asked to issue a warrant may have this discretion, but their decision not to exercise it is effectively unreviewable.

2) Telewarrants

Many warrants in the *Criminal Code* and other federal statutes can be obtained relatively quickly by phone or electronic means. Section 487.1 of the *Code* provides for "telewarrants" where "a peace officer believes that an indictable offence has been committed and that it would be impracticable to appear personally before a justice to make an application." The officer must "submit an information on oath by telephone or other means of telecommunication to a justice." An officer will fax or email an "information to obtain a warrant," but the information on oath can also be conveyed orally—in which case, the exchange is recorded and a transcript is made for later review.[57] The telewarrant provisions in section 489.1 apply to warrants under section 487 of the *Code*, along with a few other *Code* warrants, including those for DNA and blood samples.[58] Warrant provisions in the *Code* and other federal statutes will permit use of a telewarrant by virtue of reference to section 489.1. An example can be found in section 11 of the *Controlled Drugs and Substances Act*.[59]

A telewarrant may be not be issued unless it is "impracticable" to apply for one in court. In *R v Daniels*, the Ontario Superior Court held

56 *Araujo*, above note 40 at para 54.

57 *R v Passon*, 2009 BCSC 192 at para 49.

58 For DNA warrants, see s 487.05(3) and for blood, s 320.29(3) of the *Criminal Code*, above note 4.

59 SC 1996, c 19 [*CDSA*].

that "the term 'impracticable' requires that personal attendance before a justice be more than merely inconvenient for the affiant, but it need not be impossible for the affiant."[60] The British Columbia Court of Appeal has held that impracticability does not require a showing of urgency.[61] The affiant should address in the ITO why it is impracticable to apply for the warrant in person.

3) Assistance Orders and Sealing Orders

Before moving on to the warrant provisions, we note an important set of tools commonly used to assist officers carrying out a search with a warrant.

The *Criminal Code* provides for "assistance orders," which compel third parties to assist law enforcement with the execution of a warrant.[62] They only work in tandem with a warrant or a wiretap authorization and remain valid as long as the warrant or authorization is valid. They can be granted where a person's assistance "may reasonably be considered to be required to give effect to the authorization or warrant."[63] The *Code* provision is silent on whether an assistance order can compel the subject of an investigation to assist with executing a warrant.[64] In two cases where police obtained a warrant to search a suspect's phone, courts have declined to issue an assistance order that would compel the suspect to provide their password to police—on the basis that it would violate the right to silence and the right against self-incrimination.[65]

---

60 *R v Daniels*, 2015 ONSC 283 at para 14

61 *R v Le*, 2009 BCCA 14 and *R v Clark*, 2015 BCCA 488, aff'd 2017 SCC 3.

62 *Criminal Code*, above note 4, s 487.02.

63 *Ibid.*

64 By contrast, *Code* provisions for "preservation demands" and "production orders" for data state that a demand or order "may not be made to a person who is under investigation for the offence" at issue (ss 487.012(3) and 487.014(4), discussed further below). The reasoning in *R v Kukemueller*, 2018 ONSC 6306 [*Kukemueller*] suggests that an assistance order compelling an accused to assist may constitute a violation of the right to silence or the right against self-incrimination. In that case, police, in the process of executing a search, compelled an accused—who had not been cautioned under s 10(b) of the *Charter*—to assist them by guiding them through his house to locate various items seized. The court held the assistance could only be authorized by valid consent, which includes being told of a right to refuse consent (citing the test in *R v Wills* (1992), 7 OR (3d) 337 (CA).

65 *R v Talbot*, 2017 ONCJ 814 and *R v Shergill*, 2019 ONCJ 54. See also Robert Diab & Marshall Putnam, "Is Password Compulsion Constitutional in Canada? Two Views" (2019) 77 *Advocate* (Vancouver) 513.

The *Code* also provides for a "sealing order" that can be sought when applying for a warrant—for the purpose of keeping the content of a warrant application (the ITO) confidential after the warrant is executed.[66] The *Code* provision provides a framework for displacing the presumption at common law that once a warrant is executed, the contents of the "sealed packet" (the warrant and the ITO) are to become publicly accessible.[67] The test in section 487.3 is whether "the ends of justice would be subverted by the disclosure" for one of several reasons, including comprising a confidential informant or an ongoing investigation or investigative technique, and whether the reason "outweighs in importance the access to the information." The sealing order may be varied or terminated, with the unsealed information partially edited if necessary.[68] In cases involving a warrant for an interception (a wiretap), section 187 of the *Code* requires that the warrant and ITO be sealed until trial, at which point the accused is entitled to disclosure of it—with possible edits to protect the identity of informants, ongoing investigations, or police techniques.[69] The Supreme Court has set out a process by which non-accused persons, after receiving notice that they have been the subject of an interception, may apply for access to the sealed packet.[70]

4) Section 487: The Standard Warrant

The warrant police seek and obtain most commonly in Canada to search a place for tangible things in a criminal investigation is the warrant issued under section 487 of the *Criminal Code*. It applies to any offence in a federal statute, but it does not apply in certain cases where other warrants are available, as discussed in this chapter and the next. In this section, we survey the basic features of the section 487 warrant, noting a number of the holdings on finer points that also apply to analogous features of other warrants.

Section 487 conforms with the requirements for a reasonable search set out in *Hunter v Southam Inc.*[71] Justice Dickson, as he then was, held that a warrant for searching a place in a criminal investigation should require that police provide "reasonable and probable grounds, established

---

66 Section 487.3 of the *Code*, which applies to "a warrant under this or any other Act of Parliament, an order under any of sections 487.013 to 487.018 or an authorization under section 529 or 529.4."

67 *AG (Nova Scotia) v MacIntyre*, [1982] 1 SCR 175.

68 *Criminal Code*, above note 4, ss 487.3(3) and (4).

69 *Ibid*, ss 187(1.4) and 187(4).

70 *Michaud v Québec (AG)*, [1996] 3 SCR 3.

71 *Hunter*, above note 5.

upon oath, to believe that an offence has been committed and that there is evidence to be found at the place of the search."[72] To arrive at this standard, Dickson J drew in part on the earlier equivalent to section 487.[73] Both the earlier and the current version in section 487 requires a belief that evidence will *likely* be found in the place to be searched. He cautioned that:

> To associate [the standard] with an applicant's reasonable belief that relevant evidence *may* be uncovered by the search, would be to define the proper standard as the *possibility* of finding evidence. This is a very low standard which would validate intrusion on the basis of suspicion, and authorize fishing expeditions of considerable latitude.[74]

The main provision, section 487(1), might be understood in three parts. First, it requires a justice to be "satisfied by information on oath in Form 1 [the ITO] that there are reasonable grounds to believe" that one or more kinds of evidence listed in the section will be found in a "building, receptacle or place." The kinds of evidence are set out in four subsections of section 487(1):

a) "anything on or in respect of which" an offence has been committed;
b) anything that will "afford evidence with respect to the commission of an offence" or will "reveal the whereabouts of a person who is believed to have committed an offence;"
c) anything "there are reasonable grounds to believe is intended to be used for the purpose of committing any offence against the person for which a person may be arrested without warrant;" or
c.1) "any offence-related property."

"Offence-related property" is defined in section 2 of the *Code* to mean any property used in the commission of an indictable offence under the *Code* or "that is intended to be used for committing such an offence." Finally, if there are reasonable grounds to believe one of the listed kinds of evidence will be found, the justice may issue a warrant to "search the building, receptacle or place for any such thing and to seize it." The officer must then "as soon as practicable, bring the thing seized before, or make a report in respect thereof to, the justice or some other justice for the same territorial division in accordance with section 489.1."

---

72 *Ibid* at 167. In *Morelli*, above note 41 at para 39, Fish J cites this sentence from *Hunter* to encapsulate what s 487 required of police to obtain the warrant at issue in that case.

73 *Hunter*, above note 5 at 167, citing what was then s 443 of the *Criminal Code*.

74 *Ibid* at 167 [emphasis in original].

The first two kinds of evidence listed in section 487(1)(a) and (b) include evidence of any offence in a federal statute. The first two subsections also involve evidence of a previous offence, whereas section 487(1)(c) and (c.1) contemplate evidence of potential future offences.[75] In most cases, police rely on section 487(1)(b), which requires a reasonable belief that it is probable that (1) an offence has occurred and (2) evidence relating to it will be found in the place to be searched. As noted above, a justice satisfied that these grounds are met may issue a warrant in Form 1, which sets out the grounds, items to be searched or seized, and other conditions for executing the warrant. A number of issues arise.

Once issued, the warrant must identify the offence being investigated, or the substance of it, with "sufficient particularity" to permit "a reasonable person faced with a search warrant" to be able to determine "the nature of the offence or the manner of its commission."[76] It need not contain the particulars necessary for an indictment.[77] A "[f]ailure to state the nature of the offence is a fatal omission" rendering the warrant invalid.[78]

Section 487 authorizes the search of a "building, receptacle or place," not persons.[79] A warrant must set out a "precise description of the place to be searched" to provide police with guidance and avoid "leaving them to fill in the blanks with their own knowledge, or to pursue attractive leads at their own discretion."[80] This also allows the person whose place is being searched to "readily apprehend that executing officers have legal authority to enter and conduct the search, reducing the risk of conflict and violent resistance to the search."[81] In *R v Ting*, the Ontario Court of Appeal held that "what constitutes an adequate description will vary with the location to be searched and the circumstances of each case."[82] In the case of a "multi-unit, multi-use building" the warrant needs to be more specific than merely the building number; "[t]he description must adequately differentiate the units within the building, as those in

---

75 Section 487(1)(c) refers to "anything . . . intended to be used"; (c.1) points to the definition in s 2, which includes any property "that is intended to be used."

76 *Re PSI Mind Development Institute Ltd et al and The Queen* (1977), 37 CCC (2d) 263 at 267 (Ont SC) [*Re PSI*].

77 *Ibid* at 268, citing *Royal American Shows Inc v The Queen, ex rel Hahn et al*, [1975] 6 WWR 571 at 573 (Alta SC).

78 *Regency Realities Inc v Loranger* (1961), 36 CR 291 at 298–99 (Qc SC).

79 Caselaw on point is discussed further below.

80 *R v Saint*, 2017 ONCA 491 at para 7 [*Saint*]; *R v Ting*, 2016 ONCA 57 at paras 48–49 [*Ting*], *R v Le*, 2011 MBCA 83 at para 77 [*Le*].

81 *Saint*, above note 80.

82 *Ting*, above note 80 at para 51.

a multi-unit dwelling have the same expectation of privacy as those in a single-unit dwelling."[83]

The Supreme Court in *R v Campbell* held that a person's "expectation of privacy in his room within the townhouse is just as high as that of a resident of a single dwelling unit."[84] Justice Charron noted that "[i]n drafting ITOs proposing to search more than one unit within a multi-unit dwelling, this principle should be reflected by clearly setting out reasonable and probable grounds for each unit to be searched."[85] A warrant permitting entry and search of a discrete or separate unit of a building could be challenged on the basis that it was issued without reasonable grounds specific to that unit.[86]

In some cases, a warrant might specify a home or building at a given address and leave uncertain whether police are authorized to search other parts of the property. In *Caslake*, Lamer CJ held that "the scope of [a] search is limited to the area and to those items for which the law has granted the authority to search. To the extent that a search exceeds these limits, it is not authorized by law."[87] Where a warrant authorizes search of a dwelling-house, this will include what is referred to at common law as "curtilage." This is defined as the area immediately surrounding a home and considered to be an "integral part" of it.[88] Canadian cases often draw on Fourth Amendment jurisprudence on curtilage, where it has been defined as "generally the area so immediately and intimately connected to the home that within it, a resident's reasonable expectation of privacy should be respected."[89] Section 2 of the *Criminal Code* defines "dwelling-house" as a structure "kept or occupied as a permanent or temporary residence" and includes

> (a) a building within the curtilage of a dwelling-house that is connected to it by a doorway or by a covered and enclosed passageway, and
>
> (b) a unit that is designed to be mobile and to be used as a permanent or temporary residence and that is being used as such a residence.

---

83 *Ibid.*

84 *R v Campbell*, 2011 SCC 32 at para 15 [*Campbell*].

85 *Ibid.*

86 See further discussion of *Campbell* below in Section C(1).

87 *Caslake*, above note 17 at para 12.

88 *R v NM*, 2007 CanLII 31570 at para 368 (ON SC).

89 *Le*, above note 80 at para 81, citing *American Jurisprudence* 2d at para 69. *R v NM*, *ibid*, cites *US v Dunn*, 480 US 294 (1987) at 301 for four factors for ascertaining what falls within curtilage: "the proximity of the area claimed to be curtilage to the home, whether the area is included within an enclosure surrounding the home, the nature of the uses to which the area is put, and the steps taken by the resident to protect the area from observation by people passing by."

Caselaw is divided on whether detached garages not specified in a warrant are searchable.[90] Other detached structures on the property not mentioned in the warrant may not be searchable. In *R v LaPlante*, a garage converted to a workshop situated forty feet from the house was found not to be part of the house and required a separate warrant.[91] The Supreme Court held in *Sleeth v Hurlbert* (1896) that a description of a clearly defined parcel of land permits the search of all buildings on it—though in the post-*Charter* period, this would need to be applied with caution, likely requiring probable grounds for any building searched.[92]

Section 487(1)(b) permits the search of anything that will "afford evidence with respect to the commission of an offence." The Supreme Court in *CanadianOxy* held that this is to be broadly construed, "encompassing all materials which might shed light on the circumstances of an event which appears to constitute an offence."[93] This includes "anything relevant or rationally connected to the incident under investigation, the parties involved, and their potential culpability."[94] In a warrant under section 487, "things" searched for can include fingerprints and blood samples.[95] But "things" cannot be intangible. In *Re Bell Telephone Company of Canada*, the court held invalid a warrant that authorized the "seizure" of telephone lines and other equipment that would have remained in place—an attempt to engage in an interception or wiretapping of the lines.[96] A credit balance in a bank account is an intangible and could not be seized under an earlier equivalent to a section 487 warrant.[97] Where the subject matter of the search is sensitive, the justice issuing the warrant may impose reasonable conditions on the manner of search and what can be sought.[98]

---

90 *R v LaPlante*, 48 DLR (4th) 615 (Sask CA) [*LaPlante*]; *R v Hutmann*, [1996] AWLD 1105 (Alta Prov Ct); *R v Hall*, 2003 BCSC 1433; *R v M(N)*, 2007 CanLII 31570 (ON SC); *R v Vo*, 2011 ABQB 701; *R v Moser*, 2012 ONCJ 209.

91 *LaPlante*, above note 90 at 5–6, 31–32. See also *R v Burkoski*, 2017 ONSC 7399 holding unlawful a search in which police broke open a separate structure not named in the warrant.

92 *Sleeth v Hurlbert*, [1896] 25 SCR 620.

93 *CanadianOxy*, above note 35 at para 15.

94 *Ibid*.

95 *R v Millard and Smich*, 2015 ONSC 7500 at paras 25–28.

96 *Re Bell Telephone Company of Canada* (1947), 89 CCC 196 (Ont SC).

97 *Attorney General of Quebec v Royal Bank of Canada et al* (1985), 18 CCC (3d) 98 (QC CA).

98 *Descôteaux et al v Mierzwinski*, [1982] 1 SCR 860 at 883, confirming that a justice may be "more demanding before authorizing a search of a lawyer's office or one of his files and will lead him, where necessary, to set out special procedures for the execution of the warrant in order to limit what is absolutely inevitable the breach of confidentiality."

A warrant must be reasonably specific about what things police expect to find. In *Solloway Mills & Company (Re)*, the Court of Appeal for Alberta found a description in a warrant of "books of account, documents, securities . . . correspondence, papers and goods and chattels" to be insufficiently precise.[99] Yet in *Re Lubell and The Queen*, the court held that "[a] search warrant is not intended to be a carte blanche, but at the same time the applicants must be afforded a reasonable latitude in describing the things they have reasonable ground to believe they might find."[100] The Ontario Court of Appeal has held that documents can be validly described by class where "by the very nature of the things to be searched for it is not possible to describe them with precision or great particularity."[101] If police come across items not specified in the warrant, section 489(1) of the *Code* authorizes them to seize items they believe on reasonable grounds will afford evidence of an offence in the *Code* or other federal statute.[102] Police authorized under a warrant to search a place for evidence of a specified offence may not begin looking for evidence of another offence.[103]

R v Vu gave rise to a rule pertaining to computers.[104] The Supreme Court recognized that computers and phones are not like filing cabinets or other receptacles. They can contain enormous amounts of deeply personal information rendering a search of them highly invasive.[105] For this reason, when police have a warrant to search a place or thing, they are not authorized to search the content of a computer they find in the course of the search unless the warrant explicitly permits them to search a computer found there. This in turn would require specific grounds supporting a belief that evidence of an offence is likely to be found on the device. Where police come across a computer not mentioned in a warrant, *Vu* provides police authority to seize the device (if believed to

---

99 *Solloway Mills & Company (Re)*, [1930] 3 DLR 293, (Alta CA), finding the warrant invalid on other grounds.

100 *Re Lubell and The Queen* (1973), 11 CCC (2d) 188 (Ont SC). See also *Re PSI*, above note 76 at 270, upholding a warrant seeking documents in a fraud investigation containing the words "and other materials of every nature" on the basis that "there [were] many documents referring to various individuals and money transactions" and police could not be more specific at that stage.

101 *Church of Scientology and The Queen (No 6), Re* (1987), 2 ACWS (3d) 292 (Ont CA).

102 A "plain view" power is also found in s 11(8) of the *CDSA*, above note 59, and at common law; see the discussion of these powers in Chapter 6, Section B(1) and Chapter 6, Section D(2) respectively.

103 *R v Jones*, 2011 ONCA 632, applying this rule to a warranted search of a computer for evidence of fraud, holding that police were not authorized to begin looking for evidence of child pornography.

104 *R v Vu*, 2013 SCC 60.

105 *Ibid* at paras 40–45.

contain evidence of an offence) and take steps to preserve the data, but they must obtain a separate warrant to search it.[106]

As we noted earlier, a warrant under section 487 does not authorize police to search a person found within the place named in the warrant.[107] By contrast, the *CDSA* permits a peace officer executing a warrant issued under that Act to search a person found in a place named in the warrant where they have reasonable grounds to believe the person may have on their person "any controlled substance, precursor, property or thing set out in the warrant" and may seize it.[108]

A warrant under section 487 of the *Criminal Code* also differs from a *CDSA* warrant in that it need not be directed to a specific officer named in the warrant.[109] A warrant under section 11 of the *CDSA* must name a specific officer who will oversee the execution of the search.[110] The Supreme Court has held this to be an "important" requirement, the breach of which would not be considered minor or technical.[111] A warrant to search a home for drugs under the *CDSA* is a "significantly broader" power than the warrant under section 487 of the *Code*.[112] The latter is usually executed in the day; a *CDSA* warrant can be executed at any time; and different post-search reporting requirements apply in the case of a *CDSA* search with a warrant.[113]

---

106 *Ibid* at para 49, Cromwell J writing for the Court:

> If police come across a computer in the course of a search and their warrant does not provide specific authorization to search computers, they may seize the computer (assuming it may reasonably be thought to contain the sort of things that the warrant authorizes to be seized), and do what is necessary to ensure the integrity of the data. If they wish to search the data, however, they must obtain a separate warrant.

For further discussion of *Vu* and the search of computers, see Section B(4) below.

107 While there are no appellate authorities on point, a number of trial courts and commentators have held this view; see the survey of sources in *R v Kirby*, 2001 CanLII 18488 at paras 77–86 (MB PC).

108 *CDSA*, above note 59, s 11(5).

109 *R v Benz* (1986), 27 CCC (3d) 454 (Ont CA) at 462, an earlier version of s 487 "does not require that the peace officers to whom it is directed be specifically named." *R v Lucas*, 2009 CanLII 69326 (ON SC), holding at para 12: "Both in the former section and in the current section, the naming requirement does not apply to a peace officer but only to a person other than a peace officer who may be authorized to conduct a search."

110 Section 11(1) of the *CDSA*, above note 59, allows for "a warrant authorizing *a* peace officer, at any time, to search the place for any such controlled substance" (emphasis added).

111 *R v Genest*, [1989] 1 SCR 59 at 84.

112 *Ibid* at 85.

113 *Ibid*; *R v Strachan*, [1988] 2 SCR 980 at 996. See the discussion in Chapter 6, Section B(1) of the post-search reporting requirements under the *CDSA*, above note 59.

At least one court has held that a person present when a search warrant is executed owes no duty to assist police in its execution. In *Kukenmueller*, police asked the accused to guide them through his home to "minimize police interference with his property."[114] Justice Woodley, for the Ontario Superior Court of Justice, held that the assistance required the accused's informed consent. Without valid consent, the accused's compelled assistance rendered the search unreasonable under section 8 on the basis of being carried out in an unreasonable manner.[115]

A warrant under section 487 can be exercised anywhere in Canada, by a peace officer or someone with that authority.[116] Section 29 of the *Criminal Code* imposes a duty on a person executing a warrant to "have it with him, where it is feasible to do so, and to produce it when requested to do so." In *R v Cornell*, a team of officers executed a warrant but only the lead officer down the block had a copy.[117] He was at the residence four minutes later. The Supreme Court affirmed the finding at trial that it sufficed that a member of the team had a copy.[118] Justice Cromwell, for the majority, held that "the purpose of s. 29(1) of the Code is to allow the occupant of the premises to be searched to know why the search is being carried out, to allow assessment of his or her legal position and to know as well that there is a colour of authority for the search, making forcible resistance improper."[119] This is accomplished by having one member of the team with a copy of the warrant, but he suggested "it is a better practice for someone among the first group of officers in the door to have a copy on his or her person."[120]

A search must begin within the time parameters specified in the warrant, but it need not be completed within that time.[121] Appeal courts have held that "[t]here is an implied requirement that warrants be

---

114 *Kukemueller*, above note 64 at para 204.

115 *Ibid* at para 206; the discussion of consent appearing under the heading "Section 8 of the *Charter*—Manner of Search" at para 179.

116 Section 487(2) states "[a] warrant issued under subsection (1) may be executed at any place in Canada. A public officer named in the warrant, or any peace officer, who executes the warrant must have authority to act in that capacity in the place where the warrant is executed." Prior to amendments in 2019, s 487(2) required that a warrant to search a place in another province or territory had first to be endorsed by a justice in that jurisdiction.

117 *R v Cornell*, 2010 SCC 31 [*Cornell*].

118 *Ibid* at para 42.

119 *Ibid* at para 43.

120 *Ibid*.

121 *R v Anderson*, 2020 BCSC 2195 at para 28, citing *R v Cardinal*, 2003 BCSC 158; *R v Pickton*, 2006 BCSC 1090; and *R v Veranski and Bellotti*, 2012 BCSC 220. See also *R v Brown*, 2010 ONSC 2280; *R v Barwell*, [2013] OJ No 3743 (CJ); *R v Nurse and Plummer*, 2014 ONSC 1779.

executed within a reasonable time of being issued."[122] Section 488 of the *Code* states that a warrant under section 487 or 487.1 (a telewarrant) "shall be executed by day" unless "(a) the justice is satisfied that there are reasonable grounds for it to be executed by night; (b) the reasonable grounds are included in the information; (c) the warrant authorizes that it be executed by night." Appellate courts interpreting section 488 have held that exceptional circumstances are required to justify a nighttime search.[123] The presumption in favour of daytime execution "protect[s] citizens against the frightening experience of nighttime intrusions into their privacy."[124]

The Supreme Court has held that "[e]xcept in exigent circumstances, police officers must make an announcement before forcing entry into a dwelling house."[125] In the normal course, police should "give (i) notice of presence by knocking or ringing the door bell, (ii) notice of authority, by identifying themselves as law enforcement officers and (iii) notice of purpose, by stating a lawful reason for entry."[126] *Cornell* assessed the validity of a search with a warrant in which police forced entry unannounced, wearing balaclavas and body armour, with weapons drawn. Departing from the requirement to knock and announce their presence gives rise to an onus on police to "explain why they thought it necessary to do so."[127] The decision in *Cornell* impliedly affirms that the power to search with a warrant includes the power to use force and to break open doors. We address the manner of executing a warrant in more detail in Chapter 8.

5) Post-seizure Reporting and Return of Property

Finally, section 487 of the *Code* requires police to bring to a justice anything seized and to follow requirements in section 489.1. Sections 489.1 and 490 contain a framework for post-seizure reporting, detention, and return of things seized under any search warrant issued under the *Criminal Code* "or otherwise in the execution of duties under this or any other Act of Parliament."[128] The framework recognizes that we retain a privacy

122 *Saint*, above note 80 at para 9, citing *R v Coull*, 1986 CanLII 4753 at para 12 (BC CA).

123 *R v Carstairs*, 2022 BCCA 69; *R v Lowe*, 2018 ONCA 110.

124 *Pars Oriental Rug v Canada*, [1988] 88 BCJ No 3055, 18 CER 6 (SC).

125 *Cornell*, above note 117 at para 18.

126 *Ibid*, citing *Eccles*, above note 23 at 747.

127 *Cornell*, above note 117 at para 20.

128 *Criminal Code*, above note 4, s 489.1(1). Sections 489.1 and 490 apply to the seizure of "non-chemical offence related property" under the *CDSA*, above note 59, but see Chapter 6, Section B(1) for a discussion of the different reporting

interest in things seized. Often, more serious intrusions on privacy happen after something is seized.[129] The Supreme Court has held that where police fail to fulfill these requirements, the seizure can become unlawful, resulting in a violation of section 8.[130]

When does the framework apply? Addressing this question, the Ontario Court of Appeal in *R v Backhouse* noted that it would apply to things seized without a warrant pursuant to sections 487.11 and 489 of the *Code* (exigent search and plain view seizure, both discussed below).[131] Interpreting the meaning of a seizure conducted "in the execution of duties" under an Act of Parliament, the court held that the framework in sections 489.1 and 490 does not apply to searches under provincial legislation. It applies to things seized in a search incident to arrest, the court reasoned, because while the search power itself is a common law power, the officer carries out the arrest executing duties under the arrest provisions of the *Criminal Code*.[132] One might infer from this holding that a seizure that police conduct acting strictly upon common law authority would not trigger the reporting and retention requirements in sections 489.1 and 490.

Under the framework, at the outset, a peace officer must make a decision. If they no longer need to detain a thing seized for further investigation, prosecution or "other proceeding" *and* "there is no dispute as to who is lawfully entitled to possession of the thing seized," they may return it to that person and report this to a justice.[133] If the item will be

---

requirements that apply to the seizure of controlled substances and the forfeiture of offence-related property under that Act.

129 In *R v Craig*, 2016 BCCA 154 [*Craig*], Bennett J at para 180 stated:

> Once goods or things are seized, the invasion of privacy rights does not end. They will likely be examined or further searches conducted. For example, the contents of a computer or cell phone may be extracted; the things seized may be forensically tested for DNA, fingerprints, alcohol or drug content; the things seized may be copied, and financial documents may be audited. The privacy rights of a person connected to the seized items may be significantly engaged after the search itself has concluded.

130 *R v Reeves*, 2018 SCC 56 at paras 63–65, noting the failure to comply with the reporting requirements in s 489.1 and the detention limits in s 490(2) as distinct violations of s 8 of the *Charter*. See also *R v Garcia-Machado*, 2015 ONCA 569; *R v Butters*, 2015 ONCA 783; and *Craig*, above note 129.

131 *R v Backhouse* (2005), 195 OAC 80 at para 99 (Ont CA).

132 *Ibid* at para 103: "whatever may be said about other common law powers, it seems to me that an officer would be in execution of duties under the *Criminal Code* when making a search incident to an arrest for a *Criminal Code* offence. The arrest involves the exercise of a *Criminal Code* power. The officer is in execution of a duty directly tied to the enforcement of the *Criminal Code*."

133 *Criminal Code*, above note 4, s 489.1(1)(a).

needed or it is not clear to whom it should be returned, the officer must "as soon as is practicable" either bring the item itself or provide a report on it to a justice in a prescribed form.[134] In the latter case, the justice must deal with the thing seized in accordance with section 490. That section provides that a justice must order the thing returned to its lawful owner or possessor if they are known and if a peace officer or prosecutor does not persuade them that the thing seized is still needed for investigation, prosecution, or "other proceeding."[135] The provision does not contain a notice requirement, and the hearing is typically conducted *ex parte*. The justice can order the thing detained or permit its return outright or permit its return on the condition that the owner or possessor take "reasonable care to ensure that [the thing] is preserved" until the end of the investigation or prosecution.[136] Where the court decides that it is necessary to detain a thing seized, subsections of section 490 authorize detention for various periods, but generally, the thing seized can be kept for however long once "proceedings are instituted in which the thing detained may be required."[137] Further subsections of section 490 provide for applications to be made for return of an item at later stages of a proceeding and on appeal.

C. CHALLENGING A SEARCH OR SEIZURE WITH A WARRANT

A warrant under section 487 of the *Code* may be issued on reasonable and probable grounds to believe an offence has been committed and evidence will be found in the place to be searched. The task for police, when preparing and submitting an "information to obtain" a warrant to a justice or judge (an ITO), is to establish reasonable grounds to believe a particular offence (or set of them) has been or is being committed and to identify the specific evidence of the offence that is likely to be found in a specific place they propose to search. Police, or anyone applying for a warrant, have an obligation when writing an ITO to make "full and frank disclosure of material facts."[138] As Le Bel J put it in *Araujo*:

> So long as the affidavit meets the requisite legal norm, there is no need for it to be as lengthy as *À la recherche du temps perdu*, as lively as the

134 *Ibid*, s 489.1(1)(b).
135 *Ibid*, s 490(1).
136 *Ibid*.
137 *Criminal Code*, above note 4, s 490(2), (3).
138 *Araujo*, above note 40 at para 46.

> *Kama Sutra*, or as detailed as an automotive repair manual. All that it must do is set out the facts fully and frankly for the authorizing judge in order that he or she can make an assessment of whether these rise to the standard required in the legal test for the authorization.[139]

The ITO should "never attempt to trick its readers" either by "the language used or strategic omissions."[140] Justice Fish, in *Morelli* expanded on this requirement:

> When seeking an ex parte authorization such as a search warrant, a police officer — indeed, any informant — must be particularly careful not to "pick and choose" among the relevant facts in order to achieve the desired outcome. The informant's obligation is to present all material facts, favourable or not. Concision, a laudable objective, may be achieved by omitting irrelevant or insignificant details, but not by material non-disclosure.[141]

Errors and omissions may not come to light until a warrant is challenged, though once it is, a court may find that an affiant's failure to make full and frank disclosure has rendered the warrant invalid.

One challenges a search or seizure carried out with a warrant — as with any challenge under section 8 — by making a motion at trial to have the evidence obtained as a result of it excluded (under section 24(2) of the *Charter*) on the basis that it amounted to an unreasonable search.[142] There are many bases for challenging a warranted search or seizure. The focus in what follows is on the possibility of arguing that (despite the view of the justice who issued the warrant), the ITO did not disclose what amounted to reasonable grounds. But the reader should keep in mind that a party might challenge a search or seizure conducted pursuant to a warrant for a host of other possible reasons, including the terms of the warrant being unreasonable, police exceeding these terms and thus acting without authority (as discussed earlier in this chapter),

---

139 *Ibid*.

140 *Ibid* at 47.

141 *Morelli*, above note 41 at para 58.

142 The general practice is for the accused's counsel to provide the Crown with a "*Charter* notice" setting out a brief description of the factual basis and caselaw on which they will rely in making their application. The Supreme Court in *R v Cody*, 2017 SCC 31 at para 38, approved of the process described in *R v Kutynec* (1992), 7 OR (3d) 277 (CA) and *R v Vukelich* (1996), 108 CCC (3d) 193 (BCCA) of allowing judges at the outset of a *Charter* motion to consider whether the motion has "a reasonable prospect of success" and to dismiss it summarily if the notice or summary "reveals no basis upon which the application could succeed."

or police conducting the search in an unreasonable manner (the topic of Chapter 8).

The most common kind of challenge to a search or seizure with a warrant involves a challenge to whether the ITO disclosed what amounted to reasonable and probable grounds to believe an offence has been committed and evidence of it would be found in the place to be searched or the thing to be seized. The party challenging the validity of the warrant (typically the accused in a criminal case) bears the onus of demonstrating that the ITO on which it was based was insufficient.[143] Justice Le Bel in *R v Araujo* articulated the test for a court reviewing whether the ITO was sufficient; the court should ask "whether there was reliable evidence that might reasonably be believed on the basis of which the authorization could have issued."[144] *Araujo* dealt with a challenge to a warrant for a wiretap, but the Supreme Court in *Morelli* applied the test in *Araujo* to review a warrant issued under section 487 of the *Code*.[145] Justice Fish, writing for the majority, expanded on the test by holding:

> The question is not whether the reviewing court would itself have issued the warrant, but whether there was sufficient credible and reliable evidence [in the ITO] to permit a justice of the peace to find reasonable and probable grounds to believe that an offence had been committed and that evidence of that offence would be found at the specified time and place.[146]

The reviewing court might take a different view of the ITO, but it should not substitute its view for that of the justice who issued the warrant. Only if there is no reasonable basis for finding the standard had been met will the warrant be held to have been invalidly issued.[147]

143 *Campbell*, above note 84 at para 14.

144 *Araujo*, above note 40 at para 55, citing the same test from *Garofoli*, above note 23 at 1452.

145 *Morelli*, above note 41 at para 40, Fish J, for the majority, citing the test in *Araujo*; Deschamps J for the dissent cites it at para 130.

146 *Morelli*, above note 41 at para 40.

147 This would not automatically make the search unreasonable. The question would then be whether there was other authority for the search. In most cases, however, where the court finds that a warrant was invalid, the Crown presents no alternative authority for the search and the court concludes the search was unreasonable. In some cases, depending on the facts, the Crown might rely on authority to search in exigent circumstances, consent, plain view seizure powers, or other authority (all discussed further in Chapter 6).

1) Facial and Sub-facial Challenges

The caselaw refers to two kinds of challenge to an ITO: a "facial" and "sub-facial" challenge. In a facial challenge, the court looks only at the text of the ITO itself to determine whether, on its face, the justice could have issued the warrant (i.e., whether the ITO did disclose reasonable grounds). In the course of a facial review, the challenger might establish in evidence that some of the details contained in the ITO are erroneous and these would be struck or "excised" from consideration on review.[148]

In a sub-facial challenge, the reviewing judge considers the ITO along with what are called "amplifications": further details police may testify to in the course of the *voir dire* to correct minor errors or omissions in the ITO made in good faith, or to clarify unclear details.[149] Police should not be strategic in their use of this window, deliberately withholding details or qualifications to their grounds for amplification on a challenge, because this could amount to "circumventing" the warrant requirement and "turning the authorization procedure into a sham."[150] A more probing form of sub-facial challenge may involve disclosing the identity of, or seeking to cross-examine, a confidential informant who served as a source of information for the affiant or author of the ITO. In this case, the question is whether disclosing the identity of the informant is "necessary to demonstrate the innocence of the accused."[151]

After a facial or sub-facial assessment, the reviewing judge decides whether the ITO, on its face or on the "amplified record," satisfies the test in *Araujo* of whether "there was reliable evidence that might reasonably be believed on the basis of which the authorization could have issued."[152] The assessment is contextual and must take into consideration all the circumstances.[153] As Le Bel J noted in *Araujo*, "errors, even fraudulent errors, do not automatically invalidate the warrant."[154] But if police

148 *Morelli*, above note 41 at para 41; *Araujo*, above note 40 at para 58.

149 *Morelli*, above note 41 at para 41.

150 *Araujo*, above note 40 at para 59.

151 *Leipert*, above note 44 at para 21.

152 *Araujo*, above note 40 at para 54.

153 *Ibid.*

154 *Ibid.* See also *Garofoli* above note 23 at 1452, Sopinka J, for the majority holding:

> If, based on the record which was before the authorizing judge as amplified on the review, the reviewing judge concludes that the authorizing judge could have granted the authorization, then he or she should not interfere. In this process, the existence of fraud, non-disclosure, misleading evidence and new evidence are all relevant, but, rather than being a prerequisite to review, their sole impact is to determine whether there continues to be any basis for the decision of the authorizing judge.

conduct is "so subversive" of the application process, this alone might be cause to find the warrant invalid.[155]

The Supreme Court has provided further insight into the process of challenging a warrant on the basis of an ITO in a series of cases. *Garofoli* involved a challenge to a wiretap or interception under Part VI of the *Code*, but many of its holdings apply to challenging warrants more broadly.[156] Justice Sopinka, for the majority, sought to resolve disparities and complexities in the process for gaining access to the sealed packet (the ITO and warrant) and for challenging a wiretap. He did so largely by affirming the trial judge's authority to consider various possible challenges to the validity of a wiretap authorization, along with the scope and manner of the surveillance carried out (rather than having to return before the issuing judge or court).[157] Parliament has since amended the *Code* to further clarify the role of the trial judge in Part VI interceptions and to codify the accused's entitlement to the unsealed packet in advance of trial.[158] Yet *Garofoli* continues to be relevant to the process of unsealing a warrant application, examining affiants, and the grounds on which the warrant may be challenged.

The holdings in *Garofoli* turn in part on the slightly different test for issuing a "standard" third-party authorization under Part VI of the *Code* from the one for granting a warrant under section 487.[159] The applicant must meet the *Hunter*-compliant standard of showing "reasonable and probable grounds to believe that an offence has been, or is being, committed and that the authorization sought will afford evidence of that offence."[160] But they must also persuade the court that a wiretap is in the "best interests of the administration of justice" and that "other investigative procedures" have failed, are unlikely to succeed, or urgency renders them impracticable.[161]

As with the standard on review for section 487 warrants, when reviewing an ITO for a wiretap warrant, the question is not whether the reviewing judge would have issued the authorization but whether "the

155 *Araujo*, above note 40 at para 54.

156 *Garofoli*, above note 23.

157 *Ibid* at 1445–51.

158 See the discussion about s 187(1.4) and (4) of the *Criminal Code*, above note 4, in Section A(2)(d) of Chapter 6.

159 Interceptions under Part VI of the *Code* are discussed in more detail in Chapter 6, Section A(2).

160 *Garofoli*, above note 23 at 1444, citing La Forest J for the majority in *R v Duarte*, [1990] 1 SCR 30 at 45.

161 *Criminal Code*, above note 4, s 186(1); *Garofoli* considered an earlier version of the provision that was substantially the same.

authorizing judge could have granted the authorization."[162] That judge could not have granted one only where the trial judge concludes "on the material before the authorizing judge, there was no basis upon which he could be satisfied that the pre-conditions for granting of the authorization exist."[163] The majority here overturned an earlier, more stringent standard of having to establish fraud, misleading, or new evidence as a precondition to review.[164] In the course of a review, hearsay from an informant may provide grounds, but a tip from a single informant to police would not, on its own, constitute reasonable grounds, unless in the totality of the circumstances there were further indicia of reliability supporting the tip. This might include the degree of detail, the informer's source, their past performance, or confirmation from other sources.[165]

Justice Sopinka also considered the form in which the ITO should be disclosed to the accused. Section 187 of the *Code* permits a judge unsealing a wiretap authorization to provide an edited version that protects the identity of informants, ongoing investigations, or police techniques.[166] But the section does not speak to the principles informing this exercise. Considering an earlier equivalent to this list of factors at common law, Sopinka J held that deciding what to include or redact in an unsealed ITO "will require the balancing of the relevance of the identity of the informer to the accused's case against the prejudice to the informer and to the public interest in law enforcement which disclosure would occasion."[167] He then proceeded to set out a process to follow on an application under section 187(4) by which the Crown first suggests redactions to the judge, who then produces a version to provide to counsel for the accused and if necessary a "judicial summary as to the general nature of the deletions."[168] The judge must balance two conflicting needs. The Crown needs the court to consider enough of the excised material "as is necessary to support the authorization." But the accused needs to be "sufficiently aware of the nature of the excised material to challenge it."[169] If the judge is not satisfied that the judicial summary provides the accused enough to work with, more detail may need to be disclosed. If they order an amount of information that would incline the Crown to

162 *Garofoli*, above note 23 at 1452.

163 *Ibid*, adopting the test Martin JA of the Ontario Court of Appeal set out in the decision below.

164 *Ibid*, rejecting the approach in *Wilson v The Queen*, [1983] 2 SCR 594.

165 *Garofoli*, above note 23 at 1456–57.

166 *Criminal Code*, above note 4, s 187(4).

167 *Garofoli*, above note 23 at 1460, citing the factors in *R v Parmar* (1987), 34 CCC (3d) 260 at 281–82 (Ont HC), which serve as the source for those in s 187(4).

168 *Garofoli*, above note 23 at 1461.

169 *Ibid*.

believe "the public interest would be prejudiced," they may "withdraw tender of the wiretap evidence."[170]

Garofoli also addressed the issue of when an accused is entitled to cross-examine the affiant or author of an ITO. Lower courts had required proof of deliberate falsehood or reckless disregard for truth before allowing cross-examination.[171] Justice Sopinka affirmed a less restrictive test. The accused must first seek and may then be granted leave to cross-examine an affiant when the court is "satisfied that cross examination is necessary to enable the accused to make full answer and defence."[172] To establish necessity, the accused must demonstrate that cross-examination will "elicit testimony tending to discredit the existence of one of the preconditions to the authorization, as for example the existence of reasonable and probable grounds."[173] Questions should be limited to showing "there was no basis upon which the authorization could have been granted."

The accused in *Garofoli* took issue with information the affiant claims he received from a confidential informer who had proved reliable in the past. The informer advised the affiant that the accused had offered to supply him with cocaine in Hamilton in December 1982. The accused contended that this could not have happened since he was not in Hamilton that month and that the officer in charge of the investigation knew this. Had the affiant made inquiries, this would have become readily apparent. The Court held that the accused was entitled to cross-examine the affiant given the disparity in his whereabouts and the fact that the information about the offer of supply came from an informant.[174] Discrediting the informer would undermine the entire ITO. However, as Sopinka J noted, in order to examine an *informer* himself (rather than the affiant), the accused must bring themselves within the "innocence at stake" exception—a matter the Court would focus on in *Leipert*.[175]

---

170 Justice Sopinka, for a majority of the Court in *R v Durette*, [1994] 1 SCR 469 at 495, held that the accused is presumptively entitled to full disclosure of an ITO under s 187 and that the Crown must establish that redactions are necessary "by showing that the public interest in non-disclosure outweighs the accused's interest in disclosure." In that case, the ITO disclosed to the accused had redacted information that had been made public in an earlier proceeding and did not relate to the factors in s 187(4).

171 *Garofoli*, above note 23, Sopinka J summarizing the cases at 1463.

172 *Ibid* at 1466.

173 *Ibid* at 1465. The Court clarified in *R v Pires*; *R v Lising*, 2005 SCC 66 at para 3, that the "*Garofoli* threshold test requires that the defence show a reasonable likelihood that cross-examination of the affiant will elicit testimony of probative value to the issue for consideration by the reviewing judge."

174 *Garofoli*, above note 23 at 1466.

175 *Ibid* at 1465; *Leipert*, above note 44.

In *Araujo*, police investigating a drug case obtained a wiretap warrant on the basis of a 130-page ITO.[176] The affiant detailed information gathered through other officers from ten confidential informants labelled A through J. In the course of being cross-examined on the ITO in a *voir dire* at trial, the affiant conceded that in various places he referred mistakenly to E when he meant to refer to F. Later in his evidence, he indicated the correct source in these passages was C. The affiant was aware of the error weeks prior to trial, had forgotten it, and was only reminded in cross-examination. The trial judge found the affiant to lack credibility to an extent that "permeate[d] the issue of reasonable and probable grounds," rendering the entire ITO "unreliable."[177] He held the wiretap evidence to be obtained unreasonably and excluded it. Justice Le Bel for the Supreme Court held that the errors at issue were minor and did not affect the substance of the information in the affidavit.[178] A reviewing court must "look at non-disclosure of any material fact . . . 'with respect to the affidavit considered as a whole, or even with respect to the remaining parts of it.'"[179] Even without detail from sources C or E, the affidavit provided "ample evidence . . . of probable grounds and investigative necessity."[180] Despite the drafting errors in the ITO, the warrant was validly issued.

Morelli offers a helpful contrast to *Araujo*.[181] In *Morelli*, police obtained a warrant to search an accused's computer for the offence of possessing child pornography. A majority of the Supreme Court held that the ITO was so deficient that the warrant should not have been issued. In contrast to *Araujo*, the discrepancies in the ITO were not minor and they undermined the necessary basis for believing the offence at issue had even occurred.

The accused in *Morelli* had ordered a high-speed internet connection to be installed in his home. A computer technician came to his home unannounced, while he was home alone with his three-year-old daughter. The accused's computer was located in a spare bedroom where the child was playing with toys on the floor. The computer was online and when the technician checked Morelli's web browser, he noticed links to adult and child pornography in the "favourites" list. Two were labelled "Lolita Porn" and "Lolita XXX."[182] He saw a pornographic image but

176 *Araujo*, above note 40.

177 *Ibid* at para 8.

178 *Ibid* at para 60.

179 *Ibid* at para 57, citing *R v Bisson*, [1994] 3 SCR 1097 at 1098, affirming the reasons of Proulx JA in the Quebec Court of Appeal, (1994), 60 CAQ 173.

180 *Araujo*, above note 40 at para 61.

181 *Morelli*, above note 41.

182 *Ibid* at para 118.

could not recall whether it was within the browser or on the computer's desktop. He also took notice of videocassettes of home videos and a webcam placed on a tripod, connected to a video recorder, and pointed at toys and the child rather than the seat in front of the computer. The technician could not complete the task and had to return the next morning. When he did so, the room had been tidied up, toys and videotapes had been put away, and the webcam was pointed at the computer user's chair. The computer appeared to be reformatted, with desktop icons no longer present. After the visit, the technician looked up some of the websites mentioned in the favourites list and saw that they depicted what he believed to be child pornography. A while later, he contacted a social worker who contacted police. Two months later, an officer obtained a statement from the technician, consulted other officers with experience investigating computer crimes, and drafted the ITO. A warrant was quickly issued and executed, with police finding child pornography.

Justice Fish, writing for the majority, first clarified that in order to possess child pornography under the *Code*, the Crown must establish "possession of the underlying data files in some way."[183] The ITO in this case alleged that the accused had possessed child pornography—rather than that he had *accessed* it, which Parliament had chosen to treat as a discrete and separate offence.[184] The majority found numerous errors and omissions in the ITO, concluding that it "could not possibly have afforded reasonable and probable grounds to believe that the accused possessed child pornography and that evidence of that crime would be found on his computer."[185] The affiant in the ITO misleadingly characterized the technician as having himself viewed the child pornography on the computer rather than having seen only bookmarks and icons.[186] In making certain omissions, the officer's summary of the technician's information was less than full and frank. He did not mention that "Lolita" bookmarks were "just scattered through the [list of] favourites" that also included adult pornographic websites, nor the point that the only graphic image the technician did see directly was a lawful adult image—suggesting, instead, a person "particularly inclined towards child pornography."[187] Computer details in the ITO were followed closely by discussion of the "web-cam pointing towards [children's] toys," a

183 *Ibid* at para 14, discussing s 163.1(4) of the *Criminal Code*, above note 4.

184 This is found in s 163.1(4.1) of the *Code*.

185 *Morelli*, above note 41 at 44.

186 This was partly implied by the assertion that when the technician returned the next day "all the child porn off the computer was gone" (*ibid* at para 47).

187 *Ibid* at paras 50–51.

point on which the ITO had "placed great emphasis."[188] Framing the observations in this way strongly suggested the accused was making and possessing his own child porn.[189] The ITO did not identify the child present as the accused's daughter, nor mention that his wife also lived with them. It also failed to mention the child was clothed and that there was no evidence of abuse.

Justice Fish held that when the ITO in *Morelli* was "amplified" to include these and other omitted facts, an innocent explanation was more likely: the accused was capturing images of his daughter for posterity. The officer had a duty to make full and frank disclosure, to be careful not to omit material facts, nor to "invite an inference that would not be drawn or a conclusion that would not be reached if the omitted facts were disclosed."[190] He may not have been intentionally misleading here, but he was "selective" in his presentation. On review, the gaps in the ITO must be filled in, and there could then be only two bases on which the warrant *could* have been issued: (1) the bookmarks and (2) other information about "types of offenders" who gather images and reasons to believe the accused was of this type.[191] On the evidence, both were purely speculative grounds. The bookmarks were not evidence of possessing files. The assertion that there is a "type" of child porn collector rested on evidence of two police officers who referred to a tendency to categorize and store material on disks—evidence that seemed tenuous on its own.[192] As Fish J held, "[t]o permit reliance on broad generalizations about loosely defined classes of people is to invite dependence on stereotypes and prejudices in lieu of evidence."[193] Cleaning up the room added nothing to the grounds; it was perfectly consistent with the possibility that the accused wanted to avoid a guest seeing the home in a disorderly state. The warrant should not have been issued, and the search and seizure violated section 8.

A further case to consider in relation to warrant applications is *Campbell*, which deals with the common problem of searches involving buildings or dwellings with multiple and separate residences.[194] In this case, police obtained a warrant to search a four-bedroom townhouse being used as a rooming house. Police found a sawed-off shotgun and ammunition in a room in the basement the accused was renting,

188 *Ibid* at para 53.
189 *Ibid* at para 54.
190 *Ibid* at para 58.
191 *Ibid* at para 63.
192 *Ibid* at para 72.
193 *Ibid* at para 79.
194 *Campbell*, above note 84.

resulting in weapons charges. The accused had to walk through the first floor to reach his room. There were three further rooms on the second floor; a shared kitchen, living room, and dining room on the first floor; and a separate kitchen and bathroom in the basement. The four bedrooms were rented and each had a lock on the door. Police discovered the remains of the body of a female tenant of the upper floor 100 metres from the house, inside a "large black sports bag," and found that she had been stabbed to death.[195] They also found a receipt near the body with the name and townhouse address of another upper-floor tenant, IR. Campbell told police he had never been to the second floor and IR told them that Campbell used black bags when moving into the house. At trial, Campbell argued the ITO did not disclose sufficient grounds to justify searching his room.

The trial judge agreed with Campbell, finding the ITO deficient on various grounds, including that the affiant had "overstated the tenants' knowledge of each other's comings and goings," misleadingly suggesting a greater likelihood of cooperation or co-involvement in the offence.[196] The affiant's suggestion that the units may not have been "properly secured" was speculative. The ITO was also drafted in a way that seemed "intentionally confusing and opaque." Justice Charron, for a unanimous Court, agreed with the assessment of the majority of the Ontario Court of Appeal, which held that the trial judge was too selective in her analysis. The trial judge had also discounted important facts, including that Campbell was the only person connected to the black bag and the only tenant with a history of violence against women. Justice Charron recognized that a tenant's "expectation of privacy in his room within [a] townhouse is just as high as that of a resident of a single dwelling unit."[197] She held more broadly that "[i]n drafting ITOs proposing to search more than one unit within a multi-unit dwelling, this principle should be reflected by clearly setting out reasonable and probable grounds for each unit to be searched."[198] In this case, the shared space throughout the home made the "tenants' residences . . . connected and overlapping" in ways not found in a larger apartment building.[199] The ITO had plausibly suggested a likelihood of Campbell's involvement in the offence, given his record, ease of access and opportunity, and tie to the black bag.[200]

---

195 *Ibid* at para 7.

196 *Ibid* at para 10.

197 *Ibid* at para 15.

198 *Ibid*.

199 *Ibid*, citing Doherty JA's dissent in the court below.

200 *Ibid* at paras 11 and 15.

2) Challenging Multiple Searches

In Chapter 2, we noted a procedural point it may be helpful to reiterate here. Police often use the fruit of one search as grounds for obtaining a warrant to carry out a second search, which might in turn furnish grounds for yet a further search. When reviewing the validity of these searches, the court may find that the first search was carried out unlawfully and in violation of section 8. If so, the fruit of this search will be removed from consideration when assessing the validity of the warrant issued for the second search. And if this too is found invalid, information obtained from this search must be removed from consideration of the validity of a further search—leading to a possible domino effect, with one unlawful search rendering all later searches unreasonable. Put another way, after concluding that a first search was unreasonable, the court will not stop to conduct an assessment under section 24(2) about excluding evidence to decide whether police in the second search were entitled to rely on information obtained in the first search.

The example we cited in Chapter 2 was found in *R v Evans*, where police carried out a search by knocking on the accused's front door to sniff odours emanating from within and used this information to obtain a warrant to search the home.[201] The initial (sniff) search was held to be unreasonable; the grounds obtained from this search had to be excised from the grounds for obtaining the warrant; the warrant was invalid, rendering the second search (of the home) unreasonable.

201 *R v Evans*, [1996] 1 SCR 8.

CHAPTER 6

SEARCHES AND SEIZURES AUTHORIZED BY LAW 2: OTHER AUTHORITY

This chapter continues the overview we began in the previous chapter of sources in law that authorize police or other state actors to conduct a search or seizure. As we noted in Chapter 5, whether a search or seizure violates section 8 of the *Charter* turns in part on whether it was authorized.[1] A person challenging a search or seizure must first establish that they had a reasonable expectation of privacy in the place or thing a state actor has searched or seized. The burden then shifts to the Crown to establish the search or seizure was reasonable. To do so, the Crown must prove the search or seizure was authorized by law, the law was reasonable, and the search or seizure was conducted in a reasonable manner.[2]

In the previous chapter we looked at one of the most common sources of authority to search or seize: the standard warrant under section 487 of the *Criminal Code*,[3] the process and standard for issuing it, and how to challenge a search with a warrant. In this chapter, we survey other authority to search and seize in the *Criminal Code*, along with powers in other federal statutes, provincial legislation, and at common law. Our aim here is to provide an overview of the wide range of powers available and to highlight their basic features.

1 *Canadian Charter of Rights and Freedoms*, Part I of the *Constitution Act, 1982*, being Schedule B to the *Canada Act 1982* (UK), 1982, c 11 [*Charter*].

2 *R v Collins*, [1987] 1 SCR 265 at 278.

3 *Criminal Code*, RSC 1985, c C-46 [*Criminal Code* or *Code*].

A. OTHER *CRIMINAL CODE* POWERS

1) General Warrants (Section 487.01)

The general warrant provisions in section 487.01 of the *Code* permit a kind of catch-all form of warrant—a warrant of last resort when no other investigative tool will suffice. We place it here rather than later in our survey because the wiretap provisions of the *Code*, which we turn to next, make frequent reference to the general warrant provisions.

Section 487.01(1) allows the police to obtain a warrant to use "any device or investigative technique or procedure or do any thing described in the warrant that would, if not authorized, constitute an unreasonable search or seizure in respect of a person or a person's property." The issuing judge must be satisfied there are reasonable grounds to believe a federal offence has been committed and "information concerning the offence will be obtained through the use of the technique, procedure or device or the doing of the thing"; it would be "in the best interests of the administration of justice"; and there is "no other provision in this or any other Act of Parliament that would provide for a warrant, authorization or order permitting the technique, procedure or device to be used or the thing to be done." A general warrant may not authorize "interference with bodily integrity."[4] It may contain "such terms and conditions as the judge considers advisable to ensure that any search or seizure authorized by the warrant is reasonable in the circumstances."[5] Section 487.01(4) and (5) provide for a general warrant involving video surveillance. Police applying for it must meet the test in section 487.01(1) and also the requirements of Part VI of the *Code*—which we discuss further in the next section. A general warrant may be issued by a provincial or superior court judge (though a video warrant would, in some cases, require a superior court judge).[6] The application for a general warrant may be made by telewarrant as set out in section 487.1. And where a general warrant authorizes police "to enter and search a place covertly," it must require police to give notice of this, after the fact, at a time the court considers reasonable in the circumstances.[7] No time limits are set on the duration of a general warrant, but renewal may not exceed three years.[8]

Parliament added the general warrant provisions to the *Code* in 1993 partly in response to the Supreme Court's holdings in *R v Duarte*

4 *Ibid*, s 487.01(2).

5 *Ibid*, s 487.01(3).

6 See the discussion of Part VI authorizations in Section A(2) below.

7 *Criminal Code*, above note 3, s 487.01(5.1).

8 *Ibid*, s 487.01(5.2).

and *R v Wong*.[9] In *Duarte*, police installed audiovisual surveillance on a wall in an apartment in which an undercover officer and an informer spoke with the accused. The Court held that even with the consent of two parties to the conversation (the officer and the informer), police required a warrant.[10] In *Wong*, acting without a warrant, police installed video surveillance behind the curtain in a hotel room in the course of investigating a suspected illegal gaming operation. The majority found a reasonable expectation of privacy in the circumstances and held that police needed a warrant to conduct surreptitious video surveillance of a private communication, and that it could not be authorized by the wiretap provisions of Part VI of the *Code*.

The Supreme Court shed some light on the application of general warrants in *R v TELUS Communications Co*.[11] Police had obtained a general warrant under section 487.01 ordering Telus to disclose any text messages sent and received between two accounts for two weeks. Police had sought a general warrant for disclosure because, in distinction to other service providers, Telus happened to temporarily copy and store text messages on its servers. Five members of a seven-member panel of the Court held the warrant invalid and that the search required authorization under the wiretap provisions in Part VI of the *Code*. For Abella, Fish, and LeBel JJ, this was an intercept because the use of the word "intercept" in Part VI "implies that the private communication is acquired in the course of the communication process."[12] The warrant here allowed for the capture of ongoing communications. Part VI should not be read in a narrow technical fashion, as was done here, but in a manner consistent with Parliament's broader intention of protecting private communications from surreptitious state interception. Justices Moldaver and Karakatsanis resisted defining what occurred here as an interception but held that it was "substantially equivalent."[13] A general warrant should not have been issued, given the precondition for issuing one, set out in section 487.01(1)(c), that there be "no other provision" for such a search.[14] This requirement "ensures that the general warrant is used sparingly as a warrant of limited resort" and that it not become an "easy

9 *R v Duarte*, [1990] 1 SCR 30 [*Duarte*]; *R v Wong*, [1990] 3 SCR 36.

10 We discuss *Duarte* further in Section A(2), below.

11 2013 SCC 16 [*TELUS*].

12 *Ibid* at para 37.

13 *Ibid* at para 52.

14 *Ibid* at para 55.

back door for other techniques that have more demanding pre-authorization requirements."[15]

Another requirement in section 487.01 — that the warrant be "in the best interests of the administration of justice" — borrows language from older provisions on wiretaps in Part IV of the *Code*. In *R v Finlay and Grellete*, involving an early *Charter* challenge to a warrant provision of Part VI, Martin JA for the Ontario Court of Appeal held:

> Although the term "in the best interests of the administration of justice" is incapable of precise definition it imports, in my view, in the context, two readily identifiable and mutually supportive components. The first component is that the judge must be satisfied that the granting of the authorization will further or advance the objectives of justice. The second component imports a balancing of the interests of law enforcement and the individual's interest in privacy.[16]

2) Wiretaps and Other Electronic Surveillance

The Supreme Court held in *Duarte* and *Fliss* that where police record a private conversation, they carry out a search.[17] Part VI of the *Code* contains an extensive scheme for authorizing surveillance by state agents, though there are provisions in other parts of the *Code* allowing for other forms of surveillance or electronic monitoring (discussed below).

First added to the *Code* in 1974, Part VI has three key features.[18] Section 184(1) makes it an offence to "intercept" or eavesdrop on a "private communication" between other people *with a device*. Section 184(2) sets out exceptions to the offence, allowing for "interceptions" with a device in certain cases — most importantly, with the consent of one party to the communication or with authorization (i.e., involving state agents using a device).[19] And third, Part VI provides three kinds of warrants ("authorizations to intercept"): what have been called standard or "full-blown" third-party interceptions; consent interceptions; and emergency interceptions.[20]

---

15 *Ibid* at para 56, citing Scott C. Hutchinson et al, *Search and Seizure Law in Canada*, vol 1 (Toronto: Carswell, 2005).

16 *R v Finlay and Grellette*, 52 OR (2d) 63 (CA) [*Finlay and Grellette*].

17 *Duarte*, above note 9 at 42–43; *R v Fliss*, 2002 SCC 16.

18 What is now Part VI of the *Criminal Code* was initially Part IV.1 and became Part VI in 1985.

19 The other exceptions set out in s 184(2) provide for interceptions in the course of technical maintenance of a communication system, "quality of service," or state agents involved in "frequency spectrum management."

20 We adopt the phrases "standard intercepts" and "consent intercepts" from c 11 of James A. Fontana & David Keeshan, *The Law of Search & Seizure in Canada*, 12th ed (Toronto: LexisNexis Canada, 2021).

The interceptions provided for in warrants under Part VI are for listening to or recording *oral* communications with a device. A warrant for video surveillance is available in section 487.01(4)—though, as discussed below, section 487.01(5) incorporates the same limitations and requirements of Part VI authorizations.[21]

Wiretap warrants in Part VI ("authorizations") are available for investigations of certain offences set out in section 183. The list is long and includes offences in the *Code* and other federal statutes involving violence, fraud, conspiracy, sexual assault, terrorism, and organized crime.[22]

Section 183 defines terms that apply in Part VI. A "private communication" is an oral communication or a "telecommunication"— a term defined in the *Interpretation Act* to be anything transmitted by an "electromagnetic system"—by or to a person in Canada where the originator reasonably expects that it will not be received by anyone other than their intended recipient.[23] An "intercept" includes the act of "listen[ing] to, record[ing] or acquir[ing] a communication" or "the substance, meaning or purport thereof."[24]

As noted earlier, in *TELUS Communications Co*, the Supreme Court held that a general warrant authorizing disclosure of text messages temporarily stored on Telus servers was invalid because it permitted capture of texts to be sent in the future.[25] The majority held that authorization should have been sought under Part IV of the *Code*, though members of the panel offered different reasons: for three judges, what police sought to do here amounted to an intercept; for two judges, it was "substantially equivalent." By contrast, in *R v Jones*, the Supreme Court addressed whether data obtained pursuant to a production order under section 487.014 of the *Code* (discussed below) constituted an intercept under section 183.[26] The majority held that because the order only permitted access to stored messages rather than future messages, it was not

---

21 Under s 186 of the *Criminal Code*, police often apply for two or more separate warrants simultaneously to facilitate multiple forms of electronic surveillance.

22 Some authorities contend that the offences set out in s 183 limit only non-consent interceptions on the basis that the provision allowing for consent interceptions, s 184.2(2), refers to "an offence" whereas s 183 defines the meaning of "offence." Section 185, permitting non-consent interceptions, refers in s 185(1)(e) to "the offence." We do not see the merit in these distinctions and suggest that the more plausible way to read these sections is to assume that all authorizations under Part VI are limited to the list of offences in s 183. For further perspective on this point, see Steve Coughlan, *Criminal Procedure*, 4th ed (Toronto: Irwin Law, 2020) at 156, n 347 [Coughlan].

23 *Interpretation Act*, RSC 1985, c I-21, s 35(1) [*Interpretation Act*].

24 *Criminal Code*, above note 3, s 183.

25 *TELUS*, above note 11.

26 *R v Jones*, 2017 SCC 60 [*Jones*].

an intercept. A production order rather than an authorization under Part VI was appropriate.

As noted, Part VI of the *Code* provides three forms of authorization for state agents seeking to lawfully intercept a communication with a device. They fall within the following three categories.

a) Standard Interceptions

Where police seek to intercept a conversation—to listen or record—without the consent of any of its parties, they must apply for a warrant under sections 185 and 186 of the *Code*. Only a superior court judge can issue these warrants, and the application must be signed personally by the provincial attorney general or the federal minister of public safety (if either is prosecuting) or by an agent specially designated in writing.[27] The affidavit to obtain the warrant requires a demonstration of reasonable grounds to believe the interception would assist the investigation.[28] It must also describe the manner of interception, the parties, and time period at issue. A judge may not issue the warrant unless satisfied that it is in the "best interests of the administration of justice" and that "other investigative procedures" have failed, are unlikely to succeed, or urgency renders them impracticable.[29]

The Supreme Court in *Duarte* and *R v Garofoli* held that wiretaps are forms of search or seizure and, given their intrusiveness, granting one will be in the "best interests of the administration of justice" where an application establishes "reasonable and probable grounds to believe that an offence has been, or is being, committed and that the authorization sought will afford evidence of that offence."[30] In addition, for a standard interception, as noted, an applicant must also meet the requirements in section 186(1) of showing it to be in the best interests of the administration of justice and that other investigative procedures have failed or

---

27 *Criminal Code*, above note 3, s 185(1).

28 Section 185(1)(e) uses the phrase "may assist the investigation" but the Supreme Court held in *Duarte*, above note 9 at 45, that a reasonable authorization under (the earlier equivalent to) Part VI requires "reasonable and probable grounds to believe that an offence has been, or is being, committed and that the authorization sought *will* afford evidence of that offence" (emphasis added). Appeal courts have noted this requirement in relation to earlier equivalents of ss 185 and 186: *R v Finlay and Grellette*, above note 16; *R v Madrid* (1994), 48 BCAC 271 (CA); *R v Mahal*, 2012 ONCA 673.

29 *Criminal Code*, above note 3, s 186(1); under s 186(1.1), the court need not be satisfied the warrant is in the best interests of the administration of justice if issued in relation to a terrorism or organized crime offence.

30 *R v Garofoli*, [1990] 2 SCR 1421 at 1444 [*Garofoli*], citing La Forest J for the majority in *R v Duarte*, above note 9 at 45.

are unlikely to succeed or would be impractical.[31] The Court in *Araujo* cautioned that the test with respect to "other investigative procedures" is not which measures are "most efficacious," as some lower courts had held, but which are left when there is "no other reasonable alternative method of investigation, in the circumstances."[32]

A warrant under section 186 may be valid for up to sixty days.[33] It may be renewed for a further sixty days if circumstances set out in the initial application "still obtain."[34] The Court in *R v Lyons* affirmed a series of implied powers for executing an intercept warrant[35]—some of which are now codified in section 186(5.1), including the authority to "install, maintain or remove the device covertly." A judge may not authorize an interception involving a solicitor, their office, or household, unless there are reasonable grounds to believe they or a person in those locations have been or are about to become a party to an offence.[36]

The Court in *Garofoli* and in *R v Thompson* held that, as a general rule, wiretap authorizations are not invalid for lacking "minimizing conditions" that avoid "a high number of irrelevant interceptions."[37] Justice Sopinka reasoned that capturing innocent third parties is "an unfortunate cost of electronic surveillance, but one that Parliament has judged is justified in appropriate circumstances in the investigation of serious crime."[38] The question in any case will be whether "the cost [is] so great that it renders the authorization unreasonable."[39] The wiretap in *Garofoli* allowed agents to intercept 950 irrelevant telephone calls. The Court held "[t]his invasion of privacy is regrettable, but is at least limited in its effects to persons visiting Garofoli's home."[40] Justice Sopinka contrasted this with "a public pay telephone, where the privacy of the public at large is threatened."[41] The authorization in *Thompson* allowed wiretapping public telephone booths suspects might use. Police, he held, "cannot simply install a listening device and leave it running indiscriminately in the hope that a target may come along."[42] The requirement when applying

31 *Garofoli*, above note 30, discussing an earlier equivalent to s 186(1) of the *Criminal Code*.

32 *R v Araujo*, 2000 SCC 65 at paras 29,39 [*Araujo*].

33 Section 186.1 of the *Criminal Code* permits authorizations of up to a year in the case of terrorism or organized crime offences.

34 *Criminal Code*, above note 3, s 186(7).

35 *R v Lyons*, [1984] 2 SCR 633.

36 *Criminal Code*, above note 3, s 186(2).

37 *Garofoli*, above note 30 at 1467; *R v Thompson*, [1990] 2 SCR 1111 [*Thompson*].

38 *Garofoli*, above note 30 at 1467.

39 *Ibid*; see also *Thompson*, above note 37 at 1144.

40 *Garofoli*, above note 30 at 1467.

41 *Ibid*.

42 *Thompson*, above note 37 at 1145.

for a wiretap warrant to name the place a target will be intercepted may include a public pay phone.[43] But police must have "reasonable and probable grounds for believing that a target was using the telephone at the time that the listening device was activated."[44] The failure to include a requirement in the warrant in this case limiting surveillance of the phone booths to calls on which police had grounds for believing a target would be involved rendered this authorization unreasonable.[45] A condition to use live monitoring would be preferable in such a case but is not constitutionally required.[46]

The only feasible method of avoiding the capture of a high number of irrelevant communications would be to impose a general requirement, in wiretap warrants, that police engage in live monitoring. The Court considered and rejected this requirement in *Thompson* on the basis that it would impose "too heavy a burden on Canadian law-enforcement officials."[47] Justice Sopinka added to this reasoning in *Garofoli* a doubt that live monitoring would be effective in screening out irrelevant calls, since these cannot be determined until some portion of the conversation is overheard.[48] A wiretap warrant should instead be tailored to the circumstances known to police so as to conduct the surveillance with "a minimum invasion of privacy."[49] This may include a condition that an agent engage in some live monitoring, or other terms that would narrow the scope of the possible conversations captured.[50]

b) Consent Interceptions

Section 184.2 provides for a warrant to intercept on a less onerous set of conditions where police have consent of one or more parties to the conversation.[51] Parliament added the provision to the *Code* in response to the holding in *Duarte* recognizing the need for a warrant even where police

43 Section 178.13(2)(c) of the *Criminal Code* at the time *Thompson* was decided, now s 185(1)(f) of the *Criminal Code*.

44 *Thompson*, above note 37 at 1145.

45 *Ibid*.

46 *Ibid* at 1145–46.

47 *Ibid* at 1146.

48 *Garofoli*, above note 30 at 1468.

49 *Ibid*.

50 *Ibid* at 1468–69.

51 Section 183.1 of the *Criminal Code* provides police a further possibility in stating: "Where a private communication is originated by more than one person or is intended by the originator thereof to be received by more than one person, a consent to the interception thereof by any one of those persons is sufficient consent for the purposes of any provision of this Part." If police did not obtain the consent of a person directly involved in a communication, they might ask a person who is *intended* to receive the communication.

have the consent of one party.[52] While the *Charter* does not protect us from the risk of speaking to a "tattletale," La Forest J wrote in that case, the risk of our interlocutor "making a permanent electronic record" is a risk of a "different order of magnitude."[53] Section 184.2 requires police to apply to a provincial or superior court judge and to establish reasonable grounds to believe an offence has been or will be committed, the intercept will afford evidence of the offence, and police have the consent of one party.[54] If granted, the authorization can be valid for no longer than sixty days.[55] The judge may make an additional order under other provisions of the *Code* allowing for warrants, including general warrants and video surveillance.[56] Consent interceptions can be authorized by telewarrant where certain conditions are met and "it would be impracticable in the circumstances for the applicant to appear personally before a judge."[57] These warrants are valid for up to thirty-six hours.

c) Emergency Interceptions

Part VI authorizes emergency interceptions without a warrant in three situations. In the first case, an "agent of the state" may intercept without a warrant where they have the consent of a party to the communication, a reasonable suspicion of a risk of harm, and the purpose is to prevent the bodily harm.[58] The evidence gathered in this case is inadmissible in any proceedings (including an application for a warrant) other than "proceedings in which actual, attempted or threatened bodily harm is alleged."[59] Police must otherwise "destroy" any recordings, transcripts, and notes "as soon as is practicable in the circumstances."[60]

Second, a "police officer" may intercept without a warrant on reasonable grounds to believe it is "immediately necessary to prevent an offence that would cause serious harm to any person or to property," "an authorization could not, with reasonable diligence, be obtained" under other provisions, and at least one party is either the potential aggressor

52 *Duarte*, above note 9.

53 *Ibid* at 44 and 48.

54 *Criminal Code,* above note 3, s 184.2(3).

55 Section 186.1 of the *Criminal Code* permits authorizations of up to a year in the case of terrorism or organized crime offences.

56 Section 184.2(5) of the *Criminal Code* lists ss 487, 487.01, 487.014–487.018, 487.02, 492.1 & 492.2 as possible sources of additional warrants.

57 *Criminal Code,* above note 3, ss 184.2(5), and 184.3.

58 *Criminal Code,* above note 3, s 184.1(1); s 184.1(4) defines "agent of the state" as "a peace officer" or "a person acting under the authority of, or in cooperation with, a peace officer."

59 *Ibid*, s 184.1(2).

60 *Ibid*, s 184.1(3).

or victim.[61] The Supreme Court in *R v Tse* held that the requirement for reasonable grounds to believe the interception is "immediately necessary" involves two distinct elements.[62] An officer must have grounds to believe there is an immediate threat and "it must be likely that interception will be an effective means of preventing the unlawful act."[63] The Court, assessing an earlier version of the provision, found it unconstitutional for its lack of a requirement to provide after-the-fact notice to parties intercepted. In response, Parliament amended the *Code* to add a requirement for notice and also for periodic reports to government on police use of the provision.[64]

A third case is found in section 188 of the *Code*, which allows for an emergency warrant to be issued "if the urgency of the situation requires interception of private communications to commence before an authorization could, with reasonable diligence, be obtained under section 186."[65] This contemplates a wiretap to prevent the imminent destruction of evidence, rather than harm to a person's safety. Depending on the offence, the peace officer applying for the warrant must be designated in writing by the provincial attorney general or the federal minister of public safety. The warrant may only be issued by a superior court judge designated by the chief justice of the court and may last up to thirty-six hours.[66]

d) Sealed Packets and Notice Requirements

Section 187 of the *Code* requires that "[a]ll documents relating to an application" under Part VI are confidential and must be "placed in a packet and sealed by the judge to whom the application is made immediately on determination of the application." The packet is to remain inaccessible to the public and only opened for limited purposes, including a renewal of the authorization.[67] The accused receives a redacted copy that protects confidential informants and ongoing investigations.[68] The *Code* makes it an offence to disclose information obtained from a wiretap, except for a narrow set of purposes, including to give evidence in a court or other proceeding where a person is required to give evidence; to share evidence with foreign investigative authorities; or to facilitate technical aspects of

61 *Ibid*, s 184.4.

62 *R v Tse*, 2012 SCC 16 [*Tse*].

63 *Ibid* at para 42.

64 *Criminal Code*, above note 3, ss 195(2.1) and 196.1.

65 *Ibid*, s 188(1).

66 *Ibid*, s 188(2).

67 *Ibid*, s 187(1.2).

68 *Ibid*, s 187(5).

the wiretap.[69] A person can apply to destroy wiretap evidence and the Crown must be given a chance to respond to the application.[70]

The content of a private communication obtained from an interception is inadmissible unless the Crown or party adducing it provides the accused with "reasonable notice of the intention" to admit it, along with a transcript or, if the substance of the communication is to be given in *viva voce* evidence, a summary of it with "full particulars."[71] The *Code* also provides that where an interception captures privileged communications, they remain "privileged and inadmissible as evidence without the consent of the person enjoying the privilege."[72]

Finally, we note sections of the *Code* that contain notice and reporting requirements—sections that do not set out powers to search or seize *per se* but are important parts of what make the various powers under Part VI reasonable under section 8 of the *Charter.* Section 196 of the *Code* requires the provincial attorney general or the minister of public safety, where either has obtained a warrant under section 185 (a standard, non-consent wiretap), to provide notice within ninety days after the wiretap has ended to any person who was "the object of the interception" and to certify to the court they have done so. Section 196.1 imposes a similar requirement in the case of an emergency warrantless non-consent intercept. Under both provisions, a person is an "object of the interception" if they were named in the warrant. The Crown need not contact a person whose communications were intercepted because they happened to speak to a person named in the warrant. In this sense, the provision does not extend notice to everyone whose privacy may have been violated by the intercept. Section 195 requires the federal minister of public safety to report to Parliament on the number and nature of non-consent emergency wiretaps carried out without a warrant and the number and nature of third-party wiretap warrants granted.[73]

e) Video Surveillance, Tracking Devices, and Transmission Data

Provisions in the *Code* outside of Part VI allow for other forms of surveillance. Section 487.01(4) addresses video surveillance specifically. It is a species of the "general warrant" power in section 487.01 discussed earlier. To obtain a warrant for video surveillance, police must meet two sets of requirements. First, they must meet the test set out in

69 *Ibid*, s 193.

70 *Ibid*, s 187(1.5).

71 *Ibid*, s 189(5).

72 *Ibid*, s 189(6).

73 Section 195(1) of the *Criminal Code* requires reporting for warrants under ss 184.4, 185, and 188.

section 487.01 of establishing reasonable grounds to believe a crime has occurred and "information concerning the offence will be obtained"; the warrant is "in the best interests of the administration of justice"; and there is "no other provision" that would provide for the form of surveillance at issue. The court must include "such terms and conditions as the judge considers advisable to ensure that the privacy of the person or of any other person is respected as much as possible."[74] Additionally, video warrants are subject to all of the requirements and limitations of warrants under Part VI of the *Code*.[75] As noted above, police would need a warrant for video surveillance only if what the camera would capture is something over which the accused (or *Charter* claimant) enjoys a reasonable expectation of privacy.

The Supreme Court in *R v Wise* recognized a reasonable expectation of privacy in a person's movement in a motor vehicle, and it held the use of a tracking device to be a form of search requiring a warrant.[76] In response, Parliament amended the *Code* to include warrants for "tracking devices" to be surreptitiously installed on a vehicle or other thing—or on anything a person might carry or wear.[77] Prior to further amendments in 2014, a warrant to install a tracking device on a person or thing required only reasonable suspicion. The updated provisions recognize the possibility of people or things already carrying GPS tracking technology with them, such as an iPhone. The *Code* now provides for two warrants. One allows for tracking the movement of a vehicle or other thing by use of a device on reasonable suspicion of a federal offence and the possibility that the tracking will assist in the investigation.[78] Another warrant allows for tracking people through the use of a device on reasonable grounds to believe a federal offence has been committed and the tracking will assist in the investigation.[79]

---

74 *Ibid*, s 487.01(4).

75 Section 487.01(5) states:

> The definition offence in section 183 and sections 183.1, 184.2, 184.3 and 185 to 188.2, subsection 189(5), and sections 190, 193 and 194 to 196 apply, with such modifications as the circumstances require, to a warrant referred to in subsection (4) as though references in those provisions to interceptions of private communications were read as references to observations by peace officers by means of television cameras or similar electronic devices of activities in circumstances in which persons had reasonable expectations of privacy.

76 *R v Wise*, [1992] 1 SCR 527.

77 *Criminal Code*, above note 3, s 492.1.

78 *Ibid*, s 492.1(1). A federal offence here means an offence under the *Criminal Code* or other Act of Parliament.

79 *Ibid*, s 492.1(2). After these provisions were amended, the court in *R v Grandison*, 2016 BCSC 1712 [*Grandison*], considered the constitutionality of the earlier

The *Code* had long provided for warrants to monitor phone numbers dialled on a given line, and the provisions were amended in 2014 to provide warrants for a broader category of "transmission data."[80] This is defined as including "data" relating to "the telecommunication functions of dialling, routing, addressing or signalling" but "does not reveal the substance, meaning or purpose of the communication."[81] The provision provides for a warrant on reasonable suspicion of a federal offence and the possibility that it will assist in the investigation. The warrant authorizes police to "identify the type, direction, date, time, duration, size, origin, destination or termination of a communication."[82]

3) Preservation Demands, Orders, and Production Orders

In 2014, Parliament added to the *Code* powers to enable law enforcement to preserve data from being lost or deleted before a warrant can be obtained. A peace officer can make a "preservation demand" of a person (i.e., a telecommunications service provider) to "preserve computer data that is in their possession or control when the demand is made."[83] The provision requires the officer to have reasonable suspicion that a federal offence has been committed or an investigation in another country is being conducted and the data will assist the investigation.[84] An officer may not make a demand of a person being investigated.[85] The order lasts for twenty-one days for domestic investigations and ninety days for

---

versions of ss 492.1 and 492.2 that allowed for tracking warrants for a device on a thing or person on the standard of reasonable suspicion. The court held that despite Parliament's decision to increase the grounds for tracking a device on a person to probable grounds, the earlier standard of reasonable suspicion was reasonable under s 8. The tracking in this case involved traces of a cellphone being "pinged" from a nearby cell tower. This did not allow police to "follow the accused from place to place with significant precision," giving rise to a limited privacy intrusion at paras 69–72. The court distinguished the pinging process for tracking used in this case from police use of GPS technology a person may carry on a phone to obtain more precise tracking of their whereabouts. By implication, had the law not been changed to require a higher standard for tracking a person's cellphone (probable grounds), and tracking were to involve more precise coordinates through GPS technology or otherwise, a tracking warrant would not be reasonable under s 8 on reasonable suspicion.

80 *Criminal Code*, above note 3, s 492.2.

81 *Ibid*, s 492.2(6).

82 *Ibid*, definition of "transmission data."

83 *Ibid*, s 487.012(1).

84 *Ibid*, s 487.012(2).

85 *Ibid*, s 487.012(3).

foreign cases.[86] It may contain reasonable conditions, including an order to not disclose the fact that a demand has been made.[87] If investigators, in a domestic case, seek an order lasting longer than twenty-one days, they may apply to a justice of the peace or a judge for a "preservation order."[88] The order functions in a similar way and is available on the same grounds as a preservation demand (reasonable suspicion), with the further condition that the officer applying must also have applied for a warrant in relation to the data sought or intend to do so.[89] A preservation order is valid for up to ninety days.[90] A person subject to either a preservation demand or order must destroy the data at issue "as soon as feasible after the order expires or is revoked"—and failure to do so is a summary offence.[91]

Not to be confused with preservation demands and orders is an older tool called the "production order." First added to the *Code* in 2004 and amended in 2014, production orders are warrants for the disclosure of a "document containing data" held by service providers and other third parties. The 2014 amendments created a general production order and four specific kinds of order: for tracing communications (e.g., metadata attached to email or phone calls); transmission data (call or text histories); tracking data (location data); and financial data.[92] The general production order requires a peace officer to satisfy a justice of the peace or a judge that there are reasonable grounds to believe a federal offence has been committed and a "document or data" in a person's "possession or

86 *Ibid*, s 487.012(4) .

87 *Ibid*, s 487.012(5) .

88 *Ibid*, s 487.013.

89 *Ibid*, s 487.013(2).

90 *Ibid*, s 487.013(6).

91 *Ibid*, ss 487.0194(1), (2), and 487.0199.

92 The general production order is found in s 487.014; tracing orders in s 487.015; transmission data, s 487.015; tracking data, s 487.17; and financial data, s 487.018. Prior to the 2014 amendments, production orders could be obtained on reasonable suspicion (under what was then s 487.012). Courts were divided on the constitutionality of this power. In *R v Fedossenko*, 2014 ABCA 314, leave refused [2014] SCCA 516, the Alberta Court of Appeal reversed lower court holdings that found the provision to require probable grounds to be reasonable. The British Columbia Supreme Court in *Grandison*, above note 79, held that the production order was used in that case to obtain information that went to the biographical core of the subject, including a "considerable volume of information as to who the accused communicated with by means of a cellular telephone over a lengthy period of time." The provision should be "read down" to require the standard of probable grounds. The amended production order powers are now consistent with *Grandison*.

control will afford evidence respecting the commission of the offence."[93] The four specific kinds of orders can be issued on reasonable suspicion, reflecting the lower privacy interest engaged by the orders.[94] And with respect to all five production orders, the person under investigation may not be the subject of the order (as is the case with preservation demands and orders).[95] Also, here too, the person subject to a production order must destroy the document or data "as soon as feasible after the order expires or is revoked," and they commit a summary offence for failing to do so.[96]

Parliament did not create the production order power to authorize police to obtain subscriber information attached to a person's internet account. But following the Supreme Court's decision in *R v Spencer*, they have been used in this way.[97] In *Spencer*, the Court held that the accused had a reasonable expectation of privacy in the subscriber information attached to his internet protocol address, and that police conducted a search when they asked his provider, Shaw, for this.[98] Powers in the *Personal Information Protection and Electronic Documents Act* (*PIPEDA*) permitting the service provider to give the information to police did not authorize the search—and since it was conducted without authority, it was unreasonable under section 8.[99] The Court did not address what a reasonable search power for obtaining subscriber information would entail. As noted earlier, the general production order power in the *Code* requires police to establish probable grounds. Police use of these orders may keep the issue from reaching the Supreme Court for the time being.

Law scholars and privacy advocates have vigorously debated whether the probable grounds standard is either necessary (should it be reasonable suspicion?) or adequate (should there not also be post-search

---

93 *Criminal Code*, above note 3, s 487.014(1). As we noted above, the Supreme Court in *Jones*, above note 26, distinguished the production order power in s 487.014 from an interception or wiretap under Part VI of the *Code* on the basis that a production order authorizes access to stored messages or data rather than future messages or data.

94 *Criminal Code*, above note 3, ss 487.015(2), 487.016(2), 487.017(2), and 487.018(3).

95 *Ibid*, s 487.014(4).

96 *Ibid*, ss 487.0194(1),(3), and 487.0199.

97 *R v Spencer*, 2014 SCC 43 [*Spencer*]; on the use of production orders to obtain subscriber information, see Tamir Israel, "Law Enforcement Access to Subscriber Data in Canada Backgrounder" (March 2017), online: *Canadian Internet Policy and Public Interest Clinic* www.cippic.ca/uploads/20170303-Subscriber_data_in_Canada-Backgrounder.pdf [Israel].

98 The rationale for finding a privacy interest in this information is discussed in Chapter 4, Section C(1).

99 *Personal Information Protection and Electronic Documents Act*, SC 2000, c 5 [*PIPEDA*].

reporting requirements?).[100] The Supreme Court in *Spencer* does give us some guidance. The Court held that "the police request to Shaw for subscriber information corresponding to specifically observed, anonymous Internet activity engages a high level of informational privacy."[101] This would support a probable grounds standard for a production order. The Court also suggested the possibility of a demand for subscriber information without a warrant being reasonable in exigent circumstances, to prevent imminent bodily harm.[102] A court at some point may have to decide whether powers to issue a production order in the *Code* are reasonable under section 8 despite not including a requirement to inform the target of the search, where they are not prosecuted, that they were subject to an order. The Supreme Court in *Tse* found powers to conduct a wiretap without a warrant in exigent circumstances to be unreasonable for their lack of after-the-fact reporting requirements to the target of the search (similar to ones found elsewhere in Part VI).[103] Police use production orders to obtain subscriber information frequently—according to one source, the Vancouver police did so more than 25,000 times in a three-year window.[104] We suggest that the intrusive nature of the search, combined with the frequency of unnecessary searches, would support an argument that the use of production orders on probable grounds alone may be unreasonable under section 8.

4) Computers

Special rules apply to the search and seizure of computers, phones, or electronic devices and the information they contain. As a general rule, police and other state agents need authority to seize a computer and a warrant to search its contents. A warrant to search a device is typically sought under section 487 of the *Code*. The Supreme Court in *R v Vu*

---

100 See, e.g., sources surveyed in Israel, above note 97, and Steven Penney, "The Digitization of Section 8 of the Charter: Reform or Revolution?" (2014) 67 *Supreme Court Law Review* (2d) 505.

101 *Spencer*, above note 97 at para 51.

102 *Ibid* at para 74.

103 *Tse*, above note 62, assessing powers in s 184.4 of the *Code*. See the discussion of this decision in Chapter 7, Section C(3).

104 Israel, above note 97 at 2, noting "Halifax Regional Police, for example, compelled production of telecommunications subscriber identification data approximately 4,507 times while only relying on voluntary disclosure by service providers 2,354 in the largely pre-Spencer period spanning January 2011–December 2014. During the same period, the Vancouver Police Department obtained 25,189 production orders for subscriber identification data while relying on voluntary disclosure only 13,407 times."

held that if state authorities have a warrant to search a place or thing, they are not authorized to search the content of a computer they find in the course of the search unless the warrant explicitly permits them to do so.[105] *Vu* is the leading decision on the search of computers more generally. Before exploring *Vu* in more detail, two notable exceptions to the requirement for a warrant to search an electronic device can be found in the context of search incident to arrest and search at the border. We canvass authority for both of those kinds of search later in this chapter.

Police in *Vu* were investigating a suspected marijuana grow operation and obtained a warrant to search a residence. The warrant authorized police to look for evidence of electricity theft, including documents that would identify the owners or occupants. The warrant contemplated a search for "computer generated notes" but not computers, and it did not explicitly authorize the search of any devices. In the course of the search, police found marijuana, two computers, and a cellphone—and searching these devices revealed the accused was an occupant. Writing for the Court, Cromwell J held that unless a warrant specifically authorizes the search of a device found in the space or thing to be searched, a separate warrant is necessary. Computer searches engage a heightened privacy interest. Computers are different from physical receptacles in terms of both the quantity and quality of personal information they contain.[106] This gives rise to "distinctive privacy concerns" that require a separate assessment of whether an intrusion is justified.[107]

The Court in *Vu* also considered whether warrants to search a computer should be required to contain "search protocols" or conditions on what can be searched—but decided against this.[108] A judge may include directions in a warrant on the scope of a computer search, i.e., what files or apps police may access. But directions are not required under section 8 of the *Charter* because of the "difficulty of predicting in advance where relevant files might be found on a computer" and the likelihood

105 *R v Vu*, 2013 SCC 60 [*Vu*].

106 *Ibid* at paras 40–45. This portion of *Vu* contains an extended discussion of the ways in which computers are different from physical receptacles. Justice Cromwell offers a succinct summary of the discussion in *R v Fearon*, 2014 SCC 77 at para 51 [*Fearon*]:

> As outlined in *Vu*, computers—and I would add cell phones—may have immense storage capacity, may generate information about intimate details of the user's interests, habits and identity without the knowledge or intent of the user, may retain information even after the user thinks that it has been destroyed, and may provide access to information that is in no meaningful sense "at the location of the search."

107 *Vu*, above note 105 at para 47.

108 *Ibid* at paras 53–56.

of adding "significant complexity and practical difficulty" to the application process.[109] A court conducting a later review of the search might find that it was too broad and not carried out in a reasonable manner, as the Quebec Court of Appeal held in *R v Boudreau-Fontaine*.[110] The Court in *Vu* also declined to require police to take notes about what they happened to search on a device; but Cromwell J suggested that taking them or failing to take them will be relevant to assessing whether the search was conducted reasonably.[111]

If police lack specific authority to search a computer they come across in the course of a warranted search, the Court in *Vu* held that police may seize the device where "it may reasonably be thought to contain the sort of things that the warrant authorizes to be seized."[112] Police may then "do what is necessary to ensure the integrity of the data" before obtaining a separate warrant to search it.[113] This in turn requires the issuing justice to be satisfied there are reasonable grounds to believe the computer's content will afford evidence of an offence.[114]

Once police obtain a warrant to search a computer, they are authorized under the *Code* to copy and print data they find on it.[115] Notably, police may search not only the data on any computer named in a warrant in section 487 but also any data "available to the computer system" at issue.[116] This permits police to access and search not only a phone named in a warrant, for example, but also the iCloud or Gmail account that may be accessible on it, and the data found there that is related to the scope of the search authorized by the warrant.

5) Firearms

Powers to search for or seize firearms are found in both the *Firearms Act* and the *Criminal Code*.[117] Powers in the Act (discussed below) are meant to assist police in enforcing the regulatory and licensing framework for firearms; powers in the *Code* are meant to aid in the investigation of criminal offences. The *Code* contains powers to search or seize firearms with and without a warrant, and sets out a process for having guns

109 *Ibid* at paras 57–58.
110 *Ibid* at para 55, citing *R v Boudreau-Fontaine*, 2010 QCCA 1108, involving a search for evidence of an offence other than the one mentioned in the warrant.
111 *Vu*, above note 105 at para 70.
112 *Ibid* at para 49.
113 *Ibid*.
114 *Ibid* at para 48.
115 *Criminal Code*, above note 3, ss 487(2.1) & (2.2).
116 *Ibid*, s 487(2.2)(a).
117 *Firearms Act*, SC 1995, c 39 [*Firearms Act*]; *Criminal Code*, above note 3.

returned to a person when seized for safety concerns and without a belief that they were being used in the commission of an offence.

The main provision in the *Code* is found in section 117.02, which allows a peace officer to carry out a warrantless search or seizure in two circumstances. One is where they have reasonable grounds to believe that one of a certain class of items *was used in* the commission of an offence.[118] The other is where an officer has reasonable grounds to believe an offence is being committed, or has been, *involving* one of a different, larger class of items.[119] In both cases, the officer must also believe, on reasonable grounds, the item "is likely to be found" on the person, in their vehicle, or anywhere other than a dwelling house, and "conditions for obtaining a warrant exist but, by reason of exigent circumstances, it would not be practicable to obtain a warrant."[120]

A peace officer may seize—but not search for—a prohibited weapon or ammunition where a person in possession fails on demand to produce a licence or authorization for it.[121] A person from whom the item is seized may recover it by producing the licence or authorization within fourteen days.[122]

The *Code* provides for a warrant on reasonable grounds to believe a person possesses "a weapon, a prohibited device, ammunition, prohibited ammunition or an explosive substance" in a place and that "it is not desirable in the interests of the safety of the person, or of any other person" to possess the item.[123] The warrant may also permit seizure of the person's licence or registration certificate. A distinguishing feature of the warrant is that it does not require a belief that an offence has been committed. A peace officer may seize *without* a warrant where "the grounds for obtaining a warrant under subsection (1) exist but, by reason of a possible danger to the safety of that person or any other person, it would not be practicable to obtain a warrant."[124] The items seized in either instance must be brought to the issuing justice "forthwith."[125] The

---

118 Section 117.02(1)(a) of the *Code*, listing "a weapon, an imitation firearm, a prohibited device, any ammunition, any prohibited ammunition or an explosive substance."

119 *Ibid*, s 117.02(1)(b), listing, "a firearm, an imitation firearm, a cross-bow, a prohibited weapon, a restricted weapon, a prohibited device, ammunition, prohibited ammunition or an explosive substance."

120 *Ibid*, s 117.02(1).

121 *Ibid*, s 117.03.

122 *Ibid*, s 117.03(2).

123 *Ibid*, s 117.04(1).

124 *Ibid*, s 117.04(2).

125 *Ibid*, s 117.03(3).

person from whom items were seized can apply for a hearing to decide the disposition of the items. The test here is the same as for the warrant: whether "it is not desirable in the interests of the safety of the person from whom the thing was seized or of any other person that the person should possess" the item.[126] If it is not desirable, the item will be forfeited to the Crown and destroyed, and a prohibition order of up to five years can be imposed.

6) DNA, Impressions, Breath, and Blood

In *R v Stillman*, the Supreme Court held that police need a warrant to take bodily impressions and samples from a suspect—in that case hair samples, dental impressions, and buccal swabs.[127] Parliament has since amended the *Code* to provide various warrants for DNA, bodily impressions, and samples.

The DNA provisions are extensive and fall into two categories: those allowing for a warrant to seize DNA for investigative purposes and those allowing for a seizure from persons convicted of designated offences for inclusion in a national DNA databank. Briefly, warrants in the first category are granted by a provincial court judge and can be issued only in relation to a designated offence (most of which are sexual, violent, or drug related).[128] The judge must be satisfied there are reasonable grounds to believe the offence has been committed and a "bodily substance" has been found "on or within" the victim or another person or place associated with the offence and that DNA analysis will provide evidence about a person who is a party to the offence.[129] In addition, the judge must be satisfied that "it is in the best interests of the administration of justice" to grant the warrant.[130] The Supreme Court considered whether these investigative DNA warrant provisions are reasonable under section 8 of the *Charter* in *R v SAB*.[131] The Court found them reasonable for striking an appropriate balance between state interests in law enforcement and individual interests in privacy and dignity.[132] In tandem with a DNA

126 *Ibid*, s 117.05(1),(4).

127 *R v Stillman*, [1997] 1 SCR 607, 144 DLR (4th) 193 [*Stillman*].

128 *Criminal Code* above note 3, s 487.05(1), referring to "designated offences" in s 487.04.

129 *Ibid*.

130 *Ibid*.

131 2003 SCC 60.

132 See the discussion of this Court's reasons in this case in Chapter 7, Section C(1)(b).

warrant, other provisions allow for the taking of hair samples,[133] buccal swabs,[134] or blood[135] in the course of an investigation.

Provisions in the second category relate to the national DNA databank. They contemplate two kinds of case. When a court convicts a person of a "primary designated offence" (which includes murder, various sexual and weapons offences, and kidnapping), the *Code* mandates the court to issue an order for a sample to be taken (the order serving as the warrant for this purpose).[136] When a court convicts a person (or finds them not criminally responsible due to mental disorder) of certain other "primary designated offences" or for "secondary designated offences" (a wide and disparate range of offences in both cases), the court has discretion as to whether to order that a DNA sample be taken.[137] Where the court has discretion in relation to a "primary designated offence," the offender must establish the order would have a "grossly disproportionate" impact on their privacy and security of person in relation to the public interest in protecting society.[138] For a "secondary designated offence," the court must weigh a person's criminal record, the nature of the offence, and the impact on privacy and security.[139]

The *Code* authorizes the taking of bodily impressions. A peace officer may obtain from a justice of the peace or a judge a warrant for "any handprint, fingerprint, footprint, foot impression, teeth impression or other print or impression of the body or any part of the body" on reasonable grounds to believe an offence has been committed and information about it will be obtained by the print or impression.[140] Granting the warrant must also be in the "best interests of the administration of justice."[141]

For breath, blood, and saliva samples, police can rely on the impaired driving provisions of the *Code*. This too is a large topic. How the search and seizure provisions work here is closely related to the driving offences for which they serve as investigative tools. A detailed analysis is beyond the scope of this chapter. We highlight commonly used provisions under

133 *Criminal Code*, above note 3, s 487.06(1)(a).

134 *Ibid*, s 487.06(1)(b).

135 *Ibid*, s 487.06(1)(c).

136 *Ibid*, s 487.051(1), referring to the definition of "primary designated offences" in s 487.04(a) and (c.02).

137 *Ibid*, s487.051(2) referring to ss (a.1)–(c.01) and (c.03)–(d) of the definition of primary designated offences in s 487.04, and s 487.051(3), referring to definition of "secondary designated offences" in s 487.04.

138 *Ibid*, s 487.051(2).

139 *Ibid*, s 487.051(3).

140 *Ibid*, s 487.092(1).

141 *Ibid*.

what is now Part VIII.1 of the *Code*.[142] Police often make demands for samples in two situations.[143] On reasonable suspicion that a person has alcohol or a drug in their body and has operated a "conveyance" (which includes a vehicle or boat) in the past three hours, a peace officer may demand that a person perform a coordination test or provide a breath sample using an "approved screening device" (ASD) or a sample of a bodily substance using "approved drug screening equipment."[144] Police usually give the "ASD demand" at roadside, using a small device that registers a "pass," "warn," or "fail" depending on the concentration of alcohol detected in the sample. An officer may use a fail reading to form grounds to detain or arrest for further investigation, but the reading is inadmissible at trial as evidence of impairment or alcohol concentration.[145]

A controversial new power, which Parliament added to the *Code* in 2018, permits police to make an ASD demand on no grounds.[146] The section requires only that police be acting "in the course of the lawful exercise of powers" under federal, provincial, or common law—powers that include the ability to arbitrarily pull a person over to check for insurance.[147] The Supreme Court has yet to assess whether this constitutes a reasonable law for the purposes of section 8.

Where a person blows a fail on an approved screening device, this provides reasonable grounds for a more invasive search.[148] The *Code* authorizes police to make a demand for a sample where an officer has reasonable grounds to believe that a person has operated a conveyance while their ability to operate it was "impaired to any degree by alcohol" or has "within two hours after ceasing to operate a conveyance, a blood alcohol concentration that is equal to or exceeds 80 mg of alcohol in 100 mL of blood."[149] In this case, the officer may demand that the person accompany them (usually to the police station), "as soon as practicable" to provide a sample of breath on an approved instrument

---

142 Prior to 2018 amendments, similar powers were found in s 254 of the *Code*.

143 Where police are authorized to make a demand in the sections discussed here, it is an offence under s 320.15(1) of the *Criminal Code* to fail or refuse to comply with a demand without reasonable excuse.

144 *Ibid*, s 320.27.

145 *R v Orbanski; R v Elias*, 2005 SCC 37.

146 *Criminal Code*, above note 3, s 320.27(2).

147 *R v Ladouceur*, [1990] 1 SCR 1257, recognizing a power to conduct random stops under provincial motor vehicle legislation violates s 9 of the *Charter*, but constitutes a reasonable limit under s 1.

148 *R v Bernshaw*, [1995] 1 SCR 254, holding that a fail on an ASD may serve as reasonable grounds to demand a sample using a Breathalyzer in the absence of a reason to doubt the accuracy of the ASD reading.

149 *Criminal Code*, above note 3, s 320.28.

(usually a Breathalyzer) or, if there are reasonable grounds to believe the person is incapable of providing a breath sample, for the taking of a blood sample.[150] To be clear, an officer may form reasonable grounds to make a demand under this power without a fail on the ASD, by drawing on other indicia of impairment. The demand for a sample constitutes a seizure under section 8,[151] and refusal to comply with a lawful demand constitutes a distinct offence under the *Criminal Code*.[152]

The *Code* provides for a warrant for taking a blood sample in a suspected case of impaired driving. A justice or judge may issue a warrant to take a blood sample to measure alcohol or drug concentration where there are reasonable grounds to believe a person has operated a vehicle in the past eight hours involving an accident that caused bodily harm or death; there are reasonable grounds to suspect they have alcohol or a drug in their body; and a "qualified medical practitioner" believes the person is unable to consent and taking the sample will not endanger their health.[153]

7) Exigent Circumstances and Feeney Warrants

The *Code* includes a broad power to enter, search, and seize without a warrant in exigent circumstances. Section 487.11 states that a peace officer "may, in the course of his or her duties, exercise any of the powers described in subsection 487(1) [the standard warrant] or 492.1(1) [tracking warrants] without a warrant if the conditions for obtaining a warrant exist but by reason of exigent circumstances it would be impracticable to obtain a warrant." Parliament added this provision to the *Code* after the Supreme Court decision in *R v Silveira*, a case in which police entered a home without a warrant to prevent the destruction of evidence, while waiting for a warrant to be obtained.[154] The Court held that the search violated section 8 because it was not authorized by law—which is to say, it declined to recognize that police have a power at common law to do what they did in this case.[155]

---

150 *Criminal Code*, above note 3, s 320.28(a)(ii).

151 *Goodwin v British Columbia (Superintendent of Motor Vehicles)*, 2015 SCC 46 at para 50: "It is undisputed before this Court that the roadside breath demand constitutes a seizure within the meaning of s. 8 of the *Charter*."

152 *Criminal Code*, above note 3, s 320.15(1).

153 *Ibid*, s 320.29(1).

154 *R v Silveira*, [1995] 2 SCR 297 [*Silveira*].

155 Note that police do have a power at common law to enter a home without a warrant in exigent circumstances where safety is at issue, rather than the preservation of evidence. This power is discussed in Section D(3) below.

Section 487.11 does not define "exigent circumstances," nor is it defined elsewhere in Part XV of the *Code*. In *R v Grant*, the Court held that exigent circumstances arise where there is an "imminent danger of the loss, removal, destruction or disappearance of the evidence if the search or seizure is delayed."[156] The Court in *R v Feeney* held that "exigent circumstances arise usually where immediate action is required for the safety of the police or to secure and protect evidence of a crime."[157] The Court there also held that exigent circumstances includes officers in hot pursuit of a suspect.[158] More recently, the Court in *R v Paterson* interpreted the exigent search power in section 11(7) of the *Controlled Drugs and Substances Act*—a power worded in similar terms to those in section 487.11.[159] Justice Brown, for the majority, held that in addition to a requirement for urgency, section 11(7) contains a requirement that a warrant be "impracticable to obtain," which suggests something close to "impossible in practice or unmanageable to obtain."[160] This holding has since been applied to section 487.11.[161]

The *Code* includes a further power for warrantless entry to a dwelling house in particular. Parliament added the provision in response to the Supreme Court's holding in *Feeney*.[162] Police had entered a residence without a warrant or consent to arrest a murder suspect but were not in "hot pursuit." The Court held that entering a home to make an arrest requires a warrant, unless in hot pursuit, and also reasonable grounds to arrest.[163] The *Code* now provides for two forms of what is called a "Feeney warrant."[164] Where police already have an arrest warrant (under another provision of the *Code* or other federal law) they may obtain an additional warrant under section 529 of the *Code* to enter a dwelling house to carry out the arrest if there are reasonable grounds to believe the person sought will be found there.[165] In order for a warrant under section 529 to be lawfully executed, the officer must also have reasonable grounds to believe the person is present immediately before they enter.[166] Where police do not already have an arrest warrant, section 529.1 provides

156 *R v Grant*, [1993] 3 SCR 223 at 243 [*Grant*].

157 *R v Feeney*, [1997] 2 SCR 13 at para 52 [*Feeney*].

158 *Ibid* at para 47.

159 *R v Paterson*, 2017 SCC 15 [*Paterson*], citing the *Controlled Drugs and Substances Act*, SC 1996, c 19, s 11(7) [*CDSA*], discussed further below.

160 *Paterson*, above note 159 at para 36.

161 See, e.g., *R v Zekarias*, 2018 ONSC 4751 at paras 45–46.

162 *Feeney*, above note 157.

163 The Court's reasoning in *Feeney* is discussed in Chapter 7, Section C(2)(b).

164 *Criminal Code*, above note 3, ss 529 and 529.1.

165 *Ibid*, s 529(1).

166 *Ibid*, s 529(2).

a warrant for entry and arrest where there are reasonable grounds to believe the person sought will be present and there are grounds to arrest under the *Code* or other federal law.[167]

Lastly, Parliament has codified the power recognized in *Feeney* in section 529.3 of the *Code*, which allows a peace officer to enter a residence without a warrant where there are reasonable grounds to believe they will be there and "the conditions for obtaining a warrant under section 529.1 exist but by reason of exigent circumstances it would be impracticable to obtain a warrant." Section 529.3 includes a definition of "exigent circumstances" that applies to this section. The officer must have a reasonable suspicion that entry is necessary to prevent "imminent bodily harm of death to any person," or reasonable grounds to believe evidence of an indictable offence will be found within and entry is necessary to prevent its imminent loss or destruction.[168] The Court in *Paterson* was asked to apply the definition of exigent circumstances in section 529.3 to a search conducted in a drug case under section 11(7) of the *CDSA*—but declined to do so, limiting the definition in section 529.3 (and its particular requirements) to that provision.[169]

8) Plain View

Canadian law contains three notable sources of authority for police to seize incriminating evidence they happen to come across when executing a warrant (which does not include those items) or when acting without a warrant. Powers to seize in "plain view" are found in the *Code*, the *CDSA*, and at common law.[170] In practical terms, the powers in section 489(1) and (2) of the *Code* are broad enough to apply in most cases where the other powers may not.

Section 489(1) of the *Code* permits any person executing a warrant to seize (not search) any "thing" not mentioned in the warrant that they have reasonable grounds to believe was obtained by, used in, or will afford evidence of a federal offence. The warrant itself must be lawful and the person must be acting within its scope when they come across the items. Section 489(2) sets out a broader power. It permits a peace officer, acting on reasonable grounds, to seize the same items in section

---

167 *Ibid*, s 529.1. In this case, police do not need to have reasonable grounds, immediately upon entry, that the person sought will be present. This can be a condition attached to the warrant under s 529.2.

168 *Ibid*, ss 529.3(2)(a) & (b).

169 *Paterson*, above note 159 at paras 30–31.

170 Plain view powers under the *CDSA*, above note 159, are discussed in Section B(1) below and plain view powers at common law are discussed in Section D(2) below.

489(1) where they come across them when "lawfully present in a place pursuant to a warrant or otherwise in the execution of duties." The latter, for example, might include items seen inside a car in plain view during a routine traffic stop. Briefly, by contrast to the *Code* powers, the plain view powers in the *CDSA* are limited to items related to offences under the Act.[171] The common law imports requirements of "inadvertence" and "immediacy," discussed below.

9) Other *Code* Warrants

In the interests of space, we note only briefly here the availability of three other warrant powers in the *Code*.

a) Proceeds of Crime

The first is another large topic on its own: the proceeds of crime. Added to the *Code* in 1989 and expanded in 2000 with the passage of the *Proceeds of Crime (Money Laundering) and Terrorist Financing Act*,[172] provisions in Part XII.2 of the *Code* contain an extensive framework for seizing assets obtained from criminal activity and for adjudicating their forfeiture to the Crown and their restitution.[173] "Proceeds of crime" are defined as "any property, benefit or advantage, within or outside Canada, obtained or derived directly or indirectly" through the commission of a "designated offence," which, in practical terms, includes most indictable offences.[174] The *Code* authorizes a "special search warrant" for the search and seizure of movable property or chattels and "restraint orders" over real property or proceeds (e.g., in bank accounts).[175] A court may issue an order seizing or restraining the movement or transfer of interests in relation to the item pending trial,[176] and for its forfeiture.[177] Applications for seizure and restraint orders depend on the likelihood that the property at issue will be subject to forfeiture.[178] The Supreme Court in *Quebec (Attorney General) v Laroche* considered the scope of these provisions and the test on review of warrants and orders issued under them.[179] Justice LeBel, for the majority, held that on review of these warrants or

171 *CDSA*, above note 159, s 11(6).

172 SC 2000, c 17 [*Proceeds of Crime Act*].

173 On the rationale for introducing these powers, see *Quebec (Attorney General) v Laroche*, 2002 SCC 72 at paras 23–27 [*Laroche*].

174 *Criminal Code*, above note 3, ss 462.3 and 462.37.

175 *Ibid*, ss 462.32 & 462.33.

176 *Ibid*, ss 462.32(1) and 462.33(3).

177 *Ibid*, s 462.37.

178 *Ibid*, ss 462.32(1) and 462.33(3).

179 *Laroche*, above note 173.

orders, given the wording in section 462.34(6) of the *Code*, the question is not whether the warrant or order *could* have been made (as is the test on review of a wiretap warrant under *Araujo*),[180] but whether it *should* have been made.[181] Even if the reviewing judge can identify a "sufficient basis for belief on reasonable and probable grounds," they must overturn the issuing judge's warrant or order if they "do not share the opinion of his or her colleague" as to whether it should have issued.[182]

A court may impose a forfeiture order in three cases: where a person has been found guilty of a designated offence, on proof on a balance of probabilities that the property is the proceeds of crime;[183] where they have not been found guilty of a designated offence, on proof beyond a reasonable doubt that the property is the proceeds of crime;[184] and where the person is convicted of a criminal organization or drug trafficking offence and the person has engaged in a pattern of criminal activity in the past decade for the purpose of receiving a material benefit or possesses property for which their income (unrelated to the offence) cannot reasonably account.[185]

b) Hate Propaganda

The *Criminal Code* criminalizes the incitement of hatred against an identifiable group that is likely to lead to a breach of the peace.[186] Police may obtain a warrant on reasonable grounds for the seizure of "copies" of "any publication . . . kept for sale or distribution" of "hate propaganda." This can include material in purely electronic form.[187] The court may then decide whether seized material should be forfeited to the Crown in a proceeding at which the owner and author of the material have standing to oppose this.[188]

c) Law Office Searches

The *Code* sets out an extensive framework for issuing a warrant and conducting the search of a law office.[189] The Supreme Court in *Lavallee, Rackel & Heintz v Canada (Attorney General); White, Ottenheimer &*

180 *Araujo*, above note 32; the *Araujo* test also applies to review of the standard warrant under s 487 of the *Code*: *R v Morelli*, 2010 SCC 8 at para 40 [*Morelli*].

181 *Laroche*, above note 173 at paras 65–66.

182 *Ibid* at para 66.

183 *Criminal Code*, above note 3, ss 462.37(1), 462.37(2), 462.37(2.01).

184 *Ibid*, s 462.37(2).

185 *Ibid*, s 462.37(2.01).

186 *Ibid*, s 319.

187 *Ibid*, s 320.1.

188 *Ibid*, ss 320(2),(3); 320.1(2) & (3).

189 *Ibid*, s 488.1.

Baker v Canada (Attorney General); R v Fink struck down the provisions as unreasonable under section 8 of the *Charter* for not adequately protecting solicitor-client privilege, and held they were not saved under section 1.[190] The Court set out "guidelines" for what would constitute a reasonable search of a law office and the seizure of items found within it. Parliament has not amended the provision to reflect this holding. Police have since sought warrants to search law offices under other authority, such as section 487 of the *Code*, with judges relying on the guidelines in *Lavallee* to craft the parameters of a reasonable search. We highlight here only some of *Lavallee*'s many requirements:[191]

- A warrant should not authorize the search or seizure of documents known to be protected by solicitor-client privilege;
- Unless otherwise directed by the warrant, documents in a lawyer's possession must be sealed before being examined or seized;
- Efforts must be made to contact the lawyer and the client when the search warrant is executed, or a representative of the bar to oversee the sealing and seizure of documents;
- Privilege holders should be given a reasonable opportunity to assert a claim of privilege and, if that claim is contested, to have the issue judicially decided;
- The Crown may make submissions on the issue of privilege but should not be permitted to inspect the documents beforehand, and the prosecuting authority can only inspect the documents if and when a judge determines the documents are not privileged; and
- Where documents are found to be privileged, they are to be returned immediately to the holder of the privilege, or to a person designated by the court.

The Supreme Court had cause to revisit the subject of law office searches in *Canada (Attorney General) v Federation of Law Societies of Canada*.[192] This case involved a challenge to provisions of the *Proceeds of Crime (Money Laundering) and Terrorist Financing Act* that authorized searches by investigators from the Financial Transactions and Reports Analysis Centre of Canada.[193] Under the Act, an investigator may enter a law office without a warrant to examine and copy records required under the Act.[194] It also permits entry into a dwelling house (a home office)

190 *Lavallee, Rackel & Heintz v Canada (Attorney General); White, Ottenheimer & Baker v Canada (Attorney General); R v Fink*, 2002 SCC 61 [*Lavallee*].

191 For the complete list, see para 49, *ibid*.

192 2015 SCC 7.

193 *Proceeds of Crime Act*, above note 172.

194 *Ibid*, s 62.

for the same purpose with a warrant.[195] The provisions also apply to a wide range of professional offices that fall within the scope of the Act. The Court found the application of them in the context of law office searches to be unreasonable under section 8 for their failure to conform with the guidelines set out in *Lavallee*, including the requirement to give the holder of solicitor-client privilege notice that documents had been searched or seized. The violation could not be justified under section 1, and the Court's remedy was to read down the provisions to "exclude legal counsel and legal firms from the scope of their operation."[196]

B. POWERS IN OTHER FEDERAL LEGISLATION

1) *Controlled Drugs and Substances Act*

The *CDSA* contains in section 11 an analogous warrant power to the one found in section 487 of the *Criminal Code*, with two key differences.[197] A warrant under section 11 of the *CDSA* authorizes police to search and seize only items related to offences in the Act, along with items that would afford evidence of the *Code* offences of money laundering and being in possession of property obtained by committing an indictable offence.[198] It may be obtained by telewarrant.[199] Unlike a warrant under section 487, a *CDSA* warrant permits a peace officer executing it to search a person found in a place named in the warrant, where the officer has reasonable grounds to believe the person may have on their person "any controlled substance, precursor, property or thing set out in the warrant" and, if so, the officer may seize it.[200]

The *CDSA* also codifies two further powers noted earlier. One is a "plain view" seizure power, permitting an officer to seize any item they come across in the course of executing a section 11 warrant that they have reasonable grounds to believe will afford evidence of an offence under the Act.[201] The other is power is found in section 11(7) of the

---

195 *Ibid*, s 63.

196 *Federation*, above note 192 at para 63.

197 *CDSA*, above note 159 and *Criminal Code*, above note 3.

198 Section 11(1) of the *CDSA*, above note 159, referring in s 11(1)(d) to ss 354 and 462.31 of the *Criminal Code*, above note 3.

199 *CDSA*, above note 159, s 11(2).

200 *Ibid*, s 11(5).

201 *Ibid*, s 11(6).

CDSA, permitting a warrantless search in exigent circumstances, similar to the power found in section 489 of the *Code*.[202]

The power to search in exigent circumstances in section 11(7) states that a peace officer may exercise any of the three powers just described (search and seizure with a warrant, a person found within, plain view) "without a warrant if the conditions for obtaining a warrant exist but by reason of exigent circumstances it would be impracticable to obtain one." Interpreting this provision in *Paterson*, Brown J, for a majority of the Supreme Court, held that "'impracticability' suggests on balance a more stringent standard, requiring that it be impossible in practice or unmanageable to obtain a warrant."[203] The *CDSA* explicitly provides that in exercising these powers an officer may "enlist such assistance as the officer deems necessary" and "use as much force as is necessary in the circumstances."[204]

Distinct from the criminal investigation powers in the *CDSA* are a set of regulatory or administrative powers in that same Act. Health Canada inspects entities that are licensed to produce, package, transport, or sell controlled substances to ensure compliance with the *CDSA*.[205] The Act empowers "inspectors" to conduct on-site inspections of inventory, records, and security measures.[206] The inspectors may enter upon property, open and search containers, and seize items.[207] They may only enter a dwelling house with a warrant.[208]

The *CDSA* imposes a special set of reporting requirements. Police must report seizures of controlled substances to the minister of health (i.e., to Health Canada) and seizures of "non-chemical offence-related property" to a justice under sections 489.1 and 490 of the *Criminal Code*.[209] A further report to Health Canada is required after police destroy chemical offence-related property.[210]

---

202 *Ibid*, s 11(7). In *Grant*, above note 156, the Supreme Court assessed an earlier equivalent to this provision (s 10 of the *Narcotic Control Act*, RSC 1985, c N-1, repealed 1996, c 19), which permitted warrantless entry and search of a place other than a dwelling house on reasonable grounds to believe evidence of a drug offence would be found. The Court held that it was consistent with s 8 of the *Charter* if read down to permit searches only where there were exigent circumstances.

203 *Paterson*, above note 159 at para 36.

204 *CDSA*, above note 159, s 12.

205 Government of Canada, "Inspection Strategy for Licensed Dealers of Controlled Substances and Class A Precursors (CS-POL-002)" (December 2019).

206 *CDSA*, above note 159, ss 30,31.

207 *Ibid*, s 31.

208 *Ibid*, s 31(2).

209 *Ibid*, ss 12.1 and13(2).

210 *Ibid*, s 29.

Finally, the *CDSA* contains a set of provisions for the restraint, management, and forfeiture of offence-related property under the Act. The Crown may apply for a restraining order in relation to a house, a car, or other thing on reasonable grounds to believe it is offence-related property—and the court may order a person not to dispose of or otherwise deal with an interest in it except as directed.[211] A court may order that any item seized (a car, computer, weapon), or any property subject to a restraining order be managed or dealt with as the court directs.[212] Once a person is convicted or discharged of a designated substance offence, the Crown may seek to obtain an order forfeiting to the Crown non-chemical offence-related property (for example, an amount of cash seized from or a house used to conduct a grow operation).[213] For property other than real property, the court may order a forfeiture where satisfied, on a balance of probabilities, that the property is "related to the commission of the offence."[214] For real property, the court must consider additional factors, including the impact on family members or residents in the case of a dwelling house, and whether the forfeiture would be "disproportionate to the nature and gravity of the offence," the circumstances, and the criminal record of persons involved.[215] The forfeiture provisions are better understood as punishment or sentencing provisions rather than powers to make a further seizure under section 8. In essence, they concern what should happen with an *interest* in property at the end of a prosecution, rather than a physical taking of, or continued possession of, an item.

2) *Firearms Act*

In distinction to the *Code*, which deals with firearms offences, the *Firearms Act* regulates the possession and use of guns, with a view to maintaining public safety through licensing and inspection.[216] It contains a set of powers under which an "inspector" may search for and seize firearms with or without a warrant.[217] Under the main "inspection" power, an inspector may, without a warrant, "at any reasonable time enter and

---

211 *Ibid*, s 14.

212 *Ibid*, s 15.1.

213 *Ibid*, ss 16 and 19.1. Section 17(2) contemplates "*in rem* forfeitures" where a person has only been charged with an offence but has died or absconded.

214 *Ibid*.

215 *Ibid*, s 19.1(3).

216 *Firearms Act*, above note 117, s 101.

217 *Ibid*, s 101 defines "inspectors" to include "firearms officers" and others designated by a provincial minister, while s 2 defines "firearms officers" to include officers designated by either the provincial minister or the federal minister of public safety.

inspect" any place they believe on reasonable grounds will contain a "gun collection," a prohibited firearm, or "more than 10 firearms."[218] They may open any container there on reasonable grounds to believe it will contain a firearm, examine a firearm, and "conduct any tests or analyses or take any measurements."[219] The inspector may not use force here.[220] They may not enter a dwelling house for this inspection, except on reasonable notice to the occupant and with their consent.[221] The Act imposes a duty to give "all reasonable assistance" to the inspector,[222] and to provide a receipt for things taken.[223]

The *Firearms Act* also provides for a warrant to search a dwelling house, but the requirements are notably restrictive. A justice must be satisfied that the conditions for entry under the main inspection power are met (reasonable grounds to believe the residence will contain a "gun collection," a prohibited firearm, or "more than 10 firearms"); entry is "necessary" for enforcement of the Act or regulations; and entry has been or is likely to be refused.[224] The warrant can only authorize inspection of "that part of a room of the dwelling-house in which the inspector believes on reasonable grounds" there are firearms, parts of them, or ammunition—or where a business is being carried on, parts of a room where there are reasonable grounds to believe ammunition or records are to be found.[225] Curiously, items seized under the warrant provision of the Act are not subject to a receipt requirement, but they would be subject to the reporting and detention requirements of sections 489.1 and 490 of the *Criminal Code* (discussed at the end of this chapter).

A final search power to note is one that permits an inspector who believes on reasonable grounds that a person possesses a firearm to demand that the person "within a reasonable time" produce the firearm to enable the inspector to verify the serial number or, if the gun is a prohibited or restricted firearm, a valid certificate.[226]

---

218 *Ibid*, s 102(1).

219 *Ibid*.

220 *Ibid*, s 102(3).

221 *Ibid*, s 104(1); the inspector need not give reasonable notice if the dwelling house is also a place of business: s 104(1)(b); they do not need consent if they have a warrant under s 104(2).

222 *Ibid*, s 103.

223 *Ibid*, s 102(4).

224 *Ibid*, s 104(2).

225 *Ibid*, s 104(3).

226 *Ibid*, s 105.

3) *Customs Act*

The *Customs Act* provides officers of the Canada Border Services Agency (CBSA) a primary source of authority to search and seize[227]—but the CBSA is also authorized to do so under other Acts, including the *Criminal Code* and the *Immigration and Refugee Protection Act*.[228] Powers under the *Customs Act* include the authority to conduct a cursory search of goods without reasonable grounds and more invasive searches of persons and goods on reasonable suspicion. The Supreme Court in *R v Simmons* held that search at the border on lower standards than would normally apply is reasonable under section 8 in light of a compelling state interest in search at the border and a person's lower expectation of privacy, in this context, in their effects and in their body.[229]

For cursory searches, the Act permits customs officers, without grounds, to "examine any goods that have been imported and to open or cause to be opened any package or container of imported goods and take samples of imported goods in reasonable amounts."[230] The CBSA has stirred debate in recent years by taking the position that data on a device brought into Canada constitutes a "good" under this power, given that "goods" are defined in the Act to include "any document in any form."[231] On this basis, courts have decided a number of cases in which officers have searched a phone or laptop on no grounds, discovering evidence of an offence (in most instances, child pornography).[232] The Alberta Court of Appeal in *R v Canfield* held that the routine search of devices at the border on no grounds (under section 99(1)(a) of the *Customs Act*) is unreasonable under section 8, rendering the provision unconstitutional in this respect.[233] But the court declined to decide what such a search requires to be reasonable.[234] The same court has since held that in the

227 *Customs Act*, RSC 1985, c 1 (2nd Supp) [*Customs Act*].

228 SC 2001, c 27 [*IRPA*].

229 *R v Simmons*, [1988] 2 SCR 495 [*Simmons*].

230 *Customs Act*, above note 227, s 99(1)(a).

231 *Ibid*, s 2.

232 See, e.g., *R v Canfield*, 2018 ABQB 408; *R v Gibson*, 2017 BCPC 237; *R v Buss*, 2014 BCPC 16. For an overview of the caselaw and issues, see Robert Diab, "Does the State Have a Compelling Interest in Searching Device Data at the Border? Emerging Approaches to Reasonable Search in Canada and the United States" (2018) *Oxford University Comparative Law Forum* 1.

233 *R v Canfield*, 2020 ABCA 383, leave to appeal refused, 39376 (11 March 2021). See also *R v Pike and Scott*, 2022 ONSC 2297, finding s 99(1)(a) unconstitutional as a basis for routine device searches on no grounds.

234 *R v Canfield*, *ibid*, suggesting, in *obiter*, at para 75: "in our view the threshold for the search of electronic devices may be something less than the reasonable grounds to suspect required for a strip search under the *Customs Act*."

immigration context, customs officers may carry out a limited search of a device on no grounds for "identification and admissibility purposes."[235]

Officers are also authorized under the *Customs Act* to conduct, without grounds, a "non-intrusive examination of goods" in the "custody or possession" of a person in a "customs controlled area" (CCA).[236] That is, in a CCA, an officer can search any goods in a person's possession, not just "those that have been imported." CCAs are spaces in an airport or seaport designated by regulation. Added to the *Customs Act* in 2001 and amended in 2009, CCAs were meant to address concerns about airport staff colluding with organized crime.

For more invasive searches of things, customs officers can obtain a warrant under the *Customs Act* to search and seize items within a building or receptacle on reasonable grounds to believe it may contain items in contravention of the Act.[237] These powers permit the seizure of a wide range of items, including a "conveyance" or vehicle.[238] Officers have a "plain view" seizure power, to seize items they come across not mentioned in a warrant, on reasonable grounds to believe they will afford evidence of a contravention of the Act.[239] The Act permits a warrantless search of a building or receptacle in exigent circumstances.[240]

Finally, customs officers may also, without a warrant, conduct more invasive searches in two notable instances. They may open mail or sealed goods or packages when they reasonably suspect violations of customs tariffs or the importation of an illicit substance or good.[241] Officers may conduct a strip search of any person "within a reasonable time after his arrival in Canada" or "about to leave Canada" on reasonable suspicion

---

235 *R v Al Askari*, 2021 ABCA 204, addressing powers under s 16 of *IRPA*, above note 228, holding at paras 59–60:

> Routine and suspicionless searches of personal electronic devices under *IRPA* must be limited to the purposes provided in the text: identification and admissibility. . . . [U]nder s 16, officers may review documents on personal electronic devices where necessary for identification and admissibility purposes. For example, an officer could ask a refugee claimant to locate the relevant documents on their device instead of independently searching for them. In this situation, a search would only occur if the person could not meet the request. . . . [A] justifiable search of a personal electronic device for the purposes of identification and admissibility must limit the invasion of privacy by conducting the search in a manner that is tailored, and only where the officer is unable to otherwise satisfy themselves of identity and admissibility.

236 *Customs Act*, above note 227, s 99.3(1).

237 *Ibid*, s 111.

238 *Ibid*, s 111(3).

239 *Ibid*.

240 *Ibid*, s 111(6).

241 *Ibid*, s 99(1)(c.1)–(f).

that the person has "secreted on or about his person anything" that might violate the Act or afford evidence of a federal offence.[242] The Supreme Court in *Simmons* upheld these strip search provisions as reasonable under section 8 partly on the basis, as noted, of the higher state interest in search at the border and lower personal interest in privacy here, but also on the basis of two additional requirements.[243] One is to provide a detainee, upon request, confirmation by a senior officer that there are reasonable grounds to suspect an offence—a second opinion.[244] The search must also be conducted by an officer (or "any suitable person") of the same sex.[245]

4) Other Federal Statutes

A number of other federal statutes contain powers to search and seize. We briefly note here only a few of the more commonly encountered (or contentious) powers and their general scope.

The *Income Tax Act* provides for a warrant on reasonable grounds to search any place for evidence of a criminal offence under the Act and to seize documents.[246] It also contains a host of inspection or audit powers to ensure compliance with the Act, including powers to demand documents or information and to enter a place where business is carried on and conduct a search.[247] An auditor may enter a dwelling house only with consent or a warrant on reasonable grounds to believe a search (an "inspection" or "examination") is necessary to enforce the Act.[248] The Supreme Court in *R v Jarvis* considered when tax officials may rely on the "investigative" or criminal powers of the Act rather than its "enforcement" or administrative powers.[249] They may do so when the "predominant purpose of the official's inquiry is the determination of penal liability."[250]

The *Corrections and Conditional Release Act* contains an extensive set of what may be the most intrusive and permissive search powers in Canadian law.[251] Routine frisk and strip searches of inmates may be conducted "without individualized suspicion," so long as the latter are

242 *Ibid*, s 98(1).

243 *Simmons*, above note 229 at 530–31.

244 *Customs Act*, above note 227, s 98(3).

245 *Ibid*, s 98(4).

246 *Income Tax Act*, RSC 1985 (5th Supp), c 1 [*Income Tax Act*], s 231.3(1) to search for offences in s 239.

247 *Ibid*, ss 231.2(1) and 231.1(1).

248 *Ibid*, s 231.1(a) and (c).

249 *R v Jarvis*, 2002 SCC 73 [*Jarvis*].

250 *Ibid* at para 2. This case is discussed further in Section B(5) below.

251 *Corrections and Conditional Release Act*, SC 1992, c 20, ss 46–67.

conducted by an officer of the same sex.[252] Non-routine searches—where a person is singled out—require reasonable grounds to believe the person possesses evidence of a disciplinary or criminal offence.[253] Further provisions allow for urinalysis, cell searches, and strip searches of an entire prison population on reasonable grounds to believe there is a "clear and substantial danger to human life or safety or to the security of the penitentiary."[254] Further provisions provide for routine frisk search of visitors and strip search on reasonable grounds.[255]

The *Canadian Security Intelligence Service Act* permits CSIS agents to obtain search warrants and to conduct electronic surveillance in limited circumstances.[256] A judge of the Federal Court may issue a warrant on reasonable grounds to believe a search is required to enable the service to investigate a "threat to the security of Canada" or perform its duties under the Act.[257] The duties defined in the Act include "the collection of information or intelligence relating to the capabilities, intentions or activities" of a foreign state or a person *other than* a Canadian citizen, permanent residence, or corporation.[258] However, as the Federal Court has noted, the service is authorized to act where it incidentally intercepts communications involving Canadians speaking with targeted foreigners.[259] This would require ministerial authorization under the Act and would be subject to a host of other safeguards and accountability mechanisms in the Act and in CSIS operational policies.[260]

Finally, the current government has tabled in Parliament a bill to amend the framework for protecting the privacy of information gathered by federal entities and institutions.[261] In both the existing framework (under *PIPEDA*[262]) and the framework in Bill C-27, there are various provisions dealing with the disclosure of information to law enforcement

252 *Ibid*, ss 47, 48, and 49(3)(b).

253 *Ibid*, s 49.

254 *Ibid*, ss 53, 54, and 58.

255 *Ibid*, ss 59 & 60.

256 *Canadian Security Intelligence Service Act*, RSC 1985, c C-23, s 21.

257 *Ibid*, s 21(1) using the term "judge," which is defined in s 2 of the Act to mean "a judge of the Federal Court designated by the Chief Justice thereof for the purposes of this Act."

258 *Ibid*, s 16(1).

259 *Canadian Security Intelligence Services Act (CA) (Re)*, 2020 FC 697 at para 77.

260 *Ibid* at paras 75–92.

261 Bill C-27, *An Act to enact the Consumer Privacy Protection Act, the Personal Information and Data Protection Tribunal Act and the Artificial Intelligence and Data Act and to make consequential and related amendments to other Acts*, 1st Sess, 44th Parl, 2021 (short title: *Digital Charter Implementation Act*) proposing amendments to *PIPEDA*, above note 99.

262 *PIPEDA*, *ibid*.

or for other investigative or regulatory purposes. As the Supreme Court noted in *Spencer*, these provisions do not create powers to search; they clarify when an entity covered by the Act may disclose information to law enforcement or other agencies without a person's knowledge or consent.[263] Both the existing and proposed frameworks permit the disclosure of information without consent to state authorities pursuant to a warrant or where the party requesting the information has lawful authority to make the demand.[264] In *Spencer*, the Court held that when police, acting without a warrant, asked Shaw to provide the accused's subscriber information, they did not have lawful authority to do so, as was required under *PIPEDA*. The Court held that making the demand constituted a search because the accused had a reasonable expectation of privacy in the information. The search was not authorized by law and was therefore unreasonable under section 8.[265] As noted earlier, in the wake of *Spencer*, police obtain internet subscriber information using the "production order" powers of the *Criminal Code*.[266]

5) Shifting from Regulatory to Criminal Search

In some cases, the law sets out search powers that are meant to enable state agents to administer and enforce a regulatory framework—for example, the regime in the federal *Firearms Act* for licensing and registering firearms,[267] or powers under Ontario's *Environmental Protection Act* to reduce pollution.[268] Where officials conduct a search under these powers, a person may be convicted of a regulatory rather than a criminal offence—which is to say, an offence resulting in a fine or, occasionally, a relatively short jail sentence. Regulatory offences are meant to impose a standard of conduct that minimizes harm to public safety or welfare of otherwise lawful activities; criminal offences are meant to deter and punish acts considered inherently wrong or unacceptably dangerous.[269]

263 *Spencer*, above note 97 at paras 71–73, discussing s 7(3)(c.1)(ii), *ibid*.

264 *PIPEDA*, above note 99, s 7(3).

265 *Spencer*, above note 97 at paras 66–67 and 74. *Spencer* is discussed at greater length in Chapter 4, Section C(1).

266 See the discussion of s 487.014 of the *Code* in Section A(3) of this chapter.

267 *Firearms Act*, above note 117.

268 RSO 1990, c E19.

269 The opinion of Cory J in *R v Wholesale Travel Group Inc*, [1991] 3 SCR 154 at 216–18 [*Wholesale Travel*], contains a segment headed "The Distinction Between Crimes and Regulatory Offences" noting: "Acts or actions are criminal when they constitute conduct that is, in itself, so abhorrent to the basic values of human society that it ought to be prohibited completely" or where they are not "inherently wrongful, but . . . unregulated activity would result in dangerous conditions

Given the lower jeopardy and consequences of a conviction for a regulatory offence, powers to search and seize in this context tend to be more permissive and involve lower standards for authorization.

In some areas of the law, however, there is an overlap. Possessing a firearm or driving, for example, can lead to a regulatory or a criminal investigation, depending on the nature of the conduct. In some cases, state agents begin investigating what appears to be a regulatory offence—using more permissive search powers—then shift their focus to a possible criminal offence. In the process, they may be using powers not authorized or crafted for this purpose, and they might carry out what amounts to an unlawful and unreasonable search under section 8 of the *Charter*. How do courts decide when state actors have crossed the line separating a regulatory from a criminal investigation?

The leading case is the Supreme Court's decision in *R v Jarvis*.[270] In that case, Revenue Canada received a tip that the accused had not reported sales of his late wife's artworks in his tax returns. An auditor visited galleries, obtained information from him without cautioning him, and reviewed his records relying on the regulatory search provisions in the *Income Tax Act*.[271] The auditor then passed the file to a prosecution unit of Revenue Canada, which obtained a warrant on probable grounds for a more extensive search under the Act's criminal search powers. In a prosecution for the criminal offence of tax evasion under the Act, the Crown sought to adduce evidence the auditor had obtained using the Act's regulatory search powers, including information the accused had provided her. He argued that the auditor was carrying out a criminal investigation when she asked him for certain information, violating his right against self-incrimination (framed here under section 7 of the *Charter*), and that a search under a warrant issued in reliance on this information was unreasonable under section 8.

---

being imposed upon members of society, especially those who are particularly vulnerable." By contrast, at 219:

> The objective of regulatory legislation is to protect the public or broad segments of the public (such as employees, consumers and motorists, to name but a few) from the potentially adverse effects of otherwise lawful activity. . . . While criminal offences are usually designed to condemn and punish past, inherently wrongful conduct, regulatory measures are generally directed to the prevention of future harm through the enforcement of minimum standards of conduct and care.

270 *Jarvis*, above note 249; see also *R v Ling*, 2002 SCC 74, decided along with *Jarvis*, involving a similar fact pattern.

271 *Income Tax Act*, above note 246. See the discussion of the two sets of powers in the Act in Section B(4) above.

The Supreme Court in *Jarvis* distinguished between the Act's "administrative" or "enforcement" powers, meant for regulatory aspects of the Act, and its "investigative" powers, meant for prosecuting criminal offences in the Act.[272] The former, the Court held, are not available for prosecutions. As Iacobucci and Major JJ wrote, "officials 'cross the Rubicon' when the inquiry in question engages the adversarial relationship between the taxpayer and the state."[273] This occurs when "the predominant purpose of an inquiry is the determination of penal liability."[274] Deciding whether and when an inquiry has assumed this purpose is "contextual" and takes account of "all relevant factors," including whether officials had reasonable grounds to lay charges; whether their "general conduct" was "consistent with the pursuit of a criminal investigation"; whether they transferred files to criminal investigators; whether they acted as agents for criminal investigators; or any other circumstances suggesting the inquiry "had in reality become a criminal investigation."[275]

A further important holding in *Jarvis* involved the question of privacy in information one is obliged to disclose under a regulatory regime such as the *Income Tax Act*. The Court held that a person has a low privacy interest in information they must disclose to an auditor under the Act, as is the case with information required in other regulatory contexts.[276] Once an auditor has compelled information or obtained a document from a person, the person does not have a reasonable expectation that the auditor will not disclose the information or document to investigators who may use it to prosecute.[277] As Iacobucci and Major JJ noted: "[i]f a particular piece of evidence comes to light as a result of the information validly contained in the auditor's file, then investigators may make use of it."[278] The question, once again, would be whether, at the time the auditor obtained the information under the Act's regulatory powers, her inquiry was still regulatory in nature rather than criminal.

In this case, the Court found that the auditor had passed on to an investigator information she had validly obtained under the Act's regulatory powers, since at the time she obtained the information, she was not conducting an "investigation into penal liability."[279] However, a few

---

272 The regulatory powers are those in ss 231.1(1), 231.2(1) *ibid*, and the investigative powers are found in s 231.3(1).

273 *Jarvis*, above note 249 at para 88.

274 *Ibid* at para 93.

275 *Ibid* at paras 93–94.

276 *Ibid* at para 72, citing *Thomson Newspapers Ltd v Canada (Director of Investigation and Research, Restrictive Trade Practices Commission)*, [1990] 1 SCR 425 at 507.

277 *Jarvis*, above note 249 at para 95.

278 *Ibid*.

279 *Ibid* at para 104.

months later, when the auditor made a further inquiry for information pertaining to banking records, she did cross the Rubicon, since "the [criminal] investigation was at that point well underway."[280]

C. POWERS IN PROVINCIAL STATUTES

Under Canada's Constitution, only the federal government may enact criminal law.[281] Provincial governments may enact offences to enforce laws that fall within provincial jurisdiction.[282] Provincial offences deal with matters that are regulatory in nature. As we noted in the previous section, regulatory offences are meant to impose a standard of conduct that minimizes harm to public safety or welfare of otherwise lawful activities, while criminal offences seek to deter and punish acts considered inherently wrong or unacceptably dangerous.[283] Regulatory offences carry lesser sentences. They also often entail investigations that intrude upon a lower privacy interest. As a consequence, courts have found to be reasonable in this context powers for search and seizure that require lower grounds than for a criminal investigation or no grounds at all.[284]

Powers to search and seize can be found in countless provincial statutes (and municipal bylaws created under them) across Canada — not only to enforce offences but also for regulatory regimes in general. We make a few general observations. Where the powers involve intrusions on a reasonable expectation of privacy — which many if not most do — they engage section 8. These powers are found in a wide variety of legislation, dealing with topics that range from motor vehicles, firearms, food safety, gaming, coroner's investigations, tax audits, liquor control, securities law, and professions such as law, medicine, and engineering. Some can be found in unexpected places.[285] In each case, the powers to search and

---

280 *Ibid* at para 105

281 *Constitution Act, 1867* (UK), 30 & 31 Vict, c 3, s 91(27), reprinted in RSC 1985, App II, No 5.

282 *Ibid*, s 92(15).

283 See the discussion of Cory J's opinion on this distinction in *Wholesale Travel*, above note 269.

284 See Chapter 7, Section C(4) for a discussion of cases assessing whether search powers in the regulatory context are reasonable.

285 See, for example, powers of "inspection" found in s 174 of Quebec's *Charter of the French Language*, CQLR c C-11, authorizing inspectors to enter a place, take photographs, and search a computer for relevant documents. Another example can be found in Ontario's *Child, Youth and Family Services Act, 2017*, SO 2017, c 14, Sch 1, s 86(2), permitting in limited circumstances a child protection officer or peace officer to enter a home without a warrant, by force if necessary, to search for and remove a child.

seize—what, when, how, on what grounds—differ, depending on the context. Generally, regulatory powers to search and seize without a warrant exclude entry to a dwelling house (without consent) or search of the person, except where there are grounds to arrest under the *Criminal Code*. Finally, where no powers are provided for in a given act, catch-all powers to search and seize can be found in equivalents to British Columbia's *Offence Act* or Ontario's *Provincial Offences Act*.[286] These Acts provide for warrants analogous to the one in section 487 of the *Criminal Code*—to search a place on reasonable grounds to believe it contains evidence of a provincial offence and seize a thing named in the warrant found there.[287]

Two provincial search powers of notable scope are worth singling out. In some provinces, statutes dealing with the control of liquor or cannabis provide police the power to search a vehicle or *persons* found within a vehicle where they see an open container of liquor or cannabis not in a closed container—or have reasonable grounds to believe the statute has been violated.[288] Powers under Ontario law to search persons within a vehicle where an officer sees open cannabis have been challenged under section 8, and the Ontario Superior Court has found them reasonable.[289]

Canada's provinces also have statutes that play an analogous role to the federal *Personal Information Protection and Electronic Documents Act*.[290] These laws protect personal information that entities in the private sphere gather by setting out rules about when the entities can disclose the information.[291] In our discussion of *PIPEDA* above, we noted that provisions allowing for disclosure of information to law enforcement or other investigative agencies do not create powers to search or seize; they indicate when an entity covered by the Act may disclose information to law enforcement or other agencies without a person's consent.[292]

286 *Offence Act*, RSBC 1996, c 338; *Provincial Offences Act*, RSO 1990, c P33.

287 See, e.g., s 158 of Ontario's Act, *ibid*.

288 See, e.g., s 32(5) of Ontario's *Liquor Licence Act*, RSO 1990, c L19 and s 12(3) of Ontario's *Cannabis Control Act, 2017*, SO 2017, c 26, Sch 1; s 67 of British Columbia's *Liquor Control and Licensing Act*, SBC 2015, c 19; and s 24 of Nova Scotia's *Cannabis Control Act*, SNS 2018, c 3.

289 *R v Tully*, 2022 ONSC 1852.

290 Above note 99.

291 Examples include British Columbia's *Personal Information Protection Act*, SBC 2003, c 63 and Alberta's *Personal Information Protection Act*, SA 2003, c P-6.5.

292 See, e.g., s 18 of British Columbia's Act, *ibid*. See the discussion of *PIPEDA* in Section B(4) above.

D. COMMON LAW POWERS

In what follows, we canvass police powers to search and seize at common law in two groups: powers tied to older common law doctrines and a more recent and ever-expanding set of "ancillary police powers" the Supreme Court of Canada has recognized using the test in *Dedman v The Queen*.[293] We address the older powers first.

1) Consent

At common law, state agents are authorized to search a place or seize a thing where they have valid consent of the person authorized to provide it. In *R v Borden*, an accused consented to an officer seizing hair and blood samples.[294] The Supreme Court held that valid consent must be informed:

> In order for a waiver of the right to be secure against an unreasonable seizure to be effective, the person purporting to consent must be possessed of the requisite informational foundation for a true relinquishment of the right. A right to choose requires not only the volition to prefer one option over another, but also sufficient available information to make the preference meaningful.[295]

The Court of Appeal for Ontario in *R v Wills* set out a more extensive and commonly cited test for valid consent.[296] It requires the Crown to establish, on a balance of probabilities, that consent was given expressly or impliedly; the person who gave it had authority to do so; it was voluntary in the sense that it was "not the product of police oppression, coercion or other external conduct which negated the freedom to choose whether or not to allow the police to pursue the course of conduct requested"; the person who gave consent "was aware of the nature of the police conduct to which [they were] being asked to consent"; they were "aware of [their] right to refuse to permit the police to engage in the conduct requested"; and they were "aware of the potential consequences of giving the consent."[297]

---

293 [1985] 2 SCR 2 [*Dedman*]. See the discussion of *Dedman* and the "ancillary police powers" doctrine in Section D(4) below.

294 *R v Borden*, [1994] 3 SCR 145.

295 *Ibid* at 162.

296 *R v Wills* (1992), 7 OR (3d) 337 (CA) [*Wills*]; see also *R v Atkinson*, 2012 ONCA 380 at para 55.

297 *Wills*, above note 296.

Whether and when a person has authority to give consent is an unfolding area of the law. The Supreme Court in *R v Reeves* held that when police came to a home to seize a computer, a common law spouse who jointly owned the device could not consent to its seizure on behalf of her partner.[298] A person does not lose a privacy interest in relation to the state by virtue of sharing a device—whether through joint ownership or possession.[299] What happens if a joint owner or possessor who discovers evidence of a crime *brings* the device to police? Courts suggest that even here, police must obtain a warrant before searching the device. In *R v Cole*, school officials turned over to police a school owned laptop used by a teacher who they believed had stored child pornography on the device.[300] The Supreme Court held that police were authorized to "seize" the laptop, but required a warrant to search it, since the teacher continued to have an expectation of privacy in the device, which the school officials could not waive.[301]

A larger question the Court identified in *Reeves* but declined to address is whether a resident can consent to police entry of a shared home without the consent of the other residents.[302] Appeal courts have held that one resident can provide valid consent to police entry to common areas of the home.[303] Justice Karakatsanis noted a number of questions that would need to be considered in crafting a rule in this instance:

> Would police also be authorized to search common areas of the home? Should the privacy interests of other residents affect the authority to seize evidence, even if in plain view? Could another resident who is present object to the police entry? What if the officers seek entry for the specific purpose of investigating one of the other residents?[304]

The majority preferred to wait for a case where the issue was more central to the facts.

---

298 *R v Reeves*, 2018 SCC 56 [*Reeves*].

299 *Ibid* at paras 40–47; *R v Cole*, 2012 SCC 53 at para 51 [*Cole*].

300 *Cole*, *ibid*.

301 *Ibid* at paras 65–67. See the discussion of civilian disclosure of evidence to police in Chapter 3, Section E(3).

302 *Reeves*, above note 298 at paras 24–26.

303 *Ibid* at para 25, noting the holdings in *R v T (RMJ)*, 2014 MBCA 36 at paras 41–52; *R v Clarke*, 2017 BCCA 453 at paras 55–56 and 62–63; *R v Squires*, 2005 NLCA 51 at para 34.

304 *Reeves*, above note 298 at para 25.

2) Plain View

Earlier in this chapter we canvassed the "plain view" seizure powers in the *Criminal Code* and in the *Controlled Drugs and Substances Act*, noting the distinct powers that apply in searches with or without a warrant.[305] The common law authorizes a plain view seizure on a slightly more onerous test, recently summarized by the British Columbia Court of Appeal.[306] It has four requirements. At the time an officer notices and seizes an item, they must have had "lawful prior justification to be at the place where the evidence was found"; they must have "discovered the evidence inadvertently while exercising a lawful police power or performing a lawful police duty"; the evidence must have been "in plain view in the sense that it was detected through the unaided use of the officer's senses"; and it must have been "immediately apparent to the officer that the evidence was probably connected to criminal activity."[307] As noted earlier, the *Code* and *CDSA* provisions are slightly more permissive in that neither include a requirement that the discovery of an item be inadvertent or that it be "immediately apparent" to an officer that the item is connected to an offence.[308]

A good example of when inadvertence and immediacy might become an issue can be found in the Supreme Court's decision in *R v Law*.[309] A safe was stolen from a restaurant and recovered by police. While waiting to return it to its owner, an officer examined documents in the safe, copied them, and provided them to tax authorities for investigation. The Court held that police could not rely on the common law plain view doctrine because "the incriminating evidence was neither immediately obvious to [the officer] nor discovered inadvertently."[310]

3) Exigent Circumstances

This is another instance where a power can be found in the *Criminal Code* and in the *Controlled Drugs and Substances Act*, among other statutes, which is also found at common law. Courts have recognized a power to enter and search without a warrant in exigent circumstances—including

305 *Criminal Code*, above note 3, s 489(1), (2) and *CDSA*, above note 159, s 11(6), (8).

306 *R v Gill*, 2019 BCCA 260.

307 *Ibid* at para 33.

308 By contrast, under both the *Criminal Code* and the *CDSA*'s plain view powers, an officer needs reasonable grounds to believe the items were obtained by or used in an offence.

309 2002 SCC 10.

310 *Ibid* at para 27.

a dwelling house — as far back as *Semayne's Case* in 1604.[311] In the post-*Charter* era, the power has drawn greater scrutiny. In *Feeney*, the Supreme Court held that police may not enter a residence without a warrant to carry out an arrest unless in "hot pursuit."[312] In *Silveira*, the Court found that a warrantless entry into a home to "secure the premises and prevent the destruction of evidence" in exigent circumstances was not authorized by law.[313] At the time the Court decided *Silveira*, the earlier equivalent to what is now section 11(7) of the *Controlled Drugs and Substances Act* permitted warrantless entry on reasonable grounds to believe evidence of a drug offence would be found — but it specifically excluded entry and search of a dwelling house.[314] The majority in *Silveira* held that the common law power to enter and search in exigent circumstances did not apply here; some authority — not necessarily a warrant — was required.

In response to these decisions, Parliament amended the *Criminal Code* and the *CDSA*. As noted above, section 529.3 of the *Code* codifies the holding in *Feeney* and earlier cases permitting police to enter without a warrant to arrest in "hot pursuit" on reasonable grounds to believe a person is present. The section also allows police warrantless entry on reasonable suspicion that a person's safety is at risk or reasonable grounds to believe that evidence will be destroyed before a warrant can be obtained — though in each case authority to enter is tied to an intention to arrest. Section 11(7) of the *CDSA* no longer excludes dwelling houses, thus authorizing police in drug cases to enter and search a home without a warrant in exigent circumstances. And more broadly, section 487.11 of the *Code* permits police to "exercise any of the powers described in subsection 487(1) (the standard warrant) or 492.1(1) (tracking warrants) without a warrant if the conditions for obtaining a warrant exist but by reason of exigent circumstances it would be impracticable to obtain a warrant."

---

311 See the discussion by Dickson J, as he then was, in *Eccles v Bourque*, [1975] 2 SCR 739 at 743, of the recognition in *Semayne's Case* (1604), 77 ER 194, that an exception to the principle that "a man's home is his castle" is the power of a state agent to enter a dwelling house to arrest or (citing *Semayne*) "do other execution of the K.'s process, if otherwise he cannot enter." The Court also cites this passage in *R v Landry*, [1986] 1 SCR 145 at 156–57 [*Landry*] and in *Feeney*, above note 157, at para 39, as authority for warrantless entry to arrest.

312 *Feeney*, above note 157; see also *R v Macooh*, [1993] 2 SCR 802 and *Landry*, *ibid*, permitting warrantless entry of a dwelling house in hot pursuit.

313 *Silveira*, above note 154.

314 *Narcotic Control Act*, RSC 1985, c N-1, as repealed by *Controlled Drigs and Substances Act*, 1996, c 19, s 10.

What remaining role, if any, the common law power of entry, search, and seizure in exigent circumstances plays is unclear. The Ontario Court of Appeal in *R v Kelsy* suggested that it may still afford police authority to search a place (other than a dwelling house) to preserve evidence, but if so, police must still have grounds for obtaining a warrant.[315] In that case, police searched a knapsack on no grounds for believing contraband would be found in it, rendering it unlawful in the court's view. The holding in *Kelsy* would appear to impose a requirement on the common law power that renders it redundant in light of section 487.11 of the *Code* or section 11(7) of the *CDSA*.

4) Ancillary Police Powers

Few areas in Canadian criminal law have evolved as rapidly in the past three decades as the caselaw involving the doctrine of "ancillary police powers." The doctrine was first developed in the English Court of Appeal decision in *R v Waterfield* (1963)[316] and adopted by the Supreme Court of Canada in *R v Stenning* (1970).[317] The Supreme Court has since invoked it in *Cloutier v Langlois* to refine an earlier common law power of search incident to arrest,[318] and to recognize a host of new powers, including in *Dedman* (the R.I.D.E. program for impaired driving stops);[319] *R v Godoy* (911 home entry without a warrant);[320] *R v Mann* (investigative detention and search);[321] *R v Kang-Brown* (sniffer dog searches);[322] and *R v MacDonald* (safety searches).[323] Initially, the doctrine was not meant as a tool for recognizing or creating new police powers. The Court's use of it in this way has been controversial and gives rise to a measure of uncertainty in the law. To lend context to what follows, it may help to briefly address how this shift came about. Doing so will also shed light on how and why the doctrine continues to be used to recognize new search powers.

The English Court of Appeal decision in *Waterfield* involved the offence of assaulting an officer in the execution of his duties.[324] It was unclear in that case whether the officer was acting in the course of his

315 *R v Kelsy*, 2011 ONCA 605 at para 30.

316 [1963] 3 All ER 659 [*Waterfield*].

317 [1970] SCR 631 [*Stenning*].

318 *Cloutier v Langlois*, [1990] 1 SCR 158 [*Cloutier*].

319 *Dedman*, above note 293, assessing the Reduced Impaired Driving Everywhere program in Ontario.

320 *R v Godoy*, [1999] 1 SCR 311 [*Godoy*].

321 *R v Mann*, 2004 SCC 52 [*Mann*].

322 *R v Kang-Brown*, 2008 SCC 18 [*Kang-Brown*].

323 *R v MacDonald*, 2014 SCC 3 [*MacDonald*].

324 *Waterfield*, above note 316.

duties. He sought to examine a vehicle that had been in an accident. Finding the accused in the vehicle in a parking lot, about to drive away, the officer directed the accused to stop, which he declined to do, "coming into slight contact" with the officer as he drove away.[325] Justice Ashworth set out a test to decide whether the officer was acting "within his duty" at this time. A court should ask "whether (a) [the officer's] conduct falls within the general scope of any duty imposed by statute or recognised at common law and (b) whether such conduct, albeit within the general scope of such a duty, involved an unjustifiable use of powers associated with the duty."[326] Police here had a duty to prevent and investigate crime, but the duty did not permit unauthorized "interference with the person or property of a private person." In this case, the accused was not under arrest and police had no authority to detain the vehicle. The officer was therefore not acting "within his duty" when briefly assaulted.

The *Waterfield* test made a distinction between duty and authority.[327] An officer is "justified" in executing a duty only where he is authorized to do so. Failing this, he cannot lawfully act "in the execution of his duties." From the outset of its adoption of the test, the Supreme Court of Canada has overlooked this distinction. It has used *Waterfield* to recognize an officer's authority to do something based on a duty to do it—rather than discerning the limits of a duty from the lack of authority, as in *Waterfield* itself. The Court turned the test on its head.

It did so initially in cases involving charges of assaulting or obstructing a peace officer in the execution of his duties. In *Stenning*, the Supreme Court invoked *Waterfield* to find that an officer who had no authority to enter a building was "engaged in the execution of his duties" because he had to investigate a crime.[328] In *R v Knowlton*, police had no authority to close a portion of a public street in front of a hotel, but they were acting within their duty in doing so because they had to protect a visiting Soviet dignitary.[329] Lost in the analysis in both cases was original use of the test: i.e., deciding whether police had acted within their duty based on whether they were "authorized."

By the time the Court decided *Dedman* in 1985, the *Waterfield* test was no longer confined to cases of assault or obstruction—it had become a general test for whether police had authority to act.[330] The question

---

325 Waterfield was not the driver, but the owner of the car who advised Lynn, a co-accused, to drive away.

326 *Waterfield*, above note 316.

327 See Coughlan, above note 22 at 19.

328 *Stenning*, above note 317.

329 *R v Knowlton*, [1974] SCR 443.

330 *Dedman*, above note 293.

in the second prong of *Waterfield*—whether police were "justified" (i.e., authorized) to carry out a duty—had transformed into the question of whether "the police action [at issue] is reasonably necessary for the fulfillment of the duty."[331] The Court in *Dedman* set out a broad test for when an act is reasonably necessary: "The interference with liberty must be necessary for the carrying out of the particular police duty and it must be reasonable, having regard to the nature of the liberty interfered with and the importance of the public purpose served by the interference."[332] Applying *Dedman*, the Court would go on to create a wide range of new police powers by recognizing an authority to act based on a duty to act.

In light of the open-ended nature of the *Dedman* inquiry, in many situations we can no longer know whether what police have done is lawful—until a court decides, after the fact, that it was reasonably necessary.[333] Where police lack authority to carry out a search or seizure, the Court might recognize a new authority and apply it retroactively—as the Court has done in some of the cases below.[334] Having said this, the cases we canvass here do capture a wide swath of police conduct and offer a stable—if not entirely precise—set of rules about search and seizure.

a) Search Incident to Arrest (Including Vehicles, Devices, Homes)

When police arrest a person, they have the power to search the person and their immediate surroundings. The power to "search incident to arrest" requires no further grounds than those required for a lawful arrest.[335] In order for the search to be lawful, the arrest itself must be

---

331 *Fleming v Ontario*, 2019 SCC 45 at para 47 [*Fleming*].

332 *Dedman*, above note 293 at 35; cited in *Fleming*, *ibid* at para 47.

333 See, e.g., *Fleming*, above note 331, the Court's most recent extended engagement with *Waterfield/Dedman*, in which the Crown had sought recognition of "a common law power to arrest individuals who have not committed any offence, who are not about to commit any offence, who have not already breached the peace and who are not about to breach the peace themselves." The Court declined to find this "reasonably necessary." A majority of the Ontario Court of Appeal had held that it was: *Fleming v Ontario*, 2018 ONCA 160.

334 For a more detailed critique of the Court's use of *Waterfield* and *Dedman*, see James Stribopolous, "In Search of Dialogue: The Supreme Court, Police Powers and the *Charter*" (2005) 31 *Queen's Law Journal* 1.

335 There are many sources of law authorizing a state agent to arrest, but most commonly, police rely on the powers in s 495(1) of the *Criminal Code*, above note 3. This provision allows for arrest in three situations: where a peace officer has reasonable grounds to believe a person has committed or is about to commit an indictable offence (which includes a hybrid offence); where an officer finds a person committing a "criminal offence" (i.e., which includes a strictly summary offence); or where there are reasonable grounds to believe a warrant is outstanding. The reference to "indictable offences" in s 495(1) includes hybrid offences by

lawful. The reason for the search and the scope of the search must be tied to the reasons for the arrest. The leading cases provide guidance on each point.

The Supreme Court decided the initial proposition—that a search on arrest requires no further grounds—in *Cloutier v Langlois*.[336] In this case, police pulled over a Montreal lawyer for a traffic violation, then discovered he was subject to an outstanding warrant for unpaid traffic tickets. An officer carried out a brief frisk search incident to Cloutier's arrest. Cloutier launched a private prosecution for assault against the two officers involved, arguing that police needed grounds to search in addition to those for the arrest. He did not frame his case, nor did the Court approach it, as a section 8 breach.[337] Justice L'Heureux-Dubé, writing for the Court, conducted an extensive review of authority in US, UK, and Canadian common law to find that without requiring further grounds, "police have a power to search a lawfully arrested person and to seize anything in his or her possession or immediate surroundings to guarantee the safety of the police and the accused, prevent the prisoner's escape or provide evidence against him."[338]

To ascertain the scope of the power, L'Heureux-Dubé J in *Cloutier* cited the test in *Dedman*, noted above.[339] This resulted in three qualifications to search on arrest. Police have discretion not to search and should not do so as a matter of "duty" or routine.[340] The search "must be for a valid objective in pursuit of the ends of criminal justice—such as the discovery of an object that may be a threat to the safety of the police, the accused or the public, or that may facilitate escape or act as evidence against the accused."[341] And third, the search "must not be conducted in an abusive fashion, and in particular, the use of physical or psychological constraint should be proportionate to the objectives sought and the other

---

virtue of the definition of an indictable offence in s 34(1)(a) of the *Interpretation Act*, above note 23. For more detail on these powers, see Steve Coughlan & Glen Luther, *Detention and Arrest*, 2d ed (Toronto: Irwin Law, 2017) at 264–74.

336 *Cloutier*, above note 318.

337 Justice L'Heureux-Dubé does, however, consider the *Charter* at one point in her analysis, suggesting, at 184, that common law search powers should be developed "in a manner consistent with the fundamental values enshrined in the Constitution" (quoting *RWDSU v Dolphin Delivery Ltd*, [1986] 2 SCR 573 at 603).

338 *Cloutier*, above note 318 at 180–81. The Court in *R v Caslake*, [1998] 1 SCR 51 [*Caslake*] held, at para 13, that the power to search on arrest is premised on a lawful arrest: "since the legality of the search is derived from the legality of arrest, if the arrest is later found to be invalid, the search will be also."

339 *Cloutier*, above note 318 at 181.

340 *Ibid* at 186.

341 *Ibid*.

circumstances of the situation."[342] *Cloutier* was not entirely clear on the physical scope of a search on arrest. As noted, L'Heureux-Dubé J held that police could search a person and "anything in his or her possession or immediate surroundings." The search in *Cloutier* involved only a brief pat down. Precisely what was permitted beyond this was unclear.

In *R v Caslake*, the Court suggested that what falls within a person's "possession or immediate surroundings" turns on the question of whether and when a search is *incidental* to an arrest.[343] Where there is a sufficient nexus between an arrest and a search, an arrestee's possessions or immediate surroundings can include a vehicle, and police may search it incident to arrest well after they have carried out the arrest.

Police in *Caslake* impounded the accused's car after arresting him for a drug offence. Six hours later, without a warrant, an officer conducted an inventory search of the vehicle—under a policy to do so routinely with impounded vehicles—and found packages of cocaine. The trial judge found the search to be "too thorough" to accept that it was a mere inventory search, with police checking the glove compartment and under the seats, but held that it fell within the power set out in *Cloutier*.[344] Chief Justice Lamer, writing for a majority of the Court, held that the power to search on arrest in *Cloutier* is premised on a search being "truly incidental" to the reason for the arrest itself. He noted the "three main purposes" of search on arrest that L'Heureux-Dubé J had identified—safety and the protection or discovery of evidence. An officer must be searching for one or more of these purposes and the purposes must be reasonable in relation to the offence for which a person is being arrested.[345] This involves both an objective and a subjective element.[346] After an officer stopped a person for a traffic violation and was satisfied safety was not at issue, it would make no sense objectively to continue to search for evidence. Conversely, in this case, while it may have been objectively reasonable to search a vehicle for drugs after arresting a person for a drug offence, this was not the officer's subjective purpose for the search (he did so to comply with the inventory policy).[347] A search will be "truly incidental" to an arrest where an officer subjectively decides to search for a reason consistent with the reason for arrest, and where that

342 *Ibid.*

343 *Caslake*, above note 338.

344 *Ibid* at para 5.

345 *Ibid* at para 19.

346 *Ibid.*

347 Justices L'Heureux-Dubé, Gonthier, and Bastarache held that the requirement for both objective and subjective purposes tied to the reason for arrest had the effect of surreptitiously reimposing a requirement for separate and additional reasonable grounds for search incident to arrest—and thus, impliedly, overturning *Cloutier*.

intention involves the search for evidence, the intention will be objectively reasonable if there is a "reasonable prospect of securing evidence of the offence for which the accused is being arrested."[348] The officer need not have separate and additional reasonable grounds for the search; they need only "some reasonable basis for doing what [they] did."[349]

How much later in space and time can a search still be incident to an arrest? The majority in *Caslake* left this open-ended, with Lamer CJ asserting that the "limits [on search] will be no different for automobiles than for any other place" and that the "scope of that search will depend on a number of factors, including the basis for the arrest, the location of the motor vehicle in relation to the place of the arrest, and other relevant circumstances."[350] Temporal limits work the same way. There is no "firm deadline on the amount of time that may elapse" before a search is no longer incidental:

> As a general rule, searches that are truly incidental to arrest will usually occur within a reasonable period of time after the arrest. A substantial delay does not mean that the search is automatically unlawful, but it may cause the court to draw an inference that the search is not sufficiently connected to the arrest. Naturally, the strength of the inference will depend on the length of the delay, and can be defeated by a reasonable explanation for the delay.[351]

As a result of *Caslake*, officers in the field are often unclear whether a search incident to arrest will be authorized by law. Courts need to assess, after the fact and on a case-by-case basis, whether a search was truly incidental. In many instances, the possibility opened up in *Caslake*—to search at some distance in space and time—gives rise to uncertainty and inconsistency in the decisions.[352]

Another crucial space that attracts a high privacy interest is the one contained in our phones and laptops, and these too engage a special set of rules about search on arrest. As Fish J held in *Morelli*, "[i]t is difficult to imagine a search more intrusive, extensive, or invasive of one's privacy than the search and seizure of a personal computer."[353] Prior to the Supreme Court's decision in *Fearon* in 2014, lower courts were divided

---

348 *Caslake*, above note 338 at para 22.

349 *Ibid* at paras 20, 23.

350 *Ibid* at para 23.

351 *Ibid* at para 24.

352 See, e.g., *R v Ellis*, 2016 ONCA 598, finding the search of a trunk in a careless driving case not incidental, while in *R v Pearson*, 2017 ONCA 389, search of a trunk on arrest for impaired driving involving drugs was incidental.

353 *Morelli*, above note 180 at para 2.

as to whether police could search a phone or device on arrest without a warrant. That year, the United States Supreme Court held in *Riley v California* that police could not (they need a warrant),[354] and given the Supreme Court of Canada's pronouncements about privacy and computers in *Morelli*, *Vu*, and *Cole*,[355] it seemed likely the Court would follow *Riley* with a similar rule in *Fearon*. The Court chose not to do so and crafted its own rule instead.

In *Fearon*, two men had robbed a jewellery merchant loading her car, and one of the men had a handgun.[356] When police arrested two suspects later that evening, neither the gun nor the jewellery had yet been found. They located a cellphone in the accused's pocket—a relatively primitive flip phone with limited storage.[357] They searched it within two hours of the arrest, finding incriminating texts and photos of a handgun. In a 4:3 decision, Cromwell J for the majority held that police may search a device incident to arrest, without a warrant, on certain conditions. The conditions are shaped in part by Cromwell J's reasons for extending the power of search on arrest to include devices. The majority held that even though phones and other devices engage a high privacy interest, the state interest in immediate access on arrest to the data they contain is also pressing because devices might be used to notify parties to an offence of police involvement, potentially endangering police, or evidence might be remotely destroyed. The dissent took a more skeptical view, consistent with the US Supreme Court's holding in *Riley*. Devices might in theory be used to "summon violent backup" or be wiped remotely, but both scenarios are likely to be rare and best dealt with under an exigent circumstances exception.[358]

Fearon authorizes police to search a phone incident to arrest on four conditions.[359] The first two are that the arrest must be lawful and the search of the device must be "truly incidental to the arrest in that the

---

354 *Riley v California*, 134 S Ct 2473 (2014).

355 *Vu* above note 105 at paras 41–44; *Cole* above note 299 at paras 47–49.

356 *Fearon*, above note 106.

357 In a commentary on *Fearon*, Jordan Fine notes that "Fearon's phone is described in the trial court judgment as a Telus LG285, a discontinued flip phone within the 'burner' class of devices, lacking a touchscreen, high-resolution camera, and social media application capabilities." Jordan Fine, "Leaving Dumb Phones Behind: A Commentary on the Warrantless Searches of Smartphone Data Granted in *R v Fearon*" (2015) 13 *Canadian Journal of Law and Technology* 171 at 179.

358 Justice Cromwell, at para 84 of *Fearon*, above note 106, conceded that the balance struck by the majority here may not be the only way to craft a reasonable law on point: "This may be an area . . . in which legislation may well be desirable. The law enforcement and privacy concerns may be balanced in many ways and my reasons are not intended to restrict the acceptable options."

359 The four rules are summarized at para 83, *ibid*.

police have a reason based on a valid law enforcement purpose to conduct the search, and that reason is objectively reasonable." The valid purposes for searching a device include safety of police or others and preserving or discovering evidence. The majority added a qualification here that police may only search to *discover* evidence when "the investigation will be stymied or significantly hampered absent the ability to promptly search the cell phone incident to arrest."[360] Third, the "nature and the extent of the search" must be "tailored to the purpose of the search." Justice Cromwell noted that "[i]n practice, this will mean that, generally, . . . only recently sent or drafted emails, texts, photos and the call log may be examined as in most cases only those sorts of items will have the necessary link to the purposes for which prompt examination of the device is permitted. But these are not rules, and other searches may in some circumstances be justified."[361] Fourth, "police [must] take detailed notes of what they have examined on the device and how it was searched." A failure to meet any one of these conditions will result in the search not being authorized by law.

In the wake of *Fearon*, commentators have questioned whether the rule would soon be rendered moot in most cases by the nearly ubiquitous use of password protection and encryption on personal devices.[362] In practice, many phones seized on arrest are not searched immediately, or not successfully even once a warrant is obtained. However, as a cursory search of the CanLII or Quicklaw databases will show, there continue to be a number of trial court decisions in which police have searched devices on arrest and the court applies *Fearon* to assess whether the search was reasonable.

The Supreme Court has recently added a further chapter to search incident to arrest in *R v Stairs*.[363] The question in this case was whether police can search an area within a dwelling house incident to arrest and on what grounds. In response to a 911 call reporting a man hitting a woman repeatedly in a car, police soon located the vehicle on the driveway of a house. Running the plate, police were cautioned that the accused had a history of violence and was deemed a "high-risk offender."[364] Police knocked on the door several times and "loudly announced their presence." Receiving no response, they entered the home and a

---

360 *Ibid*.

361 *Ibid* at para 76.

362 Colton Fehr & Jared Biden, "Divorced From (Technological) Reality: A Response to the Supreme Court of Canada's Reasons in *R. v. Fearon*" (2015) 20:1 *Canadian Criminal Law Review* 93.

363 *R v Stairs*, 2022 SCC 11 [*Stairs*].

364 *Ibid* at para 12.

woman with injuries to her face approached them coming up a set of stairs from the basement. Police then saw the accused run across the landing of the staircase, heading from a living room area to a laundry room, where they arrested him. Following the arrest, an officer went to the living room to "make sure there was no one else there and that there were no other hazards."[365] There, he conducted a "visual clearing search," scanning the table, couch, television, and cabinets.[366] To see what was behind the couch, he walked behind it and saw a clear plastic container and a bag containing what he believed was methamphetamine. The accused was charged with possession for the purpose of trafficking, assault, and breach of probation. He challenged the search of the room as exceeding the scope of search incident to arrest but was unsuccessful.

A majority of the Court of Appeal for Ontario in *Stairs* saw the officer's decision to go back to the living room as authorized under the safety search power in *R v MacDonald*.[367] Police here had a reasonable belief in an imminent threat to police or public safety. Justice Nordheimer in dissent held that there was neither a reasonable basis to believe nor to suspect that other people or weapons might be found in the room. A majority of the Supreme Court opted to recognize two new and distinct powers to search incident to arrest within a home.

Justices Moldaver and Jamal, for the majority in *Stairs*, held that a search within a home engages a higher degree of privacy than searches on arrest elsewhere, but is not as invasive as a strip search or penile swab.[368] Police objectives are also pressing here, since "arrests within the home are often volatile and dynamic."[369] On this basis, when police carry out a lawful arrest within a home, they may search the area "within the arrested person's physical control at the time of the arrest" on no additional grounds, as set out in *Cloutier*.[370] Police may also search the area "outside the arrested person's physical control at the time of the arrest" but "sufficiently proximate to the arrest" where police have "reason to suspect that the search will further the objective of police and public safety, including the safety of the accused."[371] In this latter case, "the key consideration is the link between the location and purpose of the search and the grounds for the arrest."[372] Justices Moldaver and Jamal

365 *Ibid* at para 22.
366 *Ibid* at para 16.
367 2020 ONCA 678, citing *MacDonald*, above note 323.
368 *Stairs*, above note 363 at paras 51 and 54.
369 *Ibid* at para 52.
370 *Ibid* at para 82.
371 *Ibid.*
372 *Ibid* at para 79, citing *R v Nolet*, 2010 SCC 24 at para 49.

also noted that "the nature and the extent of the search must be tailored to the purpose of the search and the heightened privacy interests in a home."[373] They cautioned that when police go beyond the space within the physical control of an arrestee, they are "highly constrained" and may not engage in "windfall searches"; they may not search "every nook and cranny of the house"; and the search should be "no more intrusive than is necessary to resolve the police's reasonable suspicion."[374] When assessing whether a search of this nature was conducted in a reasonable manner, the Court may consider notes the officer took on the "places searched, the extent of the search, the time of the search, its purpose, and its duration."[375] The Court may draw an adverse inference about reasonable conduct of a search where an officer fails to take notes.[376]

In this case, the majority held that the trial judge did not err in finding that the officer's decision to return to the living room was based on a reasonable suspicion of a risk to safety, given the uncooperative nature of the victim, the fact of her being injured, and the uncertainty about others being present or other hazards remaining.[377] Justice Karakatsanis, writing in dissent (joined by Brown and Martin JJ), held the privacy interest in a home to be high enough to warrant a higher standard for search incident to arrest here: reasonable suspicion of an *imminent* threat to police or public safety—a standard not met in this case.[378]

Both the majority and the dissent left an important issue unaddressed: whether and how the plain view doctrine should apply on a search incident to arrest in a dwelling house, as contemplated in this case.[379] The dissent held it was unnecessary to address the issue because it found the entry and search of the living room to be unlawful. The majority held that it was unnecessary given findings of the trial judge and counsel's concession that if the applicable standard for a search incident to arrest in a home were modified to require reasonable suspicion, the plain view doctrine would apply.[380] Without having heard submissions on the role of the plain view power here, the majority declined to rule on it. The balance struck by the majority in crafting the safety

373 *Ibid* at para 82.
374 *Ibid* at paras 79–80.
375 *Ibid* at para 81.
376 *Ibid*.
377 *Ibid* at para 95.
378 *Ibid* at paras 107–8. Justice Côté authored a further dissent, agreeing with Karakatsanis J on the standard to be applied for a safety search on arrest in a home, and it not being met here, but disagreeing on s 24(2); she would have admitted the evidence.
379 *Ibid* at paras 102, 126, and 151.
380 *Ibid* at para 102.

search power on arrest depended in large part on the pressing state interest in preventing harm—i.e., a pressing enough interest to prevail over a high privacy interest in a home. One commentator has argued that the same would likely not be said of allowing police to rely on the plain view doctrine in the course of a safety search on arrest in a home.[381] The state has a lower interest in discovering or preserving evidence than in protecting safety. The solution, however, is unclear. The majority, in passing, pointed to the possibility that a plain view seizure might only be authorized in the course of a search on arrest in a home on reasonable suspicion that the evidence might otherwise be destroyed.[382] This would authorize a seizure, but would it warrant admission of the evidence? The balance between individual and state interests would likely shift to the terrain of section 24(2) of the *Charter*, with trial courts asking whether the impact on privacy in a given case outweighs other concerns and compels exclusion.

b) Strip Search and Penile Swab Incident to Arrest

In *R v Golden*, the Supreme Court held that the power in *Cloutier* permitting police to search incident to arrest without requiring further grounds does not extend to a strip search.[383] Police are authorized to conduct a strip search on arrest only where—in addition to having grounds for arrest—they have further reasonable grounds to believe a strip search is necessary for safety or to obtain evidence. And if police wish to conduct a strip search *in the field*, they need still further reasonable grounds to believe that exigent circumstances make it necessary to conduct it there. The Court extended this reasoning in *R v Saeed* to a strip search involving a penile swab.[384]

In *Golden*, police carried out a strip search at a Subway restaurant in Toronto. After observing the accused engaged in what appeared to be drug trafficking, officers arrested him and conducted a pat down but found nothing. They took him into a stairwell where they visually inspected his underwear and buttocks and saw protruding from his buttocks clear plastic wrap containing a white substance. Following a struggle with him to retrieve it, officers brought the accused to a seating booth at the back of the restaurant where they forced the accused to bend over a table and lowered his pants and underwear in the presence of several

381 Colton Fehr, "Defending the Castle: Search Incident to Arrest after *R v Stairs*" (2022) 26 *Canadian Criminal Law Review*.

382 *Ibid* at para 9.

383 *R v Golden*, 2001 SCC 83 [*Golden*], referring to *Cloutier*, above note 318 (which is discussed in the previous section of this chapter).

384 *R v Saeed*, 2016 SCC 24 [*Saeed*].

other officers and co-accused.[385] Using a pair of rubber gloves that were used to clean the restaurant's washrooms, an officer removed the package from the accused, finding crack cocaine. Trial and appellate courts found the search reasonable under section 8.

A narrow majority of the Supreme Court held that the search violated section 8 on the basis that it was neither authorized by law nor carried out in a reasonable manner. Justices Iacobucci and Arbour, for the majority, held that strip searches "represent a significant invasion of privacy."[386] They are "inherently humiliating and degrading for detainees regardless of the manner in which they are carried out and for this reason they cannot be carried out simply as a matter of routine policy."[387] Police do not have authority to conduct a strip search incident to arrest on no further grounds, as they do with a pat-down search. Police are only authorized to carry out a strip search if they have reasonable and probable grounds to believe it would yield "evidence related to the reason for the arrest" or "weapons in the detainee's possession."[388]

The majority also formulated a discrete rule for strip searches in the field. A strip search "should generally only be conducted at the police station except where there are exigent circumstances."[389] To conduct one in the field, police need "reasonable and probable grounds to believe that it is necessary to conduct the search in the field rather than at the police station" which entails "a demonstrated necessity and urgency to search for weapons or objects that could be used to threaten the safety of the accused, the arresting officers or other individuals."[390] In this case, while

---

385 *Golden*, above note 383 at paras 30–33.

386 *Ibid* at para 83.

387 *Ibid* at para 90. The majority defined a "strip search" at para 47 as involving "the removal or rearrangement of some or all of the clothing of a person so as to permit a visual inspection of a person's private areas, namely genitals, buttocks, breasts (in the case of a female), or undergarments."

388 *Ibid* at para 99: "the police must establish reasonable and probable grounds justifying the strip search in addition to reasonable and probable grounds justifying the arrest." And at para 94, noting: "Whether searching for evidence or for weapons, the mere possibility that an individual may be concealing evidence or weapons upon his person is not sufficient to justify a strip search."

389 *Ibid* at para 102.

390 *Ibid*. Interpreting this passage, the Ontario Court of Appeal, in *R v Pilon*, 2018 ONCA 959 held at para 27:

> Notwithstanding the broad statement in para. 102 of *Golden*, that exigent circumstances are limited to safety concerns, and the absence of case law considering preservation of evidence as an exigent circumstance justifying a field strip search, it is at least arguable that the Supreme Court in *Golden* left open the possibility that the need to preserve evidence could qualify as exigent circumstances that permit a field search.

there were grounds to conduct a strip search, there were no grounds to do so at the restaurant rather than at a police station some two minutes away.[391] The searches at the restaurant—taking them together as a single event—were also conducted in an unreasonable manner.[392] To establish what would constitute both a lawful and reasonably conducted strip search, the majority set out a set of criteria that we canvass in Chapter 8.[393]

The Court has had cause to revisit strip searches in a brief decision in *R v Ali*.[394] Justice Moldaver, for the majority, affirmed the finding at trial and the Court of Appeal that the strip search in this case complied with section 8. Police had received a tip from a confidential source that the accused was in possession of a large quantity of cocaine and kept most of his drugs on his person. Police found the accused next to a table with drugs (not cocaine), a scale, money, and a cellphone. As he was arrested, his pants were partially pulled down and an officer saw him reach toward the back of his pants. Collectively, this consisted reasonable and probable grounds to believe he had concealed evidence in his buttocks, justifying a strip search.

In *Saeed*, the Court addressed when police may obtain a penile swab. The case involved an arrest following an allegation of sexual assault.[395] Police obtained a swab from the accused roughly two hours after the arrest, while he was in custody. They had not sought a warrant under the assumption that they were authorized to obtain the sample under the power to search incident to arrest set out in *Cloutier*.[396] The swab was found to contain the complainant's DNA. Lower courts had held the swab to fall outside the power to search incident to arrest. A majority of the Supreme Court found that it does fall within this power, with some qualification.

One aspect of the reasons in *Golden* supports this reading. At para 108 of *Golden*, above note 383, Iacobucci and Arbour JJ note that the police station was a two-minute drive away from the shop:

> This fact alleviated any sense of exigency in this case. In our view, it seems highly improbable that the appellant, who was handcuffed, could have somehow surreptitiously ridded himself of the evidence concealed on his person during the very brief time it would have taken police to relocate him to 51 Division.

This would imply that had the station been much farther away, exigent circumstances might have justified a search for evidence.

391 *Golden*, above note 383 at paras 107–12.

392 *Ibid* at para 113.

393 *Ibid* at para 101. See the discussion of *Golden* in Chapter 8, Section B(1)(a).

394 2022 SCC 1.

395 *Saeed*, above note 384.

396 *Cloutier*, above note 318.

The Court in *Saeed* distinguished a penile swab from the taking of a bodily sample, which under *Stillman* requires a warrant.[397] A penile swab is meant to capture the complainant's rather than the accused's DNA.[398] It is invasive, given the need to expose a man's genitals, but less invasive than taking bodily impressions or hair samples because it does not involve a potentially painful impression or penetration.[399] And since DNA samples degrade over time, or the accused could remove or destroy the sample, there is a measure of urgency to such a seizure.[400] The privacy interest engaged in the act of taking a penile swab is high, but it can be reasonably balanced against law enforcement interests in light of two safeguards. One is a requirement that police may take a sample only if they have "reasonable grounds to believe that the search will reveal and preserve evidence of the offence for which the accused was arrested."[401] The other is to require police to conduct the swab in a reasonable manner, by following guidelines analogous to those set out in *Golden* for a reasonable strip search.[402] These include giving the accused a chance to remove his clothes and take the swab himself; having male officers take the swab somewhere in private; having no more of them involved than is reasonably necessary; and taking a "proper record" of the reasons for and manner in which the swab was conducted.[403]

In separate opinions, Karakantsanis and Abella JJ dissented. Justice Karakatsanis held the privacy interest here and the indignity entailed in the swabbing process—being handcuffed to a pipe in a dry cell—outweighed the state interest in obtaining the evidence. The common law should not be expanded to include a warrantless penile swab power on arrest. The swab in this case was not authorized by law, but Karakatsanis J would have admitted the evidence under section 24(2) of the *Charter*. Justice Abella agreed with Karakatsanis J that police do not have the power to take a penile swab on arrest given the heightened privacy and dignity interests, but would have excluded the evidence in this case under section 24(2).

---

397 *Saeed*, above note 384 at paras 43–51 distinguishing *R v Stillman*, above note 127.

398 *Ibid* at para 45. At para 48, Moldaver J held that "if an accused's DNA is obtained through a penile swab and the swab was taken without a warrant authorizing such seizure, or the accused's consent, the accused's DNA cannot be used for any purpose."

399 *Ibid* at para 49.

400 *Ibid* at paras 50 and 59.

401 *Ibid* at paras 6 and 64.

402 *Ibid* at paras 64 and 78.

403 *Ibid* at para 78.

c) Search Incident to Investigative Detention

Drawing on the test in *Dedman*, discussed above, the Supreme Court in *Mann* recognized a police power to conduct an investigative detention on reasonable suspicion of involvement in an offence and a further power to conduct a brief pat down search for weapons where there are additional reasonable grounds to suspect that safety is at issue.[404]

The facts in *Mann* help illustrate the scope of the search power created here. Late at night, responding to a dispatch about a break and enter, police came across the accused who closely matched the suspect's description given over police radio. Police stopped the accused and briefly patted him down for tools he might have used in the break-in that could be used as weapons. The officer felt a soft object in one of the accused's pockets and, reaching into it, found a small bag of marijuana and, in the other pocket, a number of small bags—resulting in a charge of trafficking. The Court held that police have a power to detain a person where there are reasonable grounds to suspect that the person is connected to an offence under investigation and where the detention is "reasonably necessary on an objective view of the totality of the circumstances."[405]

Where an officer conducts a lawful investigative detention, they may carry out a search with two key limitations. First, the officer must "believe on reasonable grounds that his or her own safety, or the safety of others, is at risk."[406] Justice Iacobucci's formulation of these grounds has been the cause of some confusion and debate.[407] "Reasonable grounds to believe" normally denotes "reasonable probability," but he refers in the same sentence to "risk"—a possibility—that safety might be at issue.[408] Further in his reasons, Iacobucci J notes that there was "a logical *possibility* that the [accused] . . . was in possession of break-and-enter tools,

---

404 *Mann*, above note 321.

405 *Ibid* at para 34.

406 *Ibid* at para 40.

407 See the dissenting opinion of Moldaver J and Wagner J, as he then was (joined by Rothstein J) in *MacDonald*, above note 323, beginning at para 64, offering a lengthy argument in support of the view that despite the wording used in *Mann*, Iacobucci J meant the standard to be "reasonable suspicion" of a risk to safety.

408 As Moldaver and Wagner JJ write in *MacDonald*, above note 323 at paras 69–70:

> Read in isolation, the "reasonable grounds to believe" language connotes the "reasonable and probable grounds" standard. . . . But one cannot stop reading there, because the concept of being "at risk" inherently builds in the concept of possibility. . . . The language of *Mann* thus appears to stack a *probability* on top of a *possibility*—a chance upon a chance. In other words, *Mann* says a safety search is justified if it is *probable* that something *might* happen, not that it is *probable* that something *will* happen. As this Court only recently explained, the former is the language of "reasonable suspicion" . . . . The latter is the language of "reasonable and probable grounds".

which could be used as weapons."[409] Therefore, despite Iacobucci J's use of the language of "reasonable belief," the standard in *Mann* might best be understood as a reasonable suspicion that safety is at risk.[410] In addition to meeting this standard, Iacobucci J adds that "[t]he officer's decision to search must also be reasonably necessary in light of the totality of the circumstances." It cannot be based on "a vague or non-existent concern for safety, nor can the search be premised upon hunches or mere intuition." The decision to search for anything that may be used as a weapon must be "grounded in objectively discernible facts to prevent 'fishing expeditions' on the basis of irrelevant or discriminatory factors."[411] Furthermore, the search is limited in scope to a "protective pat-down search of the detained individual" and it "should be brief in duration."[412] In this case, feeling a soft object in the detainee's pocket, the officer had no reasonable basis for assuming safety was at issue. The search here did not fall within the scope of the power to search incident to investigative detention.

Justice Iacobucci in *Mann* asserted repeatedly and unequivocally that the power to search on an investigative detention recognized in that case was a power to conduct a pat-down search. Yet the Ontario Court of Appeal in *R v Batzer* read Iacobucci J to have left open the possibility that the power could extend beyond a pat down, since he did not explicitly rule it out.[413] In *R v Plummer*, the same court affirmed this reading of *Mann* and held that police detaining a passenger standing near a vehicle were also authorized under *Mann* to search a bag within the vehicle.[414] Other courts have followed *Plummer*, extending the scope of a search on investigative detention to include the trunk of a car.[415] Debate about the limits of *Mann* may now be moot in light of the Supreme Court's recognition in *MacDonald* (discussed in the next section) of a stand-alone "safety search" power. Although that power requires the higher standard

409 *Mann*, above note 321 at para 48 [emphasis added].

410 As the dissent notes in *MacDonald*, above note 323 at para 76, the majority in *R v Clayton*, 2007 SCC 32, applies the standard in *Mann* in these terms. Justice Abella, at para 46 of that case, finds the two accused were detained on a "reasonable suspicion" they possessed firearms and "the lives of the police officers and of the public were at risk." Nothing further than a suspicion of this risk grounded the brief search in that case, which was found to be authorized by *Mann*.

411 *Mann*, above note 321 at para 43.

412 *Ibid* at para 45.

413 *R v Batzer*, 2005 CanLII 33026 at paras 14–16, 202 OAC 87.

414 *R v Plummer*, 2011 ONCA 350, noting, at para 53, that "there is nothing in *Mann* confining a search incidental to an investigative detention to only the person detained."

415 *R v Lee*, 2017 ONCA 654 (trunk search); *R v Webber*, 2019 BCCA 208 (search of the front console of a vehicle) [*Webber*].

of "probable grounds to believe that safety is at stake," on the facts in the vehicle search cases extending the limits in *Mann*, the standard would likely have been met.

d) Emergency Response and Safety Searches

The Supreme Court in *Godoy* recognized a police power to enter and search a residence without a warrant in response to a 911 distress call, but only for the purpose of finding a person and ensuring that they are safe.[416] The Court in *MacDonald* recognized a power to conduct a "safety search" of a person's immediate surroundings on reasonable grounds to believe in an imminent safety risk.[417] The Court crafted both powers by applying the ancillary police powers doctrine in *Dedman v The Queen* and finding these searches to be "reasonably necessary" under certain conditions.[418] The majority in *MacDonald* crafted the "safety search" power in reference to the power of search incident to investigative detention in *Mann*, suggesting that it serves as a kind of modified extension of it and an authority to use it outside of an investigative detention (on the higher standard of reasonable grounds).[419] The circumstances in these cases help illuminate the scope and limit of these powers.

Officers in *Godoy* received a dispatch at 1:30 in the morning about a 911 call from the accused's apartment.[420] The caller hung up before speaking. Four officers attended the apartment. The accused opened the door slightly and in response to being asked if things were all right said "Sure, there is no problem." One officer asked if they could enter to investigate, but the accused tried to close the door. The officer put his foot in the way and four police entered. Once inside, one officer could hear a woman crying. He found the accused's common law spouse in their bedroom, "curled in the fetal position and sobbing" with a swollen eye, reporting that the accused had hit her.[421]

Writing for the Court in *Godoy*, Lamer CJ held that the high privacy interest in a dwelling house must be balanced against the "public interest in maintaining an effective emergency response system."[422] This justifies a police power to "investigate [a] 911 call and, in particular, to locate the caller and determine his or her reasons for making the call and provide such assistance as may be required."[423] However, he also noted, "the

---

416 *Godoy*, above note 320.

417 *MacDonald*, above note 323.

418 *Dedman*, above note 293.

419 *MacDonald*, above note 323 and *Mann*, above note 321.

420 *Godoy*, above note 320.

421 *Ibid* at para 3.

422 *Ibid* at para 22.

423 *Ibid*.

police authority for being on private property in response to a 911 call ends there." Police do not have "further permission to search premises or otherwise intrude on a resident's privacy or property." And the power itself is conditional: if police can locate the caller "without entering the home with force, obviously such a course of action is mandated. Each case will be considered in its own context, keeping in mind all of the surrounding circumstances."[424] In this case, police were justified in entering "considering the totality of the circumstances," including the fact that they had no knowledge of the nature of the distress or the reason for the call and the accused's attempt to shut the door.

Courts have applied *Godoy* with an emphasis on assessing the totality of the circumstances to decide whether entry to a home was justified in response to a distress call—or, more broadly, a report about safety concerns. Generally, unless there is a real possibility that someone within a home is at serious risk or poses a risk to others, courts do not find police entry to be authorized under *Godoy*. For example, in *R v Larson*, the British Columbia Court of Appeal held that *Godoy* did not authorize entry to a home in response to a report by its delusional owner that he had been the victim of a home invasion—where there were no external signs of forced entry and a neighbour could not confirm anything untoward occurring.[425] In *R v Timmons*, the Nova Scotia Court of Appeal held that *Godoy* did not authorize entry and search where police responded to a report by a mother about her daughter in distress.[426] The daughter had answered the door and told police that "everything was fine," no assault had taken place, and that she had only had an argument with her boyfriend. By contrast, in *R v Lowes*, the Ontario Court of Appeal held that *Godoy* did authorize entry and search where a neighbour called 911 to report "banging and crashing" next door and heard a female crying and pleading "please don't kill me."[427] When police knocked at the door minutes later, there was no answer. Eventually a woman came to the window; police explained why they were there and she told them she was alone, in bed, and asked them to leave. But it was obvious to police that she was speaking to someone behind her. In *R v Ahmed-Kadir*, the British Columbia Court of Appeal found entry to an apartment in response to a domestic dispute justified under *Godoy*, but not the further search of spaces that included a closet after the accused had been arrested and the other occupant located.[428]

424 *Ibid.*

425 *R v Larson*, 2011 BCCA 454.

426 *R v Timmons*, 2011 NSCA 39.

427 *R v Lowes*, 2016 ONCA 519.

428 *R v Ahmed-Kadir*, 2015 BCCA 346.

In *MacDonald*, police attended the accused's home in response to a noise complaint.[429] The accused opened the door "about 16 inches," making visible only the right side of his body, and an officer noticed a "black and shiny" object in his hand, but it was "in a shadow and partially hidden" by his leg.[430] The officer asked the accused twice what was in his hands, believing it could be a knife, and the accused did not respond. The officer then pushed open the door "a few inches further" to see and noticed it was a handgun.[431] The two men struggled and the officer disarmed the accused. The Supreme Court held that pushing open the door to get a better look constituted a search and found authority for it here by crafting a new common law power to conduct a "safety search."[432] Citing *Dedman* and *Waterfield*, LeBel J, for the majority, found that the officer was acting within the general scope of a police duty at common law to protect life and safety. A search under these circumstances was "reasonably necessary" interference with liberty given the importance of protecting life and safety, a reasonable belief that the accused was armed, and the brief extent of the interference. The power to conduct a "safety search" "will be authorized by law only if the police officer believes on reasonable grounds that his or her safety is at stake and that, as a result, it is necessary to conduct a search."[433] Safety is "at stake" where officers have a reasonable belief in "an imminent threat" to themselves or to the public. Justice LeBel offered no guidance on the physical scope of the power to carry out a safety search, suggesting, more broadly, that the "legality of the search . . . turns on its reasonable, objectively verifiable necessity in the circumstances of the matter."[434] In this case the officer did have probable grounds to believe the accused was armed (only the *kind* of weapon was unclear), posed an imminent threat, and a further search was necessary.[435]

In their dissenting opinion in *MacDonald*, Moldaver and Rothstein JJ and Wagner J (as he then was), argued that the majority's opinion had the effect of overturning the standard in *Mann* to carry out a warrantless search for protective purposes.[436] The majority purported to be applying the same standard to the "safety search" as the one crafted in *Mann* for search incident to investigative detention—reasonable

429 *MacDonald*, above note 323.
430 *Ibid* at para 6.
431 *Ibid* at para 7.
432 *Ibid* at para 32.
433 *Ibid* at para 41.
434 *Ibid*.
435 *Ibid* at paras 48–49.
436 *Ibid* at para 65.

grounds to believe safety was at risk—but had in fact imposed a higher standard of reasonable grounds to believe safety is "threatened" or "at issue." This is a belief that safety is *probably* threatened rather than possibly threatened. As noted above, in our discussion of *Mann*, the dissent in *MacDonald* suggested that Iacobucci J in *Mann* may have used the phrase "reasonable grounds to believe" but by referring to a "risk," he clearly intended the standard of a reasonable possibility, a reasonable suspicion, that safety is at issue.[437] The majority's choice in *MacDonald* of avoiding the language of risk and requiring a belief in a probable "threat" has made the test for authorizing a safety search more onerous for police to meet, contrary to the balance struck in *Mann* in its application of *Dedman*. The higher standard is also counter-intuitive. If police have grounds to believe a person is probably armed and dangerous, the dissent in *MacDonald* points out, police would have authority to arrest for the *Criminal Code* offence of possessing a weapon for a purpose dangerous to the public peace—and could then carry out a more invasive search.[438] Moreover, in the dissent's view, the standard of reasonable grounds was not met here; officers in this case—as the trial judge had found—had no more than a suspicion the accused "might" be armed and dangerous.[439]

The dissent's criticisms in *MacDonald* are powerful, but the majority's opinion can be reconciled with them. The safety search power crafted here should require a higher standard than the one in *Mann* because it is a free-standing power—a power not premised on a lawful investigative detention or limited to that context. It can lead to more invasive searches. It is also not rendered redundant by requiring the same standard for an arrest itself. If the officer here had grounds to arrest, he might have skipped a search and proceeded directly with an arrest, but in the heat of the moment *this is not what he did*. He made a spit-second decision to push open the door a few inches further—to carry out a search—rather than stage an arrest. In many cases, this will be the prudent choice. And it will give rise, only after the fact, to the question of whether police had authority for the search. The merit of the majority's holding in *MacDonald* is that a search may well have been justified even if police might instead have carried out an arrest.

In the wake of *MacDonald*, confusion has arisen over the standard to be applied in safety searches—despite the clarity of the majority's opinion on this (reasonable grounds rather than reasonable suspicion). Surveying the caselaw on safety searches in the wake of *MacDonald*,

---

437 *Ibid* at paras 69–70.

438 *Ibid* at para 79.

439 *Ibid* at paras 83 and 85

Mainella JA of the Manitoba Court of Appeal in *McKenzie* offered a helpful summary.[440] He noted that three schools of thought have emerged. One view holds that the higher test the majority set out in *MacDonald*—reasonable grounds to believe safety is at issue—"applies only to free-standing safety searches and does not apply to other contexts" including investigative detention, where the reasonable suspicion of a safety risk in *Mann* still applies.[441] Another view holds that the minority in *MacDonald* is not correct that the majority opinion had the effect of altering the standard from reasonable suspicion; "all that happened was the majority in *MacDonald* used the same unclear language that was used in *Mann*."[442] The standard for all safety searches, on this view, remains reasonable suspicion. A third view holds that the dissent in *MacDonald* was correct about the effect of the majority's opinion: it raised the standard for all safety searches to probable grounds to believe safety is at issue—including search incident to investigative detention.[443] At the time of this writing, appellate courts remain divided, but we suggest the first view is the most plausible. The majority in *MacDonald* deliberately avoided adopting Iacobucci J's formulation of a reasonable belief that safety is "at risk" in favour of the language of probability: a reasonable belief (i.e., in the probability) that safety *is* "at stake." The majority opinion can be read as intentionally raising the standard for "free standing" safety searches by virtue of the much broader scope of their possible use by police, including limited searches of a dwelling house. It might have been helpful had the majority opinion been more explicit on this point. The lingering uncertainty as to how to interpret *MacDonald* is an issue the Court will hopefully soon revisit and clarify.

e) Sniffer Dogs

The Supreme Court in *Kang-Brown* and *AM* recognized a police power at common law to conduct an olfactory search using a sniffer dog.[444] Police in *Kang-Brown* used sniffer dogs to search a person's bag at a bus station and, in *AM*, to sniff bags in a high school gym. The Court in *R v Chehil* affirmed police use of sniffer dogs to search a person's

440 *R v McKenzie*, 2022 MBCA 3 at paras 38–40 [*McKenzie*].

441 *Ibid* at para 39, citing *R v Peterkin*, 2015 ONCA 8 at para 59; *R v Smith*, 2019 SKCA 126 at paras 13–15; and *R v Stairs*, 2020 ONCA 678 at paras 54–55.

442 *McKenzie*, above note 440 at para 40, citing *Webber*, above note 415 at para 65 and *R v McGuffie*, 2016 ONCA 365 at para 52.

443 *McKenzie*, above note 440 at para 40, citing *R v Del Corro*, 2019 ABCA 156 at para 49.

444 *Kang-Brown*, above note 322; *R v AM*, 2008 SCC 19 [*AM*]. The quotation above is from Moldaver J's decision in *R v MacKenzie*, 2013 SCC 50 [*MacKenzie*], noting when the power in *Kang-Brown* and *AM* applies.

baggage at an airport and, in *R v MacKenzie*, to sniff odours emanating from a vehicle during a highway traffic stop.[445] Justice Moldaver, for the majority in *MacKenzie*, suggested the broad application of this power in writing that "police may use sniffer dogs for routine crime prevention in contexts where individuals have a reasonable, but lesser, expectation of privacy, such as bus terminals and schools, and the police have reasonable grounds to suspect that a search will reveal evidence of a criminal offence."[446] A majority of the Court in *Kang-Brown* and *AM* crafted the power to search with sniffer dogs by applying the test for recognizing new ancillary police powers in *Dedman*, discussed above.[447] The facts and reasons in these two cases help explain the majority's rationale for crafting the power and when it applies. It may help to begin with the facts of each case and then turn to the reasoning by drawing from both decisions.

Police in *Kang-Brown* were conducting an operation to investigate possible drug couriers transiting through bus stations. The accused, getting off a bus, gave an officer a lengthy stare and looked back at him as he entered the station. The officer approached him, asked if he was carrying drugs, and he said no. The officer asked to look inside the accused's bag, the latter began to unzip it, and when the officer reached to touch the bag, the accused pulled it away. The officer called another officer to approach with a sniffer dog, who gave a signal to indicate that drugs were in the bag. The accused was arrested for possession and trafficking, searched, and police found narcotics in the bag. In *AM*, police took up a "long-standing" invitation from the principal of a high school to bring sniffer dogs to school to search for drugs. Police were not acting on suspicion that there were drugs present on the day in question. While students were in class, a sniffer dog searched backpacks in the gym and gave a signal indicating that one contained drugs. Without a warrant, police opened the bag and found illicit substances and the student was charged with trafficking.

The Supreme Court in *Kang-Brown* was unanimous in finding the use of sniffer dogs at the bus station to constitute a search under section 8; in *AM*, seven of nine judges held that the search of a bag in a high school engaged section 8.[448] In both cases, four judges were inclined to defer to Parliament the task of crafting new powers for sniffer dog searches.[449] Five judges applied the *Dedman* test to find the use of sniffer dogs a justified and reasonably necessary use of police power in these

445 *R v Chehil*, 2013 SCC 49 [*Chehil*]; *MacKenzie*, above note 444.

446 *MacKenzie*, *ibid* at para 2.

447 *Dedman*, above note 293.

448 *Kang-Brown*, above note 322; *AM*, above note 444; Deschamps and Rothstein JJ were the dissenters.

449 Justices LeBel, Fish, Abella, and Charron held this view.

contexts.[450] In the opinion of Binnie J and McLachlin CJ, the power is justified in light of the lower privacy interest in odours emanating from bags in public spaces, the brief and non-invasive nature of the search, the exigency of the circumstances involved in such searches (even a telewarrant would take too much time given the fleeting contact with suspects not detained or arrested), and given the high degree of accuracy dogs exhibit in detecting illicit substances.[451] All five agreed that an adequate standard is reasonable suspicion that the individual has committed an offence and evidence relating to it may be found by use of an olfactory search. Justice Bastarache would have gone further in permitting use of sniffer dogs (in high schools) on the standard of generalized suspicion (i.e., the person searched is transiting an area or fits a general pattern that raises a reasonable suspicion).[452] The four justices in dissent held that a reasonable search under section 8 involving sniffer dogs would require reasonable and probable grounds, except in exigent circumstances.

The majority in the two decisions were not specific as to where police may use the power to carry out a sniffer dog search. Justice Binnie (joined by McLachlin CJ) in *Kang-Brown* stated generally that police "possess the common law authority to make use of sniffer dogs in places to which they have lawful access for the purpose of criminal investigations."[453] Justice Deschamps (joined by Rothstein J) acknowledged that police were using dogs in the program involved in *Kang-Brown* at "bus terminals, train stations and airports" in contexts where drug traffickers were known to transit.[454] Justice Moldaver's comment in *MacKenzie*, noted above, should also be considered: "the police may use sniffer dogs for routine crime prevention in contexts where individuals have a reasonable, but lesser, expectation of privacy."[455]

The majority in *Kang-Brown* and *AM* also reached no agreement as to the scope of a sniffer dog search on reasonable suspicion. Justice Binnie and McLachlin CJ held that a positive detection by a dog authorized a further search of the area signalled by the dog—i.e., the content of the bag—without a warrant and prior to arrest.[456] In *Kang-Brown*,

---

450 In *Kang-Brown*, above note 322; at paras 48–57, Binnie J (joined by McLachlin CJ) applies *Dedman*; Deschamps J (joined by Rothstein J) at paras 149–53 and 182 invokes *Dedman*; and Bastarache J does so at para 232.

451 *AM*, above note 444, at paras 12–14, 90.

452 *Kang-Brown*, above note 322 at para 245.

453 *Ibid* at para 57; he repeats the statement at para 41 of *AM*, above note 444.

454 *Kang-Brown*, above note 322 at para 182.

455 *MacKenzie*, above note 444 at para 2.

456 *AM*, above note 444 at para 14; *Kang-Brown* above note 322 at para 101:

> Sergeant Bouey acknowledged that the dog alerts to the odour of narcotics, not to their actual presence. Ordinary currency and coins sometimes carry a

Deschamps and Rothstein JJ, and writing separately Bastarache J, found that a positive indication by the dog gave police reasonable grounds to arrest, and they could have searched the bag incident to arrest.[457] Soon after the Court decided *Kang-Brown* and *AM*, the Manitoba Court of Appeal in *R v Frieburg (TL)* followed the holding of Binnie J and McLachlin CJ in permitting the search of the inside of the trunk of a car parked on a public street that had been indicated by a sniff search.[458] In her decision on behalf of the Court in *Chehil*, Karakatsanis J acknowledged this holding but cast doubt on its validity.[459]

Chehil and *MacKenzie* involved sniffer dog searches, but the central issue in each case was whether the constellation of observations police made amounted to a reasonable suspicion authorizing the search.[460] In *Chehil*, Karakatsanis J addressed the scope of a sniffer dog search in *obiter*. Once a dog has given a positive indication, police have two choices: obtain consent for a further verification search (opening a bag or container) or decide whether they have probable grounds for an arrest and conduct the verification search using the power to search incident to arrest.[461] In *Chehil* itself, police did the latter. Justice Karakatsanis acknowledged that Binnie J and McLachlin CJ in *Kang-Brown* and *AM* had held that a verification search is permitted once a dog gives a positive indication, but noted that this was not a view adopted by the majority.[462] This would entail a more invasive search than the one contemplated by the majority when it recognized the power to carry out a sniff search without a warrant as reasonable.[463]

f) School Searches

In *R v M(MR)*, the Supreme Court recognized a power on the part of high school administrators to conduct a warrantless search or seizure of a student or their locker or bag on a reasonable belief that they have violated

---

> residual odour of cocaine or other drugs. Accordingly, I believe the arrest of the appellant in this case was in any event premature. The police should first have confirmed the presence of narcotics by a hand search of the gym bag. In my view, if reasonable cause had existed, and given the positive alert and Chevy's history of accuracy, the RCMP would have been entitled to perform such a verification search on-the-spot and without prior judicial authorization, as discussed in *A.M.*

457 *Kang-Brown* above note 322 at paras 200, 218.

458 *R v Frieburg (TL)*, 2013 MBCA 40 [*Frieburg*].

459 *Chehil*, above note 445 at paras 55–58, citing *Frieburg*, *ibid*, n 4.

460 *Chehil*, above note 445; *R v MacKenzie*, above note 444.

461 *Chehil*, above note 445 at para 55.

462 *Ibid* at para 57.

463 *Ibid.*

school rules.[464] The search may include a pat down of the student, and the "reasonable belief" that school officials require may entail something less than what police need for an arrest.

M(MR) involved a search at a junior high school, following a tip several students had given to a vice principal about the accused intending to deal drugs at school. The vice principal called an RCMP officer to be present and summoned the accused and his friend to his office. The vice principal asked the two students if they had drugs in their possession and told them he was going to search them. The officer then arrived, identified himself to the students, but sat passively as the vice principal searched both students. He found a bag of marijuana on the accused and gave it to the officer, who arrested the student for drug possession. The officer searched the accused's locker, uncovering nothing further.

In an 8:1 decision, Cory J, for a majority of the Supreme Court in *M(MR)*, held that the vice principal may have cooperated with police, but he did not, by virtue of this, act as an agent of the police; he would have conducted the search regardless and in the same manner.[465] Students have a reasonable expectation of privacy in their person, bags, and lockers at school, but a diminished expectation.[466] School officials are responsible for maintaining a safe environment, to foster both safety and learning. Having drugs or weapons at school hinders these goals. Administrators need to be able to respond to disciplinary problems with some flexibility, and in some cases promptly.[467] A power to carry out searches and seizures for prohibited items on something less than probable grounds would be reasonable under section 8. Teachers and administrators are authorized to search on "reasonable grounds to believe that a school rule has been or is being violated, and evidence of the violation will be found in the location or on the person of the student searched."[468] Valid grounds may consist of information from a single student who school officials believe to be credible, several students, or a "combination" of information and observations "assessed by the school authority in the context of the circumstances existing at the particular school."[469] The scope of the search will "vary with the gravity of the infraction that is suspected," and where serious — involving a gun, in Cory J's example — the search may be "swift, thorough and extensive."[470]

---

464 *R v M(MR)*, [1998] 3 SCR 393 [*M(MR)*].
465 *Ibid* at para 29.
466 *Ibid* at paras 31–34.
467 *Ibid* at paras 35–36 and 47.
468 *Ibid* at para 48.
469 *Ibid* at para 49.
470 *Ibid* at para 52.

The search must be "conducted in as sensitive a manner as possible and take into account the age and sex of the student."[471] However, where a school official acts as an agent of the police, normal standards for search and seizure will apply.[472] The Court was explicit that the holding in this case applies to students in "an elementary or secondary school," on school property, by school officials acting "within the scope of their responsibility and authority to maintain order" and not to a search in a "college or university setting."[473]

The majority in *M(MR)* found the search and seizure in that case to be reasonable. Given the number and nature of student reports he received, the vice principal had a reasonable belief that the accused possessed drugs.[474] Writing in dissent, Major J found the search violated section 8 on the basis that the vice principal acted as a "*de facto* agent of the police" since it was school policy to engage police when a student was found to possess drugs.[475] Normal standards should have applied here and would not have been met, given the failure to corroborate the information received about the accused.

There is some authority for school officials having the power to search teachers and persons other than students, under provincial legislation. In *Elementary Teachers Federation of Ontario v York Region District School Board*, the Ontario Court of Appeal held that, in some cases, a principal's power under the province's *Education Act* to "maintain proper order and discipline" might "authorize a power of search and seizure concerning others who may be in the school, including teachers."[476] But Huscroft J added that "the rationale supporting such authority concerning students [referring to *M(MR)*] suggests that this power may seldom be exercised with teachers, and the nature of the search permitted will be limited."[477] He pointed to the Supreme Court's decision in *Jarvis* as an example, a case in which a principal seized a camera pen from a male teacher who had used it to make surreptitious video recordings of female students.[478]

471 *Ibid* at paras 52–53.

472 *Ibid* at para 56.

473 *Ibid* at paras 55 and 64.

474 *Ibid* at para 62.

475 *Ibid* at para 79.

476 *Elementary Teachers Federation of Ontario v York Region District School Board*, 2022 ONCA 476 at paras 58, 61 [*Elementary Teachers*], citing the *Education Act*, RSO 1990, c E.2, s 265.

477 *Elementary Teachers*, above note 476 at para 61.

478 *Ibid* at para 60, citing *R v Jarvis*, 2019 SCC 10.

CHAPTER 7

WHEN IS A SEARCH LAW REASONABLE?

A. INTRODUCTION

Section 8 of the *Charter* guarantees a right to be "secure against unreasonable search or seizure."[1] The Supreme Court in *R v Collins* held that a search or seizure will be reasonable under section 8 "if it is authorized by law, if the law itself is reasonable and if the manner in which the search was carried out is reasonable."[2] This chapter explores the Court's holdings on the second part of this test: when a law authorizing a search or seizure is reasonable.

In crafting the second part of the *Collins* test, Lamer J, as he then was, had in mind a passage from *Hunter et al v Southam Inc*.[3] In *Hunter*, the Court found that a statutory power authorizing a search and seizure in an office, building, or home, in the course of a criminal investigation, was unreasonable under section 8 because it did not require a warrant issued by an independent person capable of acting judicially, on the standard of reasonable grounds to believe an offence had been committed and evidence would likely be found in the place to be searched. Meeting these requirements marked the point at which the "state's interest in detecting and preventing crime begins to prevail over the individual's

1 *Canadian Charter of Rights and Freedoms*, Part I of the *Constitution Act, 1982*, being Schedule B to the *Canada Act 1982* (UK), 1982, c 11 [*Charter*].

2 *R v Collins*, [1987] 1 SCR 265 at 277–78.

3 [1984] 2 SCR 145 [*Hunter*].

interest in being left alone."[4] Justice Dickson, as he then was, held that "[h]istory has confirmed the appropriateness of this requirement as the threshold for subordinating the expectation of privacy to the needs of law enforcement."[5] But this did not settle, once and for all, the question of when a search law would be reasonable under section 8, because, as Dickson J went on to explain, in some contexts law enforcement interests might prevail over individual privacy at a different point:

> Where the state's interest is not simply law enforcement as, for instance, where state security is involved, or where the individual's interest is not simply his expectation of privacy as, for instance, when the search threatens his bodily integrity, the relevant standard might well be a different one.[6]

He was suggesting that whether a law authorizing a search or seizure is reasonable depends on context. It involves a weighing of the state and individual interests at issue and finding a reasonable balance.[7] In the normal course—a conventional criminal law case involving the search of a residence—the *Hunter* standards will apply. But as we note in Chapter 6, there are many laws that authorize state agents to conduct what amounts to a search or seizure in different contexts, involving higher or lower standards than those set out in *Hunter*. When a person challenges a search law under the second part of the *Collins* test, a court must engage in the balancing test contemplated in *Hunter* to decide whether the search law is reasonable.

The Supreme Court has been reluctant to provide a specific test for how to perform this balancing.[8] It has, however, identified a set of relevant considerations. Justice Strayer of the Federal Court of Appeal formulated these consideration in *Del Zotto v Canada*, and the Supreme Court adopted them on appeal.[9] Deciding whether a law is reasonable may depend on "the nature and the purpose of the legislative scheme . . . ,

---

4 *Ibid* at 167.

5 *Ibid* at 167–68.

6 *Ibid* at 168.

7 As Dickson J notes at the end of *Hunter*, after engaging in this balancing and finding a law unreasonable, there is little left to do under s 1 of the *Charter*. Most of the decisions canvassed in this chapter reflect this insight, with the Court neglecting to proceed to a s 1 analysis after finding a search law unreasonable, or finding, in a few cases, that it fails s 1 (usually for failing to minimally impair by not requiring a higher standard or more safeguards).

8 *Thomson Newspapers Ltd v Canada (Director of Investigation and Research, Restrictive Trade Practices Commission)*, [1990] 1 SCR 425 at 495 [*Thomson Newspapers*].

9 *Del Zotto v Canada*, [1997] 3 FC 40 (CA) [*Del Zotto* FC], Strayer JA, in dissenting reasons adopted in [1999] 1 SCR 3.

the mechanism . . . employed and the degree of its potential intrusiveness[,] and the availability of judicial supervision."[10] The Court recently re-affirmed the relevance of these considerations in *Goodwin v British Columbia (Superintendent of Motor Vehicles)*.[11]

We make two general observations about the *Del Zotto/Goodwin* factors. One is that the first factor, the "nature and purpose of the scheme," comprises two distinct considerations: whether a power relates to a criminal or regulatory investigation and how pressing is the state interest in this context. The second point is that not every case that decides whether a search or seizure law is reasonable applies all of the *Del Zotto/Goodwin* factors. They are best understood as a list of the main considerations to be found in the larger body of caselaw on whether powers to search or seize are reasonable. In many cases, courts decide a law is reasonable or unreasonable by focusing on only one or two of the factors.

We proceed in this chapter in two parts. In the first, we look in more detail at the considerations in *Del Zotto*, providing examples of what they entail. However, looking at these in isolation leaves out a sense of how the Court has carried out the balancing test in relation to various powers to search or seize. To illustrate how the Court has done this in specific cases, we turn to, in the second part of the chapter, a survey of the Court's decisions on reasonable laws, grouped by category or theme.

B. CONSIDERATIONS FOR ASSESSING A REASONABLE LAW

1) Nature of the Scheme: Criminal or Regulatory

A central consideration when deciding whether a power to search or seize is reasonable under section 8 is whether it serves as a tool for investigating a criminal rather than a regulatory offence. Discerning whether an offence is criminal or regulatory turns on the purpose of the offence or the legislative scheme of which it forms a part. Offences are criminal in nature where their primary aim is to deter and punish action that is inherently wrongful by imposing serious consequences (usually penal) and the stigma of a criminal conviction. Offences are regulatory that aim to manage acceptable but risky conduct by submitting it to a

---

10 *Del Zotto* FC, above note 9, as cited in *Goodwin v British Columbia (Superintendent of Motor Vehicles)*, 2015 SCC 46 at para 57 [*Goodwin*].

11 *Goodwin*, *ibid*.

minimum standard of care and enforcing this through fines and lesser punishments.[12]

The Court has held in a number of cases that "[w]here an impugned law's purpose is regulatory and not criminal, it may be subject to less stringent standards."[13] Explaining the rationale for this in *British Columbia Securities Commission v Branch*, Sopinka and Iacobucci JJ noted that in certain areas of activity that fall under state authority, search or seizure is so closely related to the task of regulation as to "raise virtually no expectation of privacy whatsoever."[14] These include filing requirements, an expectation of inspections or "spot checks," or requests for information on a demand basis—and often without the state agent requiring a suspicion or belief in wrongdoing. These powers are generally thought to be reasonable on the basis that "inspection may be the only means of detecting non-compliance, and that its detection serves an important public purpose."[15]

The converse is also true. Standards should remain high if the search or seizure power is criminal in nature. In these cases, courts presume the standards in *Hunter* should apply, with departures from them needing to be justified by either a lower expectation of privacy, a pressing state interest arising in the situation, or both.[16] If state agents shift their purpose in gathering evidence from a regulatory to a criminal investigation, higher standards should apply.[17]

---

12 An authoritative source on the distinction between criminal and regulatory offences can be found in Cory J's opinion in *R v Wholesale Travel Group Inc*, [1991] 3 SCR 154 at 216–22, noting at 219:

> Regulatory legislation involves a shift of emphasis from the protection of individual interests and the deterrence and punishment of acts involving moral fault to the protection of public and societal interests. While criminal offences are usually designed to condemn and punish past, inherently wrongful conduct, regulatory measures are generally directed to the prevention of future harm through the enforcement of minimum standards of conduct and care.

13 *Goodwin*, above note 10 at para 60, citing *British Columbia Securities Commission v Branch*, [1995] 2 SCR 3 at para 52 [*British Columbia Securities*]; *R v McKinlay Transport Ltd*, [1990] 1 SCR 627 at 647, Wilson J [*McKinlay*]; *R v Jarvis*, 2002 SCC 73 [*Jarvis*].

14 *British Columbia Securities*, above note 13 at para 53, citing Wilson J's opinion in *McKinlay*, above note 13 at 645–46 and A. Reid & A.H. Young in "Administrative Search and Seizure Under the Charter" (1985) 10 *Queen's Law Journal* 392 at 398–99.

15 *Ibid.*

16 *R v Grant*, [1993] 3 SCR 223 at 239–40 [*Grant*].

17 *R v Colarusso*, [1994] 1 SCR 20 at 65–67; *Jarvis*, above note 13 at para 88.

One might question this "binary" approach. As Steven Penney has argued, "there is no reason to treat privacy as categorically less important (and law enforcement more important) in regulatory investigations than criminal ones (or vice versa)."[18] Taking this approach, courts have approved of search powers that are too invasive, even in the regulatory context, and disapproved of non-intrusive powers because they apply in the criminal context. The courts have certainly embraced a "binary" approach to assessing reasonableness. Whether this skews the way judges think about the balance of interests is a question to consider as we survey the cases below.

One example of a kind of search power the Supreme Court has found reasonable due to its regulatory nature is the power to demand documents. In three cases, involving competition law, tax, and securities, the Court found that the power to demand documents constituted a search under section 8 and that it was reasonable—despite requiring no grounds—because persons subject to the regulatory scheme at issue could expect less privacy in the documents and because the power to inspect or request relevant documents was essential to effectively regulating the conduct at issue.[19]

In some cases, the nature of the legislative scheme may be unclear. In *Goodwin*, the Court considered whether a power under a British Columbia statute authorizing police to demand a breath sample at roadside, leading to an immediate driving prohibition, was reasonable.[20] Driving is a regulated activity, suggesting the power was regulatory in nature. Yet other features of the scheme had "certain criminal-like features," including its administration by a police officer acting under *Criminal Code* authorization (for the demand) and "immediate and serious" consequences that followed a "fail" reading.[21] A search power can thus be neither criminal nor regulatory, but somewhere along a spectrum, closer to one end or the other.

A further possibility is that whether a power is reasonable may depend on a principle that renders the regulatory or criminal nature of a scheme of secondary importance, if not irrelevant. In a series of cases, the Court has found powers to search law offices or demand documents

18 Steven Penney, "The Reasonableness of Regulatory Searches: Saying Goodbye to the Criminal-Regulatory Binary" (2021) 26 *Canadian Criminal Law Review* 77, arguing at 78: "The relative strength of privacy and law enforcement interests should not turn—even in part—on whether the discovery of evidence of wrongdoing leads to regulatory rather than criminal sanctions (or vice versa)."

19 *Thomson Newspapers*, above note 8; *McKinlay*, above note 13; and *British Columbia Securities*, above note 13.

20 *Goodwin*, above note 10.

21 *Ibid* at para 63, citing the *Criminal Code*, RSC 1985, c C-46 [*Criminal Code* or *Code*].

to be unreasonable due not to the regulatory or criminal nature of the scheme at issue but its failure to protect solicitor-client privilege.[22] Justice Cromwell, for the majority in *Canada (Attorney General) v Federation of Law Societies of Canada*, encapsulated the rationale running through these cases in stating "the reasonable expectation of privacy in relation to communications subject to solicitor-client privilege is invariably high, regardless of the context."[23] What determines the "elevated expectation of privacy" in this instance is "the specially protected nature of the solicitor-client relationship, not the context in which the state seeks to intrude into that specially protected zone."[24]

2) Purpose of the Scheme: State Interest

A strong or compelling state interest in carrying out a search can justify departures from the *Hunter* standards as reasonable, even in the face of serious privacy concerns.[25] The Supreme Court has applied this reasoning in areas involving bodily, territorial, and informational privacy.

For example, in *R v Simmons*, the Court found the national interest in preventing illicit goods from entering Canada to be pressing enough to justify strip searches on the standard of reasonable suspicion (along with other safeguards, discussed below).[26] In *R v Saeed*, the Court considered whether police could require or conduct a penile swab on arrest in sexual assault cases. The majority acknowledged that a swab involves a "significant intrusion on the accused's privacy because of the body part searched."[27] Yet the majority also held that a swab advances a pressing state objective by "enable[ing] police to preserve important evidence"—evidence that is "highly reliable" and "can be crucial in the case of complainants who are unable to testify, such as children, adults with disabilities, or those who have died or suffered serious injuries as a

22 *Lavallee, Rackel & Heintz v Canada (Attorney General); White, Ottenheimer & Baker v Canada (Attorney General); R v Fink*, 2002 SCC 61 [*Lavallee*]; *Canada (Attorney General) v Federation of Law Societies of Canada*, 2015 SCC 7 [*Federation of Law Societies*]; and *Canada (Attorney General) v Chambre des notaires du Québec*, 2016 SCC 20.

23 *Federation of Law Societies*, above note 22 at para 38.

24 *Ibid*.

25 *Hunter*, above note 3.

26 *R v Simmons*, [1988] 2 SCR 495 [*Simmons*]. On the meaning of "reasonable suspicion" and the higher standard of "reasonable and probable grounds to believe" (also referred to here as "reasonable grounds to believe" or "reasonable belief"), see Chapter 5, Section A.

27 *R v Saeed*, 2016 SCC 24 at para 56 [*Saeed*].

result of the offence."[28] On this basis, police can take or demand a swab on reasonable grounds and without a warrant.

Police may search a home without a warrant where the state's interest is not to investigate but to avoid imminent harm. In *Godoy*, Lamer CJ held on behalf of the Court:

> [T]he importance of the police duty to protect life warrants and justifies a forced entry into a dwelling in order to ascertain the health and safety of a 911 caller. The public interest in maintaining an effective emergency response system is obvious and significant enough to merit some intrusion on a resident's privacy interest.[29]

The majority in *R v MacDonald* similarly describes the "duty to protect life and safety" as being "of the utmost importance to the public good" and holds that it justifies a limited "safety search" in a residence, without a warrant, "to the extent that it is necessary to search for weapons."[30]

A pressing state interest can also justify a warrantless search of personal information over which we possess a high privacy interest. One example can be found in *R v Fearon*, where a majority of the Court held that under certain conditions (discussed below), police may search the content of a digital device on arrest without further grounds or a warrant.[31] Part of the reasoning involved the "important law enforcement objectives" a power to search immediately would serve, including "public safety."[32] A quick search could also help police with "identifying accomplices or locating and preserving evidence that might otherwise be lost or destroyed" or to prevent accomplices from warning off other parties so as to evade police or "call[ing] for 'back up' to help resist law enforcement."[33]

3) Measure's Intrusiveness and Reliability

Generally, a law should strive to use the least intrusive measure to advance the state interest at issue.[34] Conversely, "the more intrusive the

28 *Ibid* at para 59.
29 *R v Godoy*, [1999] 1 SCR 311 at para 22 [*Godoy*].
30 *R v MacDonald*, 2014 SCC 3 at para 39 [*MacDonald*].
31 *R v Fearon*, 2014 SCC 77 [*Fearon*].
32 *Ibid* at para 48.
33 *Ibid*.
34 See, e.g., *Goodwin*, above note 10, at para 65, noting "[t]he roadside breath demand authorized by the Criminal Code has a much less significant impact on an individual's bodily integrity and privacy interests: *R v Stillman*, [1997] 1 SCR 607 at para 90. This minimally intrusive character supports the reasonableness of the ASD seizure."

search, the greater degree of justification and constitutional protection that is appropriate."[35] Courts will also assess whether a search power is reasonable based on how reliable it is in uncovering relevant evidence.

Looking at the first of these considerations, the Court has identified certain forms of search to be highly invasive, warranting a higher degree of protection. One example is found in *R v Golden*, where the majority held that a strip search and a body cavity search in particular "involve a higher degree of infringement of personal dignity and privacy as well as additional medical concerns and, accordingly, a higher degree of justification will be required before such a search can be carried out."[36] The Court in *Stillman* found the seizure of bodily samples, including hair and dental impressions, to be very intrusive, requiring authority other than the common law power of search incident to arrest, if not a warrant.[37] Another example is found in the case of computers. Majority decisions in *R v Morelli* and *R v Vu* assert that "it is difficult to imagine a more intrusive invasion of privacy than the search of one's home and personal computer."[38] Computers are not like other receptacles. They engage privacy interests "different in both nature and extent from the search of other 'places'."[39] On this basis, the Court held in *Vu* that a warrant permitting the search of a physical space does not authorize the search of a computer found within it—without authorizing this explicitly; otherwise, a separate warrant is necessary to adequately protect the privacy interests at issue.[40] A further example can be found in the case of an interception.

---

35 *R v Golden*, 2001 SCC 83 at para 88 [*Golden*], citing *Simmons*, above note 26 at 517.

36 *Golden*, above note 35 at para 87.

37 *R v Stillman*, [1997] 1 SCR 607 at para 42, 144 DLR (4th) 193 [*Stillman*]; Cory J, for the majority:

> It has often been clearly and forcefully expressed that state interference with a person's bodily integrity is a breach of a person's privacy and an affront to human dignity. The invasive nature of body searches demands higher standards of justification. In *R v Pohoretsky*, [1987] 1 SCR 945, at p. 949, Lamer J., as he then was, noted that, "a violation of the sanctity of a person's body is much more serious than that of his office or even of his home".

On the question of authority for seizure of bodily samples, Cory J asserts at para 49 that:

> The common law power of search incidental to arrest cannot be so broad as to encompass the seizure without valid statutory authority of bodily samples in the face of a refusal to provide them. If it is, then the common law rule itself is unreasonable, since it is too broad and fails to properly balance the competing rights involved.

38 *R v Morelli*, 2010 SCC 8 at para 105; *R v Vu*, 2013 SCC 60 at para 40 [*Vu*].

39 *Fearon*, above note 31 at para 51.

40 *Vu*, above note 38.

In *R v Duarte*, the Court contrasted the invasion of privacy we risk when we speak to a person who may tattletale to police from the risk that they might be carrying a wiretap. The latter entails "a risk of a different order" involving the "much more insidious danger" of the state "record[ing] and transmit[ting] our words."[41] Even if a person consents to carrying a wire, a search this invasive should require police to obtain a warrant.

Conversely, the Court has pointed to the minimally invasive nature of a mechanism for search or seizure as a basis for finding a power reasonable under section 8. In *R v Kang-Brown* and *R v AM*, a majority found the brief and non-invasive nature of a search involving sniffer dogs of odours emanating from bags people carry in public places to justify police use of this power reasonable on reasonable suspicion.[42] In *R v SAB*, the Court described the taking of DNA samples through a buccal swab, a pinprick, or the plucking of hairs "quick and not terribly intrusive," not a "particularly serious affront to privacy or dignity"[43]—supporting the reasonableness of this form of seizure with a warrant in the *Criminal Code*. Similarly, a penile swab is "not inherently invasive," because it does not involve penetration, only touches the outer skin, and "does not cause pain or physical discomfort" or "pose any risk to the accused's health."[44] A requirement for reasonable grounds rather than a warrant to obtain a swab seemed reasonable in light of this. In *Goodwin*, the Court situated the taking of a breath sample at roadside somewhere between a demand for documents and the taking of a bodily sample, such as a blood sample or DNA swab, concluding that it has "a much less significant impact on an individual's bodily integrity and privacy interests."[45] This supported the reasonableness of a breath demand (using an approved screening device (ASD)) on reasonable suspicion.

A third consideration is reliability. The Court has held that the "reliability of a search or seizure mechanism is directly relevant to the reasonableness of the search or seizure itself."[46] A search power will not be reasonable if it "captures an inordinate number of innocent individuals."[47] Conversely, a highly accurate tool may justify searches or seizures on lower standards than those set out in *Hunter*, such as a sniffer dog search

41 *R v Duarte*, [1990] 1 SCR 30 at 44 [*Duarte*].

42 *R v Kang-Brown*, 2008 SCC 18 [*Kang-Brown*]; *R v AM*, 2008 SCC 19 at paras 12–14, 90 [*AM*].

43 *R v SAB*, 2003 SCC 60 at para 44 [*SAB*].

44 *Saeed*, above note 27 at para 55.

45 *Goodwin*, above note 10 at para 65.

46 *Ibid* at para 67, citing *R v Chehil*, 2013 SCC 49 at para 48 [*Chehil*].

47 *Goodwin*, above note 10 at para 67, citing *Chehil*, above note 46 at para 51.

on reasonable suspicion.[48] The high reliability of a DNA match was relevant to finding the *Criminal Code* warrant scheme reasonable in *SAB*,[49] and the high reliability of DNA from penile swabs was also relevant to finding a power of warrantless seizure reasonable in *Saeed*.[50] By contrast, in *Goodwin*, concerns raised about the reliability of an ASD device to take breath samples at roadside weighed against finding this search power reasonable.[51]

4) Oversight and Accountability Safeguards

In *Hunter v Southam Inc*, Dickson J, as he then was, held that "[a] provision authorizing . . . an unreviewable power would clearly be inconsistent with s. 8 of the *Charter*."[52] In a number of cases, the Supreme Court has held a power to be reasonable or unreasonable by taking into account the requirement for prior authorization with a warrant or some other means of holding police accountable for the exercise of the power.

For example, the requirement for oversight through a warrant was central in both *Duarte* and *SAB*.[53] In *Duarte*, the Court considered whether it is reasonable under section 8 for police to conduct a wiretap only on the consent of one party to a conversation.[54] Prior to this case, there was "a total absence of prior judicial supervision of this practice."[55] Allowing police to do this without a warrant would give them "unlimited discretion in defining the scope and duration of participant surveillance."[56] Given the far greater invasiveness of the state recording our conversations from that of a civilian-interlocutor doing so, it was unreasonable without a warrant. By contrast, in *SAB*, the Court pointed to the *Code*'s warrant requirement for obtaining a DNA sample as an important safeguard that rendered the scheme reasonable.[57] The *Code* also imposes further restrictions on the power: provincial court judges rather than justices of the peace may issue these warrants; they are limited to designated offences; and they require a judge to be satisfied that

48 *Kang-Brown*, above note 42 at paras 63–65 and *AM*, above note 42 at para 11; *Chehil*, above note 46 at para 48.

49 *SAB*, above note 43 at para 51.

50 *Saeed*, above note 27 at para 59.

51 *Goodwin*, above note 10 at para 66.

52 *Hunter*, above note 3 at 166.

53 *Duarte*, above note 41 and *SAB*, above note 43.

54 *Duarte*, above note 41.

55 *Ibid* at 47.

56 *Ibid* at 42.

57 *SAB*, above note 43 at paras 38–39.

issuing a DNA warrant is in the best interests of the administration of justice.[58]

The Court in *Baron v Canada* considered another form of oversight: the discretion not to issue a warrant, even where there is probable cause.[59] The Court found a provision of the *Income Tax Act* to be unreasonable under section 8 because it required a warrant when reasonable grounds were established but left courts with no residual discretion to refuse to issue a warrant. To maintain their impartiality—to act judicially—a judge issuing a warrant must retain the discretion not to issue one even where there are reasonable grounds to believe an offence has been committed and evidence will be found in the place to be searched.[60] The discretion enables a judge to strike an appropriate balance between state and individual interests in particular cases by "empower[ing] the judge to consider all the circumstances."[61] This is necessary since "[n]o set of criteria will always be determinative or sufficient to override the right of the individual to privacy."[62] Judges need "a sufficient degree of flexibility . . . in order that justice be done to the respective interests involved."[63]

In some cases, a law might include adequate oversight and transparency by imposing after-the-fact forms of review. Some search laws do this by imposing a standard for exercising a power—requiring reasonable suspicion or reasonable grounds to believe an offence has occurred.[64] Examples of a standard factoring into the Court's assessment of reasonableness include its treatment in *R v Mann* of search incident to investigative detention;[65] strip search on arrest in *Golden*;[66] and sniffer dogs in *Kang-Brown* and *AM*.[67] Another accountability method is to impose a notice requirement. In *R v Tse*, emergency wiretap provisions of the *Code* were unreasonable for failing to include a *post facto* notice requirement to persons affected.[68] Justice Karakatsanis, for the Court in *Chehil*,

58 *Ibid.*

59 *Baron v Canada*, [1993] 1 SCR 416.

60 *Ibid* at 439.

61 *Ibid* at 437.

62 *Ibid.*

63 *Ibid.*

64 *Goodwin*, above note 10 at paras 70–75.

65 *R v Mann*, 2004 SCC 52 [*Mann*].

66 *Golden*, above note 35.

67 *Kang-Brown*, above note 42 and *AM*, above note 42.

68 *R v Tse*, 2012 SCC 16 [*Tse*], involving s 184.4 of the *Criminal Code*, above note 21. A further oversight mechanism considered in this case—but not thought to be necessary—to render the power at issue reasonable under s 8 is an annual statistical reporting requirement to Parliament, which applies to other interception powers in Part VI of the *Code*. Writing for the Court, Moldaver and Karakatsanis JJ note at para 89: "As a matter of policy, a reporting regime that keeps Parliament abreast

expressed the view that where they use a sniffer dog to search an item in the absence of its owner, "the police should generally provide notice to the owner of the item searched."[69] A further tool for oversight and transparency is notetaking. The Court in *Fearon* required police to take notes as one of a series of conditions that render the power to search a phone incident to arrest, without a warrant, both lawful and reasonable.[70]

C. HOLDINGS ON REASONABLE LAW

In this part of the chapter we turn to a survey of the Court's holdings on whether powers to search or seize are reasonable, with a view to showing how the Court has chosen to strike a balance between individual and state interests when considering one or more of the factors in *Del Zotto* and *Goodwin* together.[71]

Before we proceed, it may be helpful to distinguish two kinds of cases. In most cases, the court is asked to assess the reasonableness of a search or seizure law found in legislation. In a smaller set of cases, the court is confronted not with a statutory provision but a form of police conduct—something police have already done—and must decide: is this or should this be "authorized by law"? (i.e., the first part of the *Collins* test). In the process of grappling with *whether* police should have the power to carry out some form of search or seizure, judges will also consider *what* would make it reasonable (the second part of *Collins*). They often do so simultaneously and indistinguishably from applying the second part of the two-part test for recognizing new "ancillary police powers" set out in *Dedman v The Queen* (in which the Supreme Court drew on the English Court of Appeal's decision in *R v Waterfield*).[72] The *Dedman* test requires a court to ask whether the police conduct at issue falls within a duty imposed under statute or at common law, and whether the conduct is reasonably necessary for carrying out the duty. This in turn requires a consideration of the "importance of the performance

---

of the situation on the ground would seem to make good sense. That said, we do not see it as a constitutional imperative."

69 *Chehil*, above note 46 at para 58.

70 *Fearon*, above note 31 at para 82. Justice Cromwell, writing for the majority in *Fearon*, notes in this paragraph that the Court "encouraged this sort of note keeping" for the search of a computer in *Vu*, above note 38 at para 70 and in *Golden*, above note 35 at 101.

71 *Del Zotto* FC, above note 9 and *Goodwin*, above note 10 at para 57.

72 See Chapter 6, Section D(4) for a discussion of the Court's test for recognizing new powers in *Dedman v The Queen*, [1985] 2 SCR 2, 20 DLR (4th) 321 [*Dedman*], drawing on *R v Waterfield*, [1963] 3 All ER 659 [*Waterfield*].

of the duty to the public good"; "the necessity of the interference with individual liberty for the performance of the duty"; and "the extent of the interference with individual liberty."[73] The question of whether a search power is reasonable under section 8 is often subsumed in the assessment of whether the power is reasonably necessary to carry out a police duty. Examples of this approach include the analyses in *Mann*, *Godoy*, and *MacDonald*.[74] In practical terms, the difference is only relevant to how the court frames its discussion of the reasonableness issue. In the cases where they deal with a statutory provision, judges refer explicitly to the balancing test in *Hunter* noted at the outset of this chapter. In some of the cases where the court recognizes a new police power, the balancing happens tacitly or by implication—in ways to be explored below.

1) Search Involving the Body

a) Search Incident to Arrest and Detention

The Supreme Court's decisions in this area involve a mix of approaches—in some cases asking how best to strike a balance between individual and state interests (as in *Hunter*) and in others asking whether a search power is reasonably necessary (as in *Dedman*).[75]

In *Cloutier v Langlois*, the Court addressed whether the power to arrest contains a power to carry out a limited search—without requiring further grounds in addition to those for the arrest itself.[76] As L'Heureux-Dubé J wrote:

> [T]he common law as recognized and developed in Canada holds that the police have a power to search a lawfully arrested person and to seize anything in his or her possession or immediate surroundings to guarantee the safety of the police and the accused, prevent the prisoner's escape or provide evidence against him.[77]

Yet, later in the decision, L'Heureux-Dubé J asserted the need to "apply and develop the common law in a manner consistent with" *Charter* values.[78] The main value at issue is the individual's right to be free from

---

73 Justice LeBel, for the majority, in *MacDonald*, above note 30, provides a summary of the test in paras 35–37.

74 *Mann*, above note 65; *Godoy*, above note 29; and *MacDonald*, *ibid*.

75 *Hunter*, above note 3 and *Dedman*, above note 72.

76 *Cloutier v Langlois*, [1990] 1 SCR 158, 105 NR 241 [*Cloutier*]. The case was not framed as a *Charter* challenge to the search but as a private prosecution against the arresting officers for assault.

77 *Ibid* at 180–81.

78 *Ibid* at 184.

"constraint and coercion."[79] The Court found a "proper balance" between this right and a police interest in being safe when enforcing the law by authorizing police to carry out a "frisk" search on arrest without additional grounds.[80] Justice L'Heureux-Dubé spoke here of a "relatively non-intrusive procedure" in which "outside clothing is patted down to determine whether there is anything on the person of the arrested individual."[81] She added "[p]ockets may be examined but the clothing is not removed and no force is applied. The duration of the search is only a few seconds."[82] A close reading of the case suggests that the Court found a proper balance of interests consistent with the *Charter* by permitting the search of a more limited scope than what was allowed under the common law: a search of the *person* of the arrestee—though L'Heureux-Dubé J did not rule out that police could also search immediate surroundings. In *R v Caslake*, the Court would treat *Cloutier* as having settled this matter, and then proceeded to hold that search on arrest could extend to portions of a vehicle searched several hours later.[83] Clearly, no longer a search taking "only a few seconds."

Cloutier may not have been clear on the spatial scope of a search incident to arrest, but it was clear on another point the Court would affirm in many later cases. A search incident to arrest will be lawful only where it is done for "a valid objective in pursuit of the ends of criminal justice, such as the discovery of an object that may be a threat to the safety of the police, the accused or the public, or that may facilitate escape or act as evidence against the accused."[84] A search done to "intimidate, ridicule or pressure the accused" would be unlawful. The Court in *Cloutier* thus held search on arrest (on no further grounds) to be reasonable given the spatial, temporal, and purpose-related limitations.

The Court has continuously extended the limits of this power. As noted, the majority in *Caslake* recognized that the power to search incident to arrest outlined in *Cloutier* could include the search of a vehicle, so long as the search is "truly incident to the arrest" in the sense of the officer having subjective and objective reasons for the search that are tied to the reasons for the arrest (safety, discovering or preserving evidence).[85] Yet *Caslake* makes only passing mention of the notion of

---

79 *Ibid.*

80 *Ibid* at 185.

81 *Ibid.*

82 *Ibid.*

83 *R v Caslake*, [1998] 1 SCR 51 [*Caslake*]. See the discussion of *Caslake* in Chapter 6, Section D(4)(a).

84 *Cloutier*, above note 76 at 186.

85 *Caslake*, above note 83 at para 25.

a balance of interests, noting that cars are "legitimately the objects of search incident to arrest, as they attract no heightened expectation of privacy" that would warrant a different rule from the one in *Cloutier*.[86] By contrast, in a number of other post-*Cloutier* cases, the Court is clear that in extending the scope of search incident to arrest, it is recognizing a new power to search or seize that reflects a careful balance of interests.

One important example of where this balance could not be found is in *Stillman*,[87] where the Court held that police may not seize bodily samples pursuant to the power to search or seize incident to arrest affirmed in *Cloutier*. Police in *Stillman* took hair samples and teeth impressions, along with a discarded tissue from the accused while in custody following arrest. Justice Cory, for the majority, cited earlier decisions of the Court to the effect that "state interference with a person's bodily integrity" is "an affront to human dignity" and an intrusion "much more serious than [a search] of his office or even of his home."[88] Parliament had recently added DNA warrant provisions to the *Criminal Code*, which implied a recognition of both the more intrusive nature of seizing bodily samples and the need for a more stringent justification for it.[89] The state does not have a pressing interest in seizing samples without a warrant. Samples are "usually in no danger of disappearing," nor would things like teeth impressions change or hair follicles "present a different DNA profile with the passage of time."[90] The evidence would not be lost or destroyed if not immediately seized. A common law power to seize bodily samples on arrest would not "properly balance the competing rights involved."[91]

The Court in *Golden* considered whether and when police are authorized to carry out a strip search on arrest.[92] Does the power recognized in *Cloutier*—to carry out a search incident to arrest without additional grounds—include strip searches? Rights advocates had argued before the Supreme Court in *Golden* that in light of the excessive frequency of strip searches and their disproportionate use against minorities, the Court should impose a warrant requirement.[93] Intervenors representing police argued against this, emphasizing the potential for violence in

86 *Ibid* at para 15.

87 *Stillman*, above note 37.

88 *Ibid* at para 42, citing *R v Pohoretsky*, [1987] 1 SCR 945 at 949; *R v Dyment*, [1988] 2 SCR 417 at 431–32; and *Simmons*, above note 26 at 517.

89 *Stillman*, above note 37 at para 43.

90 *Ibid* at para 49.

91 *Ibid*.

92 *Golden*, above note 35.

93 Kent Roach, *Canadian Policing: Why and How It Must Change* (Toronto: Delve Books, 2022) at 57 [Roach].

every arrest, and contended that a warrant scheme would be unworkable for strip searches.[94] The trial court and Ontario Court of Appeal in *Golden* had held that police could conduct a strip search on no further grounds.[95] The Supreme Court was divided 5:4 on the issue, with the dissenting judges agreeing with the courts below. The majority struck a compromise in declining a warrant requirement but imposing additional requirements for a strip search to be reasonable under section 8.

The majority's point of departure was the notion in *Hunter* that because the purpose of section 8 is to "protect individuals from unjustified state intrusions upon their privacy, it is necessary to have a means of preventing unjustified searches before they occur, rather than simply determining after the fact whether the search should have occurred."[96] This need, in Iacobucci and Arbour JJ's view, is "particularly acute" in the case of strip searches given their "significant and very direct interference with personal privacy." They can also be "humiliating, embarrassing and degrading" in ways that "any *post facto* remedies. . . cannot erase."[97] They cannot, therefore, be carried out "as a matter of routine policy."[98] They can only be conducted lawfully and reasonably where the arrest is lawful; the purpose for the search is related to the reason for the arrest (for safety or to discover or preserve evidence); and, most crucially, there are reasonable and probable grounds for believing a search for one of these purposes is necessary—i.e., a belief in a probability in finding a weapon or evidence rather than a possibility.[99] The higher degree of justification before searching is appropriate here given the "higher degree of interference with individual freedom and dignity."[100] The majority also held that police may not conduct a strip search in the field, which entails "a much greater invasion of privacy and pose[s] a greater threat to the detainee's bodily integrity," unless police have "reasonable and probable grounds to believe that it is necessary to conduct the search in the field rather than at the police station."[101] This kind of search can only be done where there is "a demonstrated necessity and urgency to search for weapons or objects that could be used to threaten the safety of the accused, the arresting officers or other individuals."[102]

94 *Ibid.*
95 *Golden*, above note 35, summarizing the decisions at para 42.
96 *Ibid* at para 89, citing *Hunter*, above note 3 at 160.
97 *Golden*, above note 35 at para 89.
98 *Ibid* at para 90.
99 *Ibid* at paras 91–93 and 98.
100 *Ibid* at para 98.
101 *Ibid* at para 102.
102 *Ibid.*

The majority in *Golden* added a further important feature to rendering a strip search both lawful and reasonable: the requirement to conform with a set of "guidelines" on how police should conduct them.[103] A search should be carried out by an officer of the same gender and should involve the fewest officers as is reasonably necessary; the detainee should not be entirely undressed at any point; and the detainee should be given the option to remove secreted items on their own.[104] For the majority, placing the power to carry out a strip search within these special parameters rendered this search law reasonable under section 8.

Professor Roach has recently surveyed statistics on the impact of *Golden* over the past two decades, and they make clear that even the majority's compromise failed to get the balance right. Neither the standard imposed in the case (additional grounds to those for the arrest) nor the guidelines have made much of a difference in reducing the frequency or manner in which strip searches have been conducted. Quite the contrary. Three years after the Court decided *Golden*, Toronto police were "strip searching 37.4% of the more than 61,000 people they arrested."[105] In 2014 and 2015, this had increased to 40% of all arrests—compared to having strip searched a quarter of all persons arrested in 2000 (prior to *Golden*). As Professor Roach writes:

> In the three years after the decision, Toronto police had strip searched more than 50,000 people—the equivalent of a crowded SkyDome. The population searched, however, would not have resembled a Blue Jays sellout. Over 27 percent of those searched were Black, almost 14 percent were Brown, and over 4 percent were Aboriginal.[106]

But "[w]ere the strip searches successful?" Between 2014 and 2016, Toronto police found evidence in less than 3 percent of strip searches.[107] Roach also notes that a 2019 report by Ontario's police complaints agency found that the province's policing standards had still not been updated to include the *Golden* guidelines and only 26 percent of police services had annual courses on limits of strip search powers.[108] A 2020 report of the Royal Canadian Mounted Police's Civilian Review and Complaints Commission found similar deficiencies on the part of the RCMP's

103 *Ibid* at para 104.

104 See para 104, *ibid* for the complete list of guidelines.

105 Roach, above note 93 at 57, drawing on statistics from Office of the Independent Police Review Director, "Breaking the Golden Rule: A Review of Police Strip Searches in Ontario" (March 2019), online (pdf): www.oiprd.on.ca/wp-content/uploads/OIPRD_Breaking-the-Golden-Rule_Report_Accessible.pdf

106 Roach, above note 93 at 57.

107 *Ibid.*

108 *Ibid* at 58.

implementation of *Golden* standards, undermining the Court's intention in *Golden* of setting out national standards.[109]

In light of the evidence, the rule in *Golden* should be overturned. Police need clear rules. Without them, police will continue to routinely violate the privacy and dignity of many thousands of people in Canada every year. A disproportionate percent of them will be Black, Brown, or Indigenous. At the very least, on revisiting the issue in *Golden*, the Court should pay closer attention to the state interest in such searches. Given how few of these searches yield evidence, is the state interest in a warrantless search truly pressing? Is it as high as the individual interest in dignity and privacy? In *Golden* itself, as Iacobucci and Arbour JJ noted, the officer who decided to search the accused "admitted to having found evidence hidden in an individual's private parts in merely five percent of [over 200] drug arrests" he had conducted.[110] The evidence suggests the Court in *Golden* placed too much weight on the state interest in strip searches, did not strike the right balance between privacy and law enforcement, and the miscalculation continues to have a serious impact on a core human right.

A further strip search case to note is the Court's earlier decision, *Simmons*.[111] This did not involve a challenge to the common law power of search incident to arrest or detention, but to provisions of the *Customs Act* permitting a strip search on detention at the border on reasonable suspicion that a person has "prohibited goods, secreted about the person."[112] Chief Justice Dickson, for the majority, found the power reasonable in light of the balance of interests at the border. On the one hand, "the degree of personal privacy reasonably expected at customs is lower than in most other situations."[113] On the other hand, "the national interests of sovereign states in preventing the entry of . . . prohibited goods, and in protecting tariff revenue" are "important" and a "compelling component in the calculus."[114] The strip search provisions also contained important safeguards. Along with a requirement for reasonable suspicion, the Act allowed the detainee to ask that the grounds be

---

109 *Ibid*, citing the Civilian Review and Complaints Commission for the RCMP, "Review of the RCMP Policies and Procedures Regarding Strip Searches" (July 2020) at 29–30, online (pdf): www.crcc-ccetp.gc.ca/pdf/Strip_Search_Final_Report-eng.PDF.

110 *Golden*, above note 35 at para 109.

111 *Simmons*, above note 26, assessing ss 143 & 144 of the *Customs Act*, RSC 1970, c C-34.

112 *Ibid*, s 143.

113 *Simmons*, above note 26 at 528.

114 *Ibid* at 527–29.

confirmed by a police magistrate or justice of the peace and required the search to be conducted by a person of the same sex.[115]

Returning to the caselaw on the common law power of search incident to arrest, the Court in *Saeed* addressed whether police have authority in sexual assault cases to take a penile swab on arrest.[116] Police in this case had assumed that the power in *Cloutier* to search incident to arrest authorized this form of search and directed the accused to conduct the swab. A test revealed that it contained the complainant's DNA. In a 7:2 decision, the majority recognized a power to take a swab by distinguishing the privacy interests and law enforcement objectives at issue here from those in *Stillman*.[117] Writing for the majority, Moldaver J held that while the accused has a high privacy interest in his own bodily samples, penile swabs involve samples belonging to the complainant.[118] Concerns about the sample capturing the accused's DNA can be addressed by the holding in this case that where police obtain a swab without a warrant or the accused's consent "the accused's DNA cannot be used for any purpose."[119] And although the taking of a penile swab is invasive, it is less so than taking dental impressions or removing hair by force.[120] It is quick, not penetrative, does not cause pain or discomfort, and poses no risk to the accused's health.[121] The state interest here is pressing. The complainant's DNA degrades quickly; the accused can easily remove or destroy it; and there is a real danger of it disappearing if not seized immediately.[122] DNA is also "highly reliable" evidence rendered all the more important in light of how "notoriously difficult" sexual assaults are to prove.[123] Two further safeguards can be imposed to render the power to take a swab on arrest reasonable. One is a requirement that police may take a sample only if they have "reasonable grounds to believe that the search will reveal and preserve evidence of the offence for which the accused was arrested."[124] The other is a set of guidelines police must follow for taking a swab in a reasonable manner, analogous to those set out in *Golden* for

115 *Ibid* at 529. In the present version of the Act, a detainee may seek a second opinion on reasonable suspicion from a "senior officer" rather than a judge, and it still requires that the search be conducted by a person of the same sex: *Customs Act*, RSC 1985, c 1 (2nd Supp.), s 98(3), (4).

116 *Saeed*, above note 27.

117 *Ibid*, distinguishing *Stillman*, above note 37.

118 *Saeed*, above note 27 at para 44.

119 *Ibid* at para 48.

120 *Ibid* at para 44.

121 *Ibid* at para 55.

122 *Ibid* at para 50.

123 *Ibid* at para 59.

124 *Ibid* at paras 6 and 64.

strip searches.[125] These include taking the swab somewhere in private; giving the accused a chance to remove his clothes and take the swab himself, or having male officers do so; having no more of them involved than is reasonably necessary; and taking a "proper record" of the reasons for and manner in which the swab was conducted.[126]

Dissenting in *Saeed*, Karakatsanis J held that the seizure of a penile swab required a warrant to be reasonable, given that "a swab of the genital area is far more damaging to personal dignity and privacy than a swab of the inside of the mouth or a pluck of hair from the head."[127] The majority's prohibition on the use of the accused's DNA obtained in the course of a swab was still a concern given that it would "remain in the hands of police, available for undetermined future use."[128] Justice Abella, also dissenting, held that taking the swab violated section 8, but was unclear as to what would render a penile swab reasonable. She noted that no *Code* provision permits it, including the general warrant in section 489.01, which states that "[n]othing . . . shall be construed . . . to permit interference with the bodily integrity of any person."[129] She appeared to suggest that a swab may be so invasive as to require a set of conditions or guidelines, in addition to a warrant, to render such a search reasonable.[130]

In *Fearon*, the majority recognized a new police power to search a cellphone incident to arrest without a warrant.[131] An important part of the context of this case was the decision of the Supreme Court of the United States on the same issue earlier the same year in *Riley v California*.[132] The Court in that case undertook a similar balancing of interests but declined to find that police have a pressing interest in being able to search a phone *immediately* on arrest—a position with which the dissent in *Fearon* agreed.

By contrast, a primary consideration for the majority of Canada's Supreme Court in *Fearon* was a belief that police cannot respond

---

125 *Ibid* at para 62, citing *Golden*, above note 35.

126 *Saeed*, above note 27 at para 78.

127 *Ibid* at para 101.

128 *Ibid* at para 105.

129 *Ibid* at para 148, citing s 487.01(2) of the *Criminal Code*, above note 21. Justice Karakatsanis also makes this observation at para 110.

130 *Saeed*, above note 27 at para 152, noting:

> A genital swab does not just require the individual to expose his or her genitals to state scrutiny, it asks that individual to violate his or her own bodily integrity by collecting potentially self-incriminatory evidence from that most private of areas. The impact on Mr. Saeed's privacy interests is as profound as one can imagine, leaving far in its wake the prior "ultimate" baseline from *Stillman*.

131 *Fearon*, above note 31.

132 134 S Ct 2473 (2014) [*Riley*].

effectively to a violent crime — in this case, a robbery with a gun — without searching an arrestee's phone without delay, so as to locate accomplices or evidence that could be lost or destroyed.[133] Justice Cromwell conceded that phones and computers engage a high degree of privacy, but held that "not every [device] search is inevitably a significant intrusion."[134] A limited search of a person's data is "completely different" from seizing bodily samples or conducting a strip search.[135] A person also has a lower expectation of privacy on arrest.[136] In light of the weight of interests falling in favour of the state, the majority held that police could conduct a limited search of a phone on arrest without a warrant and without requiring additional grounds — on certain conditions. The arrest itself must be lawful; the search must be carried out for a valid objective (protecting police and preserving or discovering evidence); the nature and extent of the search must be tailored to the purpose; and police must take detailed notes of what they searched.[137] A further qualification applies where the purpose of the search is to discover evidence, including locating additional suspects. Police can only search for this purpose "in situations in which the investigation will be stymied or significantly hampered absent the ability to promptly search the cell phone incident to arrest."[138]

In *Riley*, the US Supreme Court held the view that a nuanced rule of the kind the majority in *Fearon* adopted — one allowing for limited searches — would entail "few meaningful constraints."[139] The Court imposed a warrant requirement for searching phones on arrest, preferring

133 *Fearon*, above note 31 at paras 46–48 and 59–65.

134 *Ibid* at para 54.

135 *Ibid* at para 55.

136 *Ibid* at para 56.

137 *Ibid* at para 83.

138 *Ibid*. The majority's position in *Fearon* has drawn considerable criticism, questioning its merits in light of the rapid development of cellphone technology; see, e.g., Colton Fehr & Jared Biden, "Divorced From (Technological) Reality: A Response to the Supreme Court of Canada's Reasons in *R v Fearon*" (2015) 20:1 *Canadian Criminal Law Review* 93, arguing at 100, that "identity protection functions" such as touch and face-ID, "raise additional constitutional concerns about the rights to silence and against self-incrimination, as well as provide additional privacy interests that were not given weight by either the majority or the dissent in *Fearon*." See also Jordan Fine, "Leaving Dumb Phones Behind: A Commentary on the Warrantless Searches of Smartphone Data Granted in *R v Fearon*" (2015) 13 *Canadian Journal of Law and Technology* 171, and Pierre-Luc Déziel, "Windows to Our Inner Private Lives: Cell Phones, Informational Privacy and the Power to Search Incident to Arrest in Canada" (2015) 20:1 *Lex Electronica* 51.

139 *Riley*, above note 132 at 2492.

"clear guidance to law enforcement through categorical rules."[140] The dissent in *Fearon* proposed a middle ground: permitting a warrantless phone search on arrest on a reasonable suspicion of imminent bodily harm or a reasonable belief that it is necessary to prevent imminent loss or destruction of evidence.[141]

In *R v Stairs*, the Supreme Court considered whether police have the power to search a portion of a home incident to arrest—the area surrounding where a person is arrested, or areas they traverse in the lead up to or course of the arrest.[142] The majority noted the longstanding recognition at common law of a heightened privacy interest in a dwelling house, yet also held that area searches on arrest are "less intrusive than strip searches and penile swabs, which inevitably impact a person's dignity."[143] Police have various interests in a search of this kind, including looking for accomplices or potential victims, and these are "likely to be more pressing than those involved in strip searches and penile swabs" since they face a lower risk of losing evidence in the former case and a lower risk to safety in the latter case.[144] The majority held that a pair of new police powers would strike a proper balance between a person's privacy in their home and public safety. Police may search "areas of the home outside the arrested person's physical control" but "proximate to the arrest" where they have a reasonable suspicion that the safety of police or others is at risk and the search is conducted in a reasonable manner, "tailored to the heightened privacy interests in a home."[145] Police may not conduct the search to preserve or discover evidence (as they may on arrest otherwise). Officers have an additional power to search the "area within the physical control of the person arrested at the time of arrest."[146] In this case, they need no further grounds and may search for all three of the purposes set out in *Cloutier*: safety and the preservation or discovery of evidence related to the reason for the arrest.[147]

Justice Karakatsanis held in dissent, along with Brown and Martin JJ, that there should be only one standard for search incident to arrest within a home, aside from a frisk search of the arrestee themself, and it should

---

140 *Ibid* at 2491.
141 *Fearon*, above note 31 at paras 178–79.
142 *R v Stairs*, 2022 SCC 11 [*Stairs*].
143 *Ibid* at para 51.
144 *Ibid* at paras 52–53.
145 *Ibid* at para 56.
146 *Ibid* at para 59.
147 *Ibid* at paras 61 and 82.

be reasonable suspicion of an *imminent* threat to police or public safety.[148] They arrived at this position by taking a different view of the interests at issue. Where a home search ranks relative to a strip search or the seizure of a bodily sample seemed "tangential" to the more fundamental point that in entering a home, police intrude upon a heightened privacy interest.[149] And while police may have a pressing interest in immediate search on arrest given the safety risks involved, "home searches in the domestic violence context may cut both ways."[150] A search might "revictimize victims or uncover evidence of unrelated offences, which may discourage individuals from reporting."[151] Powers too permissive might "compound that reluctance." The majority responded to these concerns by noting that a higher standard—suspicion of imminent harm—would "prevent the police from acting promptly" and have the effect of "restat[ing] the exigency exception."[152] If police had a suspicion of imminent harm, they could rely on exigent circumstances for authority.[153]

Turning from arrest to investigative detention, the Court in *Mann* recognized a power to carry out a limited search incident to detention.[154] Justice Iacobucci relied on the *Dedman/Waterfield* test to recognize such a power,[155] noting that "[u]nderlying this discussion is the need to balance the competing interests of an individual's reasonable expectation of privacy with the interests of officer safety."[156] A power to search incident to detention fell within the scope of a police duty to protect life and property, and the interference on liberty it entails was reasonably necessary in part because it could be crafted to be limited in scope.[157] An officer may conduct a search only where he "believe[s] on reasonable grounds that his safety, or the safety of others, is at risk."[158] Drawing from the United States Supreme Court decision recognizing an analogous power in *Terry v Ohio*, Iacobucci J held that the officer "must not be acting solely on a hunch, but rather is required to act on reasonable and specific inferences

148 *Ibid* at paras 107, 135; the latter paragraph containing an explicit rejection of the majority's distinction between "areas inside and outside the arrested person's physical control."

149 *Ibid* at para 120.

150 *Ibid* at para 123.

151 *Ibid.*

152 *Ibid* at para 77.

153 *Stairs* above note 142, left the important question of whether and how the plain view doctrine applies in the course of a search incident to arrest in a dwelling house. See the discussion of this issue in Chapter 6, Section D(4)(a).

154 *Mann*, above note 65.

155 *Waterfield*, above note 72; *Dedman*, above note 72.

156 *Ibid.*

157 *Mann*, above note 65 at paras 39–40.

158 *Ibid* at para 40.

drawn from the known facts of the situation."[159] And the search would involve only a "protective pat-down" for things that may be used as weapons.[160] Later courts would extend the limits of this "safety search" power in ways explored below.

b) DNA, Fingerprints

In *SAB*, the appellant challenged the reasonableness of provisions in the *Criminal Code* allowing for the seizure of DNA samples for investigative purposes.[161] A DNA warrant, he argued, should only be issued as a last resort. Justice Arbour, writing for the Court, disagreed, finding the scheme reasonable in light of the nature of the interests at issue and a number of safeguards it included. Taking a DNA sample through a buccal swab or a pinprick interferes with bodily integrity in a "relatively modest" way.[162] The process can be rendered less invasive by imposing conditions that "respect the offender's privacy" and precluding the removal of pubic hair.[163] A DNA sample engages a person's right over informational privacy but the sample is collected for the limited purpose of "forensic analysis."[164] It does not reveal "any medical, physical or mental characteristics"; it is used only as a means of "identifying information that can be compared to an existing sample."[165] The *Code* makes it an offence to use information from a DNA analysis under these provisions for any use other than an investigation of a designated offence.[166] Moreover, the state's interest in taking a sample is "significant" given the "enormous utility and power of DNA as an investigative tool"—the "virtual certainty" with which a DNA match can eliminate a person as a suspect, helping to "avoid wrongful convictions."[167] Parliament made a reasonable decision not to require the Crown to establish the need for a DNA sample as an investigative avenue of last resort because it put in place other safeguards. Only a provincial court judge can issue a DNA

159 *Ibid* at para 41, citing *Terry v Ohio*, 392 US 1 (1968) at 27.

160 *Mann*, above note 65 at paras 42–43.

161 *SAB*, above note 43, considering the warrant power in s 487.05 of the *Criminal Code*, above note 21, and related provisions (from ss 487.04–487.09). The investigative DNA warrant power is distinct from a second kind of warrant for seizure of DNA for inclusion in the national DNA databank where persons are convicted of designated offences: s 487.051(1), (2) & (3). Both powers are discussed in Chapter 6, Section A(6).

162 *SAB*, above note 43 at para 44.

163 *Ibid* at paras 44–46.

164 *Ibid* at paras 48–49.

165 *Ibid* at para 49.

166 *Ibid* at para 50, noting ss 487.05(1)(b), 487.08(1) & (2).

167 *Ibid* at para 51.

warrant, not a justice of the peace; the judge must be satisfied there are reasonable grounds to believe a designated offence has been committed; and they must conclude it is in the best interests of the administration of justice to issue the warrant.[168] The scheme strikes an "appropriate balance between the public interest in effective criminal law enforcement for serious offences and the rights of individuals to control the release of personal information about themselves, as well as their right to dignity and physical integrity."[169]

R v Beare; R v Higgins addressed the reasonableness of the power under the *Identification of Criminals Act* to take fingerprints upon arrest.[170] Justice La Forest, on behalf of the Court, dispensed with the appeal by dealing mostly with section 7, but did find the power reasonable under section 8.[171] The balancing favoured the state interest here. An arrestee has a diminished privacy interest on arrest and "must expect that incidental to his being taken in custody he will be subjected to observation, to physical measurement and the like."[172] Fingerprinting is "insubstantial, of very short duration, and leaves no lasting impression."[173] It does not involve "penetration into the body and no substance is removed from it."[174] It is, however, "an invaluable tool of criminal investigation because of the ease and rapidity of the process and because it is virtually infallible, no two persons' fingerprints being alike."[175] Prints also serve a variety of purposes in criminal justice, including "linking the accused to the crime" or to evidence; indicating if the accused has been charged with or convicted of other offences for the purpose of deciding on bail; discerning whether the accused is "unlawfully at large" or has outstanding charges; and "assisting in the apprehension of an accused should he fail to appear."[176] They can also be used to "identify prisoners with suicidal tendencies, sex offenders, career criminals and persons with a history of escape attempts so that they can be segregated or monitored as may appear appropriate."[177] The restriction of this power to persons lawfully arrested strikes an appropriate balance of interests.

---

168 *Ibid* at paras 38–39.

169 *Ibid* at para 52.

170 *R v Beare; R v Higgins*, [1988] 2 SCR 387 [*Beare*], considering s 2 of the *Identification of Criminals Act*, RSC 1970, c I-1.

171 The decision assumes that taking a fingerprint constitutes a search or seizure without addressing how it does so.

172 *Beare*, above note 170 at 413.

173 *Ibid.*

174 *Ibid.*

175 *Ibid* at 399.

176 *Ibid* at 399–400.

177 *Ibid* at 400.

2) Searches of Homes and Other Places

Hunter serves as a starting point for defining where a reasonable balance is struck between individual and state interests in a law that authorizes a search or seizure that occurs within a private physical space, which could include a building such as a dwelling house or an office, a portion of land or the perimeter of a building, or a closed container. The Court in *Hunter* set out standards that need to be met to make these searches reasonable, but it permitted exceptions to them where the weight to be accorded to individual or state interests differs in dissimilar contexts.

a) *Hunter*

As the reader may recall from Chapter 2, Dickson J, as he then was, took an important step in framing the Supreme Court's approach to section 8 of the *Charter* by citing the opinion of the majority in the US Supreme Court in *Katz v United States* for the point that "the Fourth Amendment protects people, not places" or, more broadly, their right to privacy, which Stewart J described as the "right to be let alone" by the state.[178] In the most general sense, any search a state agent conducts of a private or civilian space engages an individual interest in being "let alone," while the search itself advances a state interest in finding evidence of an offence so as to uphold the law. A search would be reasonable under section 8, or a law authorizing a search, where the "state's interest in detecting and preventing crime begins to prevail over the individual's interest in being left alone."[179] In the normal course, where police enter a private building or space, the balance is tipped in the state's favour where three conditions are met. First, police or state agents must obtain a warrant or some form of prior authorization. This supports the purpose of section 8—to protect the right to privacy—by "preventing unjustified searches before they happen" rather than "determining, after the fact, whether they ought to have occurred in the first place."[180] Second, the warrant should only be issued by a person in a position to decide "in an entirely neutral and impartial manner" whether the standard for granting a warrant has been met.[181] The person need not be a judge, but they must "at a minimum be capable of acting judicially."[182] And finally, the warrant should be issued on a sufficiently stringent standard to prevent unjustified intrusions into

---

178 *Hunter*, above note 3 at 158–59, citing *Katz v United States*, 389 US 347 (1967) at 351, then 350.

179 *Hunter*, above note 3 at 167.

180 *Ibid* at 160

181 *Ibid* at 162.

182 *Ibid*.

privacy. The statute in *Hunter* allowed for a warrant on the basis of a mere possibility that evidence would be found. Justice Dickson held:

> Such an amorphous standard cannot provide a meaningful criterion for securing the right guaranteed by s 8. The location of the constitutional balance between a justifiable expectation of privacy and the legitimate needs of the state cannot depend on the subjective appreciation of individual adjudicators. Some objective standard must be established.[183]

The common law, the *Criminal Code*, and the Fourth Amendment all pointed to the same longstanding test for intrusions into homes, offices, and other spaces: "information upon oath that there is 'reasonable ground to believe' that there is evidence of an offence in the place to be searched."[184]

Meeting the three requirements in *Hunter* marks the point at which state interests begin to prevail over individual interests, rendering the search of a place or the seizure of a thing in a criminal case presumptively reasonable under section 8. But where individual or state interests are more or less pressing—strip searches, border searches, searches in exigent circumstances, among others—a court might strike a different balance.[185] In what follows, we turn to cases where the Supreme Court has found searches or seizures in private spaces—all of them homes—to be reasonable on lesser standards due to more pressing state interests.

b) Dwelling Houses

In *Grant*, the Court dealt with a law authorizing a search around the perimeter of a home.[186] Acting on a tip, police carried out two warrantless perimeter searches of the accused's residence on a belief that he was setting up a marijuana grow operation, and then used observations made in the course of that search to obtain a warrant to enter the home. At the time of the offence, section 10 of the *Narcotic Control Act* permitted police to search a place other than a dwelling house without a warrant on reasonable grounds to believe a narcotics offence had been committed.[187] The Court found the power in section 10 unreasonable. Justice Sopinka, writing on behalf of the Court, held that in light of the potential criminal consequences that could flow from a conviction under the Act, the search power had to be "assessed in strict accordance with

---

183 *Ibid* at 166.

184 *Ibid* at 167.

185 *Ibid* at 168.

186 *Grant*, above note 16.

187 *Narcotic Control Act*, RSC 1985, c N-1.

the approach set out in *Hunter*."[188] The power was invasive; it allowed police not only to "intrude into places where individuals may have very high expectations of privacy," but also to "break down walls and doors, seize a wide variety of evidence and search the person of individuals found in the place searched."[189] The common law has long recognized the privacy interest in a home to be high and to include a "freedom from trespass on private property."[190] Although the state has a pressing interest in fighting the "pernicious scourge" of the "illicit drug trade," given the "suffering" it inflicts, a law that strikes a reasonable balance with individual interests is one that imposes more stringent limits on a warrantless search.[191] The Court read down section 10 to require a reasonable belief in "an imminent danger of the loss, removal, destruction or disappearance of the evidence sought in a narcotics investigation if the search or seizure is delayed in order to obtain a warrant."[192] The analogous power found today in the *Controlled Drugs and Substances Act* incorporates this limitation.[193]

In the 1990s, the Supreme Court decided three cases involving police entering homes without a warrant in exigent circumstances, prompting the Court to articulate *Charter*-compliant limits on this power. In *R v Macooh*, an officer entered an apartment in hot pursuit of what he believed was an impaired driver who had given chase.[194] The case was not framed as a potential section 8 violation, but rather a breach of sections 7 and 9 of the *Charter*. The Court recognized as consistent with the *Charter* the longstanding common law exception to the law of trespass allowing police entry into a home to effect an arrest when in hot pursuit. A person in flight may pose a danger to others; the officer has personal knowledge of the facts justifying the arrest; flight suggests an awareness of guilt (and impliedly a lesser privacy interest, as on arrest generally); and police have a pressing interest in gaining entry so as to identify a suspect or avoid having evidence lost or destroyed.

In *R v Silveira*, police entered a home without a warrant to prevent the destruction of evidence of drug offences.[195] A majority of the Court refused to recognize a common law police power to enter a residence to prevent the imminent destruction of evidence, but Parliament

188 *Grant* above note 16 at 240.

189 *Ibid.*

190 *Ibid* at 241.

191 *Ibid.*

192 *Ibid* at 241–42.

193 *Controlled Drugs and Substances Act*, SC 1996, c 19, s 11(7) [*CDSA*].

194 *R v Macooh*, [1993] 2 SCR 802 [*Macooh*].

195 *R v Silveira*, [1995] 2 SCR 297.

soon responded by codifying powers of warrantless entry in exigent circumstances.[196]

In *R v Feeney*, police entered the accused's trailer without a warrant to locate and arrest him.[197] The Court had held in *R v Landry* (1986) that police may enter a dwelling house to arrest a person on reasonable grounds to believe they had committed an indictable offence and would be present.[198] Exigent circumstances were not required. Writing for the majority in *Feeney*, Sopinka J held that *Landry* had not struck the right balance between "privacy and the effectiveness of police protection" since "in the *Charter* era . . . the emphasis on privacy in Canada has gained considerable importance."[199] Privacy now "outweighs the interest of the police" in carrying out warrantless arrests in homes, with one exception.[200] In *Macooh* the Court had held that the balance of interests favours police in the case of hot pursuit of a suspect into a home, for the reasons canvassed above.[201] A warrant requirement would not be justified in that instance, but it was "well worth the additional protection" to privacy in homes in the normal course.

One concern in *Landry* justifying police entry was the possibility of a suspect taking refuge in a home to avoid arrest. A warrant, Sopinka J reasoned in *Feeney*, would slow police down but not allow homes to be used to evade police. As Sopinka J held, "privacy rights under the *Charter* demand that the police, in general, obtain prior judicial authorization of entry into the dwelling house in order to arrest the person."[202] Having a warrant requirement would avoid the "ex post facto analysis of the reasonableness of an intrusion that *Hunter* held should be avoided under the *Charter*."[203] At the time *Feeney* was decided, no such warrant could be found in the *Code* or elsewhere and so "such a provision should be read in."[204] The warrant would "only be authorized if there are reasonable grounds for the arrest, and reasonable grounds to believe that the person will be found at the address named."[205] Parliament responded to this ruling by adding sections 529 and 529.1 to the *Code*, which

196 *Criminal Code*, above note 21, s 487.11; *CDSA*, above note 193, s 11(7). See the discussion of these sections in Chapter 5, Section B(5) and Chapter 6, Section B(1).

197 *R v Feeney*, [1997] 2 SCR 13 [*Feeney*].

198 *R v Landry*, [1986] 1 SCR 145.

199 *Feeney* above note 197 at para 42.

200 *Ibid* at para 44.

201 *Macooh*, above note 194, cited in *Feeney*, above note 197 at para 47.

202 *Feeney* above note 197 at para 48.

203 *Ibid* at para 49.

204 *Ibid* at para 48.

205 *Ibid* at para 49.

allow for a warrant on precisely these grounds.[206] Drawing from *Landry*, Sopinka J also imposed a further requirement to render a search here both lawful and reasonably conducted: the need, before entering with force, to make a "proper announcement."[207]

Writing in dissent in *Feeney*, L'Heureux-Dubé J, together with Gonthier J and McLachlin J, as she then was, would not have overturned *Landry* and would also have recognized as reasonable under section 8 a police power to enter and search where there are grounds to believe evidence may soon be destroyed.[208] The Court in *Eccles v Bourque* and *Landry* had recognized exceptions to the requirement to obtain a warrant before entering a home, in both cases for the purpose of arrest.[209] If the Court in *Macooh* limited warrantless entry to hot pursuit, L'Heureux-Dubé J held, "I would note that, in a real sense, 'hot pursuit' is actually nothing more than a variety of exigent circumstances, and not really a separate doctrine."[210] It was also "part of the basis upon which the 'hot pursuit' exception to the arrest warrant requirement [was] founded."[211] The majority in *Feeney* did not address exigent circumstances as a further exception, because it did not find them to be present here. Section 529.3(2) codifies the dissent's holding in *Feeney*, by permitting warrantless entry *to effect an arrest* in a dwelling house on reasonable grounds to believe it "necessary to prevent the imminent loss or imminent destruction" of evidence.[212]

In *Godoy*, the Court drew on the *Dedman/Waterfield* test to recognize a new power to enter a dwelling house without a warrant in response to a disconnected or disrupted 911 distress call.[213] An emergency call was made from the accused's apartment but the line was disconnected before the caller spoke. Police knocked and the accused answered and said there was no problem. An officer asked to enter and the accused attempted to shut the door. Police forced their way in, heard a woman crying, and found her in a bedroom with a swollen eye, reporting the accused had assaulted her. Chief Justice Lamer, writing on behalf of the Court, held that when a 911 call is disrupted it is "imperative" that "police assume that the caller is in some distress and requires immediate assistance."[214] To do otherwise "would seriously impair the effectiveness

206 We discuss these powers in Chapter 6, Section A(7).

207 *Feeney*, above note 197 at para 50, also found in ss 529 and 529.4 of the *Criminal Code*, above note 21.

208 *Ibid* at paras 143 and 154–56.

209 *Eccles v Bourque*, [1975] 2 SCR 739, cited *ibid* at para 144.

210 *Feeney*, above note 197 at para 147, citing *Macooh*, above note 194.

211 *Feeney*, above note 197 at para 155.

212 This provision is discussed further in Chapter 6, Section A(7).

213 *Godoy*, above note 29; *Dedman*, above note 72; *Waterfield*, above note 72.

214 *Godoy*, above note 29 at para 16.

of the [emergency response] system and undermine its very purpose."[215] Acting upon this assumption, police had met the first part of the test in *Dedman/Waterfield*: they were acting under a statutory duty to protect life. The second part of the test asks whether police were justified in making a warrantless entry with force. Whether this was reasonably necessary to fulfilling the duty involves a test similar to the balancing in *Hunter*: the Court considers, on the one hand, the nature and extent of the interference with liberty that the police conduct entails and, on the other, the importance of fulfilling the duty to the public good.[216] In this case, police had to enter without delay because there was "no reasonable alternative" to ensuring the caller would receive "necessary assistance in a timely manner." It would have been "dangerous" to simply wait in the hall for "further signs of distress."[217] The home attracts a high privacy interest, but a disconnected 911 call also engages interests in "dignity, integrity, and autonomy . . . in a most immediate and pressing nature," tipping the balance in favour of this police power being reasonable.[218]

In *MacDonald*, the Court recognized a power that is closely related to the one in both *Godoy* and *Mann*.[219] Police attended the accused's home in response to a noise complaint. He opened the door and an officer could see that the accused had an object in his hand, hidden behind his leg. The officer, believing it could be a knife, asked what it was. Not receiving a reply, he pushed open the door a few inches to get a better look. A struggle ensued, with police discovering the accused had a loaded handgun. Was the "safety search" police conducted here — pushing the door open slightly — reasonable under section 8? As in *Godoy*, the majority in *MacDonald* answered the question by applying the *Dedman/Waterfield* test to ascertain whether the use of the safety search power was authorized by law. Doing so entailed, once again, asking whether the power was "reasonably necessary," which subsumed the question of whether it would constitute a reasonable law under section 8. Here too, under the first part of *Dedman*, police were acting under a duty to "protect life and safety."[220] The infringement on liberty a safety search in these circumstances entails was reasonably necessary. It served an important duty in terms of the public good: protecting life and safety. It was a necessary infringement on liberty because police needed to "interact with an individual who they have reasonable grounds to believe is

215 *Ibid.*
216 *Ibid* at para 18.
217 *Ibid.*
218 *Ibid* at para 19.
219 *MacDonald*, above note 30; *Godoy*, above note 29; *Mann*, above note 65.
220 *MacDonald*, above note 30 at para 35.

armed and dangerous."[221] And it was limited in its extent, ending as soon as the search for weapons ended.[222] Justice LeBel, for the majority, was clear that the safety search power could apply in situations other than merely pushing open a door, but cautioned that "such a search will be lawful only if all aspects of the search serve a protective function."[223] The authority "runs out at the point at which the search for weapons is finished."[224] In light of the high privacy in a home, the majority imposed a further important safeguard: "the search will be authorized by law only if the police officer believes on reasonable grounds that his or her safety [or the safety of others] is at stake and that, as a result, it is necessary to conduct a search."[225]

Writing in dissent in *MacDonald*, Moldaver J and Wagner J, as he then was (joined by Rothstein J), agreed that a new, free-standing "safety search" power should be recognized but held the standard should be reasonable suspicion of an imminent threat to safety—consistent with the standard for a safety search on investigative detention in *Mann*.[226] Police had reasonable suspicion to believe in a threat to safety here, and that was enough to justify the search. If they had probable grounds to believe safety was at issue, they would have had grounds to arrest and would not have needed a new power to authorize this search. The majority does not address the dissent's claim that its ruling in this case has the effect of overturning the standard in *Mann*. One way to read the difference of opinion in *MacDonald* is to infer that the majority sought to impose a higher standard in light of the recognition of the safety search as a distinct, *free-standing* power—one that could authorize the search of a home. On this reading, the majority's ruling leaves the safety search power in *Mann* untouched; it applies only on investigative detention.

As we suggested in Chapter 5, the majority's higher standard for safety searches in *MacDonald* is appropriate in light of the more invasive nature of these searches. They may involve extensive, if brief and cursory, searches of entire homes. Whether these are reasonable will turn on the facts in each case, but by requiring probable grounds, the majority in *MacDonald* compels police and courts on review to establish a clear basis in the surrounding facts for concerns about safety. However, the caselaw to date suggests that, in practice, the line courts are drawing (to justify or not) residential safety searches falls closer to reasonable suspicion than

221 *Ibid* at para 39.
222 *Ibid*.
223 *Ibid*.
224 *Ibid*.
225 *Ibid* at para 41.
226 *Mann*, above note 65.

probability. Cases in which courts find a safety search to be reasonable are ones in which there *might* still be someone found inside a house or a loaded weapon found (rather than that being *probably* the case, as is required on the reasonable belief standard).[227] Cases finding the search unreasonable are ones in which police had no grounds whatsoever.[228] In this regard, the dissenting opinion in *MacDonald* reflects a more intuitive sense of the balance between privacy and security that both police and courts find reasonable in urgent situations. Where there is a real *possibility* of danger, police should err on the side of caution.[229]

c) Sniff Searches

The Supreme Court in *Kang-Brown* and *AM* recognized a police power to conduct a sniff search of odours emanating from a bag or locker using a sniffer dog.[230] Police in *Kang-Brown* had used sniffer dogs to search a person's bag at a bus station and, in *AM*, to sniff bags in a high school gym, in both cases on a suspicion that they contained an illicit substance. Both of these decisions involved multiple opinions. In both cases, four judges deferred to Parliament to create new powers for sniffer dog searches.[231] Five judges applied the *Dedman/Waterfield* test to find the use of sniffer dogs a justified and reasonably necessary use of police power in some contexts, and that it would be reasonable under section 8 on the standard of reasonable suspicion.[232] Justice Binnie, joined by McLachlin CJ, held that police are justified in exercising this power in light of the lower privacy interest in odours emanating from bags in public spaces, the

---

227 See, e.g., *R v McPake*, 2019 BCSC 751 (finding reasonable a safety search of an entire one-bedroom apartment in response to the discharge of a gun and after the resident was in custody).

228 See, e.g., *R v Ahmed-Kadir*, 2015 BCCA 346 (going into bedroom and closet on a "clearing search" following a domestic dispute was unreasonable given that the couple residing there were accounted for and there was no reason to believe others would be present in the room or closet); *R v Kennett*, 2019 NBCA 52 (considering whether to exclude evidence from a safety search held unreasonable at trial involving the search of "every room" of a house); and *R v Thompson*, 2020 SKPC 39 (finding unreasonable entry and a safety search of an entire home and gun safe without any basis for believing there was an imminent danger to anyone's safety).

229 Or, as Groberman JA held in *R v Larson*, 2011 BCCA 454 at para 26, "in matters involving the protection of life and physical safety, the police have no realistic choice but to err on the side of caution."

230 *Kang-Brown*, above note 42; *AM*, above note 42.

231 Justices LeBel, Fish, Abella, and Charron held this view.

232 In *Kang-Brown*, above note 42, at paras 48–57, Binnie J (joined by McLachlin CJ) applies *Dedman*; Descamps J (joined by Rothstein J) at paras 149–53 and 182 invokes *Dedman*; and Binnie J does so at para 232.

brief and non-invasive nature of the search, the high degree of accuracy dogs exhibit in detecting illicit substances, and the fact that "[i]n sniffer-dog situations, the police are generally required to take quick action guided by on-the-spot observations searches."[233] Justices Deschamps and Rothstein held the power to be justified by placing emphasis on the lower privacy interest in odours and the finding in earlier cases of reasonable suspicion as an adequate standard in other contexts, including strip search at the border and search incident to investigative detention.[234] Justice Bastarache thought the power would have been reasonable on the standard of generalized suspicion (i.e., the person searched is transiting an area or fits a general pattern that raises a reasonable suspicion).[235] The four justices in dissent held that a reasonable search under section 8 involving sniffer dogs would require at least reasonable and probable grounds, except in exigent circumstances.

d) Schools

In *R v M(MR)*, the Supreme Court, in an 8:1 decision, recognized a special power of authorities in high schools to conduct warrantless searches and seizures in that context.[236] In this case, a vice principal, acting on information from several students, searched a student, finding marijuana in his possession. Justice Cory, for the majority, affirmed that young people at school have a privacy interest in their person and their effects, but a lower one than in other places. They must reasonably assume that school officials "are responsible for providing a safe environment and maintaining order and discipline" in schools and that this "may sometimes require searches of students and their personal effects and the seizure of prohibited items."[237] Minding the safety of young persons is a pressing state objective, since "without an orderly environment learning will be difficult if not impossible" and education is important.[238] Possession of drugs and weapons in schools has increased to the point of "challeng[ing] the ability of school officials to fulfill their responsibility to maintain a safe and orderly environment."[239] Administrators need "flexibility" to deal with discipline issues as they arise; they must be "able to act quickly and effectively to ensure the safety of students and to prevent

---

233 *Ibid* at paras 48–60, noting his discussion in *AM*, above note 42, at paras 12–14 and 90.

234 *Kang-Brown*, above note 42 at paras 160–69 and 186.

235 *Ibid* at para 245.

236 *R v M(MR)*, [1998] 3 SCR 393, 166 DLR (4th) 261.

237 *Ibid* at para 33.

238 *Ibid* at para 36.

239 *Ibid.*

serious violations of school rules."[240] In some cases, waiting for a warrant could be dangerous.

For the majority in *M(MR)*, the heightened safety concerns in schools coupled with the lower privacy interest supported the recognition of a new common law power to search or seize, on a unique standard. As Cory J held, "[a] search by school officials of a student under their authority may be undertaken if there are reasonable grounds to believe that a school rule has been or is being violated, and that evidence of the violation will be found in the location or on the person of the student searched."[241] Reasonable grounds here has a specific meaning: they "may well be provided by information received from just one student that the school authority considers credible."[242] Or they may derive from "information from more than one student or from observations of teachers or principals, or from a combination of these pieces of information which considered together the relevant authority believes to be credible."[243] More invasive searches for "health and safety" may require higher standards, but in any case, "[a]ll the circumstances surrounding a search must be taken into account in determining if the search is reasonable."[244]

A further limitation in *M(MR)* that speaks to all three parts of the *Collins* test for school searches under section 8 is the manner of conduct. "The permissible extent of the search," Cory J held, "will vary with the gravity of the infraction that is suspected."[245] It will also take into consideration age and gender. Male teachers searching female students "may well be inappropriate and unreasonable."[246] A search at school must be carried out "in a sensitive manner and be minimally intrusive."[247] Finally, school officials are not authorized to exercise the power recognized here where they act as agents of the police.[248] Justice Major, in dissent, agreed on the need for a new power but thought it would not apply in this case since the trial judge had found that the vice principal had acted as an agent for the police.

240 *Ibid*.
241 *Ibid* at para 48.
242 *Ibid* at para 50.
243 *Ibid*.
244 *Ibid*.
245 *Ibid* at para 52.
246 *Ibid* at para 53.
247 *Ibid* at para 54.
248 *Ibid* at para 56.

e) Law Offices

The Supreme Court's decisions in *Lavallee* and *Federation of Law Societies* deal with statutory powers authorizing the search of a law office.[249] The two cases stand apart from the pattern of all other decisions in this chapter. The Court in those cases decides whether a law allows for a reasonable search by applying the balancing test in *Hunter v Southam Inc* that weighs the state interest in search against the individual's interest in privacy.[250] In these two cases, the Court considers reasonableness in light of solicitor-client privilege.

In *Lavallee*, a 6:3 decision, the Court found unreasonable under section 8 the framework for law office searches in the *Criminal Code*, for failing to protect solicitor-client privilege.[251] Justice Arbour, for the majority, held that the interests engaged in this search called for a different approach from other section 8 cases. Solicitor-client privilege "favours not only the privacy interests of a potential accused, but also the interests of a fair, just and efficient law enforcement process."[252] The privilege is therefore "a positive feature of law enforcement, not an impediment to it."[253] And it must "remain as close to absolute as possible if it is to retain relevance."[254] A more appropriate tool in this context is not the balancing in *Hunter* but minimal impairment.[255] A power to search a law office will be reasonable where it does not "interfere with solicitor-client privilege more than is absolutely necessary."[256] Powers in section 488.1 fail to do this in various ways, including by permitting a privileged document to be searched if counsel fails to claim privilege over it; forcing counsel to name a client to initiate the process of having a document sealed; and failing to provide notice of the search to the privilege holder.[257] The majority held the shortcomings to be too extensive to remedy by reading in qualifications.[258] It instead struck down the provision and invited Parliament to re-write it in accordance with a set of "general principles" that serve as the criteria for a reasonable law office search, now typically conducted under a warrant in section 487 (on

---

249 *Lavallee*, above note 22; *Federation of Law Societies*, above note 22.

250 *Hunter*, above note 3.

251 *Criminal Code*, above note 21, s 488.1. At the time of this writing, s 488.1 remains in the *Code*.

252 *Lavallee*, above note 22 at para 36.

253 *Ibid*.

254 *Ibid*.

255 *Ibid*.

256 *Ibid*.

257 *Ibid* at paras 39–45.

258 *Ibid* at para 48.

terms reflecting the principles).[259] Justice LeBel, on behalf of the dissent, believed that lawyers were capable and diligent enough in practice to provide adequate protection of solicitor-client privilege in the course of a search under section 488.1 and only took issue with the requirement to name a client in one of the subsections. The provision at issue could be read to allow a client to be designated without being named or identified, and was therefore—along with the rest of the scheme—not unreasonable.[260]

The Court returned to the subject of law office searches in *Federation of Law Societies of Canada*.[261] The case concerned provisions of the *Proceeds of Crime (Money Laundering) and Terrorist Financing Act* that authorized searches by investigators from the Financial Transactions and Reports Analysis Centre of Canada.[262] The Act permitted an investigator to enter an office (including a law office) without a warrant to examine records required under the Act and make copies of them, or a home office with a warrant.[263] A seven-judge panel of the Court was unanimous in finding the application of these provisions in the context of law office searches to be unreasonable under section 8. Justice Cromwell held the legislation to be criminal rather than regulatory in nature, meriting a higher standard, and that it authorizes "sweeping law office searches which inherently risk breaching solicitor-client privilege."[264] The provisions do not conform with the guidelines set out in *Lavallee*, including a requirement to give the holder of solicitor-client privilege notice that documents had been searched or seized; provision for court oversight over claims of privilege; and a requirement to consider reasonable alternatives to a search.[265] He asserted that a "law office search power is unreasonable unless it provides a high level of protection for material subject to solicitor-client privilege," citing *Lavallee* for this proposition rather than providing further rationale specific to this context.[266] The violation of section 8 could not be justified under section 1, and the Court's remedy was to read down the provisions to "exclude legal counsel and legal firms from the scope of their operation."[267]

259 These principles are canvassed in Chapter 6, Section A(9)(c).
260 *Ibid* at para 80.
261 *Federation of Law Societies*, above note 22.
262 *Proceeds of Crime (Money Laundering) and Terrorist Financing Act*, SC 2000, c 17.
263 *Ibid*, ss 62, 63.
264 *Federation of Law Societies*, above note 22 at paras 34–35.
265 *Ibid* at paras 48, 51–52, and 54.
266 *Ibid* at para 36.
267 *Ibid* at para 63.

3) Interceptions

Police powers for wiretapping private communications are found in Part VI of the *Criminal Code* and predate the *Charter*. In *Duarte*, *R v Araujo*, and *Tse*, the Supreme Court considered whether some of the powers under Part VI are reasonable under section 8.[268] In each case, the Court found the powers to be unreasonable and pointed to further safeguards the law would need to incorporate in order to strike an appropriate balance between privacy and law enforcement interests.

Duarte concerned the *Criminal Code*'s "one-party consent" provisions.[269] The *Code* makes it an offence to record a private conversation to which one is not a party,[270] but sets out as an exception to the offence recording with the consent of one party.[271] The question in *Duarte* was whether police could lawfully wiretap a suspect by having an informant consent to using a wire.[272] The Ontario Court of Appeal, in a decision of Cory JA, as he then was, held that police could do this lawfully because the conversation did not engage section 8.[273] The target of the wiretap did not have a reasonable expectation of privacy in his conversation with the informant, since it entailed the risk that arises in any conversation that the interlocutor might divulge it. In a 6:1 decision, the Supreme Court rejected this risk-based approach.[274] The accused did have a reasonable expectation of privacy against the state, and police use of the one-party consent provisions, in lieu of obtaining a warrant, rendered the search unreasonable.

Writing for the majority in *Duarte*, La Forest J was emphatic about the privacy interest engaged by "surreptitious electronic surveillance of the individual by an agency of the state."[275] As he put it, "one can scarcely imagine a state activity more dangerous to individual privacy."[276] The possibility that someone we speak to might divulge our secrets or even record our words is one thing; but the possibility of being wiretapped presents "a risk of a different order, i.e., not the risk that someone will repeat our words but the much more insidious danger inherent in

268 *Duarte*, above note 41, *R v Araujo*, 2000 SCC 65 [*Araujo*], and *Tse*, above note 68.

269 *Duarte*, above note 41; *Criminal Code*, above note 21.

270 *Criminal Code*, above note 21, s 184(1).

271 *Ibid*, s 184(2)(a). Wiretap powers are discussed in Chapter 6, Section A(2).

272 *Duarte*, above note 41, considering s 178.11(2)(a) of the *Code*, above note 21, which was an earlier version of s 184(2)(a).

273 *R v Sanelli, Duarte and Fasciano*, 61 OR (2d) 385, 22 OAC 307.

274 Justice Lamer, as he then was, in dissent, dismissed the appeal for the reasons given by Cory JA in the court below.

275 *Duarte*, above note 41 at 42.

276 *Ibid* at 43.

allowing the state, in its unfettered discretion, to record and transmit our words."[277] If police had unfettered discretion to do this, we would never be free from the possibility or risk of being recorded by the state. We would become a society in which "privacy no longer had any meaning."[278] Surveillance can play an "indispensable role in the detection of sophisticated criminal enterprises" and does advance a pressing objective.[279] The wiretap provisions of the *Code* strike a "reasonable balance" by "providing that police must always seek prior judicial authorization before using electronic surveillance."[280] These warrants can only be issued by a superior court judge on the stringent standard of probable grounds and the need to be satisfied that "other investigative methods would fail, or have little likelihood of success, and that the granting of the authorization is in the best interest of the administration of justice."[281] These "external and objective" criteria restrain police and hold them to a high measure of accountability.[282] The participant or consent surveillance provisions of the *Code* contain none of these protections. Justice La Forest could see no material difference between state and participant surveillance that would justify police use of the latter; the question of authorization, he asserted "cannot . . . turn on the location of the hidden microphone."[283] Wiretapping on the basis of nothing more than participant consent would not be reasonable under section 8. Police should need a warrant.[284]

In *Arauajo*, the Court considered the need to establish "investigative necessity" in *Code* provisions that allow for a standard or "full blown" interception (i.e., between two or more unknowing parties).[285] Among the various conditions for obtaining the authorization is the requirement that "other investigative procedures have been tried and have failed, other investigative procedures are unlikely to succeed or the urgency of the matter is such that it would be impractical to carry out the investigation of the offence using only other investigative procedures."[286] The question was how to interpret this provision in a manner that would render

---

277 *Ibid* at 43–44.

278 *Ibid* at 44.

279 *Ibid*.

280 *Ibid* at 45.

281 *Ibid*.

282 *Ibid*.

283 *Ibid* at 47.

284 Parliament amended the *Criminal Code*, above note 21, to include the "consent wiretap" provisions in s 184.2, discussed in Chapter 6, Section A(2)(b).

285 *Araujo*, above note 268 considering s 186(1)(b) of the *Criminal Code*, above note 21. We discuss these provisions in Chapter 6, Section A(2)(a).

286 *Ibid*.

the search power reasonable. Justice LeBel, for the Court, held that the "appropriate balance" here between "privacy interests and the realities and difficulties of law enforcement" is not to be found in requiring police to establish surveillance as a "last resort" since this would "turn the process of authorization into a formalistic exercise that would take no account of the difficulties of police investigations targeting sophisticated crime."[287] Unjustified searches or fishing expeditions could be effectively avoided where police are instead required to establish that a wiretap is "necessary" and there is "no other reasonable alternative method of investigation, in the circumstances."[288]

Tse involved new powers added to the *Code* after *Duarte* had been decided, powers authorizing police to conduct a wiretap without a warrant in exigent circumstances.[289] Section 184.1 allows for a warrantless wiretap with one party's consent in order to prevent a risk of bodily harm to that party. Section 184.4 permits this where necessary to prevent imminent and serious harm to persons or property. At issue in this case was section 184.4, but Moldaver and Karakatsanis JJ, writing for the Court, assessed whether this was a reasonable law under section 8 by contrasting it with features of sections 184.1 and 188(1). Under the latter provision, a specially appointed judge may permit a wiretap of up to thirty-six hours where "the urgency of the situation requires interception of private communications before an authorization could, with reasonable diligence, be obtained under section 186." Sections 184.1 and 188(1) imposed important limits on police not found in section 184.4. In the one case, police have to obtain the potential victim's consent and the purpose of the interception is limited to preventing the bodily harm.[290] In the case of section 188(1), in addition to the standard set out in the provision, state agents are subject to two after-the-fact accountability mechanisms: a requirement to provide notice of wiretap evidence the Crown intends to use against a person in evidence and an annual statistical reporting requirement to Parliament on the use of the provision.[291] The justices pointed to a further limit in the case of warrants for a standard interception under sections 185 and 186: the requirement to provide after-the-fact notice to the target of surveillance.[292] The powers in sections 184.1 and 184.4 lacked any after-the-fact accountability mechanisms, but section 184.4 entailed the fewest constraints. It did, however, impose a

287 *Araujo*, above note 268, at paras 22 and 29.

288 *Ibid* at para 29.

289 *Tse*, above note 68; *Duarte*, above note 41.

290 *Criminal Code*, above note 21, s 184.1(1)(c).

291 *Ibid*, ss 189 and 195.

292 *Ibid*, s 196, noted in *Tse*, above note 68 at para 23.

stringent set of standards: reasonable grounds to believe in imminent and serious harm and a belief that a warrant would not be obtainable under Part VI with "reasonable diligence."[293] Moreover, the provision required that the originator or recipient of the communication be the person likely to cause harm or the intended victim.[294]

The Court in *Tse* considered the *Code*'s inclusion of these standards to be important protections of privacy, but they were not enough to render the power reasonable. To do so, Parliament would have to impose at least a notice requirement similar to the one applicable to standard interceptions (under sections 185 and 186), in which after-the-fact notice must be given to the target of a wiretap.[295] A requirement to report to Parliament on the use of section 184.4 would make "good sense" but was not necessary under section 8, nor was a record keeping requirement on the part of police, given that police would often be "focussed on the emergency and it would be impractical to require contemporaneous detailed record keeping in such situations."[296] The power could not be saved under section 1 of the *Charter* for not minimally impairing the right under section 8. It could have done so by requiring notice to affected parties. Parliament has since amended the *Code* to include a requirement to provide written notice to targets of surveillance under section 184.4 within ninety days.[297]

A further decision to consider here is *Wakeling v United States of America*,[298] a case that involved the use made in a cross-border drug trafficking investigation of information obtained through wiretaps authorized under the *Criminal Code*. The appellant had challenged the constitutionality of provisions of the *Code* and the *Privacy Act* for enabling disclosure to a foreign state without adequate protections. Justice Moldaver, along with two other members of the panel of seven judges, held that the governing provision in this case was section 193(2)(e) of the *Code*, which sets out a series of exceptions to the offence of disclosing information obtained through a wiretap, and found that it "implicitly authorizes" cross-border disclosures.[299] The disclosure did not amount to a second search, as counsel had argued. But it engaged section 8 by virtue of forming "part of the context in which courts must assess the reasonableness of the law

293 *Criminal Code*, above note 21, ss 184.4(a), (b).

294 *Ibid*, s 184.4.

295 *Tse*, above note 68 at paras 84 and 86, noting the requirement in s 196(1) of the *Code*, *ibid*.

296 *Tse*, above note 68 at paras 89 and 92.

297 *Criminal Code*, above note 21, s 196.1.

298 2014 SCC 72.

299 *Ibid* at para 32. Justice Moldaver was joined by LeBel and Rothstein JJ.

authorizing the search."[300] Looking at the wiretap regime in its totality, including the requirement for a warrant and after-the-fact notice, Moldaver J found the framework reasonable despite the various disclosures it permits. Three dissenting justices held the disclosure provisions to be unreasonable for failing to include adequate safeguards and protections.[301] Chief Justice McLachlin declined to consider the constitutionality of the provision on the view that the disclosure did not engage section 8. Section 193(2)(e), she held, does not authorize disclosure; it excludes certain disclosures from being an offence.

4) Regulatory Searches

In a series of decisions beginning with *Thomson Newspapers* and *McKinlay*, the Supreme Court has grappled with whether search powers under regulatory statutes are reasonable under section 8.[302] A central issue in each of these cases is whether the power at issue, or the larger legislative scheme of which it forms a part, is distinctly regulatory rather than criminal in nature, falls somewhere in between, or is closer to the latter. The more clearly regulatory the thrust of a statute or power, the heavier the state interest is in search or seizure and the lower the privacy interest. The Court has consistently held that a regulatory search power involving lower standards or fewer safeguards is reasonable under section 8.

Thomson Newspapers involved a challenge to a provision of the *Combines Investigation Act* allowing investigators of competition law offences to demand the disclosure of documents without a warrant or specific grounds, aside from relevance to an investigation under the Act.[303] The 3:2 judgment contains four opinions on section 8, with a majority of the Court holding that the power at issue entails a seizure but is reasonable. Justice La Forest recognized that the powers considered in *Hunter v Southam Inc* may have pertained to criminal offences but held that other powers in the *Combines Investigation Act*, including the one at issue, were regulatory in nature, despite carrying jail sentences.[304] The Act was concerned not with inherently or morally wrongful conduct, such as theft or violence, but "economy and business" and the "preservation of the competitive conditions which are crucial to the operation of a free

300 *Ibid* at para 36.

301 Justices Abella, Cromwell, and Karakatsanis.

302 *Thomson Newspapers*, above note 8 and *McKinlay*, above note 13.

303 *Thomson Newspapers*, above note 8, considering the *Combines Investigation Act*, RSC 1970, c C-23, s 17.

304 *Thomson Newspapers*, above note 8 at 519–20, noting *Hunter* above note 3.

market economy."[305] This gave rise to a broader reflection about search in the regulatory context that would be cited in a number of later cases:

> In a modern industrial society, it is generally accepted that many activities in which individuals can engage must nevertheless to a greater or lesser extent be regulated by the state to ensure that the individual's pursuit of his or her self-interest is compatible with the community's interest in the realization of collective goals and aspirations. In many cases, this regulation must necessarily involve the inspection of private premises or documents by agents of the state.[306]

We come to expect this scrutiny. Business documents still retain a measure of privacy but tend not to contain detail about our "lifestyle, intimate relations or political or religious opinions."[307] Document demand powers on a standard lower than those set out in *Hunter* are reasonable in the competition law context given both the lower privacy interest and the fact that offences under the Act are often difficult to detect, "typically tak[ing] the form of subtle alterations in otherwise perfectly legal business practices."[308] To require investigators to have a belief or even a suspicion of wrongdoing before making inquiries would "immunize perpetrators of anti-competitive offences from discovery and prosecution."[309] Investigators are not completely unfettered. A demand under section 17 must pertain to "matters in respect of which the Director or Commission can conduct inquiries," or relevant to the regulatory scope of the Act.[310]

Justice L'Heureux-Dubé's opinion largely overlapped with that of La Forest J. She also held the power to demand documents constitutes a seizure; the *Combines Investigation Act* is regulatory in nature; the document demand power is necessary to advance the important objective of protecting citizens in the marketplace and it engages a low privacy interest.[311] A warrant requirement would set too high a standard.[312] The provision contains an adequate safeguard in the fact that a person may hold off on making a disclosure before seeking judicial review of a disclosure order in Federal Court, on the standard of relevance to the "regulatory aims of the Act."[313] Justice Sopinka disagreed that an order for

305 *Thomson Newspapers*, above note 8 at 510.
306 *Ibid* at 506–7.
307 *Ibid* at 517.
308 *Ibid* at 520.
309 *Ibid.*
310 *Ibid* at 535.
311 *Ibid* at 589–97.
312 *Ibid* at 596.
313 *Ibid* at 595.

disclosure under the provision constitutes a seizure, given the possibility of challenging the validity of a demand or the extent of the documents one is required to disclose.[314] Justice Lamer, as he then was, agreed with Wilson J who authored an opinion that the provision did entail a seizure because it contemplates taking something against a person's will and that it was not reasonable under section 8.[315] In light of the penalties available under the *Combines Investigation Act* and the "moral overtones" of the offences it seeks to target, the investigatory powers in the Act were "criminal or quasi-criminal in nature."[316] In order for section 17 to be reasonable, the "criteria set forth in *Hunter* must be substantially if not completely met."[317]

In a companion decision to *Thomson Newspapers*, the Court in *McKinlay* considered the reasonableness of document demand powers in a provision of the *Income Tax Act*.[318] Reading the demand provisions together with their accompanying enforcement provisions, four members of the Court found them reasonable under section 8. Justice Sopinka, the fifth member of the panel, held that the demand power here did not involve a seizure, for the reasons set out in *Thomson Newspapers*,[319] and therefore did not engage section 8. Justices Wilson and Lamer, as he then was, held that when read together, the demand and enforcement provisions are regulatory rather than criminal in nature, and that the random monitoring they allow for was essential to maintaining the integrity of the tax system.[320] The privacy in the documents is low and disclosures were protected by a prohibition on disclosing information to other persons or agencies.[321] The *Hunter* standards would be inappropriate here. Justices La Forest and L'Heureux-Dubé concurred with Wilson J's opinion in this case and pointed to their opinions in *Thomson Newspapers* for further rationale in finding the power at issue reasonable.[322]

---

314 *Ibid* at 610–15.

315 *Ibid* at 493.

316 *Ibid* at 494, pointing back to a discussion at 453, citing Dickson J, as he then was, in *Attorney General of Canada v Canadian National Transportation Ltd*, [1983] 2 SCR 206 at 250.

317 *Thomson Newspapers*, above note 8 at 498. The "*Hunter* criteria" include a requirement to obtain a warrant, from a neutral and impartial decision maker, on the standard of reasonable (probable) grounds to believe an offence has been committed and evidence is likely to be found in the place or thing searched or seized. *Hunter* is canvassed in detail in Chapter 2, Section B(1).

318 *McKinlay*, above note 13; considering the *Income Tax Act*, RSC 1952, c 148, ss 231(3) and 238(2).

319 *McKinlay*, above note 13 at 651.

320 *Ibid* at 641 and 648–49.

321 *Ibid* at 650.

322 *Ibid* at 650–51.

The Court considered a further document demand power in *British Columbia Securities Commission v Branch*.[323] The power was found in a provision of the British Columbia *Securities Act* compelling a person to attend for examination and "produce records and things" relating to an investigation under the Act.[324] The Court was unanimous in finding the power reasonable under section 8, with Sopinka and Iacobucci JJ authoring a majority opinion and L'Heureux-Dubé J concurring on this issue separately. Justices Sopinka and Iacobucci characterized the Act as regulatory in nature, with the aim of protecting investors, "capital market efficiency," and "public confidence in the system."[325] The industry requires careful and close regulation, given the need to ensure that those trading in securities or offering advice "be of honest and of good repute," and the need to discourage "detrimental forms of commercial behaviour."[326] Being well aware of this, people involved in securities do not have a high privacy expectation in their business documents.[327] The power to demand documents at issue here was minimally invasive in not involving an intrusion into a private home or space, and it was limited in scope to documents relating to trading and securities.[328] The pressing state interest here, coupled with the low privacy expectation and relatively non-intrusive nature of the seizure rendered the power reasonable under section 8.[329]

In *Comité paritaire de l'industrie de la chemise v Potash*, the Court considered powers under a Quebec labour and employment statute to enter a workplace and examine documents relating to payroll.[330] Under Quebec's *Act respecting Collective Agreement Decrees* (*ACAD*), the government could issue a decree imposing a standard or a "collective agreement" on all employers within an industrial sector.[331] Under section 22(e) of the Act, an inspector "may, as of right and at any reasonable time, examine the registration system [and] . . . the pay-list of any employer, [and] take copies or extracts therefrom" for the purpose of verifying wages, hours worked, and other such details. An employer had refused to allow an

323 *British Columbia Securities*, above note 13.

324 *Securities Act*, SBC 1985, c 83, s 128(1).

325 *British Columbia Securities*, above note 13 at para 54. Justices Sopinka and Iacobucci do not address whether and how the document compulsion power here constitutes a seizure under s 8; their analysis of the s 8 issue simply proceeds on the assumption that it does.

326 *Ibid* at paras 57 and 59.

327 *Ibid* at para 58.

328 *Ibid* at paras 60 and 62.

329 *Ibid* at para 64.

330 *Comité paritaire de l'industrie de la chemise v Potash*, [1994] 2 SCR 406 [*Comité*].

331 RSQ, c D-2, s 2.

inspector to enter without a warrant and was fined for obstructing the inspection. The Quebec Court of Appeal held the provision to violate section 8 of the *Charter* for not at least requiring probable grounds to believe the employer is covered by a decree issued under the Act.[332] The Supreme Court found the power reasonable under section 8, issuing two concurring opinions, by six and five judges respectively (McLachlin J, as she then was, and Sopinka J signed both) and no dissent. The opinions largely overlap and both hold that section 22(e) was reasonable without requiring a warrant or grounds to believe an employer is covered by a decree under the Act.

Both La Forest and L'Heureux-Dubé JJ's opinions in *Comité* held that section 8 applied here because the power to enter a place of employment constitutes a search, the power to copy documents amounts to a seizure, and both engage a measure of privacy.[333] The purpose of *ACAD*, La Forest J held, is to "ensure decent working conditions in certain sectors of industry (textiles, clothing, shoes, furniture, and so on) where employees are among the most vulnerable."[334] Compliance with decrees "depends first and foremost on employer honesty."[335] This in turn depends on "[i]nspection—or the threat of it—especially if it is done without notice."[336] And since the point of conducting inspection is to find out if there are grounds to believe an offence has been committed, it should not be required as a condition.[337] Warrantless inspections on no grounds thus have a pressing purpose, while the privacy interest in both the documents and the space where they are found—in La Forest J's view, even if it happens to be in a residence—is low.[338] A key factor for La Forest J in finding a lower degree of privacy or intrusiveness here was the fact that employers are aware that their affairs are regulated, while L'Heureux-Dubé J emphasized the limited scope and purposes of a search under the provision: it could be done only during "reasonable times" and the inspector could search only for certain documents listed.[339] The *Hunter* standards are inappropriate here in light of this balance of interests and also, for La Forest J, due to the consequences flowing from a search:

---

332 *Potash c Comité paritaire d' l'industrie de la chemise*, [1992] RJQ 1743 (CA).

333 *Comité*, above note 330; La Forest and L'Heureux-Dubé JJ disagreed on whether the power to copy amounted to a seizure, with the former finding, at 416, that it was a seizure since it was analogous to a requirement to produce documents and the latter finding, at 437–38, that it was not analogous since nothing is "taken."

334 *Ibid* at 419.

335 *Ibid*.

336 *Ibid*.

337 *Ibid* at 452.

338 *Ibid* at 420–21, 424, and 442–43.

339 *Ibid* at 420–21 and 449–50.

not a stigma or a penal sentence but a "very modest" fine for a limited range of regulatory offences.[340] Both opinions also held that it would also be impractical to require inspectors to have reasonable grounds to believe an employer was subject to a decree since the *ACAD* applied to all employers in Quebec and in some cases an inspection would need to be carried out to see whether work being done by employees triggered the application of a decree.[341]

In *Goodwin*, the Court assessed the reasonableness of a power under a British Columbia impaired driving law.[342] The power at issue involved police use of an ASD to take a breath sample at roadside. Police have the power to demand the ASD sample under the *Criminal Code*'s impaired driving provisions.[343] A person who blows a fail on an ASD may be asked to provide a further breath sample at a police station using a Breathalyzer instrument, and this may or may not lead to charges under the *Code*. The province added to its *Motor Vehicle Act* the Automatic Roadside Prohibition (ARP) scheme as a means of imposing a set of consequences for refusing to blow, or blowing a warn or a fail at roadside — regardless of what happens beyond that point. The consequences include having a car immediately impounded and three-day, thirty-day, or ninety-day prohibitions, depending on a person's driving record. Was the power to demand an ASD sample at roadside, on reasonable suspicion that a driver has alcohol in their body, a reasonable law, when used in the ARP scheme?

In a 6:1 decision, a majority of the Court held that the use of the ASD demand power here constituted an unreasonable law under section 8 and the violation could not be saved under section 1 of the *Charter*. Justice Karakatsanis, for the majority, recognized at the outset the "compelling purpose of preventing death and serious injuries on public highways" and the scheme's effect in reducing drunk driving fatalities in British Columbia by 35 percent from its introduction in 2010 to 2013.[344] She framed the ARP scheme itself as regulatory in nature, due to its location within the *Motor Vehicle Act* and its regulatory purpose of highway safety.[345] Yet she agreed that the use of the ASD power within the ARP scheme was a power closer in nature to criminal law for two reasons. A

340 *Ibid* at 421–22 and 444–47.

341 *Ibid* at 423–24 and 455.

342 *Goodwin*, above note 10.

343 Section 320.27 of the *Criminal Code*, above note 21, allows a peace officer to make an ASD demand "on reasonable grounds to suspect that a person has alcohol or a drug in their body and that the person has, within the preceding three hours, operated a conveyance."

344 *Goodwin*, above note 10 at paras 58–59.

345 *Ibid* at para 63.

police officer administered the ASD search under *Criminal Code* authorization, and the results of an ASD sample could be "severe."[346] By contrast, the ASD result in the *Criminal Code*'s scheme only serves as a first step in an investigative process and the result alone cannot establish the offence of impaired driving.[347] Turning to assess the mechanism of the seizure, Karakatsanis J found the demand power not as intrusive as other powers to seize bodily samples, such as blood or DNA.[348] However, the evidence suggested that the results of an ASD sample are not highly reliable, given the tool's inability to accurately assess levels of mouth alcohol.[349] Added to this concern was the lack of "meaningful safeguards" on the use of the ASD as a basis for imposing serious consequences.[350] The scheme allowed a driver to ask for a second sample, but the officer was not obliged to advise of this right. The Act provided that the second result would apply whether or not it was higher or lower than the first result.[351] Finally, there was a lack of judicial oversight. Drivers could seek review of a suspension based on a sample, but the superintendent of motor vehicles could only consider whether the applicant was the driver and whether the ASD had registered a fail or warn, or the applicant refused to provide a sample. There was no means to challenge the accuracy of the sample, i.e., no way to cast doubt on the fail or warn result on the basis of having had a lower blood alcohol level than was required in either case.[352] The lack of accuracy and limited scope for review rendered the power unreasonable under section 8.

Turning to section 1, Karakatsanis J recognized the scheme had a pressing and substantial objective in seeking to "remove impaired drivers from the highway."[353] Automatic prohibitions based on a roadside ASD test were rationally connected to the goal of highway safety.[354] But the scheme's measures were disproportionate to its aims. It failed to minimally impair the right under section 8 by providing a wider ambit for review.[355] Amendments to the scheme in 2012 had demonstrated this possibility as a reasonable alternative means of achieving the scheme's objectives by requiring the superintendent to be satisfied the driver was advised of a right to a second test; the second test was performed using a

346 *Ibid* at para 61.
347 *Ibid* at para 62.
348 *Ibid* at para 65.
349 *Ibid* at para 66.
350 *Ibid* at para 68.
351 *Ibid*.
352 *Ibid* at para 73.
353 *Ibid* at para 80.
354 *Ibid* at para 81.
355 *Ibid* at paras 82–83.

different ASD; the prohibition was based on the lower of the two results; and that the result itself was reliable.[356]

Chief Justice McLachlin, in dissent, found the scheme reasonable under a new test she proposed for assessing the reasonableness of a law under section 8. She invited the Court to adopt a different, more precise test for reasonableness than the balancing of state and individual interests the Court had used since *Hunter*. She was concerned that the balancing test considering only individual and state interests is too narrow. A compelling enough state purpose may detract from considering "restraint and procedures that permit judicial review."[357] Conversely, in much of the Court's analysis of the privacy interest in the reasonable law cases, privacy has been "conceived in terms of how 'secret' or closeted the thing searched for or seized is."[358] As a consequence, searches or seizures of things not secret tend to be more easily justified. Instead, the Court should understand privacy not in terms of secrecy but in terms of "what falls within the private sphere of the individual within which the individual reasonably expects to be free from state intrusion absent a higher state purpose and legal safeguards."[359] Rather than balancing state interests and individual privacy, the Court should decide whether a power is reasonable under section 8 by "examin[ing] three requirements . . . : (1) a state objective capable of overriding individual private interests, (2) restraint of the incursion on the private interest to what is reasonably necessary to achieve the object, and (3) the availability of judicial supervision."[360] In this case, all three requirements were met. The state aim of preventing death or serious harm justified the intrusion into "the private sphere of the individual's bodily substances."[361] The seizure did not go beyond what is reasonably necessary to achieve the state's goal: i.e., by requiring a sample at the police station or a blood sample.[362] And third, the scheme provided adequate judicial supervision: a driver could apply to the superintendent for review and seek judicial review of that decision. The ambit of review was broad enough, given the many ways to address a lack of accuracy, including through a request for a second sample and presenting evidence in support of one's challenge.[363]

356 *Ibid* at para 84.
357 *Ibid* at para 102.
358 *Ibid* at para 103.
359 *Ibid*.
360 *Ibid* at para 92.
361 *Ibid* at para 105.
362 *Ibid* at para 106.
363 *Ibid* at para 107.

The Court has not chosen to adopt the chief justice's proposal for reform of the "reasonable law" analysis. Her concerns about the test have merit: the privacy or state interest in a case can be so strong as to easily sway judgment about where the balance is best struck. Yet her proposed test raises concerns of its own. It skews the analysis in the state's favour by reducing privacy to one of three considerations. It also suggests that the right balance can be struck where there is a state interest "capable of overriding individual private interests" and adequate judicial supervision—when these factors depend on having *already* worked out the balance at issue. The merit of Dickson J's formulation in *Hunter* and its persistence for close to four decades is its clarity and simplicity. In the final analysis, whether a search power is reasonable turns on a basic and fundamental question about whether, in the circumstances, the state's interest should prevail over the individual's interest in being let alone by government. By adopting the factors in *Del Zotto*, the majority opinion in *Goodwin* offers a clearer set of criteria for thinking through this balancing. It is not clear that a more complex, three-part test would be preferable.

CHAPTER 8

WHEN IS A SEARCH REASONABLY CONDUCTED?

A. INTRODUCTION

Our focus in this chapter is the third part of the Supreme Court's test in *R v Collins* for when a search or seizure under section 8 of the *Charter* will be reasonable. Under *Collins*, a search or seizure will be reasonable and comply with section 8: "if it is authorized by law, if the law itself is reasonable and if the manner in which the search was carried out is reasonable."[1] What, then, constitutes a search or a seizure conducted in a reasonable manner?

We explore the various answers to this question courts have provided in three main areas: searches and seizures involving the person and their effects, territory or buildings, and information. Before embarking on this survey, however, we briefly address the origin and nature of this criterion of legality.

When Lamer J, as he then was, invoked the idea of the "manner" in which a search is conducted in his formulation of a general test for section 8 in 1987, he was not the first judge to do so. The idea appeared three years earlier in *Hunter v Southam Inc*, when Dickson J, as he then was, remarked at the outset of the decision that it "does not concern the reasonableness or otherwise of the manner in which the appellants

---

1 *R v Collins*, [1987] 1 SCR 265 at 278 [*Collins*], holding also that once the accused establishes that s 8 is engaged, the burden shifts to the Crown to establish the search was reasonable (i.e., all three grounds) on a balance of probabilities.

carried out their statutory authority"—suggesting that he was aware of it as a possible basis for challenging a search.[2] The same year, judges in at least a few cases involving challenges to searches under the *Narcotic Control Act* had also invoked it. Justice Martin of the Ontario Court of Appeal in *R v Rao* may have been the first to do so when he held that

> [a] challenge to the reasonableness of a particular search may be made under the *Charter* on two bases. Firstly, the reasonableness of the legislation authorizing the search is subject to challenge; secondly, a search under a constitutionally valid statutory authority may be carried out in an unreasonable manner, for example, by the use of excessive force.[3]

The British Columbia Court of Appeal and Federal Court cited *Rao* in formulating a framework for assessing section 8 that included "manner of search" as a consideration, but did not make findings in relation to this ground.[4] *Collins* may be the first notable appellate decision to make substantive use of conduct as a ground, in ways to be explored further below. By then, the idea of a "reasonable search" comprising reasonable conduct as well as authority had gained a measure of recognition in the caselaw—as a fundamental rather than a marginal consideration.

The Supreme Court clarified in a general sense what is meant by "the manner in which a search is conducted" in *R v Debot*.[5] In that case, the appellant was pulled over on a tip that he was in possession of a narcotic, on his way to meet a buyer. An officer ordered him to assume a "spread eagle" position and empty his pockets and found him in possession of speed. The majority rejected the proposition that the right to counsel arose from the fact of being searched, and that a denial of counsel prior to the search rendered the "manner" in which the search was carried out unreasonable. Justice Lamer, as he then was, held that "[t]he 'manner' in which the search is conducted relates to the physical way in which it is carried out and should not, in my view be inclusive of restrictions of other rights that already receive the benefit of protection from the *Charter*."[6] The majority was staking a position against a view held by Wilson J in this case and in earlier decisions that the denial of counsel prior to search could amount to a search unreasonably conducted.[7] As

2 *Hunter v Southam Inc*, [1984] 2 SCR 145 at 154.

3 *R v Rao*, 46 OR (2d) 80 (CA). Justice Martin's dicta here may also have been a point of origin for the second prong of the *Collins* test.

4 *R v Hamill*, [1984] 6 WWR 530 (BCCA); *Danielson v Sterba*, [1985] 1 FC 821 (FC); *Minister of National Revenue et al v Kruger et al*, [1984] FC 535 (FCA).

5 [1989] 2 SCR 1140 [*Debot*].

6 *Ibid* at 1148.

7 *R v Simmons*, [1988] 2 SCR 495; *R v Strachan*, [1988] 2 SCR 980; and *R v Jacoy*, [1988] 2 SCR 548.

Lamer J would go on to note, a search found to be done in a reasonable manner might still result in the exclusion of evidence for other *Charter* breaches, but the analysis under section 24(2) of the *Charter* would involve different considerations as a result.[8]

As a final point of general application, the Supreme Court has held that the purpose of requiring that a search be conducted in a reasonable manner is that "[t]his ensures that the search is no more intrusive than is reasonably necessary to achieve its objectives."[9] Justice Cromwell's formulation of this rationale can also be read as a general principle or test for determining whether and when a search has been conducted in an unreasonable manner. The question to be asked in every context is whether police or other state agents have done more than was reasonably necessary to achieve their objective of investigating an offence or addressing a safety concern. This principle informs all the cases we canvass in this chapter, inviting us to read them as applications of this general principle or test to specific kinds of search.

B. REASONABLE SEARCH OF THE PERSON

1) On Arrest or Detention

Two common scenarios in which police search a person in ways that are held to be unreasonable involve search incident to arrest or detention. The Court's pronouncements on the reasonable conduct of these searches delineate boundaries and set out guidelines meant to assist police in avoiding and trial courts in judging unreasonable conduct.

The Supreme Court in *Cloutier v Langlois* affirmed a police power at common law to conduct a brief frisk or pat down search incident to a lawful arrest.[10] Although the search in that case was not challenged as a section 8 breach, and predates *Collins*, L'Heureux-Dubé J sought to craft the scope of this power "in a manner consistent with the fundamental values enshrined in the Constitution."[11] She set out a set of qualifications on the use of the power, including one stipulating that "[t]he search must not be conducted in an abusive fashion and in particular, the use of physical or psychological constraint should be proportionate to the

8 *Debot*, above note 5 at 1148–49.

9 *R v Vu*, 2013 SCC 60 at para 22 [*Vu*].

10 *Cloutier v Langlois*, [1990] 1 SCR 158 [*Cloutier*]. The scope of this power is discussed in Chapter 6, Section D(4)(a).

11 *Ibid* at 184, citing *RWDSU v Dolphin Delivery Ltd*, [1986] 2 SCR 573 at 603.

objectives sought and the other circumstances of the situation."[12] Given the appellant's "highly agitated and verbally abusive conduct" in the course of his encounter with police, the decision to conduct the brief pat down was reasonable.[13] And since it was quick and cursory, with police ordering Cloutier to place his hands on the hood of his car while being patted down, and did not involve "either excessive force or constraint," it was reasonably conducted.[14]

Collins involves a case of excessive force. The officer acted on a tip that the accused was a heroin dealer. Finding her seated in a pub, he tackled her to the floor and (in his words) "grabbed her by the throat" to prevent her from swallowing the evidence.[15] The officer conceded at trial that the force he used was "considerable."[16] The Supreme Court was concerned with both the authority for the search and the way it was conducted. The officer lacked sufficient grounds for an arrest and had no other authority to conduct the search. Justice Lamer, as he then was, also held that the search was "carried out with unnecessary violence"[17]—a distinct ground on which it violated section 8. However, at the end of the decision, Lamer J noted that had the officer had more certainty that the accused was a "handler of drugs," "taking a flying tackle" at her *may* not have been unreasonable.[18] We query whether, today, this amount of violence would be considered "proportionate to the objectives sought" as L'Heureux-Dubé had held in *Cloutier*.

The Court would go on to consider the scope of search on arrest in various cases that trace the limits of this power, expanding it well beyond the frisk search initially authorized in *Cloutier*.[19] *R v Stillman* marked an important limit by requiring a warrant for the seizure of bodily samples,[20] but in *R v Golden*, *R v Saeed*, and *R v Fearon* the Court declined to impose a warrant requirement for strip searches, penile swabs, and device searches incident to arrest—all forms of search that engage

---

12 *Cloutier*, above note 10 at 186.

13 *Ibid* at 187.

14 *Ibid* at 188.

15 *Collins*, above note 1 at 270–71.

16 *Ibid* at 271.

17 *Ibid* at 279.

18 *Ibid* at 288.

19 The cases are canvassed in Chapter 6, Section D(4)(a), including *R v Caslake*, [1998] 1 SCR 51, permitting the search of a car incident to arrest, hours or possibly days after the arrest has occurred, and *R v Stairs*, 2022 SCC 11 [*Stairs*], permitting a search of a person's immediate surroundings when arrested in a dwelling house.

20 *R v Stillman*, [1997] 1 SCR 607.

heightened privacy interests.[21] In each of these cases, the Court sought to address the privacy concerns at issue by imposing a requirement to satisfy further grounds or conditions for the kind of search at issue, and by setting out guidelines for their reasonable conduct.

Before turning to those cases, we note an important extension to search incident to arrest in the Supreme Court's most recent consideration of this power. In *R v Stairs*,[22] the Court recognized the power to conduct a search of the area surrounding a person when arrested within a dwelling house, including an area outside the person's physical control. At the end of their discussion of the scope of this authority for search, Moldaver and Jamal JJ, for the majority, remarked that "as a general rule, the police cannot use the search incident to arrest power to justify searching every nook and cranny of the house."[23] A search involving this power should be "no more intrusive than is necessary." They also added that "it would be good practice for the police to take detailed notes after searching a home incident to arrest."[24] These should include "places searched, the extent of the search, the time of the search, its purpose, and its duration." A court might, therefore, consider the adequacy of police notes and the degree of intrusiveness when assessing whether the search was reasonably conducted.

Finally, a brief note about the conduct of a search on an investigative detention. The Supreme Court in *R v Mann* recognized a power to conduct a brief safety search in this context, and for the majority, the brief "frisk search" contemplated in *Cloutier* was the model for its reasonable scope.[25] Justice Iacobucci cited L'Heureux-Dubé J's description of a frisk search in *Cloutier* as a "relatively non-intrusive procedure," "the duration of which is 'only a few seconds'."[26] Police are authorized to conduct a brief, non-intrusive safety search in *Mann*, but these limits also speak to the reasonable conduct of such a search.[27] When the officer in *Mann* reached into the accused's pockets to retrieve a soft object, Iacobucci J held that the officer had exceeded his lawful authority for

21 *R v Golden*, 2001 SCC 83 [*Golden*]; *R v Saeed*, 2016 SCC 24 [*Saeed*]; *R v Fearon*, 2014 SCC 77 [*Fearon*].

22 *Stairs*, above note 19.

23 *Ibid* at para 80.

24 *Ibid* at para 81.

25 *R v Mann*, 2004 SCC 52 [*Mann*].

26 *Ibid* at para 43, citing *Cloutier*, above note 10 at 185. Justice Deschamps, writing in a dissent joined by Bastarache J, would have permitted search on investigative detention for objectives other than safety, but agreed that it should be less intrusive than search on arrest, at paras 65–69.

27 See, e.g., *R v Schrenk*, 2010 MBCA 38, finding reasonable an investigative detention of eighteen minutes of a driver at roadside involving a dog search.

this form of search *and* had not carried it out in a reasonable manner.[28] Later cases that expand the scope of search on an investigative detention well beyond a pat-down have held searches to be reasonably conducted where they involved a vehicle, bag, or other item.[29]

a) Strip Searches and Penile Swabs

In *Golden*, the Supreme Court held that police have authority to conduct a strip search incident to arrest but require reasonable grounds in addition to those for the arrest. The Court also outlined the reasonable conduct of a strip search. The facts in this case offered a litany of things not to do.

Police were observing a Subway shop in downtown Toronto where they believed drug deals were taking place. After witnessing what appeared to be two transactions, they moved in to arrest Golden and two others. After patting down Golden, police carried out "a visual inspection" of his underwear and buttocks.[30] An officer brought Golden to a stairwell at the back of the shop where he undid Golden's pants and conducted a further examination of what was inside his underwear. The officer saw a plastic wrap, but before he could retrieve it, Golden hip-checked him. In response, the officer "pushed [Golden] into the stairwell, face-first."[31] Police brought Golden back into the shop to conduct a more extensive strip search. The two other suspects, a store employee, and five officers were present. Officers forced Golden to bend over a table and pulled his pants and underwear down, with his "genitalia . . . completely exposed."[32] To remove a package caught between Golden's buttocks, officers used a pair of rubber gloves which had been used to clean the shop's toilets.[33] Golden was arrested and brought to a police station roughly two minutes away, where he was strip searched again.

The judicial history of this case is notable. The trial judge held the arrest and the decision to strip search on scene to be reasonable and necessary, and conducted in a reasonable manner (had Golden not resisted, the ordeal would have been "shorter and less intrusive").[34] The Court of Appeal for Ontario was unanimous in upholding these findings.[35] All nine judges of the Supreme Court held the second search

28 *Mann*, above note 25 at para 49.

29 See, e.g., *R v Plummer*, 2011 ONCA 350 involving the search of a bag within a passenger area of a vehicle near the detainee.

30 *Golden*, above note 21, at para 30.

31 *Ibid.*

32 *Ibid* at para 32.

33 *Ibid* at para 33.

34 The decision of McNeely J is summarized *ibid* at para 41.

35 Summarized *ibid* at para 42.

(Golden bent over the table) to be unreasonably conducted. A majority of five judges went further in holding both searches at the scene unreasonable. While the dissenting four held that no further grounds should be necessary for a strip search in addition to those for the arrest itself, the majority held that a strip search requires further reasonable grounds to believe it necessary—and grounds additional to those to believe it necessary to conduct in the field.[36] For the majority, there were grounds to carry out a strip search, but not *at the shop*, with the station only two minutes away.[37]

To prevent the conduct of unreasonable strip searches in the future, the Court imposed a higher threshold but also a detailed set of guidelines for police in performing these searches.[38] A strip search should be authorized by a supervising officer and be done at the station unless there are exigent circumstances. The latter requires a "demonstrated necessity and urgency to search for weapons or objects that could be used to threaten the safety of the accused, the arresting officers or other individuals."[39] A strip search should be done by officers of the same gender as the person searched and involve no more officers than is reasonably necessary. It should involve minimal force necessary and be done in a private area. The search should be brief and avoid a person being "completely undressed at any one time." It should involve a visual inspection rather than physical contact with the person's genital and anal areas. Where police find an item, the person searched should be given a chance to remove it or have it removed by "a trained medical professional." Finally, police should keep a record of their reasons for conducting the search and the manner in which they did so.

The majority also commented on the significance of Golden's resistance during the search. They rejected the proposition that "an arrested person's non-cooperation and resistance necessarily entitles police to engage in behaviour that disregards or compromises his or

---

36 *Ibid* at para 99: "the police must establish reasonable and probable grounds justifying the strip search in addition to reasonable and probable grounds justifying the arrest"; and para 102:

> Strip searches should generally only be conducted at the police station except where there are exigent circumstances requiring that the detainee be searched prior to being transported to the police station. Such exigent circumstances will only be established where the police have reasonable and probable grounds to believe that it is necessary to conduct the search in the field rather than at the police station.

37 *Ibid* at paras 108 and 112.

38 The criteria summarized in what follows are set out *ibid* at para 101.

39 *Ibid* at para 102.

her physical and psychological integrity and safety."[40] As Iacobucci and Arbour JJ noted, "there is no requirement that anyone cooperate with the violation of his or her *Charter* rights." Police are not relieved of the requirement to follow the guidelines set out in this case when detainees resist. Applying the principle invoked in *Cloutier*, Iacobucci and Arbour JJ added that "[a]ny application of force or violence must be both necessary and proportional in the specific circumstances."

In this case, police violated virtually all of the guidelines. They confronted no exigent circumstances to justify a search in the field (the station was close by and Golden was closely watched). They did not conduct it in private and too many officers were involved. They used excessive force and unsanitary methods. They did not give Golden a chance to remove the item himself.[41] Both searches in the shop violated section 8 because they were not authorized by law (police had grounds to conduct a strip search but not at the shop) *and* not carried out in a reasonable manner.

As we noted in Chapter 6, statistics on the high frequency with which strip searches have continued to be conducted in the wake of *Golden*—and the disproportionate impact they have had on racialized detainees—cast doubt on whether additional grounds police require or guidelines are effective in avoiding unnecessary or unreasonably conducted strip searches.[42] We suggested there that in light of the evidence of *Golden*'s failure to curb police abuse of this tool, it may be time to revisit the issue and impose a warrant requirement for a strip search. If the Supreme Court were to impose a warrant requirement, this would not render the guidelines redundant. They might come to play a more central role in the conduct of police strip searches across Canada if coupled with a warrant requirement and a common practice of being included as terms of a strip search warrant.

Appellate courts have applied the standards and guidelines in *Golden* to assess the conduct of strip searches in various contexts. In *R v Poirier*,[43] police failed to conduct a strip search of the accused following arrest in private and inadvertently videotaped it. Officers then handcuffed the accused to the bars of a dry cell in which he was held for the first half of the forty-three hours it took to be brought to a justice. The court found the search unreasonable for violating the accused's privacy and involving

40 *Ibid* at para 116.

41 *Ibid* at paras 105–15.

42 See the discussion of *Golden* in Chapter 7, Section C(1)(a) and Kent Roach's comments on it in *Canadian Policing: Why and How It Must Change* (Toronto: Delve Books, 2022) at 57–58.

43 2016 ONCA 582.

a disproportionate degree of physical constraint. In *R v Muller*,[44] the court held a strip search to be unreasonably conducted where police violated several *Golden* guidelines. Officers did not obtain authorization from a supervisor. They left open a door of the room where the search took place. They made the accused remove every item of clothing, leaving him naked as he faced the open door and exposed to persons of either gender. The officers did not give him a chance to remove a contraband item himself. And they videotaped the search.

In *R v Pilon*,[45] the court assessed two strip searches of an accused in the field, one involving pulling on his waistband to view what may be in his shorts, and upon noticing an elastic band tied around the accused's penis, a second search in a bathroom to remove contraband. For the first search, police lacked reasonable grounds relating to either safety or preserving evidence, and they were not justified in conducting a further search in the field on the basis of exigent circumstances. In *R v B(B)*,[46] the court found a strip search in the field (in the accused's vehicle) unreasonable in light of the officer's rationale for conducting it. He wanted to spare the person a trip to the station in case of a negative search.[47]

In other cases, courts have found strip searches to be reasonable for substantially conforming to *Golden*. For example, in *R v Johal*,[48] the court affirmed as reasonable a strip search in which officers had not taken notes. In *R v Parchment*,[49] the court affirmed a finding of exigent circumstances to conduct a strip search in the field (on arresting the accused in his home) on the basis of feeling a hard object in the accused's pants suspected to be a weapon. In *R v Black*,[50] the court affirmed that a strip search of a male accused conducted at the station involving a female officer, with the accused completely naked, was justified on the basis of exigent circumstances. The accused had a history of violence, attempted to hide something in his pants, and became violent with officers when they tried to search him for the item. The female officer's continued involvement, after the accused was handcuffed and shackled, did not render the search unreasonable given his continued resistance.

---

44 2014 ONCA 780.

45 2018 ONCA 959.

46 2002 BCCA 388.

47 *Ibid* at para 30, Prowse JA writing: "I think it is fair to say that the majority of citizens would rather be spared the favour."

48 2015 BCCA 246.

49 2015 BCCA 417.

50 2022 ONCA 628 [*Black*].

Justice Koehnen of the Ontario Superior Court has described the line to be drawn in post-*Golden* cases in this way:

> The goal always is to determine whether the search maintained the privacy and dignity of the detainee; not to complete a check list in [a] mechanical fashion. . . . If the failure to follow a guideline has no material impact on the detainee's dignity, there is no *Charter* breach. In certain cases, the failure to adhere to a single *Golden* factor will result in a *Charter* breach, in other cases the failure to adhere to multiple factors will not result in a *Charter* breach.[51]

The court in *Black* adds to this analysis the point that where the Crown seeks to rely on exigent circumstances to justify a departure from *Golden*, "the Crown must show that the purported exigent circumstances rendered a less intrusive procedure insufficient."[52]

A further kind of invasive search that gives rise to unique considerations is taking a penile swab in sexual assault cases. Prior to the Supreme Court's decision in *Saeed*,[53] courts would approach these searches as a form of strip search and assess them using a modified form of the *Golden* guidelines.[54] In *Saeed* the Supreme Court created a distinct standard and set of guidelines for this form of search.

Following an allegation of a violent sexual assault against a young complainant, the accused in *Saeed* was taken into custody and handcuffed to a wall in a cell with no toilet or sink for roughly thirty to forty minutes. The supervising officer, assuming a penile swab fell within the scope of a search on arrest, directed two male officers to enter the cell and demand the swab from the accused who conducted it. While he did so, the officers stood blocking the cell's window. The swab contained the complainant's DNA. In a 7:2 decision, the Court held that police could conduct a swab without a warrant, but required grounds additional to those for the arrest. As in *Golden*, the majority also set out a series of guidelines for the reasonable conduct of a swab (described throughout the case as both a search and a seizure).

A swab should, "as a general rule," be done at the police station, but may be done at a hospital or in another safe space if necessary.[55] It should be "conducted in a manner that ensures the health and safety of

---

51 *R v Atule*, 2018 ONSC 5416 at paras 51–52, cited in *Black*, *ibid* at para 40.

52 *Black*, above note 50 at para 42.

53 *Saeed*, above note 21.

54 See, e.g., *R v Laporte (PLR)*, 2016 MBCA 36, holding a penile swab to be reasonably conducted on the basis of conforming in large part to a modified version of the guidelines in *Golden*, above note 21.

55 *Saeed* above note 21 at para 78, containing all the guidelines discussed here.

all involved"; be authorized by a supervising officer; and be conducted by male officers "unless circumstances compel otherwise." It should be done in "a private area such that no one other than the individuals engaged in the swab can observe it." Police should inform the accused of the nature and purpose of the procedure and police authority to do so. The accused should be given the option of removing his clothes and taking the swab himself; if he opts not to, it should be done by "a trained officer or medical professional, with the minimum of force necessary."[56] There should be "no more officers involved than are reasonably necessary." It should be done "as quickly as possible and in a way that ensures that the person is not completely undressed at any one time." Police should keep a record of the reasons why and manner in which they conducted the swab.

Justice Moldaver, for the majority, held that police in this case had conformed to all of these guidelines. They explained the purpose and nature of the procedure and carried it out "quickly, smoothly, and privately."[57] The accused took the swab himself, without contact with the officers. They minimized the violation of his privacy and carefully took detailed notes on their reasons and the process. It was reasonably conducted.

b) Device Searches

A further case to consider in this context is *Fearon*, involving the search of a device on arrest.[58] This is a personal search in the sense that a phone or other device is immediately searchable if found when searching a person or their immediate surroundings on a valid arrest. In *Fearon*, a majority of the Court held that police have authority to conduct a warrantless search of a device on arrest, without requiring further grounds, but on certain conditions.[59] Two are relevant to the manner of search. The "nature and the extent of the search" must be "tailored to the purpose of the search" and police must take "detailed notes of what they have examined on the device and how it was searched."[60] Violating either condition would mean the search was not authorized by law. But each requirement is also a guideline as to the conduct of a device search, suggesting that a failure on either ground would entail a search unreasonably conducted.

---

56 *Ibid* at para 80, Justice Moldaver cited *Golden* above note 21 at para 116, for the proposition that "[t]he fact that an accused resists does not entitle the police 'to engage in behaviour that disregards or compromises his or her physical and psychological integrity and safety.'"

57 *Ibid* at para 89.

58 *Fearon*, above note 21.

59 See the discussion of *Fearon* in Chapter 6, Section D(4)(a).

60 *Fearon*, above note 21 at para 83.

2) DNA Samples

The *Criminal Code* provides for a warrant to obtain a DNA sample from a suspect in the course of an investigation and a warrant for a DNA sample for inclusion in the national DNA databank when a person is convicted of certain offences.[61] The *Code* imposes a number of conditions on the process of taking any of the DNA samples it authorizes, and these can be read as a guide for the reasonable conduct of a seizure. Violating any of them would mean a seizure is not authorized by law and might also result in a finding that the seizure was unreasonably conducted. Before taking a DNA sample, an officer must confirm the person's DNA is not already in the DNA databank.[62] They must inform the person of the nature of, purpose for, and authority for the procedure; its possible use in evidence; rights of a young person on the taking of a sample; and they must use "no more force than is necessary for the purpose of taking the samples."[63] The officer must also "ensure that the person's privacy is respected in a manner that is reasonable in the circumstances."[64] A young person has the right to consult with and have a parent, adult relative, or counsel present and any waiver must be recorded or confirmed in writing. A further set of provisions guards against the use of the DNA sample for any purpose aside from inclusion in the databank or the investigation tied to the warrant.[65]

In *R v SAB*, a case dealing with whether a DNA warrant for investigative purposes was a reasonable law, Arbour J noted three ways in which the DNA provisions sought to minimize infringements of privacy—and each of these points can be read as indicia of a reasonably conducted seizure.[66] On the requirement that an officer ensure that a person's privacy is respected in the course of taking the sample, Arbour J cited approvingly Weiler JA's comment in *R v Briggs* that "a person would not ordinarily be required to expose a part of the body that is not ordinarily exposed to view."[67] Justice Arbour also noted that the *Criminal Code* allows a judge to impose terms in a warrant to "ensure that the seizure of a bodily

61 The investigative warrants are in sections 487.04–487.09 of the *Criminal Code*, RSC 1985, c C-46 [*Criminal Code* or *Code*] and warrants for inclusion in the national DNA databank are in ss 487.051(1)–(3). These powers are discussed in Chapter 6, Section A(6).

62 *Criminal Code*, above note 61, s 487.071.

63 *Ibid*, s 487.07(1).

64 *Ibid*, s 487.07(3).

65 *Ibid*, s 487.08.

66 *R v SAB*, 2003 SCC 60 [*SAB*].

67 *Ibid* at para 45, citing *R v Briggs* (2001), 55 OR (3d) 417 at para 35 (CA).

substance authorized by the warrant is reasonable in the circumstances."[68] And, finally, the limited purposes for which a sample taken may be used provides further protection of privacy, yet it also points to a further way in which a seizure (resulting in unlawful use) can constitute a seizure carried out unreasonably.

3) Dog Searches

The Supreme Court in *R v Kang-Brown* and *R v AM* recognized a police power to employ "sniffer dogs" to aid in detecting odours emanating from bags and sealed compartments in public spaces, and revisited the grounds for using sniffer dogs in *R v Chehil* and *R v MacKenzie*.[69] The Court offers limited guidance in these cases as to what would constitute a sniffer dog search conducted in a reasonable manner.

In their dissenting opinion in *Kang-Brown*, Deschamps and Rothstein JJ pointed to three features of the search in that case that rendered its conduct reasonable—a non-binding opinion, but one that offers a useful blueprint.[70] First, police sought permission of the bus terminal's management to employ search dogs on site. Police observed the suspect, formed a reasonable suspicion in relation to him, and only then signalled for the sniffer dog to approach him. Finally, the dog itself gave a positive indication of the presence of narcotics by simply sitting down. By implication, an unreasonably conducted sniffer dog search might be one in which dogs were brought into a privately owned but publicly accessible space without permission; police approached people with them randomly or without individualized suspicion (a requirement that may depend on the context); and/or the dog was aggressive, or in some way menacing or intimidating.

In *Chehil*, Karakatsanis J, writing for the Court, held that "[c]oncerns about the reliability and accuracy of a drug detection dog may arise at each level of the *Collins* inquiry."[71] More specifically, "the reliability of a particular dog is also relevant to determining whether a particular sniff search was conducted reasonably in the circumstances."[72] Handlers, she asserts, "should keep records of the dog and team's performance,"[73] and these should be used in assessing reliability. Yet the Crown need not

---

68 *Criminal Code*, above note 61, s 487.06(2), cited in *SAB*, above note 66 at para 46.

69 *R v Kang-Brown*, 2008 SCC 18 [*Kang-Brown*]; *R v AM*, 2008 SCC 19; *R v Chehil*, 2013 SCC 49 [*Chehil*]; and *R v MacKenzie*, 2013 SCC 50.

70 *Kang-Brown*, *ibid* at paras 196–97.

71 *Chehil*, above note 69 at para 48.

72 *Ibid*.

73 *Ibid* at para 51.

establish that "the dog is infallible, just as it does not have to prove that an informer's tip is infallible."[74] Police using a sniffer dog with a poor record for accuracy conduct a search in an unreasonable manner.

4) Search in a High School

In *R v M(MR)*, the Supreme Court recognized a power of school officials to conduct a warrantless search of students and their effects on school property.[75] Justice Cory, for the majority, held that the scope of what school officials are authorized to search is closely related to the question of how they might conduct the search in a reasonable manner.[76] Both will be assessed "in light of the circumstances presented and the nature of the suspected breach of school regulations."[77] The invasiveness of the search "will vary with the gravity of the infraction that is suspected." Suspicion of a gun or other "dangerous weapon" would justify "swift, thorough and extensive searches."[78] A search for minor infractions should be minimally invasive. All school searches should be conducted "in as sensitive a manner as possible and take into account the age and sex of the student."[79] A male teacher searching "the person of a female student . . . may well be inappropriate and unreasonable." Whether a search is authorized and conducted reasonably must be considered "in the context of all the circumstances presented including [the officials'] responsibility for students' safety."[80]

In *M(MR)* itself, Cory J held the vice principal's search of a student was "minimally intrusive" and "carried out in an appropriately sensitive manner."[81] He carried out the search in the privacy of his office, asking the student to turn out his pockets and pull up his pants legs. Seeing a bulge in his sock, the vice principal removed a cellophane bag containing marijuana and gave it to a police officer present.[82] The officer's presence did not render the search unlawful or unreasonably conducted,

---

74 *Ibid* at para 53.

75 *R v M(MR)*, [1998] 3 SCR 393. The power applies only where school officials act independently of police. On the grounds for using the power and police involvement in school searches, see Chapter 6, Section D(4)(f).

76 *Ibid* at paras 51–54.

77 *Ibid* at para 52.

78 *Ibid.*

79 *Ibid* at para 53.

80 *Ibid* at para 52.

81 *Ibid* at para 63.

82 *Ibid* at para 6.

on the view that he was merely a passive observer and the vice principal had not acted as his agent.[83]

C. REASONABLE TERRITORIAL SEARCHES

1) Hard, Dynamic (No-Knock) Entry

R v Cornell concerned the police use of a "hard" or "dynamic" entry (entry without knocking) and considerable force in the course of executing a warrant to search a home.[84] The sole issue was whether police had conducted the search reasonably. The Supreme Court was divided 4:3 on the question, with the majority deciding in favour of the Crown and granting police significant leeway in the conduct of warranted searches in potentially dangerous situations. Yet by offering widely divergent views of the facts, both the majority and dissent offer a blueprint for constructing arguments about when a territorial search is or is not reasonably conducted.

Police were investigating N and T, who they believed to be gang members involved in drug trafficking. After surveilling them for a period, police learned that the accused, C, together with N and T, were using his residence as a stash house and sought a warrant to search C's residence and two other places. In their application for a warrant to search C's house, police noted that N and T had a history of violence and were involved with a gang, and also expressed a concern about the destruction of evidence. Before entering the home, police saw C's mother and sister leave. The other warrants had been executed and N was in custody. Police chose to conduct a hard entry of C's home by ramming open the front door by surprise, "yelling 'Police, search warrant'," with nine officers wearing balaclavas and body armour and weapons drawn.[85] C's mentally challenged brother was handcuffed, became emotionally distressed, and was soon released. Members first entering did not have a copy of the warrant, but an officer down the block did and arrived four minutes later. Police caused damage throughout the house and found

83 Writing in dissent, Major J held, at para 78 *ibid*, that the vice principal was acting as an agent of the police, partly on the basis of having received instruction from the officer moments before on how to conduct the search. The officer lacked what amounted to reasonable grounds for arrest, and without lawful authority for the search, it was unreasonable on that basis alone.

84 *R v Cornell*, 2010 SCC 31 [*Cornell*].

85 *Ibid* at para 10.

cocaine in C's bedroom. Both the trial judge and a majority of the Alberta Court of Appeal found the search to have been conducted reasonably.

Agreeing with this view, Cromwell J, writing for the majority of the Supreme Court, affirmed a common law rule predating the *Charter* that "[e]xcept in exigent circumstances, police officers must make an announcement before forcing entry into a dwelling house."[86] In the ordinary course, he held, police should give notice of their presence by knocking on the door or ringing the doorbell, identify themselves as law enforcement, and state their purpose by giving "a lawful reason for entry."[87] When police depart from these rules, the Crown bears the onus of establishing police had "reasonable grounds to be concerned about the possibility of harm to themselves or occupants, or about the destruction of evidence."[88] The greater the departure, "the heavier the onus." The Crown cannot rely on "*ex post facto* justifications"; it must provide evidence supporting "grounds to be concerned about the possibility of violence."[89] Even "a low risk of weapons being present" would justify a departure.[90]

For the majority, police here had reasonable grounds to justify use of "an unannounced, forced entry while masked."[91] This involves three considerations: what police knew at the time (or should have reasonably known); being allowed "a certain amount of latitude" in deciding how to proceed; and according "substantial deference" to the trial judge's findings on point.[92] Justice Cromwell's elaboration of the second of these considerations includes the often cited assertion that "[t]he role of the reviewing court in assessing the manner in which a search has been conducted is to appropriately balance the rights of suspects with the requirements of safe and effective law enforcement, not to become a Monday morning quarterback."[93]

The accused had argued on appeal that police did not have grounds to support a hard entry. They had no reason to suspect violence at C's residence or that evidence would be destroyed without a hard entry. The majority disagreed, relying largely on the trial judge's findings. Police were reasonably concerned about their safety in light of their experience with drug traffickers and the frequency of violence in dealings

---

86 *Ibid* at para 18, citing *Eccles v Bourque*, [1975] 2 SCR 739 at 747 [*Eccles*].

87 *Ibid* at para 18, quoting *Eccles*.

88 *Ibid* at para 20.

89 *Ibid*, citing *R v Genest*, [1989] 1 SCR 59 at 89–90 [*Genest*].

90 *Cornell*, above note 84 at para 20.

91 *Ibid* at para 22.

92 *Ibid* at paras 23–25.

93 *Ibid* at para 24.

with them.[94] Cocaine could be destroyed easily. N may have been in custody and C's mother and sister may have left, but police had no knowledge of who might be inside—possibly gang members with a history of violence, given evidence of C's associations with them.[95] Yet, as the trial judge had also noted, anyone in the house—criminally involved or not—might easily have destroyed evidence upon hearing police at the door. The accused cited authority in which police had resorted to hard entry as a matter of "blanket policy" in drug cases, and Cromwell J distinguished these cases by pointing out that police here did not act on such a policy, and may have lacked reasonable grounds had they done so.[96] Police relied instead on "ample grounds to be concerned about violence and destruction of evidence." No further investigation was necessary before entering, including an attempt to ascertain who was inside, given the extensive surveillance police had conducted on the house in the days prior to and all of the day of entry itself, along with several searches in police and city databases on ownership and occupancy. A court reviewing police conduct should not ask "whether every detail of the search, viewed in isolation was appropriate."[97] To claim there was an insufficient basis for concerns about violence involving C, as the dissent in the Court of Appeal had held, was in Cromwell J's view to consider C in isolation from what police reasonably knew about the home as a base for gang-related drug dealing.

Section 29 of the *Criminal Code* requires "every one who executes a process or warrant to have it with him, where it is feasible to do so" and produce it on request.[98] No member of the tactical team making entry had the warrant with them, but Cromwell J notes that the intention was to have the team enter and secure the site and the officer overseeing the search (who had the warrant) to enter shortly thereafter, which he did within four minutes. No one asked to see the warrant in that time, and when C's mother arrived shortly thereafter, she was shown the warrant. Section 29, the majority held, does not require that "each member of the police team executing the warrant have a copy on his or her person."[99] The purpose of the provision is to enable a person to know whether there is "a colour of authority for the search, making forcible resistance

94 *Ibid* at para 27.

95 *Ibid* at paras 27 and 30.

96 *Ibid* at para 31, distinguishing *R v Lau*, 2003 BCCA 337 and *R v Schedel*, 2003 BCCA 364. See also *R v Thompson*, 2010 ONSC 2862.

97 *Cornell*, above note 84 at para 31.

98 *Criminal Code*, above note 61.

99 *Cornell*, above note 84 at para 42.

improper."[100] Having one member of the team be in possession satisfies this purpose, but it would be "a better practice for someone among the first group of officers in the door to have a copy on his or her person."[101]

Writing in dissent, Fish J held that the evidence in the record did not support the view that the force police used was "necessary in the circumstances," as stipulated in the warrant provision of the *Controlled Drugs and Substances Act* on which police had relied.[102] Police should be granted "considerable latitude" in choosing tactics to protect their safety and to preserve evidence, but their decisions must be reasonable and "informed by a fact-based assessment of the particular circumstances."[103] Neither C nor any family member had a history of violence, and police were aware from surveillance that the home was neither "a gang house nor a drug house frequented by addicts or users."[104] N and T, the targets of the initial investigation, were seldom seen in or near the home, and not with weapons.[105] What police knew about C permitted them to reasonably infer he was storing small amounts of product for N—was only marginally involved in the operation and not a gang member himself—and police had no basis for believing anyone in the home would be armed and dangerous.[106] The application for the warrant made no reference to weapons in the home or the likelihood of finding any.[107] Nor did police have a basis to believe that without a quick and violent entry, evidence would be destroyed. "Generic assertions in this regard are plainly insufficient to justify a violent entry of the kind that occurred here."[108] Wearing balaclavas—a routine practice on entry, the evidence revealed—was a form of "[g]ratuitous intimidation," of "psychological violence entirely unrelated to the particular circumstances of the search" and one that "may in itself render a search unreasonable."[109]

---

100 *Ibid* at para 43.

101 *Ibid.*

102 *Controlled Drugs and Substances Act*, SC 1996, c 19, s 12, permitting "as much force as is necessary in the circumstances;" cited in *Cornell*, above note 84 at para 47.

103 *Cornell*, above note 84 at para 48.

104 *Ibid* at para 49.

105 *Ibid* at para 76.

106 *Ibid* at para 101.

107 *Ibid* at para 50.

108 *Ibid* at para 51.

109 *Ibid* at paras 115–17:

> Moreover, anonymity in the exercise of power, particularly state power, invites in some a sense of detachment and a feeling of impunity. The wearing of masks by intruding police officers creates an unjustified risk in this regard where, as here, it is based on nothing more than an ill-considered police "policy" that has been judicially condemned on more than one occasion.

The majority and the dissent agreed that the mere *possibility* of violence or the easy destruction of evidence could justify a hard entrance and a significant degree of force. The thrust of Fish J's reasons, and the crux of the difference in opinion, is to suggest that the possibility of violence or losing evidence must be a reasonable one, with a real evidentiary basis. At one point, he speaks of police having lacked "any particularized information regarding the home and its occupants . . . that might have caused them concern for their safety."[110] Analogously, he was critical of the merely theoretical concern about the ease of destroying evidence: "police must make some attempt to ascertain whether there is a real likelihood that, without a sudden and violent entry of the kind that occurred here, the occupants will have time—and will proceed—to conceal or destroy the evidence that is the object of the search."[111] Concerns on both fronts need to be more than hypothetical. They cannot be supported by vague or tenuous fears. We agree with this view. Justice Fish outlines a plausible danger that accepting vague assertions on the part of police about risks that are speculative or remote will lead to heavy-handed, violent police tactics becoming routine.

In pointing to the need for a more solid, or less hypothetical, evidentiary basis for concerns about safety or lost evidence, Fish J did not set out to craft a new standard, but rather to reiterate what he took to be the Court's earlier holding in *Genest*, another case involving a no-knock entry.[112] Chief Justice Dickson in *Genest* held for a unanimous Court:

> The assessment of the amount of force, like the motives for the search in the first place, need not be proven on the same standard of guilt as when proving the elements of an offence. The Crown must, however, lay the evidentiary framework to support the conclusion that there were grounds to be concerned about the possibility of violence.[113]

Justice Fish in *Cornell* held this to mean that police are "bound under *Genest* to at least make reasonable inquiries to ascertain the nature of the premises they intend to search, the identities and background of its occupants, and the real risk of resistance by force."[114]

Genest had also involved a large group of heavily armed police ramming through the door of the accused's home unannounced, but in distinction to *Cornell*, the facts present a clear lack of sufficient grounds for

110 *Ibid* at para 102.
111 *Ibid* at para 106.
112 *Genest*, above note 89.
113 *Ibid* at 90, cited in *Cornell*, above note 84 at para 108.
114 *Cornell*, above note 84 at para 109.

using a hard entry.[115] Entering the home, police did not find the drugs they hoped to seize but did find weapons. The issue at the Supreme Court was the exclusion of evidence rather than the reasonableness of the search. Chief Justice Dickson's decision for a unanimous Court addressed the conduct of the search when assessing the seriousness of the violation of section 8 under section 24(2) of the *Charter*. The trial judge had found the application for the warrant to be deficient (based primarily on a tip) and the warrant invalid. The accused had convictions involving violence, but police at trial did not express concerns that he would be violent or the search dangerous. Reviewing the trial record, Dickson CJ observed that "there appear[ed] to be no factual foundation for the means used by police" in executing the warrant.[116]

The chief justice held that in assessing the seriousness of a violation under section 24(2), reasons for police use of force are relevant. But to justify the use of force, the Crown needs to "show a real threat of violent behaviour." Despite *Cornell* now being the leading authority on hard entry, the line Dickson CJ draws in *Genest* is still pertinent:

> The consideration of the possibility of violence must, however, be carefully limited. It should not amount to a *carte blanche* for the police to ignore completely all restrictions on police behaviour. The greater the departure from the standards of behaviour required by the common law and the *Charter*, the heavier the onus on the police to show why they thought it necessary to use force. . . . The evidence to justify such behaviour must be apparent in the record.[117]

To justify significant force in executing a warrant, the line is one between "real" and hypothetical or speculative risks. Police knew that Genest had a history of violence, believed him to be a Hells Angel, and saw a number of bikers gathered the night before. Yet, at trial, the officers did not point to any of these details as grounds for concerns about the possibility of violence—suggesting that if they had any, they were hypothetical at best.

The chief justice concluded that the violation of section 8 in this case was "serious" and the amount of force used "excessive."[118] He faults police for making "[n]o attempt . . . to justify the amount of force used." There are two ways to read this. On one view, he was finding fault with the failure to *try* to justify the force used rather than asserting that the facts would not have justified it. On another reading, Dickson CJ was

115 *Genest*, above note 89; *Cornell*, above note 84.

116 *Genest*, above note 89 at 70.

117 *Ibid* at 89.

118 *Ibid* at 91.

asserting indirectly that the facts did not meet the threshold of a real threat: i.e., the police were to be faulted because, had they paused to reflect, they would have realized they should not make a hard entry because in the circumstances *it could not be justified*. In our view, the ambiguity here is less important than the *ratio* itself: police, at the time of the search, need to have grounds to justify the amount of force they use, and those grounds need to be substantiated by evidence, be more than speculative or hypothetical, and be reasonable. In *Genest*, police, subjectively, lacked these grounds altogether. In *Cornell*, police had something between plausible and speculative concerns. They made a laudable effort to articulate them. Yet a concern remains, underlined in Fish J's dissent in *Cornell*, that the majority's readiness to assume that the largely speculative concerns in that case justified a hard entry may overshadow or bury the clearer, more stringent test in *Genest* (real not speculative concerns).

Appellate decisions have tended to support the concern that courts might approve of police use of hard entry tactics on risks that are more theoretical than real or evidence based. Looking first at decisions from the Ontario Court of Appeal, in *R v Burke*,[119] the court held that a hard entry was reasonable when police executed a warrant in a case involving child pornography based not on specific information supporting the suspect's likelihood of deleting relevant files, but on theoretical ease of doing so.[120] In *R v Pileggi*,[121] the court upheld a no-knock entry in a case involving a person suspected of selling oxycodone from his home. "Given the size and layout of the house," Trotter JA held, "as well as the nature of the drugs in question, there was a real likelihood that the appellant would be able to destroy the evidence quickly and with ease."[122] In *R v Rutledge*,[123] the court upheld as reasonable a hard entry involving police breaking a window and tossing in tear gas at a farmhouse where firearms were being sought. In this case, police had firmer grounds for believing the accused would be armed and potentially dangerous.

In *R v Kwiatkowski*,[124] the Court of Appeal for British Columbia upheld as reasonable a search in which an officer entered through an open door a greenhouse on a large rural property and announced his

119 2013 ONCA 424.

120 *Ibid* at paras 54–58.

121 2021 ONCA 4.

122 *Ibid* at para 32, adding at 33: "As [one officer] testified, while there may be no information indicating that weapons may be located in the place to be searched, it does not necessarily mean that weapons will not be there."

123 2017 ONCA 635.

124 2010 BCCA 124.

presence (rather than first knocking and announcing). Police also acted reasonably in drawing their weapons upon entry despite a lack of evidence that anyone in or near the greenhouse was likely to be armed. Justice Kirkpatrick, for the court, pointed to no specific basis for safety concerns, suggesting instead that "[t]o ignore the modern realities of the dangers associated with sophisticated illicit operations such as this one would, in my opinion, be extremely naive."[125] In *R v Sexton*,[126] the New Brunswick Court of Appeal considered a no-knock entry involving police use of a battering ram, balaclavas, and guns drawn. The court held it to be reasonable on the basis of cautions on a police computer database about the accused being armed and dangerous, along with the possibility that, with notice of police at the door, he might pour cocaine down a sink or toilet.

2) Safety Searches

In *R v MacDonald*, the Supreme Court recognized a police power to conduct a "safety search" in a dwelling house on reasonable grounds to believe safety is at stake and the search is necessary.[127] The Court recognized the power by applying the test for crafting new police powers in *Dedman v The Queen* and *R v Waterfield*.[128] Justice Le Bel, for the majority, held that whether a safety search is carried out in a reasonable manner is closely related to the second stage of the *Dedman/Waterfield* test, which asks whether what police did was reasonably necessary to fulfilling a police duty (which in most if not every case applying *Dedman* is a duty to keep the peace and prevent crime).[129] Determining the reasonable necessity of some action involves a consideration not just of the extent of an interference with liberty it entails, but also "how it was carried out." In *MacDonald* itself, an officer responding to a noise complaint knocked at the front door of the accused's apartment. Seeing what appeared to be a knife in the partially hidden hands of the accused, he asked twice what it was but did not receive an answer. He then pushed open the door a few inches further to get a better look and discovered it was a gun. Justice Le Bel held that the search was conducted in a reasonable manner, given that the officer had asked twice what was in the accused's hands and did not receive an answer and that the officer then did "no more than was

---

125 *Ibid* at para 62.

126 2011 NBCA 97.

127 *R v MacDonald*, 2014 SCC 3 [*MacDonald*].

128 *Dedman v The Queen*, [1985] 2 SCR 2 and *R v Waterfield*, [1963] 3 All ER 659. See the discussion of this test in Chapter 6, Section D(4).

129 *MacDonald*, above note 127 at para 47.

necessary to find out what Mr. MacDonald had behind his leg."[130] There was indeed "no less intrusive way" to address the safety threat than to push open the door slightly further.

Courts in later cases have assessed the reasonableness of a safety or "clearing" search primarily on the basis of whether police had reasonable grounds for conducting it.[131] Yet the broader principle would still apply if and when courts do address this. The manner in which a safety search is conducted will be unreasonable if it goes beyond what is reasonably necessary to achieve its intended purpose.[132] This could involve going too far in space or time: being more extensive (looking into small compartments or bags) or extending beyond the point in time when police have objective concerns about safety. A good example of this can be found in *R v Ahmed-Kadir*,[133] where police, responding to a domestic dispute call, conducted an initial clearing search of a living room and kitchen, accounted for both residents, and then conducted a further search by entering a bedroom and looking into a closet. Justice Frankel, for the British Columbia Court of Appeal, framed the second search (of the bedroom and closet) as exceeding the authority set out in *MacDonald*. But the search of those spaces might also have been considered unreasonably conducted portions of a general, continuous search the Crown invited the court to recognize here—on the basis that they went beyond what was reasonably necessary.[134] However, a safety search might still be reasonably conducted despite being thorough and extensive. In *R v Farrah (D)*,[135] the Manitoba Court of Appeal held as reasonable a safety search of an entire suite, including "any part of the suite which might provide a space for a person to hide," minutes after a report of a bank robbery in which a shotgun had been discharged.[136]

Finally, we note that another way in which a safety search might be carried out unreasonably is if it involved unnecessary property damage or destruction, or undue intimidation or hostility to persons present.

130 *Ibid* at para 48.

131 See, e.g., *R v Ahmed-Kadir*, 2015 BCCA 346 [*Ahmed-Kadir*]; *R v Kennett*, 2019 NBCA 52; *R v Thompson*, 2020 SKPC 39.

132 *Vu*, above note 9 at para 22.

133 *Ahmed-Kadir*, above note 131.

134 *Ibid* at para 69; this was also how the trial judge conceived it, finding the search of the entire apartment reasonable.

135 2011 MBCA 49.

136 *Ibid* at para 51, finding the search was both authorized and reasonably conducted.

3) Law Office Searches

In *Lavallee, Rackel & Heintz v Canada (Attorney General); White, Ottenheimer & Baker v Canada (Attorney General); R v Fink*, the Supreme Court struck down section 488.1 of the *Criminal Code*, which allows for the search of a law office, as contrary to section 8 of the *Charter*.[137] Section 448.1 authorizes an unreasonable search for failing to "interfere with solicitor-client privilege more than is absolutely necessary."[138] The scheme bore various shortcomings that could readily result in police seizing privileged documents, a client being named, or the privilege holder failing to receive notice of the search.[139] The Court invited Parliament to rectify these shortcomings and set out a series of "general principles" that have since served as conditions for a warrant sought under section 487 of the *Code*. The principles might also be read as a general guideline for what would constitute the search of a law office conducted in a reasonable manner. To highlight only a few of these requires documents in a lawyer's possession should be sealed before being examined or seized; efforts should be made to contact the lawyer or a representative of the bar to oversee the search; privilege holders should be given a reasonable opportunity to assert a claim of privilege; disputed documents should not be inspected until adjudicated; and when documents are found to be privileged, they should be returned immediately to the holder of privilege.[140]

D. REASONABLE SEARCH INVOLVING INFORMATION

A wide range of searches involve tools or techniques that may have some tangible or physical component where the real target of the search is something intangible: namely, data or information. This can include warrants to obtain a DNA sample, a tracking device for the movement of a vehicle or an item, or a production order for data about digital communications. In many if not most of these cases, the statutory framework providing authority for the search includes some form of protection against the misuse of the data or information gathered in the process.

137 *Lavallee, Rackel & Heintz v Canada (Attorney General); White, Ottenheimer & Baker v Canada (Attorney General); R v Fink*, 2002 SCC 61. See the discussion in Chapter 7, Section C(2)(e) on the reasons it was struck down.

138 *Ibid.*

139 *Ibid* at paras 39–45.

140 For the complete list, see para 49, *ibid.*

For example, as noted earlier, the DNA warrant provisions make it an offence to use DNA information gathered for any purpose beyond a narrow set of them identified in the *Code*.[141] Another example can be found in the production order or demand provisions of the *Code*, which require a person to destroy the data at issue "as soon as feasible after the order expires or is revoked" and making failure to do so a summary offence.[142] This general form of statutory protection against misuse is also a form of guidance as to what constitutes a search or seizure of information carried out unreasonably.

Another important general form of protection that also has implications for the reasonable conduct of a data search can be found in the special rules courts have developed for the search of computers, phones, and other devices. The Supreme Court held in *Vu* that a warrant to search a place does not authorize the search of a computer found within it unless it permits this explicitly.[143] The warrant in *Vu* did not do so, thus rendering unreasonable the search of two computers and a phone found within the house. The Court declined to impose a requirement that computer warrants include "search protocols" or specific limits on which files could be accessed. Justice Cromwell noted that "the manner of search is generally reviewed after the fact" due in part to not knowing where to look for things.[144] This does not mean that with a warrant police have "a licence to scour the devices indiscriminately."[145] If, when carrying out a computer search, police "realized that there was in fact no reason to search a particular program or file on the device, the law of search and seizure would require them not to do so." Where there are concerns about sensitive material—intellectual property or documents subject to solicitor-client privilege—a judge or justice could impose conditions on the ambit of the search, or a warrant could be issued to seize the device and a further warrant issued to search it on conditions after further consideration.[146] Justice Cromwell suggested that officers carrying out a search should take notes on how the search is conducted, but did not hold this to be a "constitutional prerequisite."[147] The failure to take notes, coupled with evidence of an unnecessarily extensive device search might, therefore, constitute a search unreasonably conducted, but it would depend on the facts.

---

141 *Criminal Code*, above note 61, ss 487.05(1)(b), 487.08(1) & 487.08(2).
142 *Ibid*, ss 487.0194(1), (2), and 487.0199.
143 *Vu*, above note 9.
144 *Ibid* at para 55.
145 *Ibid* at para 61.
146 *Ibid* at para 62.
147 *Ibid* at para 70.

Finally, we noted earlier in this chapter that the Court in *Fearon* imposed a set of conditions on the search of a device incident to arrest.[148] We pointed to two of these conditions as relevant to the manner of a reasonable device search. As Cromwell J held, the "nature and the extent of the search" must be "tailored to the purpose of the search," and police must take "detailed notes of what they have examined on the device and how it was searched."[149] The notetaking requirement is raised here to a requirement to render the search authorized by law, but as in *Vu*, it also serves as a factor in assessing the reasonable conduct of a search.

E. POST-COLLECTION EVENTS CONSTITUTING AN UNREASONABLE SEARCH OR SEIZURE

In Chapter 3, we noted that some powers to search or seize set out in the law place obligations on police to do things that might happen long after the initial search or seizure has taken place. These include rules about reporting, storage, sharing, or destroying evidence. We noted that these have the effect of extending the scope of what constitutes a search or seizure, giving rise to the possibility that a court might find a breach of these rules rendering the entire search or seizure, seen as a single event, unreasonable. One such example was the failure of police in *R v Reeves* to report the computer seizure in that case to a justice as soon as was practicable, resulting in a violation of section 8 on that basis.[150] We seek to draw attention to these rules once again in order to suggest that they might also be read as features of a search or seizure conducted in a reasonable manner. One might construe the breach of these rules resulting as a violation of section 8 being a search or seizure no longer authorized by law or a violation due to a breach of the third ground of the *Collins* test.

We noted that in practical terms, the post-collection rules police contend with most frequently are found in sections 487, 489.1, and 490 of the *Criminal Code*, which require police to bring to a justice anything seized, to document what they have seized, and eventually return it when certain conditions are met.[151] Further examples include provisions

148 *Fearon*, above note 21.

149 *Ibid* at para 83.

150 *R v Reeves*, 2018 SCC 56 at paras 63–65.

151 The provisions are discussed in detail in Chapter 5, Section B(5).

in Part VI of the *Code* to seal a wiretap;[152] to eventually report to a target the fact that a wiretap has taken place;[153] rules on when information obtained from a wiretap may be disclosed to other parties;[154] and rules on sealing and destroying wiretap evidence.[155] The *Code* also makes it an offence to use information obtained from a DNA warrant for any but a limited set of purposes.[156]

152 *Criminal Code*, above note 61, s 187.
153 *Ibid*, s 196.
154 *Ibid*, s 193(2), (3).
155 *Ibid*, ss 187(1.5), 193.
156 *Ibid*, ss 487.05(1)(b) and 487.08(1) & (2).

CHAPTER 9

EXCLUSION AND OTHER REMEDIES FOR UNREASONABLE SEARCH OR SEIZURE

A. INTRODUCTION

The *Charter* allows for a number of remedies in response to a finding that a search or seizure, or a law authorizing one, is unreasonable. Where a court finds that a *law* violates a *Charter* right, it will turn to section 1 of the *Charter* to decide whether the violation can be justified as a "reasonable limit" on the right in a "free and democratic society."[1] The court then applies a proportionality test found in *R v Oakes*, which, broadly speaking, considers the nature of the state interest in or purpose of the law and the extent to which it impairs the right at issue.[2] We noted in Chapter 2 that in the case of section 8, this balancing has tended to take place almost exclusively within the assessment of whether a law violates section 8 itself, as part of the assessment of whether a search law is reasonable (the subject of Chapter 7). As a consequence, as Dickson J (as he then was) predicted in *Hunter v Southam Inc*, there are few Supreme Court cases that go on to consider in much detail whether violations of section 8 can be justified under section 1 and none that have found a violation of section 8 to be saved under section 1.[3] The government tends to concede that if a law allows for an unreasonable search or seizure, it

---

1 *Canadian Charter of Rights and Freedoms*, Part I of the *Constitution Act, 1982*, being Schedule B to the *Canada Act 1982* (UK), 1982, c 11, s 1 [*Charter*].

2 *R v Oakes*, [1986] 1 SCR 103.

3 *Hunter et al v Southam Inc*, [1984] 2 SCR 145 at 169–70; for s 8 cases proceeding to s 1, see Chapter 7.

cannot be justified as a reasonable limit. In which case, the law is read down or struck down.[4]

The vast majority of the time that courts find a search or seizure to be in violation of section 8, they do so in response to an *act* on the part of police or other state officials. The court then turns to section 24 of the *Charter* for a remedy, and in most of these cases, the court turns to section 24(2) to decide whether evidence obtained from the search or seizure should be excluded or admitted at trial.[5] There are, however, other important remedies under section 24(1), which states that "[a]nyone whose rights or freedoms, as guaranteed by this *Charter* have been infringed or denied may apply to a court of competent jurisdiction to obtain such remedy as the court considers appropriate and just in the circumstances." A court of competent jurisdiction under section 24(1) and (2) includes the superior court of every province and any court or administrative tribunal provided the authority to grant a remedy under the *Charter* in the legislation constituting that court or tribunal—or where such authority is found to be "essential . . . to the effective and efficient functioning of the court or tribunal."[6] Remedies under section 24(1) include the power to grant a judicial stay of proceedings, to award monetary damages, to quash a seizure order, or to impose a reduced sentence—though in the normal course, a sentence should be reduced within the court's discretion on sentencing under the *Criminal Code*.[7] We deal first with these less common remedies before turning to exclusion in section 24(2).

A brief note on our aims in this chapter. Remedies are a distinct topic from search and seizure. There are many readily accessible and thorough sources on the topic.[8] We have chosen to include a short chapter on

---

4 The authority for the remedy of a declaration of invalidity is s 52(1) of the *Charter*, above note 1.

5 On the relation between ss 24 and 1 of the *Charter* and s 52 of the *Charter*, see *R v 974649 Ontario Inc*, 2001 SCC 81 [*974649 Ontario*], noting at para 14: "If a law is inconsistent with the *Charter*, s. 52 of the *Constitution Act, 1982* provides that it is invalid to the extent of the inconsistency. On the other hand, if a government action is inconsistent with the *Charter*, s. 24 provides remedies for the inconsistency."

6 *974649 Ontario*, above note 5 at para 44. A provincial court is a court of competent jurisdiction under s 24, but not in the course of a preliminary inquiry: *Mills v The Queen*, [1986] 1 SCR 863; *R v Rahey*, [1987] 1 SCR 588; *R v Smith (Michael Harold)*, [1989] 2 SCR 1120.

7 *Criminal Code*, RSC, 1985, c C-46 [*Criminal Code* or *Code*]; below, we discuss the Supreme Court's holding in *R v Nasogaluak*, 2010 SCC 6 [*Nasogaluak*] on the exceptional cases in which a sentence reduction should be granted under s 24(1).

8 See, e.g., the extensive treatment on s 24(2) in David Paciocco, Palma Paciocco & Lee Steusser, *The Law of Evidence*, 8th ed (Toronto: Irwin Law, 2020).

remedies to complete the account we have offered on search and seizure, on the view that a remedy for violating section 8—exclusion in particular—is an important part of the story. Our aim here is not to provide the encyclopedic survey we have attempted in earlier chapters, but rather to provide a high-level overview of the various remedies and tests that apply, and to assist readers by providing direction for further inquiry.

B. REMEDIES UNDER SECTION 24(1) OF THE *CHARTER*

1) Judicial Stay

The leading case setting out the test for a judicial stay for the violation of a *Charter* right, and one that deals with a violation of section 8 itself, is the Supreme Court's decision in *R v Babos*.[9] Justice Moldaver, writing the majority in this case, consolidated a number of relevant strands of earlier law on point before affirming the applicable test. A judicial stay, as he noted, is "the most drastic remedy" a court can order and is appropriate in only the "clearest of cases" for what amounts to an abuse of process on the part of the state.[10] Forms of abuse fall into two categories. The first is where "state conduct compromises the fairness of an accused's trial (the 'main' category)."[11] The second is where "state conduct creates no threat to trial fairness but risks undermining the integrity of the judicial process (the 'residual' category)." *Charter* breaches involving unreasonable conduct on the part of police, such as an unreasonable search, fall into the second or "residual" category.[12] The test for a stay under both categories is the same,[13] worth citing in full:

> 1) There must be prejudice to the accused's right to a fair trial or the integrity of the justice system that "will be manifested, perpetuated or aggravated through the conduct of the trial, or by its outcome" (*Regan*, at para 54);

---

9 2014 SCC 16 [*Babos*].

10 *Ibid* at paras 30–31, citing *R v Regan*, 2002 SCC 12 at para 53 [*Regan*] (a "drastic remedy") and *R v O'Connor*, [1995] 4 SCR 411 at para 68 [*O'Connor*] (the "clearest of cases").

11 *Babos*, above note 9 at para 31.

12 *Ibid* at para 35: "when the residual category is invoked, the question is whether the state has engaged in conduct that is offensive to societal notions of fair play and decency."

13 *Ibid* at para 32.

2) There must be no alternative remedy capable of redressing the prejudice; and
3) Where there is still uncertainty over whether a stay is warranted after steps (1) and (2), the court is required to balance the interests in favour of granting a stay, such as denouncing misconduct and preserving the integrity of the justice system, against "the interest that society has in having a final decision on the merits" (*ibid* at para 57).[14]

Justice Moldaver held that when considering a stay under the residual category, the court must assess whether the state conduct is "so troublesome that having a trial—even a fair one—will leave the impression that the justice system condones conduct that offends society's sense of fair play and decency."[15] If so, the first part of the test is met. The Court's prior holding in *Canada (Minister of Citizenship and Immigration) v Tobiass* adds an important qualification to this stage:[16]

> For a stay of proceedings to be appropriate in a case falling into the residual category, it must appear that the state misconduct is likely to continue in the future or that the carrying forward of the prosecution will offend society's sense of justice. Ordinarily, the latter condition will not be met unless the former is as well—society will not take umbrage at the carrying forward of a prosecution unless it is likely that some form of misconduct will continue. There may be exceptional cases in which the past misconduct is so egregious that the mere fact of going forward in the light of it will be offensive. But such cases should be relatively very rare.[17]

Justice Moldaver affirmed the distinction in this passage between past and continuing misconduct, but emphasized that the main question at this stage is "whether proceeding would lend judicial condonation to the impugned conduct."[18]

At the second stage of the test, a court considering a stay under the residual category must recognize that the question is not whether a stay would "provide redress to an accused for a wrong that has been done to

---

14 *Ibid*, citing *Regan*, above note 10. The Supreme Court first articulated this test in *O'Connor*, above note 10 at paras 75–78, deriving it there from Professor (now Justice) David Paciocco, "The Stay of Proceedings as a Remedy in Criminal Cases: Abusing the Abuse of Process Concept" (1991) 15 *Criminal Law Journal* 315 at 341.

15 *Babos*, above note 9 at para 35.

16 *Canada (Minister of Citizenship and Immigration) v Tobiass*, [1997] 3 SCR 391 [*Tobiass*].

17 *Ibid* at para 91, cited in *Babos*, above note 9 at para 36.

18 *Babos*, above note 9 at para 38.

him or her in the past" but rather "whether an alternate remedy short of a stay of proceedings will adequately dissociate the justice system from the impugned state conduct going forward."[19] For cases under the residual category, the third stage of the test "takes on added importance" in light of the need to balance a stay against having a trial despite the abuse at issue. Among the factors the court should consider here are "the nature and seriousness of the impugned conduct, whether the conduct is isolated or reflects a systemic and ongoing problem, the circumstances of the accused, the charges he or she faces, and the interests of society in having the charges disposed of on the merits."[20] The "more egregious the state conduct," Moldaver J held, "the greater the need for the court to dissociate itself from it."

The misconduct in *Babos* itself included a finding at trial that police had searched the trunk of the accused's car in violation of section 8 and that officers had colluded outside the courtroom, prior to testifying, "for the purpose of misleading the court."[21] The trial judge had excluded the firearm found in the course of the search, and one of the questions on appeal was whether excluding the evidence rather than granting a stay of proceedings, which the court eventually did, would have provided an adequate remedy. In the view of the majority of the Supreme Court, excluding the gun would have sufficed to "dissociate the court from the officers' collusion,"[22] and a stay was otherwise not warranted in the circumstances.[23]

By contrast, in *R v Bellusci*, the Supreme Court upheld a judicial stay granted at trial in a case involving an accused who had been "grievously assaulted" by a prison guard while shackled and handcuffed at the back of a van.[24] The trial judge had a reasonable doubt on the charge against the accused of assaulting the guard, but granted a stay on the count of intimidating a justice system participant (for uttering a threat against the guard).[25] The guard's assault violated the accused's rights under section 7 of the *Charter*. Assessing this as misconduct in the residual category, the trial judge found the assault to be serious enough to fall within the "exceptional" cases contemplated in *O'Connor* and *Tobiass* and that "the misconduct was 'so egregious that the mere fact of going forward in

19 *Ibid* at para 39.

20 *Ibid* at para 41.

21 *Ibid* at para 13; among the other forms of abuse here were the aggressive tactics on the part of the Crown to coerce a plea agreement from the accused.

22 *Ibid* at para 57.

23 *Ibid* at para 72, addressing the search, collusion, and other forms of misconduct at issue.

24 *R v Bellusci*, 2012 SCC 44 at para 5 [*Bellusci*].

25 *Ibid* at paras 14–15.

the light of it will be offensive.'"[26] The seriousness of the assault rendered alternative remedies inadequate. And under the balancing at the third stage of the test, the judge recognized the importance of protecting justice system participants and the seriousness of the charges, but found they were outweighed in this case by the "nature and gravity of the violation of Mr. Bellusci's rights."[27] Justice Fish, for a unanimous Supreme Court, held that, as with the Quebec Court of Appeal in this case, he "might well have granted a lesser remedy," but he saw no error of law or reviewable finding of fact in the trial judge's ruling.[28]

Two examples of cases involving a stay application for an unreasonable search under section 8 can be found in *R v Hall* and *R v Mok*.[29] In *Hall*, a female officer conducted a strip search, at the station, of a female accused of trafficking heroin and fentanyl. The officer did not have probable grounds for believing it was necessary to conduct a strip search (as *R v Golden* requires) and carried out the search after having been told that a superior officer did not authorize such a search.[30] The court granted a stay due in part to the seriousness of an unauthorized strip search, but also, under the balancing at the third stage of the *Babos* test, due to the finding of a "longstanding and ongoing pattern of conduct by the Langley RCMP with respect to cell searches of female arrestees."[31] In *Mok*, the court held that police had violated the accused's rights under section 8 by placing her in a holding cell where video surveillance captured her use of the toilet. Relevant to the findings under both sections 8 and 24(1) were the location of the camera, toilet, and toilet paper roll, which resulted in the accused having to stand up and walk across the cell, being "fully exposed to the video camera on several occasions" with male and female officers monitoring her, and a recording made which could "only be described as extremely degrading."[32] The situation was made worse, in the trial judge's view, by the fact that it was apparent from the video that "she was completely unaware that her activities in the holding cell were being videotaped." Here too, the court found a stay necessary due in part to the egregious nature of the violation but due also to the fact that video-recording all detainees in the custody of York

---

26 *Ibid* at para 21, citing *Tobiass*, above note 16 at para 91; *O'Connor*, above note 10.
27 *Bellusci*, above note 24 at para 29.
28 *Ibid* at para 30.
29 *R v Hall*, 2019 BCPC 349 [*Hall*] and *R v Mok*, 2012 ONCJ 291 [*Mok*].
30 *R v Golden*, 2001 SCC 83 [*Golden*] (discussed in Chapter 6, Section D(4)(b)).
31 *Hall*, above note 29 at para 80.
32 *Mok*, above note 29 at para 100.

Regional Police would continue.[33] The Ontario Court of Appeal affirmed the decision to impose a stay.[34]

2) Monetary Damages

The Supreme Court set out a test for when a court may grant monetary or "constitutional damages" for a *Charter* violation under section 24(1) in *Vancouver (City) v Ward*, a case involving two breaches of section 8.[35] During the prime minister's visit to a ceremony in Vancouver, police learned that a person unknown was planning to throw a pie at Mr Chrétien. The threat seemed credible in light of a person having thrown a pie at the prime minister two years prior. Ward, a Vancouver lawyer, attended the ceremony and roughly matched the physical description police were provided. Spotting him running from the scene, and apparently "avoiding interception," police detained Ward in handcuffs, which caused him to protest loudly, drawing the attention of a local television crew.[36] Police then arrested Ward for breach of the peace and took him to the station. He was strip searched but refused to remove his underwear and was not forced to.[37] He was placed in a "small cell where he spent several hours." Police impounded his car for a search, but decided they lacked grounds for a warrant or to charge Ward with assault. He was released roughly four-and-a-half hours after his arrest.[38]

Ward sued the city in tort and for breach of his *Charter* rights. The trial court found that city police had arrested Ward lawfully but searched him in violation of section 8 and kept him in custody longer than was necessary, resulting in a wrongful imprisonment.[39] The court awarded him $100 in damages for the unlawful seizure of his car, $5,000 for the strip search, and an additional $5,000 for the tort of being wrongfully imprisoned. Both the trial judge and the Court of Appeal rejected the submission that *Charter* damages were not appropriate in the absence of bad faith, an abuse of power, or tortious conduct.[40]

Chief Justice McLachlin, writing for a unanimous Court, affirmed that the power under section 24(1) to impose "such remedy as the court

---

33 *Ibid* at para 115.

34 *R v Mok*, 2015 ONCA 608.

35 *Vancouver (City) v Ward*, 2010 SCC 27 [*Ward*], distinguishing at para 22 "private law damages" from "the distinct remedy of constitutional damages" under s 24(1).

36 *Ibid* at para 7.

37 *Ibid* at para 8.

38 *Ibid*.

39 *Ward v City of Vancouver*, 2007 BCSC 3 [*Ward* trial].

40 *Ward*, above note 35 at paras 11 & 12, noting *Ward* trial, *ibid*, and *Ward v City of Vancouver*, 2009 BCCA 23.

considers appropriate and just in the circumstances" is broad enough to include monetary damages.[41] Only a court or tribunal authorized by statute or with inherent jurisdiction may award damages under section 24(1), and McLachlin CJ notes explicitly that "[p]rovincial criminal courts are not so empowered and thus do not have the power to award damages under s. 24(1)."[42] Where a court or tribunal is empowered to grant damages under section 24(1), the first step is to establish that a *Charter* right has been breached.[43] The second step involves establishing that damages would be an "appropriate and just" remedy on the basis of a "functional justification," or showing they would "serve a useful function or purpose."[44] The chief justice identified three such purposes: compensating the claimant for "personal loss" they may have suffered; "vindicating the right by emphasizing its importance and the gravity of the breach"; and "deterring state agents from committing future breaches."[45] Suffering a personal loss is not a requirement for constitutional damages; they may be awarded where it would serve any one of the three purposes.[46]

A third step is to consider "countervailing factors," which include the existence of "alternative remedies and concerns for good governance."[47] Damages would not be "appropriate and just" where other remedies, including exclusion of evidence or private remedies in tort, would "correct" the state conduct at issue.[48] The burden of establishing this falls on the state.[49] A concurrent claim in tort does not preclude the award of *Charter* damages, but courts should avoid a "duplicative" remedy.[50] Where the claimant has suffered no personal loss or harm, a declaration that one or more of their *Charter* rights have been breached may suffice.[51] A damage award under section 24(1) will also be inappropriate where they "would deter state agents from doing what is required for effective governance."[52] One such case is where damages are imposed for conduct that fails to meet "a minimum threshold of gravity."[53]

---

41 *Ward*, above note 35 at paras 14–22.
42 *Ibid* at para 58.
43 *Ibid* at para 23.
44 *Ibid* at para 24.
45 *Ibid* at para 31.
46 *Ibid* at paras 30 & 31.
47 *Ibid* at paras 32–33.
48 *Ibid* at para 34.
49 *Ibid* at para 35.
50 *Ibid* at para 36.
51 *Ibid* at para 37.
52 *Ibid* at para 42.
53 *Ibid* at para 39, noting this concern arose in *Mackin v New Brunswick (Minister of Finance)*, 2002 SCC 13.

If the court finds a breach of section 8 (or other *Charter* right) and the claimant establishes that constitutional damages would serve one or more functional purposes *and* the state fails to establish a "countervailing purpose" outweighing these purposes, the court turns to the quantum of damages. When assessing quantum, "[g]enerally, compensation will be the most important object, and vindication and deterrence will play supporting roles."[54] But in some cases, vindication or deterrence might play "a major and even exclusive role." Where the purpose is compensation, the court should aim to "restore the claimant to the position she would have been in had the breach not been committed."[55] This may include damages for pain and suffering, though "[a]bsent exceptional circumstances, compensation is fixed at a fairly modest conventional rate, subject to variation for the degree of suffering in the particular case."[56] A main consideration in deciding quantum is "the seriousness of the breach," which should be assessed on the basis of "the impact of the breach on the claimant and the seriousness of the state misconduct," applying the considerations set out in *R v Grant* under section 24(2) of the *Charter*.[57] Damages must be "fair—'appropriate and just'—to both the claimant and the state."[58] To assess this, a court should consider "the public interest in good governance, the danger of deterring governments from undertaking beneficial new policies and programs, and the need to avoid diverting large sums of funds from public programs to private interests."[59]

The Supreme Court affirmed the $5,000 in damages the trial judge granted to Ward for the strip search, which McLachlin CJ described as "egregious," noting that such searches are "inherently humiliating and degrading regardless of the manner in which they are carried out."[60] The breach was more serious given that police had conducted it as a matter of routine and without safety concerns, flouting numerous court decisions (including *Golden*) requiring grounds for a search.[61] The state had not established that alternative remedies would serve the functional purposes of compensating, vindicating, or deterring police in relation to the strip search that the award in this case advanced, nor was it contrary

54 *Ward*, above note 35 at para 47.

55 *Ibid* at para 48.

56 *Ibid* at para 50.

57 *R v Grant*, 2009 SCC 32 [*Grant*], cited in *Ward*, above note 35 at para 52.

58 *Ward*, above note 35 at para 53.

59 *Ibid*, noting that punitive damages are possible under s 24(1) but that "public law damages, in serving the objects of vindication and deterrence, may assume a punitive aspect" and that courts around the world have been reluctant to award punitive damages in this context.

60 *Ibid* at para 64, citing *Golden*, above note 30 at para 90.

61 *Ward*, above note 35 at para 65.

to good governance concerns.[62] The quantum was appropriate given that, while serious, the search was "not extremely disrespectful, as strip searches go" since it did not involve removal of underwear and Ward was not touched.[63] However, the chief justice found the $100 award for seizure of the car to be inappropriate, since it did not advance any of the three functional purposes.[64] A declaration that police violated Ward's rights under section 8 by seizing the car was a more appropriate remedy under section 24(1).[65]

3) Declarations and Orders

As we noted in the section above, the Supreme Court in *Vancouver (City) v Ward* affirmed that a further possible remedy a court may grant for the finding of a section 8 (or other *Charter*) breach is a formal declaration that the right has been breached.[66] In that case, the Court held that in response to the unreasonable seizure of Ward's car, a declaration was a more appropriate remedy than damages, since the seizure did not cause Ward a personal loss, police did not search the vehicle, and police drove Ward to pick it up.[67] Speaking in relation to the three-part test for monetary remedies (discussed above), the chief justice stated that, generally, a declaration will be an "adequate" remedy for a breach where "the claimant has suffered no personal damage."[68] Where the breach is so minor as to preclude a private law remedy, a declaration will also be adequate to vindicating the right and, depending on the circumstances, there may be no need to craft a remedy that will deter state actors.[69]

The Supreme Court in *Quebec (Attorney General) v Laroche* identified a further remedy under section 24(1): an order quashing an unreasonable seizure order or mandating that police discontinue an unreasonable seizure.[70] In this case, police had seized a number of vehicles belonging to a garage suspected of using stolen parts. A provincial court judge had issued a restraint order and "special warrants to seize" under the *Criminal Code*'s "proceeds of crime" provisions allowing for the seizure

62 *Ibid* at paras 68 and 72.
63 *Ibid* at para 71.
64 *Ibid* at para 77.
65 The appeal in this case concerned only the *Charter* damages for the searches, not the tort damages for the wrongful imprisonment.
66 *Ward*, above note 35.
67 *Ibid* at para 77.
68 *Ibid* at para 37.
69 *Ibid*.
70 *Quebec (Attorney General) v Laroche*, 2002 SCC 72 [*Laroche*].

of assets pending trial.[71] Police seized twenty-four vehicles not authorized under the warrants for seizing chattels. Laroche, the owner of the garage, applied to the Superior Court of Quebec to review the granting of the order and warrants under provisions for review in the *Code*,[72] but also on the basis that they were issued in violation of section 8 of the *Charter* and should be remedied by an order under section 24(1) terminating the seizure of all the items.[73] The superior court granted the application and quashed the restraint order and all of the warrants of seizure.[74] The Supreme Court of Canada affirmed a superior court's jurisdiction to decide *both* an application under the *Criminal Code* to terminate a restraint order or a warrant of seizure (under the proceeds of crime provisions), where certain conditions are met, and also an application under sections 8 and 24(1) of the *Charter* to terminate a seizure in this context on the basis that it was unreasonable.[75] In this case, LeBel J, writing for the majority, held that the superior court below had erred in quashing the restraint order and warrants of seizure since they were properly issued under the *Code* (i.e., officials had the requisite probable grounds tying the property to an offence).[76] But he upheld the superior court's order terminating the seizure of the twenty-four vehicles not mentioned in the restraint order or seizure warrants for having been seized without authorization and in violation of section 8. The termination order was an appropriate remedy under section 24(1). A point not stated overtly here was that since the claimant had not framed their challenge to police being in unlawful possession of the cars in tort, but rather as an unreasonable seizure under section 8, an order under section 24(1) was the only means of remedying the unlawful seizure of those vehicles.[77]

---

71 Sections 462.32 and 462.33 of the *Criminal Code*, above note 7, appear among the "proceeds of crime" provisions of the *Code* as initial steps that may lead to a forfeiture order. (For more on these powers, see Chapter 6, Section A(9)(a).)

72 *Criminal Code*, above note 7, s 462.34.

73 *Laroche*, above note 70 at paras 18–19.

74 *Ibid* at paras 19–20 and 79.

75 *Ibid* at paras 63 and 78.

76 *Ibid* at paras 80–94.

77 *Ibid* at para 95. Neither LeBel J nor the superior court decision he upheld here are overt on the point that the termination order was issued under section 24(1), but this is implied by the fact that the breach and remedy in relation to the twenty-four vehicles at issue are dealt with exclusively under the *Charter* rather than the *Code* provisions considered in relation to the other seizures.

4) Sentence Reduction

In *R v Nasogaluak*, the Supreme Court restricted but did not rule out a sentence reduction as a remedy under section 24(1) for a breach of *Charter* rights.[78] In this case, after receiving a tip about an intoxicated driver, police engaged in a high-speed chase with the accused. When he finally stopped, police needed to forcibly remove him from the vehicle and punched him in the head three times. While he was pinned to the ground, officers punched him again twice, breaking his ribs and puncturing a lung. The accused pleaded guilty to impaired driving and flight from police. At sentencing, the trial judge held that police had violated his rights under section 7 of the *Charter*, and as a remedy under section 24(1) imposed a sentence lower than the mandatory sentence for impaired driving. The Alberta Court of Appeal ruled that while sentences may be reduced as a remedy under section 24(1), the trial judge had no discretion to not impose the minimum (in this case a fine).[79] The Supreme Court agreed, but also provided some direction on the use of section 24(1) on sentencing.

Justice LeBel, writing for the Court, held that "[w]here the state misconduct in question relates to the circumstances of the offence or the offender, the sentencing judge may properly take the relevant facts into account in crafting a fit sentence, without having to resort to s. 24(1) of the *Charter*."[80] In this case, the misconduct formed part of the offence and should have been addressed as a mitigating circumstance under the sentencing provisions of the *Criminal Code*.[81] He also held:

> As a general rule, therefore, it is neither necessary nor useful to invoke s. 24(1) of the *Charter* to effect an appropriate reduction of sentence to account for any harm flowing from unconstitutional acts of state agents consequent to the offence charged. When acting within the boundaries of the statutory sentencing regime, of course, the sentencing judge must exercise his or her discretion within the parameters of the *Criminal Code*. The judge must impose sentences complying with statutory minimums and other provisions which prohibit certain forms of sentence in respect of the offence.[82]

---

78 *R v Nasogaluak*, above note 7.

79 *R v Nasogaluak*, 2007 ABCA 339.

80 *Nasogaluak*, above note 7 at para 3.

81 *Ibid* at para 47, addressing the relation between s 24(1) of the *Charter* and ss 718–718.2 of the *Criminal Code*, above note 7.

82 *Nasogaluak*, above note 7 at para 5.

However, LeBel J added the qualification that "in some exceptional cases, a sentence reduction outside statutory limits may be the sole effective remedy for some particularly egregious form of misconduct by state agents in relation to the offence and the offender."[83] Police conduct in this case was "serious," but this was not a case where a reduction under section 24(1) would be the sole effective remedy. Justice LeBel offered no comment on what this might involve.[84] The trial judge erred in imposing a sentence that did not include the mandatory minimum of a fine.

The Ontario Superior Court of Justice in *R v Donnelly* granted a sentence reduction below the statutory minimum, under section 24(1) of the *Charter*, as the "sole effective remedy" in a case involving the production of child pornography for a violation of sections 7 (security of the person) and 9 (arbitrary detention) of the *Charter*, which entailed being in custody for five days following arrest.[85] The Court of Appeal overturned the finding that *Charter* rights had been violated but held that if the brief custodial period here had breached *Charter* rights, it would not meet the "egregious" standard set out in *Nasogaluak* and would not have been the "sole effective remedy."[86] The Ontario Court of Appeal in *R v Gowdy* overturned a sentence imposed below the minimum, as a remedy under section 24(1), in a case involving child luring and a violation of section 7 (police infringing the accused's "security of the person" by publicizing information about his health).[87] Justice Watt, for the court, overturned the finding of a section 7 breach but held that even if it had been breached this was not the kind of egregious conduct for which a reduction under section 24(1) would be the sole effective remedy.[88]

C. EXCLUSION OF EVIDENCE UNDER SECTION 24(2)

Where a claimant establishes that a *Charter* right has been breached in the course of an investigation or prosecution, section 24(2) of the *Charter* allows for the exclusion of the evidence obtained as a consequence of the breach. Section 24(2) states:

---

83 *Ibid* at para 6, further discussed at para 64.

84 *Ibid* at para 65.

85 *R v Donnelly*, 2014 ONSC 6472, referring to *Charter* breaches found in *R v Donnelly*, 2013 ONSC 7798.

86 *R v Donnelly*, 2016 ONCA 988 at paras 163–73.

87 *R v Gowdy*, 2016 ONCA 989.

88 *Ibid* at para 128.

> Where, in proceedings under subsection (1), a court concludes that evidence was obtained in a manner that infringed or denied any rights or freedoms guaranteed by this *Charter*, the evidence shall be excluded if it is established that, having regard to all the circumstances, the admission of it in the proceedings would bring the administration of justice into disrepute.

The reference to subsection (1) of section 24 points to the requirement in that subsection that a claimant must make an application for a remedy to "a court of competent jurisdiction." As noted earlier, this includes a superior court, a provincial court in the course of a trial, or a tribunal where the power to issue a remedy under section 24 is consistent with legislative intent.[89] On an application under section 24(2), the accused bears the onus of establishing, on a balance of probabilities, that the admission of the impugned evidence would bring the administration of justice into disrepute.[90]

Section 24(2) requires that the evidence to be excluded be "obtained in a manner that infringed or denied any rights." In most cases under section 24(2), police obtain the evidence at issue in a manner directly connected to a *Charter* breach and there is no question about whether the evidence was "obtained in a manner" that violated a right. But in some cases, this may not be clear. As a result, courts have adopted a two-stage framework for section 24(2): a "threshold requirement" in which the court decides whether the evidence was "obtained in a manner" that violated a right and an "evaluative component" in which the court decides whether admitting the evidence would bring the administration of justice into disrepute.[91]

---

89 *974649 Ontario*, above note 5 at paras 41–47.

90 *R v Collins*, [1987] 1 SCR 265 at 280 [*Collins*], Lamer J, as he then was, holding:

> At the outset, it should be noted that the use of the phrase "if it is established that" places the burden of persuasion on the applicant, for it is the position which he maintains which must be established. Again, the standard of persuasion required can only be the civil standard of the balance of probabilities. Thus, the applicant must make it more probable than not that the admission of the evidence would bring the administration of justice into disrepute.

But we query below whether this applies to the test for exclusion in *Grant*, above note 57.

91 *R v Beaver*, 2022 SCC 54 at para 94 [*Beaver*], Jamal J, for the majority noting that Doherty JA coined these terms in *R v Plaha*, 2004 CanLII 21043 at para 44 (ON CA) [*Plaha*].

1) Threshold Requirement

Justice Moldaver set out the general test for the threshold requirement under section 24(2) in *R v Mack*:[92]

> Whether evidence was "obtained in a manner" that infringed an accused's rights under the *Charter* depends on the nature of the connection between the *Charter* violation and the evidence that was ultimately obtained. The courts have adopted a purposive approach to this inquiry. Establishing a strict causal relationship between the breach and the subsequent discovery of evidence is unnecessary. Evidence will be tainted if the breach and the discovery of the impugned evidence are part of the same transaction or course of conduct. The required connection between the breach and the subsequent statement may be temporal, contextual, causal, or a combination of the three. A "remote" or "tenuous" connection between the breach and the impugned evidence will not suffice (*Wittwer*, at para. 21).[93]

Justice Jamal, writing for the majority in *R v Tim*, recently summarized other relevant holdings on the threshold requirement.[94] Courts should take a "purposive and generous approach" to whether evidence was "obtained in a manner" that violated a *Charter* right; they should look at the "entire chain of events"; they should find the evidence is "tainted if the breach and the discovery of the impugned evidence are part of the same transaction or course of conduct"; they should assume the connection between the breach and the impugned evidence can be "temporal, contextual, causal or a combination of the three" and that "[a] causal connection is not required."[95] However, a "remote or tenuous connection between the *Charter* breach and the impugned evidence will not suffice to trigger s. 24(2)."[96]

In *Tim*, the Supreme Court applied the threshold test to find that evidence at issue was obtained in a manner that violated rights under section 8. Police encountered the accused after he had struck a road sign, lawfully detaining him to investigate the accident but then mistakenly arresting him for possessing a drug that was not illegal and searching

92 *R v Mack*, 2014 SCC 58 [*Mack*].

93 *Ibid* at para 38, citing *R v Wittwer*, 2008 SCC 33 [*Wittwer*].

94 *R v Tim*, 2022 SCC 12 at para 78 [*Tim*].

95 *Ibid*, citing *Mack*, above note 92; *Wittwer*, above note 93; *R v Strachan*, [1988] 2 SCR 980; *R v Mian*, 2014 SCC 54; *R v Goldhart*, [1996] 2 SCR 463; and *Plaha*, above note 91.

96 *Tim*, above note 94 at para 78.

him and his vehicle unlawfully.[97] In the course of these searches, police seized ammunition and found illegal drugs in his car—evidence clearly obtained as a result of breaches of sections 8 and 9. Concerned that they had "missed some items," officers then conducted two further searches in which they found a gun and more ammunition. The Supreme Court found the later searches to be lawful on the basis of Tim's initial detention having been lawful and police having grounds for a safety search at that later point. But the Court held that there were "temporal and contextual connections" between the earlier and later searches, rendering the evidence lawfully obtained in the later searches excludible under section 24(2).[98] The fact that officers were prompted to conduct the later searches on the belief arising after the illegal searches that they may have "missed some items" formed a contextual connection between the two events.[99] The later searches were also "very close in time" to the breaches and "flowed directly out of the same encounter with the police."

In *R v Mack*, the Supreme Court held that confessions to undercover officers that involved a violation of section 8 were not "obtained in a manner" that engaged section 24(2).[100] In that case, police violated the accused's rights in the course of a "Mr Big" operation by obtaining a recording of his confession in an unlawful wiretap. The trial judge found the causal connection between the unlawful wiretap authorization and the confession to be "so remote as to be insignificant."[101] He recognized a temporal connection, but considering the causal and temporal connection together, he held the evidence was not "obtained in a manner that infringed the *Charter*. The Supreme Court affirmed this finding.[102]

2) Evaluative Component

Once satisfied that the evidence was "obtained in a manner" that breached one or more *Charter* rights, the court moves to the evaluative component, which involves assessing whether admission of the evidence would "bring the administration of justice into disrepute." The leading authority on this component is *R v Grant*, to which we devote the final segment of this chapter, below.[103] However, a claimant may not reach the

97 *Ibid* at para 58, noting the officer's authority to detain to investigate the collision under Alberta's *Traffic Safety Act*, RSA 2000, c T-6 and a potential *Criminal Code* offence of failing to stop after a traffic accident.

98 *Ibid* at para 79.

99 *Ibid*.

100 *Mack*, above note 92.

101 *Ibid* at para 41.

102 *Ibid* at paras 41–42.

103 *Grant*, above note 57.

evaluative component if the court finds that police made a "fresh start" after violating a *Charter* right.

3) "Fresh Start" Doctrine

In a 5:4 decision, a majority of the Supreme Court in *Beaver* held that evidence under section 24(2) will not be "obtained in a manner" that breached a *Charter* right where police make a "fresh start" from an earlier *Charter* breach by taking steps that have the effect of "severing any temporal, contextual, or causal connection between the *Charter* breach and the evidence obtained or by rendering any such connection remote or tenuous."[104]

Justice Jamal, writing for the majority in *Beaver*, held that whether police have made a "fresh start" involves a "case-specific factual inquiry," though "potentially illustrative indicators" include:

- informing the accused of the *Charter* breach and "dispelling its effect with appropriate language";
- cautioning the accused and giving them a chance to consult counsel after the breach but before obtaining the impugned evidence;
- "[w]hether and how different police officers interacted with the accused after the *Charter* breach but before the impugned evidence was obtained"; and
- "[w]hether the accused was released from detention after the breach but before the impugned evidence was obtained."[105]

Justice Jamal resisted the use of the term "cure" to describe a "fresh start,"[106] though in a spirited dissent, Martin J suggested the doctrine amounts to precisely this and runs contrary to the "broad and generous" approach to section 24(2) in *Wittwer* and other holdings.[107]

The majority in *Beaver* found that police had made a fresh start in the case of one accused, but not the other. Police had detained the accused following a 911 call one of them made reporting a death in the home where they were tenants. Later at the station, homicide detectives placed them under arrest and cautioned them again under the *Charter*, after which they both confessed to killing the deceased. The trial judge found

104 *Beaver*, above note 91 at para 97.

105 *Ibid* at para 103.

106 *Ibid* at para 105–6.

107 *Ibid* at paras 198–200 citing *Wittwer*, above note 93, and at para 202 of *Beaver*: "By shifting the focus to the eventual *Charter*-compliant conduct, the 'fresh start' doctrine distracts from the remedial nature of s. 24(2) and allows police to insulate their conduct from review, regardless of the severity of that conduct."

that police violated their rights under sections 9 and 10(a) and (b) of the *Charter* by not having grounds to detain them initially and providing inadequate cautions. But the judge was satisfied that police had lawfully arrested and effectively cautioned the accused at the station, and that in doing so, police had made a fresh start that severed the confessions from the earlier breaches. Justice Jamal, for a majority of the Supreme Court, agreed with the trial judge's findings in relation to one of the accused, Lambert, but not the other. When police cautioned Beaver upon arrest and he declined counsel, they did not clearly "disassociate" the content of the warning from the caution he received when he was initially detained. Police had merely told him on arrest that the information he needed to know is "no different than what [the detaining officer] read to him"—which did not advise him of the jeopardy he was in, for any offence, including murder.[108] Beaver's post-arrest confession was thus "obtained in a manner" that breached sections 9 and 10(b)—but, as the majority went on to find, it should be admitted under section 24(2).

The Court's decision in *Wittwer* suggests that in 2008 the Court was prepared to recognize that police may make a "fresh start" under section 24(2) and that the majority in *Beaver* was not breaking new ground.[109] Police had obtained statements from the accused on two prior occasions in violation of section 10(b). In a third interview with the accused a few months later, police obtained a confession from him which the Court held to be voluntary. But officers had only succeeded in persuading him to confess by confronting him with incriminating information he had provided to police in an earlier, unlawful interrogation. Justice Fish, on behalf of the Court, found a temporal, causal, and contextual connection between the two statements, resulting in the later admission engaging section 24(2).[110] The accused had given the statement immediately upon being confronted with his earlier one; prior to being confronted with it, he had resisted confessing for some four hours; and the officer obtaining the statement had the benefit of the other officer's "watchful assistance."[111]

On one view, the entire analysis in *Wittwer* is premised on the Court's tacit recognition that police might have made a fresh start had the facts been slightly different. Had police obtained a statement from the accused in their third, lawful interrogation without relying on anything said in the earlier, unlawful interrogations, there would have been no meaningful connection between the prior breaches and the voluntary statement. But on another view (closer to the dissent in *Beaver*), even here, if police

108 *Beaver*, above note 91 at para 114.

109 *Wittwer*, above note 93.

110 *Ibid* at para 22.

111 *Ibid*.

had managed to obtain a confession quickly and without reference to the earlier events, their *entire investigation* would still have been tainted. Put another way, the Court in *Wittwer* may have recognized the possibility of later police conduct bearing no meaningful connection to an earlier breach, but this would be the case in only the most abstract and remote scenarios. In most cases, police will gain knowledge or understanding from breaches that significantly inform or affect their later conduct.

D. *GRANT* TEST FOR EXCLUSION

We note once again that in the vast majority of cases where a *Charter* right has been breached, the claimant seeks a remedy under section 24(2), and in the majority of these cases, there is little, if any, discussion of whether the impugned evidence was "obtained in a manner" that violated the right, since it is obvious on the facts in the form of a direct, causal connection. After finding that one or more *Charter* rights have been violated, judges proceed directly to section 24(2) and cite the test for applying it found in *R v Grant*.[112]

Before turning to that test, a brief word about the caselaw predating *Grant*, to help explain the impetus behind the reformulation of the test in *Grant*. The Court set out its first test for how to apply section 24(2) in *R v Collins* and refined the test in *R v Stillman*.[113] One part of the test involved a consideration of whether admission of the impugned evidence would affect trial fairness. The caselaw had evolved to the point where, in *Stillman*, the majority held that if the impugned evidence was "real" or physical and "conscripted" or obtained by force, coercion, or through involvement of the accused (for example, forcibly taking a hair sample from him), and it was otherwise "non-discoverable," its admission would compromise trial fairness and needed to be excluded on that basis alone "without considering the seriousness of the breach or the effect of exclusion on the repute of the administration of justice."[114] In other words, the test had become a rule for automatic exclusion. In a vigorous dissent in *Stillman*, the recently appointed McLachlin J (as she then was) argued that the caselaw on section 24(2) and the majority's holding in this case had drifted too far from the framer's desire to "avoid a rule of automatic exclusion."[115] The provision, in her view, calls for a balancing process and a multi-factor test that encompasses a wider set

112 *Grant*, above note 57.

113 *R v Collins*, above note 90; *R v Stillman*, [1997] 1 SCR 607 [*Stillman*].

114 *Stillman*, *ibid* at para 119; see also paras 72–74 and 102–11.

115 *Ibid* at para 239.

of considerations than were now routinely applied. She was alone in this view at that time, but not, two decades later, in *Grant*.

Grant involved the unlawful detention and arrest of a young man who provided an unwarned statement, leading to the discovery of a firearm in violation of sections 9 and 10(b) of the *Charter*.[116] In the older terminology, this was conscriptive, non-discoverable evidence that would have resulted, under *Stillman*, in automatic exclusion. Writing for a majority of five out of seven judges, McLachlin CJ and Charron J noted the flaw in the earlier jurisprudence and emphasized the balancing implied by the requirement in section 24(2) to consider "all the circumstances":

> Where, in proceedings under subsection (1), a court concludes that evidence was obtained in a manner that infringed or denied any rights or freedoms guaranteed by this *Charter*, the evidence shall be excluded if it is established that, *having regard to all the circumstances, the admission of it in the proceedings would bring the administration of justice into disrepute.*[117]

The purpose of the provision, in their view, is to "maintain the good repute of the administration of justice."[118] What would "bring the administration of justice into disrepute" should be understood in "the long-term sense of maintaining the integrity of, and public confidence in, the justice system."[119] The focus should not be on the "immediate reaction to the individual case" but rather whether "the overall repute of the justice system, viewed in the long term, will be adversely affected by admission of the evidence."[120] It is prospective in the sense of seeking to "ensure that evidence obtained through [the] breach does not do further damage to the repute of the justice system."[121] And it is "societal" in the sense that a remedy under the provision is "not aimed at punishing the police or providing compensation to the accused, but rather at systemic concerns."[122] The assessment is objective, asking whether "a reasonable person, informed of all relevant circumstances and the values underlying the *Charter*, would conclude that the admission of the evidence would bring the administration of justice into disrepute."[123]

116 *Grant*, above note 57.
117 *Charter*, above note 1, s 24(2), cited in *Grant*, above note 57 at para 59 [emphasis in the decision].
118 *Grant*, above note 57 at para 67.
119 *Ibid* at para 68.
120 *Ibid.*
121 *Ibid* at para 69.
122 *Ibid* at para 70.
123 *Ibid* at para 68.

Chief Justice McLachlin and Charron J then set out three "lines" or "avenues of inquiry" to help decide whether the admission of evidence obtained in violation of a *Charter* right would bring the administration of justice into disrepute. The court's role is to "balance the assessments under each of these lines of inquiry" to make a final determination.[124]

1) Seriousness of the *Charter*-Infringing Conduct

This line of inquiry asks a court to consider whether admission would bring the administration of justice into disrepute by "sending a message to the public that the courts, as institutions responsible for the administration of justice, effectively condone state deviation from the rule of law by failing to dissociate themselves from the fruits of that unlawful conduct."[125] The more "severe or deliberate" the conduct of police and other state officials, "the greater the need for the courts to dissociate themselves from that conduct, by excluding evidence linked to that conduct, in order to preserve public confidence in and ensure state adherence to the rule of law."[126] The court should not assess conduct with a view to punishing police or deterring *Charter* breaches, but rather to "preserv[ing] public confidence in the rule of law."[127] A breach where police acted in good faith will be less serious, reducing the need to dissociate from it; but "ignorance of *Charter* standards must not be rewarded or encouraged and negligence or wilful blindness cannot be equated with good faith."[128] "Wilful or flagrant disregard of the *Charter*" will require the court to dissociate from the conduct, mitigating in favour of exclusion.[129]

2) Impact on *Charter*-Protected Interests

Under this line of inquiry, the court considers "the extent to which the breach actually undermined the interests protected by the right infringed," from the "fleeting and technical to profoundly intrusive."[130] The more serious the impact, the greater the risk that admission would bring the administration of justice into disrepute by "breeding public cynicism" as to the importance of *Charter* rights.[131] By the "interests a right is meant to

124 *Ibid* at para 71. The headings that follow here are found in the opinion at paras 72–79.

125 *Ibid* at para 72.

126 *Ibid.*

127 *Ibid* at para 73.

128 *Ibid* at para 75.

129 *Ibid.*

130 *Ibid* at para 76.

131 *Ibid.*

protect," the majority refers here to interests "engaged" by a right, such as an interest in autonomy or making a free choice to speak to authorities protected in section 7 (the right to silence), or interests in privacy and dignity in relation to section 8. The more invasive a search, for example, the more serious the impact on a claimant's *Charter*-protected interest.[132]

3) Society's Interest in Adjudication on the Merits

A court asks here whether "the truth-seeking function of the criminal trial process would be better served by admission of the evidence or by its exclusion."[133] The "reliability of the evidence" is important here, in the sense of a coerced confession being unreliable and undermining the truth-seeking function of the court.[134] But excluding relevant and reliable evidence would be contrary to the court's truth-seeking function and the public interest in adjudicating a case on its merits.[135] This would be especially so if the evidence at issue is important to or essential to the Crown's case. In this case, exclusion might "impact more negatively on the repute of the administration of justice" where it effectively ends a prosecution.[136]

On the seriousness of the offence, McLachlin CJ and Charron J expressed the following reservation:

> In our view, while the seriousness of the alleged offence may be a valid consideration, it has the potential to cut both ways. Failure to effectively prosecute a serious charge due to excluded evidence may have an immediate impact on how people view the justice system. [. . .] As pointed out in *Burlingham*, the goals furthered by s. 24(2) "operate independently of the type of crime for which the individual stands accused" (para. 51). And as Lamer J. observed in *Collins*, "[t]he *Charter* is designed to protect the accused from the majority, so the enforcement of the *Charter* must not be left to that majority" (p. 282). The short-term public clamour for a conviction in a particular case must not deafen the s. 24(2) judge to the longer-term repute of the administration of justice. Moreover, while the public has a heightened interest in seeing a determination on the merits where the offence charged is serious, it also has a vital interest in having a justice system that is above reproach, particularly where the penal stakes for the accused are high.[137]

---

132 *Ibid* at paras 77–78.

133 *Ibid* at para 79.

134 *Ibid* at para 81.

135 *Ibid.*

136 *Ibid* at para 83.

137 *Ibid* at para 84, citing *R v Burlingham*, [1995] 2 SCR 206, and *Collins*, above note 90.

At the conclusion of the three lines of inquiry, a court must weigh the three outcomes in a final consideration of "all the circumstances" of the case and decide "whether, on balance, the admission of the evidence obtained by *Charter* breach would bring the administration of justice into disrepute."[138] The chief justice and Charron J added that "[n]o overarching rule governs how the balance is to be struck. Mathematical precision is obviously not possible."[139]

The majority opinion in *Grant* is notably silent on who bears the onus on a section 24(2) application. As we noted above, Lamer J, as he then was, in *Collins* held that the claimant had the burden on section 24(2) to establish, on a balance of probabilities, that the admission of impugned evidence would bring the administration of justice into disrepute.[140] But the majority in *Grant* does not frame its discussion of the new test in terms of things a claimant needs to establish. The central actor in the *Grant* test for exclusion is the court itself. The judge undertakes to weigh considerations arising from evidence tendered in the *voir dire* into whether a *Charter* right has been breached, rather than assessing whether a claimant has succeeded in meeting specific requirements under section 24(2).[141]

A detailed summary of the Court's application of the *Grant* test in later decisions is beyond the scope of this chapter. However, the Court has undertaken to apply the test (or review the application of it) in cases involving violations of section 8 in a host of contexts, including searches or seizures of items from persons or vehicles incident to detention or arrest;[142] of devices or computers;[143] of information or electronic communications;[144] of dwelling houses or portions thereof;[145] and of bodily samples.[146] The caselaw applying the Grant test in lower courts is vast.[147]

---

138 *Grant*, above note 57 at para 85.

139 *Ibid* at para 86.

140 *Collins*, above note 90 at 280.

141 On the standard of review on appeal of a decision under s 24(2) see *R v Côté*, 2011 SCC 46 [*Côté*].

142 *Tim*, above note 94; *R v Le*, 2019 SCC 34; (the dissent in) *R v MacKenzie*, 2013 SCC 50; *R v Aucoin*, 2012 SCC 66; *R v Loewen*, 2011 SCC 21; *R v Nolet*, 2010 SCC 24; *R v Beaulieu*, 2010 SCC 7; and *R v Harrison*, 2009 SCC 34.

143 *R v Reeves*, 2018 SCC 56; *R v Fearon*, 2014 SCC 77; *R v Vu*, 2013 SCC 60; *R v Cole*, 2012 SCC 53; and *R v Morelli*, 2010 SCC 8.

144 *R v Jones*, 2017 SCC 60; *R v Marakah*, 2017 SCC 59; and *R v Spencer*, 2014 SCC 43.

145 *Côté*, above note 141; *R v Stairs*, 2022 SCC 11; *R v Paterson*, 2017 SCC 15; and the dissent in *R v Cornell*, 2010 SCC 31.

146 *Goodwin v British Columbia (Superintendent of Motor Vehicles)*, 2015 SCC 46, and by the dissenting justices in *R v Saeed*, 2016 SCC 24.

147 A search on canlii.org brings up close to 5,000 citations.

Recent studies of how courts across Canada have applied section 24(2) in the decade after *Grant* have found that applicants at trial are successful in having at least some evidence excluded in roughly 70 percent of cases.[148]

148 Steven Penney & Moin Yahya, "Section 24(2) in the Trial Courts: An Empirical Analysis of the Legal and Non-legal Determinants of Excluding Unconstitutionally Obtained Evidence in Canada" (2021) 58.3 *Osgoode Hall Law Journal* 509, finding at 532 that "[t]he exclusion rate in our dataset was 70.4%; that is, in 1,472 reported exclusionary decisions from 2013–2018, trial judges who found that evidence was obtained in a manner that violated the Charter excluded at least some of the evidence in just over seven in ten instances." See also Benjamin Johnson, Richard Jochelson & Victoria Weir, "Exclusion of Evidence Under Section 24(2) of the Charter Post-Grant in the Years 2014–2017: A Comprehensive Analysis of 600 Cases" (2019) 67 *Criminal Law Quarterly* 57, finding that provincial courts had excluded evidence in 74.5 percent of cases while appeal courts had excluded in only 21 percent of cases (when the Grant test was conducted *de novo*); and Patrick McGuinty, "Section 24(2) of the Charter: Exploring the Role of Police Conduct in the Grant Analysis" (2018) 41 *Manitoba Law Journal* 273 at 288 finding evidence excluded in 67 percent of 100 cases from 2016.

TABLE OF CASES

Canadian Cases

INDEX

ABOUT THE AUTHORS

Robert Diab is a professor in the Faculty of Law at Thompson Rivers University, where he teaches criminal law, evidence, and jurisprudence. He has written extensively on constitutional rights, police powers, and civil liberties and is the author of *The Harbinger Theory: How the Post-9/11 Emergency Became Permanent and the Case for Reform* (Oxford University Press, 2015) and *Guantanamo North* (Fernwood, 2008). He has also practised as Crown and defence counsel in trial and appeal courts in British Columbia.

Chris Hunt is a professor in the Faculty of Law at Thompson Rivers University. He earned his LLM and PhD from Cambridge University, clerked for the justices of the Supreme Court of British Columbia, and practised commercial litigation in Vancouver. He teaches contract law, evidence, and unjust enrichment. He has written extensively on a range of topics, including privacy, evidence, and contracts. His work has been cited numerous times by Canadian courts, including the Supreme Court of Canada.

Printed and bound by CPI Group (UK) Ltd, Croydon, CR0 4YY

15/09/2026

14962403-0001